DEMOCRACY
in Latin America

Towards a Citizens' Democracy

Argentina, Bolivia, Brazil, Chile, Colombia, Costa Rica, Dominican Republic, Ecuador, El Salvador, Guatemala, Honduras, Mexico, Nicaragua, Panama, Paraguay, Peru, Uruguay, Venezuela

United Nations
Development Programme

© 2004 by the United Nations Development Programme
1 UN Plaza, New York, New York, 10017, United States of America
www.undp.org

Of this edition:
© 2004 by Aguilar, Altea, Taurus, Alfaguara, S.A.
Leandro N. Alem 720, (1001) Ciudad de Buenos Aires
www.alfaguara.com.ar

The translation of the Report into English was done by a team of translators, headed by Merril Stevenson, and including Joanna Richardson, Celia Vartalitis de Podestá, Elena Feeney, Isabel Onetti de Mora, and Rafaela Gunner. The text was reviewed by Thomas Scheetz. The English version of the Statistical Compendium was prepared by Gerardo Munck and Wendy Prentice. A final reading of the Report was carried out by Gerardo Noto and Myriam Mendez-Montalvo.
The English version of this Report was edited by Richard Jones, Exile: Design & Editorial Services (rmjones@onetel.com)

ISBN: 987-04-0085-X
Queda hecho el depósito legal que marca la ley 11723
Impreso en la Argentina. Printed in Argentina

Editorial Direction:	Fernando Esteves
Editorial Coordination:	Mercedes Sacchi
Cover Design Idea:	Fischer America Argentina
Desktop Composition:	Mónica Deleis and Lenguaje Claro Consultora
Proofreading:	Luz Freire and Lenguaje Claro Consultora

United Nation Development Programme.
Democracy in Latin América : towards a citizen's democracy. - 1a ed. - Buenos Aires : Aguilar, Altea, Taurus, Alfaguara, 2005.
288p. +1 CD Rom ; 30x21 cm.

Traducido por: Merril Stevenson...[et al.]

ISBN 987-04-0085-X

1. Programa de las Naciones Unidas para el Desarrollo. I. Stevenson, Merril, trad. II. Título.
CDD 307.76

First Spanish Edition: April 2004
Second Spanish Edition: December 2004
First English Edition: February 2005

This Report was prepared with the financial assistance of the European Union. Its analyses and recommendations should in no way be considered to reflect the official views of the European Union.

Note:
This publication is an English translation of the revised second edition of the Spanish version of the Report La democracia en América Latina, published on December 2004 (www.democracia.undp.org).

United Nations Development Programme

This Report could not have been written without the generous contributions of many individuals and organizations. We would like to thank all of them sincerely. A detailed list of those involved can be found on page 201 of this publication.

■ Project on Democracy in Latin America

Project Director

Dante Caputo

Consultants on Thematic Areas

Theoretical Framework
Guillermo O'Donnell, with comments provided by Bruce Ackerman, Andrew Arato, Renato Boschi, Fernando Calderón, Catherine Conaghan, Julio Cotler, Larry Diamond, José Eisenberg, Manuel A. Garretón, David Held, Céli Regina Jardim Pinto, Jennifer McCoy, Adalberto Moreira Cardoso, Juan Méndez, José Nun, Pierre Rosanvallon, Alain Touraine, Laurence Whitehead.

Opinion Study
Jorge Vargas headed the team integrated by Miguel Gómez Barrantes, Tatiana Benavides, Evelyn Villarreal and Lorena Kikut, which designed and analyzed the opinion poll Latinobarómetro/ PRODDAL 2002.

Indicators
Gerardo Munck headed the team integrated by David Altman, Jeffrey A. Bosworth, Jay Verkuilen and Daniel Zovatto.

Round of Consultations
Diego Achard, Augusto Ramírez Ocampo, Edelberto Torres Rivas, Gonzalo Pérez del Castillo, Claudia Dangond, Raúl Alconada Sempé, Rodolfo Mariani, Leandro García Silva, Adriana Raga, Luis E. González, Gonzalo Kmeid, and Pablo Da Silveira. A team that analyzed the results was led by Hilda Herzer and composed of Verónica De Valle, María M. Di Virgilio, Graciela Kisilesky, Adriana Redondo and María Carla Rodríguez.

Coordinators

Coordinator, Andean Countries
Augusto Ramírez Ocampo, with the cooperation of Claudia Dangond, Elisabeth Ungar and Amalfy Fernández.

Coordinators, MERCOSUR Countries
Dante Caputo and Raúl Alconada Sempé.

Coordinator, Central American Countries and Dominican Republic
Edelberto Torres Rivas, with the collaboration of Claudio Luján.

Institutional Coordinator
Gonzalo Pérez del Castillo.

Project Team in Buenos Aires

Programme Officer:
Rosa Zlachevsky.

Technical Team:
Leandro García Silva, Rodolfo Mariani and Thomas Scheetz.

Support Team:
María Eugenia Bóveda and Fabián de Achaval.

Special Collaboration:
Fabián Bosoer and Daniel Sazbón.

Dissemination of the Report

Milena Leivi, Milagros Olivera, Sandra Rojas and Emilio Sampietro (Spanish version).
Emilio Sampietro (English version).

Advisors

José Luis Barros Horcasitas, Fernando Calderón, Alberto Couriel, Joaquín Estefanía, Gustavo Fernández Saavedra, Enrique Ganuza, Manuel Antonio Garretón, Edmundo Jarquín, Marta Lagos, Marcos Novaro, Vicente Palermo, Arturo O'Connell, Guillermo O'Donnell and Carlos Ominami.

Consultants

Gloria Ardaya, Horacio Boneo, Sebastián Campanario, Eva Capece, Julio Godio, Luis Eduardo González, Juan Carlos Herrera, Néstor Lavergne, Norbert Lechner, Silvia Lospennato and Luis Verdesoto.

Report Readers' Group

Carmelo Angulo Barturen, Víctor Arango, Marcia de Castro, Juan Pablo Corlazzoli, Juan Alberto Fuentes, Enrique Ganuza, Freddy Justiniano (Coordinator), Thierry Lemaresquier, Carlos Lopes, Carlos F. Martínez, Magdy Martínez, Myriam Méndez-Montalvo, Gerardo Noto, William Orme, Stefano Pettinato, Juan Rial, Harold Robinson, Martín Santiago and Luis Francisco Thais.

Contents

SECOND SECTION

75   Empirical Basis of the Report

Foreword by the Administrator of the United Nations Development Programme

Latin America today presents an extraordinary paradox. From one perspective, the continent can look back with great pride on more than two decades of democratic governments. From another, the region faces a growing social crisis. Deep inequalities remain entrenched, serious levels of poverty prevail, economic growth has been insufficient, and dissatisfaction with those democracies—manifest in many places by widespread popular unrest—has been growing, often with deeply destabilizing consequences.

The Report represents an unprecedented effort to understand and overcome this paradox. By combining quantitative indicators and detailed interviews with in-depth surveys and an on-going dialogue with a cross-section of prominent leaders and opinion-formers across the region, the Report provides a comprehensive analysis of the state of democracy in Latin America. In addition, it seeks to move beyond a simple diagnosis of existing challenges and proposes new approaches to tackling many of the festering problems that now put at risk many of the region's successes of the past 25 years.

While the Report is the product of an independent team of experts and therefore not a formal statement of UNDP or United Nations policy, as an outline of the central obstacles facing, and the opportunities for, democracy in the region, we believe that it helps to frame an agenda for Latin American countries and UNDP and its development partners in the months and years to come. UNDP is very pleased to have sponsored it.

At the heart of the challenge lies the fact that while democracy has spread widely across Latin America, its roots remain shallow. Thus, the Report warns that the proportion of Latin Americans who would be willing to sacrifice a democratic government in exchange for real social and economic progress now exceeds 50 percent.

There are several reasons for this trend.

The most important is that democracy is, for the first time in Latin American history, the incumbent form of government. Incumbents get blamed when things go wrong, with jobs, income and many basic services failing to meet steadily growing public expectations.

Exacerbating matters, many of the other underpinnings of democratic governance—a free press, strong human rights protections, an independent and vigorous judiciary—still need to be significantly strengthened. This is all the more critical considering that many traditionally disenfranchised groups are denied access to power through more formal channels, leading them increasingly to express their frustrations through alternative, sometimes violent, routes.

Beneath this surface turmoil, there are some encouraging signs. First is that regardless of the crisis, the countries in the region have not sought a return to authoritarianism but broadly sustained their democratic institutions. Second, citizens are also starting to draw a distinction between democracy as a system of government and the performance of those governing in particular. Many are simply "dissatisfied democrats"—a phenomenon well known in many longer-established democracies—which partly explains why opposition movements today are tending not towards military solutions but populist "outsiders" promising a new broom and fresh approach.

At the same time, people do increasingly differentiate between organs of government in apportioning blame. While legislatures and political parties enjoy the support of less than a quarter of the population, the Judiciary, Executive and Security Services tend to do somewhat better.

Nevertheless, if democracy is to survive and flourish, Latin America needs to work much harder at ensuring democratic institutions, from legislatures through to local authorities, are transparent and accountable and have the skills and capacity to carry out critical work. That means making sure power at all levels of government is structured and distributed in a way that gives real voice and space to poor people and creates mechanisms whereby the powerful—whether political leaders, corporations or other actors—are held accountable for their actions.

There are no short cuts—entrenching democracy is a process, not an event.

But making public institutions work more effectively is only part of the story. The other part is to be able to prove to constituents that democratic governments are working on the kind of issues that matter most to them, are capable of addressing them, and are being held to account when they fail to do so.

In practice that means building a legislative institutions and a judiciary that protect human rights and give scope for the cut and thrust of vigorous—but peaceful—political debate; a police force that provides safe streets and safe borders; decentralized power so that local people can monitor and mobilize to ensure schools with well trained teachers and hospitals with proper drugs and equipment; and a thriving civil society and a free press that participate fully in entrenching democracy and that are in the vanguard of attacks on corruption and mismanagement by government and business alike.

The United Nations Millennium Development Goals (MDGs)—ranging from halving extreme poverty and hunger to putting all boys and girls in school all by the year 2015—provide a vehicle that can help address these issues at national and regional level. Because in a very real sense they are the first global manifesto for ordinary men and women and children all over the world: a set of concrete, measurable, pocket-book issues that everyone can understand and applaud.

As important, as part of a global compact between rich and poor countries, whereby the developed world is committed to provide support to developing nations that make good faith reforms, the MDGs offer a real opportunity for harnessing the external support in terms of trade access, debt relief and increased assistance that so many Latin American countries desperately need to bolster their own efforts.

If Latin America—and the world—can seize this opportunity then there is every chance of building a new virtuous circle where renewed economic growth boosts the MDGs, which in turn helps build and sustain more effective democracies better able to accelerate equitable, social and economic progress. But to make such a vision a reality, all Latin Americans, and especially the regions' leaders first have to confront these critical issues of democratic governance head on and make sure that development and democracy are no longer seen as alternatives but two sides of the same coin.

Mark Malloch Brown
Administrator of the United Nations Development Programme

Preface by the Regional Director for Latin America and the Caribbean of UNDP

There was a time not long ago when many people believed that politics had died, and that the impersonal market and technocratic know-how would lead us to development. But the market requires the juridical security that institutions provide. And technology does not answer general questions concerning why or for whom, but rather serves as a vehicle to attaining development.

That is why, in recent years, economists and development agencies have been taking a second look at institutions. In other words, they have rediscovered politics (although they prefer not to say so).

It is in the context of this rediscovery that the Report seeks to promote the reinvention of politics as an aid to development in Latin America.

Indeed, at the request of governments, UNDP has been devoting increasing attention to the challenge of deepening democracy in Latin America and the Caribbean. In fact, most of its national cooperation programs are aimed at promoting this objective through the modernization of various branches of State, political reform, local governance and effective integration into the 'global village'. In no fewer than 17 countries, UNDP has participated in dialogues designed to build consensus between authorities, political forces, civil society members and non-traditional actors. Given that UNDP is a knowledge-based organization, a number of regional and national projects have been or are concerned with the evaluation of alternatives and the dissemination of good practices on democratic governance.

Against this backdrop, the Executive Board of UNDP approved the Second Regional Cooperation Framework for the period 2001–2005, which includes "preparation of a report on the state of democracy in Latin America [which] will be the result of the joint efforts of the academics and political and social agents of the region."[1] This document, which I am honored to introduce, is the final product of that effort. Its production involved over 100 analysts, 32 presidents or former presidents, more than 200 political and social leaders and nearly 19,000 citizens surveyed in 18 different countries.

1 Executive Board of the United Nations Development Programme and United Nations Population Fund, First Regular Session, 2002.

In its most elementary sense, democracy is none other than 'government of the people'. The Report seeks to take this old idea seriously, and apply it to the present and future of the Americas:

- Government of the people means that decisions that affect everyone should be taken by everyone. In Latin America, therefore, we must welcome the emergence of governments elected by popular vote and the advances achieved in political representation and participation over the past several decades. But the challenge of how to expand politics remains. That is, how to submit for debate and resolution all of those issues that affect the collective interest. In turn, this necessitates greater diversity in terms of options and the granting of more power to the State so that it can fulfill the mandate given to it by its citizens.
- Government of the people thus means a State of citizens in the full sense of the term. A system of electing authorities but also a form of organization that guarantees the rights of all: civil rights (guarantees against oppression); political rights (part of the public or collective decision-making process); and social rights (the right to live in safety and security).

The seminal idea of the Report is to integrate the different dimensions of citizenship in the building of democracy through the expansion of politics.

Is it necessary to point out that 'politics' is not only (or always) what politicians do, but what citizens and their organizations do when they become involved in public affairs? And is it necessary to add that, viewed in this light, democracy is a form of human development? If human development, as UNDP reports have argued time and again, is "a process of enlarging people's choices to lead lives they value,"[2] then I would say that democracy is human development in the public sphere. It is the expansion of the collective options that impact on the quality of our lives. Hence the statement by Amartya Sen that "human development is the process of expansion of the real freedoms enjoyed by a people"[3] may indeed serve as a definition of democracy.

The debate is open. How does one preserve and improve the democratic system that our countries now operate under? How does one expand social citizenship and reduce the poverty and inequality that remain our great weakness and a serious threat to the democratic system? How does one expand politics or reclaim the public domain for debate and popular participation? How does one return economics to politics and, without populism, place the market in the service of citizens? How does one ensure that the State promotes the democratization of society? How does one guarantee that the State is able to prevail over other centers of power? And finally, how does one make certain that the global village is governed and that this government also represents all Latin Americans?

The Report does not seek to provide answers to these questions, but rather it helps to

2 This definition was first proposed in UNDP's Human Development Report 1990, Oxford University Press.
3 *Amartya Sen, Development as Freedom*, Oxford University Press, 1999.

elucidate them. Moreover, the Report is merely a pre-text, both in the sense of a preliminary document that needs improvement and in the sense that it offers an excuse or an opportunity to pursue a dialogue that has already begun.

This dialogue is the *raison d'être* of the Project for Democratic Development in Latin America (PRODDAL), which is being implemented by UNDP with the generous support of the European Union and of national governments, institutions and individuals, all of whom I cannot list here but whom I certainly wish to thank.

In addition to the Report, other outputs that we hope will stimulate and enrich a much needed debate (which I would call a 'debate on the democratization of our democracies') are: a book in which 26 outstanding intellectuals offer their thoughts; a statistical compendium containing a comprehensive survey of citizens; and academic essays that explore the foundations of our understanding of democracy.

Latin America is multiple yet one. Consequently the political debate must be based on the particular realities and dreams of each country. That is why UNDP has planned meetings in each of them. We also wish to pursue this dialogue through a series of regional events, through the network of governance stakeholders that supports PRODDAL and, of course, through interactive 'e-communication'. Welcome to the debate!

Elena Martínez
Assistant Administrator and Regional Director for Latin America
and the Caribbean of UNDP

Introduction by the Director of the Report

Liberty, Democracy and Politics

The Report on Democracy in Latin America offers a number of responses to questions that Latin American societies have about their democracies. We have conducted this exploration bearing in mind the needs of our women and men, which are not adequately addressed in the political debate.

Our hope is that the Report will encourage debate in society, and that it will help people to understand better their particular democracy and the need to improve it.

There is no unease about the concept of democracy, but there is disquiet within democracies. Overcoming this requires that we use the most valuable instrument that democracy affords us: freedom. Freedom to discuss the things that cause anxiety, which some would rather conceal. Freedom to say that the Emperor has no clothes and to try and understand why. Freedom to know why a system that is virtually synonymous with equality exists alongside the highest level of inequality in the world. Freedom to know if what we are discussing is what we need to be discussing or whether it is what others have forced upon us. And freedom to know our priorities and the matters that are urgent.

Indeed, while recognizing its limitations, the Report is an exercise in freedom, which in politics basically means exercising the right to know and to decide what we wish to do with our societies. In part, the crisis of political representation can be better addressed if we are aware of what to ask for, that is, what to demand of our representatives.

A text in itself will not achieve this objective. It is also essential to actively promote debate and to incorporate into the daily decision-making process of social organizations the issues highlighted here—and others that we may have omitted—in order to stimulate a new type of discussion.

To this end, the Report contains critical analysis of the state of our democracies from the standpoint of democracy. Inevitably, this has led us to point out its shortcomings and weaknesses.

But there is a danger in exploring what is lacking, while forgetting what we have. The deficits and pitfalls that threaten our democracies should not make us forget that we have left behind us the long legacy of authoritarianism—the fears of assassination, forced disappearances, and torture and the deafening silence of the absence of freedom. A history in which a few appropriated for themselves the right to interpret and determine the destiny of all.

While we have many problems, some of them very serious, we must nevertheless hold on to the memory of this past and never lose sight of it, so that our children will know that freedom did not emerge spontaneously, that the right to protest, speak, think and decide with the dignity of free men and women was achieved in a long and bitter struggle. We need to be critical of our democracy because these memories require that we preserve and improve it.

Democracy is built through politics. Yet politics also has major weaknesses, which have led to increased rejection of politicians in our societies. The Report does not shy away from highlighting the seriousness of the crisis that surrounds politics and politicians. But it is these politicians that have led the struggle, paying for their defects or failures with their prestige and honor. They do not have the purity of those who risk only expressing an opinion. Many have the courage to enter an arena in which, more often than not, what they confront are not grand ideas but passion and misfortune. Some become fearful and abandon the fight, while others commit errors and, in one way or another, pay for them. But a majority did something more than simply offer an opinion on how things should be done. Although they committed themselves and lost, many returned to try again, some successfully.

This is not a sentimental defense of politicians but a simple observation that the building of democracy is no easy task. It requires men and women who are prepared to take part in a struggle in turbulent territory where interests and passions all play themselves out.

Democracy is exercised through politics, the only activity that can bring people together in the challenging but rewarding process of struggling with the human condition to build a society based on greater dignity.

As Max Weber observes: "politics is a long and hard struggle against tenacious resistance for which both passion and moderation are needed. It is absolutely true, and history attests to this, that in this world the possible is never achieved if the impossible is not attempted again and again. But in order to do this one must not only be a leader but also a hero in the simplest sense of the word. Even those who are neither one nor the other need to first develop the strength of mind that would enable them to survive the destruction of all hope, if they wish to be able to achieve even what is possible today. Only a person who is confident that he would not give up when, in his view, the world seems too stupid or too abject for what he offers; only a person who when faced with all of this is capable of responding with a 'nevertheless', only a man built in this way has a 'vocation for politics'."[1]

Lastly, a warning about the limitations of this work. The Report on Democracy in Latin America offers an analysis of the situation in the region, provides a wealth of data and suggests an agenda for tackling the principal challenges. It is only a partial effort, however.

1 M. Weber, 1997 (in Spanish). Originally given as 'Politik als Beruf,' *Gesammelte Politische Schriften* (Muenchen, 1921), pp. 396-450. Originally a speech at Munich University, 1918, published in 1919 by Duncker & Humboldt, Munich.

Democracy is a phenomenon central to which are its human and cultural dimensions. The history we have inherited, the social impulses driven by our hopes and frustrations, and the passions that revolve around power relations often contain indications or explanations that are not fully reflected in data and analysis. We remark on this absence to show that we are aware of it and to underscore our reluctance to pigeonhole and to reduce to figures the immense complexity of human experiences. We have focused only on one segment, albeit an important and necessary one, of the vast experiment that is democracy.

Dante Caputo
Director of the Report

Overview

Introduction

Democracy in Latin America: Towards a Citizens' Democracy is an element of the strategy of the United Nations Development Programme (UNDP) to promote democratic governance and human development. Put together by the Project on Democratic Development in Latin America (PRODDAL), the Report represents an initial input into a longer-term process of analysis and social dialogue. Its purpose is to evaluate the state of democracy in Latin America, considered not only as an electoral regime, but also as a democracy of citizens. On the basis of this approach, achievements, limitations, and challenges are identified, and an agenda of reforms is suggested to encourage the deepening of democracy in Latin America.

Even though 140 countries in the world today live under democratic regimes—a fact that is seen as a great achievement—only in 82 of them is there full democracy.[1] Moreover, many democratically elected governments tend to maintain their authority through undemocratic means, such as by amending their national Constitutions to favor themselves, intervening in electoral processes and/or undermining the independence of the legislative and judicial branches of State. Hence, democracy cannot be reduced to the mere holding of elections; it requires efficient, transparent and equitable public institutions, as well as a culture that accepts the legitimacy of political opposition and recognizes and promotes the rights of all citizens.

At the same time, in many cases, the increasing frustration with the lack of opportunities, combined with high levels of inequality, poverty and social exclusion, has resulted in instability, a loss of confidence in the political system, radical action and crises of governance, all of which threaten the stability of the democratic system itself.

As the *Human Development Report 2002* argues, democracy is not only valuable in its own right, but it is also tied to human development. For UNDP, democratic governance is a key condition for human development, since it is through politics, and not just economics, that it is possible to create more equitable conditions and to expand people's options. Insofar as democracy allows for dialogue among the various social groups, and as public institutions are strengthened and become more efficient, it will be possible to achieve the Millennium Development Goals (MDGs), particularly those concerned with poverty reduction. In this sense, democracy provides the right framework for creating opportunities for political and social participation, especially for the most disadvantaged: the poor and ethnic and cultural minorities.

This Report is structured around the responses to three questions:

---

1 UNDP, *Human Development Report 2002*, Oxford University Press, Oxford and New York, 2002, p. 10.

The Report sees as positive the main achievements of democracy as a political system in Latin America and identifies inequality and poverty as its main weaknesses.

- What is the state of democracy in Latin America?
- What are the perceptions of and how strong is the support of leaders and citizens for democracy?
- What are the principal issues for a debate geared towards the deepening of a citizens' democracy?

It consists of three sections, wherein are found the attempts to answer these questions. The first section develops the conceptual framework employed in the study and puts in context the development of democracy in a region with high levels of poverty and inequality. The second section analyzes the data obtained using the various empirical instruments: indicators and indices of political, civil and social citizenship; an opinion survey to which 19, 508 citizens from the 18 countries responded; and a round of consultations with 231 leaders on the challenges to democracy in Latin America. The third section seeks to broaden the public agenda on the development of democracy, which is focused on the crisis of politics, State and economic reforms, and the impact of globalization on the region.

Democracy and the Idea of Democracy in Latin America

The 18 Latin American countries considered in this Report today fulfill the basic requirements of a democratic regime; of these, only three lived under a democratic regime 25 years ago. At the same time as the people of Latin America consolidate their political rights, however, they confront high levels of poverty and the highest levels of inequality in the world. Consequently, the argument is being made that there are severe tensions between the deepening of democracy and of the economy, as well as between the pursuit of equality and the reduction of poverty.

The Report sees as positive the main achievements of democracy as a political system in Latin America and identifies inequality and poverty as its main weaknesses. It also stresses the urgent need for policies that promote democratic power, whose goal is to make citizens full participants.

What should we understand by 'full civic participation'? As the reader will have already deduced, this notion encompasses substantially more than a political regime and its institutional rules. Full civic participation means that today's citizens must enjoy easy access to their civil, social, economic and cultural rights and that all of these rights together constitute an indivisible and interconnected whole.

While the study takes into account and highlights as important elements for analysis the marked differences between the countries of the region, it also notes that, with respect to questions of democracy, there are common regional problems and that differences exist with regard to national responses to them.

Based on its theoretical underpinnings, this Report argues that:

- democracy implies a certain way of thinking about the human being and the development of citizenship;
- democracy is a form of organization of power that implies the existence of a State and its proper functioning;
- democracy requires full civic participation, that is, complete recognition of political, civil and social citizenship;
- democracy in the region has a particular historical development that must be understood and judged in terms of its specific characteristics; and
- although the electoral system is a key element of a democratic regime, democracy cannot be reduced to the mere holding of elections.

Balance Sheet on Integral Citizenship

Progress towards full *political citizenship* was gauged using the Index of Electoral Democracy (IED), which, even though it measures only one aspect of the political system, corresponds to the minimum dimension or condition that would allow us to speak of democracy. The data show that *electoral democracies* do exist in the region today. More specifically, they reveal that:

- the *universal right* to vote is recognized in all countries;
- despite some problems, *national elections* held between 1990 and 2002[2] were *generally 'clean'*;
- during the same period, even though ten out of 70 national elections witnessed the imposition of significant restrictions on *electoral freedom*, the general trend was positive; and
- progress was made in the sense that *elections offer a means of access to public office*. The transfer of presidential power became commonplace, although in some cases this occurred against a backdrop of a severe constitutional crisis.

The data also show, however, that *participation in elections* is uneven, that in some countries levels of participation are very low and that *new entrants to the electoral contest confront barriers to entry*. One important achievement has been the opening of *political spaces for women* through reserved seats or political party quotas. The representation of indigenous peoples and Afro-descendants in parliament, though, is generally still very limited. *Political parties* as agents of representation are also experiencing a severe crisis, which is manifested by people's increasing loss of confidence in them. They are considered to be aloof and an alien and self-interested sector that offers no possibility of a shared future.

As *for mechanisms of political control in addition to elections*, in a number of countries, the executive branch continues to interfere openly in the affairs of the Supreme Court, although some progress has been made towards *constitutional reforms aimed at professionalizing and strengthening the independence of the judiciary*. Specialized oversight bodies have also been created in recent years, including agencies to monitor the use of public funds, public prosecutors and ombudsmen. However, the lack of resources available to, and, in some cases, the limited autonomy from the executive branch reduce the effectiveness of these entities. Lastly, an important achievement has been the decline in the political influence of the armed forces in nearly all countries.

Thus, although progress has been made in terms of the holding of elections and institution-building, serious deficiencies remain with regard to the control that citizens are able to exercise over the actions of the State. Political parties are deeply distrusted as representatives of the people (which is a key challenge to the deepening of democracy). As a result, representation of broad sectors of the population is generally low and participation in elections is uneven.

With respect to *civic citizenship*, important gains have been made vis-à-vis legislation, but the limited capacity of States to guarantee in practice the rights enshrined in these laws remains a matter of concern.

Most of the countries of the region have ratified the main international treaties and enacted domestic legislation concerned with *equality under the law and protection against discrimination*, as well as with women's rights. Progress has also been made in the protection of labor rights and the rights of children. Despite delays to the ratification of the Convention on Indigenous Peoples (1991), the rights of indigenous peoples have been recognized in a number of national Constitutions.

The same cannot be said of international treaties that provide protection, in particular, for *the rights to life, humane treatment and security*. The anticipated reduction in this type of human rights violation did not occur as expected, al-

---

2 In general, the information contained in this Report uses data that cover the period up to 2002.

> **The deepening of democracy requires a significant expansion of social citizenship, particularly with respect to efforts to combat poverty and inequality and to create high-quality employment opportunities.**

though such abuses are no longer committed as a matter of State policy, but rather by parastatal or criminal entities that the State has been unable to control.

Despite the progress made in the legislative realm, the right to non-discrimination is still not adequately guaranteed: marked inequalities persist in the treatment of persons belonging to different population groups, laws to protect children in the workplace are frequently ignored and social security protection for workers has been reduced. One advance in the field of labor, however, is the trend towards greater equality between men and women.

The lack of financial and human resources has weakened the *administration of justice systems*. Prison populations are thus a matter of concern, since the rights of prisoners are frequently violated, evidenced by the fact that more than 50 percent of all prisoners are being held under pre-trial detention conditions.

As for the *right to freedom of the press*, the Report notes that there are still significant shortcomings in Latin America. Progress in the area of the *right to information* has been more encouraging, since access to public sources of data is now legally recognized in most countries.

In short, although the human rights situation has improved in comparison to the undemocratic period, international agreements in the civil rights sphere have been ratified, and nation-al laws have been promulgated, the data reveal that areas of weakness remain, a fact that should serve as a warning sign. Progress in terms of respect for the right to life, humane treatment, security and non-discrimination has been uneven and, in some respects, inadequate.

Trends in the field of *social citizenship* also give cause for deep concern and pose the most serious challenge to Latin American democracies. This is because the groups most frequently excluded from fully exercising social citizenship are the same ones whose participation in other areas of citizenship is limited.

The main problems in this area are *poverty and inequality*, which prevent individuals from expressing themselves on issues of public concern (as citizens with full and equal rights) and undermine their *social inclusion*. Statistics show that the level of inequality in all of the countries of the region is higher than the global average. In 15 of the 18 countries studied, more than 25 percent of the population lives below the poverty line, and in seven of these countries more than 50 percent of the population lives below the poverty line, even though 12 countries recorded a reduction in poverty and 15 achieved some degree of per capita economic growth between 1991 and 2002.

Some progress has been achieved, though, in the areas of *health* (infant malnutrition declined in 13 of the 18 countries; infant mortality also fell while life expectancy rose) and *education* (the rate of illiteracy decreased in all countries and school attendance figures increased, although the quality of education remained generally low).

A key issue is *unemployment*, since work is one of the principal mechanisms for ensuring social inclusion and the very exercise of citizenship, which has an economic component. The rise in the level of unemployment during the 1990s is, therefore, one of the major weaknesses of democracy in Latin America. What is more, during the same period, the social protection net for workers narrowed and informal employment increased, but this was generally of low quality, of limited social value and insufficient to bring about a level of social integration that would guarantee a minimum level of well-being.

In sum, the deepening of democracy requires a significant expansion of social citizenship, particularly with respect to efforts to combat poverty and inequality and to create high-quality employment opportunities. Only by reducing inequality can poverty be truly reduced and the possibilities for economic growth expanded.

Perceptions and Support of Leaders and Citizens

Despite the advances made, albeit under very precarious conditions, it must be recognized that, in terms of progress towards democracy and economic and social development, the region is in a period of change that, in many instances, takes the form of a widespread crisis. It is therefore entering a period of transformation both in the content of democracy and in its links to the economy and to the social process in a global context, which is also characterized by change, by the concentration of wealth and by the increasing internationalization of politics.

The reality is that politics, as noted in various parts of the Report, has major limitations and is in crisis. It lacks the capacity to address the problems to which citizens demand solutions. According to the Report, politics tends to lose its effectiveness due to the diminution of the internal sovereignty of the State, on account of:

- the imbalance in the relationship between politics and the market;
- the presence of an international order that limits the capacity of States to act with a reasonable degree of autonomy; and
- the increasing complexity of societies that cannot be managed using current systems of representation.

In this regard, in their analyses of democracy, the Latin American leaders consulted agree on a number of issues. On the one hand, they welcome the democratization that has taken place over the past decade and the fact that, at least on a formal level, the countries of the region satisfy the minimum requirements of democracy. They also recognize that popular participation and checks and balances on the exercise of power have increased, while threats to democracy as a system and the classic risk of military insubordination have diminished.

On the other hand, they point to problems with political parties and de facto centers of power. With regard to the former, one of the principal difficulties noted is that political parties are failing to channel the demands of citizens effectively. The relationship between political parties and civil society organizations, moreover, is usually conflictual. For the leaders consulted, the solutions to these problems are to be found in politics, through the strengthening of political parties. As for the de facto power centers, especially the economic and financial sectors and the communications media, these are perceived as inhibiting the capacity of governments to meet the demands of citizens. The tensions with other de facto power centers have their roots in, for example, the loss of government autonomy vis-à-vis the United States and multilateral financial organizations and the threat posed by drug trafficking.

For its part, the public opinion survey carried out for this Report reveals tensions between economic development and democracy. The data obtained show that:

- the preference of citizens for democracy is relatively low;
- a large proportion of Latin Americans rank development above democracy and would withdraw their support for a democratic government if it proved incapable of resolving their economic problems;
- 'non-democrats' generally belong to less well-educated groups, whose socialization mainly took place during periods of authoritarianism and who have low expectations of social mobility and a deep distrust of democratic institutions and politicians; and
- although 'democrats' are to be found among the various social groups, citizens tend to support democracy more in countries with lower levels of inequality. However, they do not express themselves through political organizations.

Utilizing data from the survey, an Index of Support for Democracy (ISD) was constructed that offers a condensed view of support for, and the possible vulnerabilities facing, the democracies of Latin America.

In conclusion, the empirical data, the results of the opinion survey and the views of the political leaders all point to the need to recognize that the region is in a period of transformation and crisis and to appreciate the value of the true meaning of politics, namely, its capacity to create options for the promotion of new and viable collective projects. At the heart of this is the empowerment of citizens.

Elements of an Agenda

The Report argues that the starting point for the strengthening of democracy is to give new value to the content and relevance of politics. It contends that the solutions to the problems and challenges of democracy have to be sought within, not outside of, democratic institutions, and finds that a constructive role must be restored to politics, as the instrument that organizes the decisions of society.

In this sense, it maintains the line of argument that UNDP has consistently put forward. As UNDP Administrator Mark Malloch Brown states in the foreword to the Human Development Report 2002: "This Report … is first and foremost about the idea that politics is as important to successful development as economics. Sustained poverty reduction requires equitable growth—but it also requires that poor people have political power. And the best way to achieve that in a manner consistent with human development objectives is by building strong and deep forms of democratic governance at all levels of society."[3]

The re-evaluation of politics requires that policies be adopted that promote legitimate institutions, that an active civil society be developed and, above all, that a wide-ranging debate take place on the State, the economy and globalization.

The agenda proposed in the Report calls for increased participation by citizens. In order to make this sustainable it is essential to advance a type of politics that provides options, harnesses intentions and permits democratic empowerment.

While institutional reforms must continue, these initiatives require a common thread with respect to the promotion of citizen participation. Only this kind of participation can enhance the legitimacy and effectiveness of such reforms. In this regard, a key institutional element is electoral reform, to ensure a better balance between governance and representation.

While party systems are undergoing major changes, they nevertheless tend to be instrumental only in terms of gaining access to government. However, they need to be strengthened in order to enhance their effectiveness and levels of transparency and accountability. The Report concludes that this is the best way of reaffirming the indispensable role of political parties as representatives of society. To this end, political parties need to have a better understanding of the changes taking place in contemporary society, formulate new projects for society and promote public debate.

An important relationship exists between citizenship and civil society organizations, which play a major part in the strengthening of democracy, in the oversight of government stewardship and in the development of pluralism. It is essential to promote strategies for strengthening civil society and its relationship with the State and political parties. The Report argues for alternative forms of representation that complement and strengthen traditional forms of representation without replacing them.

A key proposal is to build a new legitimacy for the State, since there cannot be sustainable democracy when a State does not have the capability to promote and guarantee citizenship. For weak and ineffective States, hopes are limited to the preservation of electoral democracy. A citi-

3 UNDP, *Human Development Report 2002, op. cit*, p. v.

zens' democracy requires a State capable of guaranteeing the universality of rights.

The Report, therefore, calls for a debate on the need for a State that can determine the general direction of society, settle conflicts in accordance with democratic rules, effectively guarantee the functioning of the legal system, maintain legal security, regulate the markets, establish macroeconomic balances, strengthen social security systems based on the principle of universality and uphold the primacy of democracy as the organizing principle of society. According to the Report, State reform should be aimed at answering the following question: what type of Nation is a given society aspiring to build? The Report thus proposes a citizen-centered State.

Another key issue for debate concerns the possibilities for developing an economy in partnership with democracy—in other words, an economy that promotes diversity in order to strengthen the options of citizens. From this perspective, the debate on the diversity of forms of market economy organization must be included in the agenda of public discussion. No discussion on the future of democracy can ignore economic options. The economy is critical, because the development of social citizenship depends on it.

The study asserts that the State and the market can be combined in various ways to create a range of models that can be adapted to promote human development. The type of economy must be at the center of the public debate, as opposed to being only the focus of technical discussion. In short, the Report suggests that progress towards democracy and the establishment of clear and legitimate macroeconomic norms must be seen as mutually reinforcing.

The Report proposes a broadening of the debate on globalization. It notes that it is dangerous to adopt a sort of fatalistic approach to this phenomenon. On the contrary, it is necessary to examine its real impact on the internal sovereignty of States and to develop better strate-

> **For weak and ineffective States, hopes are limited to the preservation of electoral democracy. A citizens' democracy requires a State capable of guaranteeing the universality of rights.**

gies for strengthening the position of the countries of Latin America within the 'global village'. Politics is precisely the force that can create autonomous space.

Methodology and Structure of the Report

In preparing this Report, PRODDAL benefited from the support of the Latin American and Caribbean Division of UNDP and from the collaboration of distinguished intellectuals and academics, as well as of former Presidents and many other distinguished figures from the region.

The study covered 18 countries (Argentina, Bolivia, Brazil, Chile, Colombia, Costa Rica, Dominican Republic, Ecuador, El Salvador, Guatemala, Honduras, Mexico, Nicaragua, Panama, Paraguay, Peru, Uruguay and Venezuela).[4] Extensive consultations were held on the conceptual framework, which oriented the search for empirical data, involving:

- the carrying out of a regional opinion survey (in collaboration with Latinobarómetro);
- the elaboration of indicators on the state of democracy; and
- the holding of interviews with Latin American leaders and intellectuals.

---

4 These countries have democratic regimes—established, for the most part, as a result of processes of transition that have taken place over the past 25 years—and their governments agreed to participate in the project PRODDAL

The Report begins with a conceptual and historical analysis of the democracies in Latin America, based on a broad review of numerous national studies. Discussion workshops were convened on the various components of the project and views and papers were solicited from academics and political figures on numerous aspects of the development of democracy in the region.

The study does not attempt to critique governments or countries. Nor does it attempt to develop some sort of national *ranking* of democracies. Its purpose is to identify the major challenges to democracy and to promote a broad debate on them.

It also recognizes the difficulty of addressing the dilemmas of democracy, since these are influenced by multiple factors (political, economic and social, national and international), some of which were either not addressed or were addressed in a very cursory manner.

In addition to the Report, various supplementary items have been prepared for wide dissemination, including:

- a book containing articles written by outstanding political and academic figures, who have contributed their ideas and positions to the debate on the development of democracy in Latin America;

- a statistical compendium containing information, until now dispersed, on democracy and full citizen participation in Latin American countries, together with the indices developed for this Report and the results of the regional opinion survey;

- the materials used to develop the conceptual framework for the project and its definition of democracy, along with the critical opinions of distinguished analysts; and

- the results of the round of consultations with Latin American leaders.

In conclusion, the Report shows that the gains made in consolidating democracy in Latin America, while highly laudable, are not sufficient. It is necessary to strengthen democratic governance—understood as the institutional strengthening of the system—and, above all, the political culture, which requires the creation of spaces to ensure equitable participation, primarily for the most disadvantaged groups in Latin American societies. This will require not only political will, but also that leaders are committed to their countries and the region, and that citizens are determined to confront the problems and challenges outlined in this Report for a better democracy.

The Development of Democracy in Latin America

This section sets out the main argument of the Report. It highlights the fact that democracy has taken root in Latin American societies where there are high levels of poverty and inequality. A cursory glance at these democracies shows that many basic civil rights are not safeguarded, and that levels of poverty and inequality are among the worst in the world.

The Report begins by outlining the development of democracy in the region and its principal shortcomings and comparing the reforms that have been implemented with political and economic realities. A number of questions arise from this: how much poverty and inequality can democracies tolerate? How do these variables affect social cohesion in the countries concerned? How relevant is democracy for Latin Americans? Opinion polls show that 54.7 percent of Latin Americans would accept an authoritarian government if it could solve their economic problems (see the second section of the Report, "How Latin Americans see their democracy"). The main reasons underlying this worrisome statistic are to be found in the contrasts highlighted here.

This section also briefly explains the theoretical bases of the Report. The practical consequences of the theoretical framework adopted here are important because they provide systematic and rigorous support for the descriptions, analysis and proposals.

The challenges to democracy in Latin America are specific to the region. Meeting them requires fresh understanding and an open dialogue, to which it is hoped this Report will contribute. This means defining with precision its theoretical bases: the concepts of democracy, citizenship and individuals in a democracy, the State and the political regime. The four central arguments are set out below.

a. Democracy is based on a certain concept of the human being and implies the development of citizenship.

b. Democracy is a means of organizing power in society, requiring the existence and healthy functioning of a State.

c. The electoral regime is a basic and fundamental element of democracy, but democracy involves more than the mere holding of elections.

d. The experience of democracy in Latin America is of a particular and historically specific nature, which must be recognized and valued, and measured and developed as such.

The Challenge: from a Democracy of Voters to a Democracy of Citizens[1]

Democracy is a vast human experience. It is linked to the historical search for freedom, justice and material and spiritual progress. Thus it is an experience that never ends.

This is a Report on the unfinished task of democracy, and on the challenges that it faces. Additionally, it seeks to determine what will be the goals for the next stage, the development of which will test the sustainability and durability of democracy.

The search for liberty, justice and progress is a central theme of all human social history, although the form, pace and outcome have varied. *Latin Americans* have been part of this search, with sometimes greater, sometimes lesser awareness of our objectives, at times taking steps forward or back. Even in the most adverse circumstances, and despite long periods of disregard, the struggle has been renewed time and time again. It will continue to renew itself, whether to pass from slavery to the condition of free persons, or to expand the scope of freedom on a daily basis.

But, as the most diverse aspects and areas of our lives show, we also possess another instinct, and one that is as important as those mentioned above: to dominate others and to accumulate power that will permit that control.

To a great extent, our life in society is built on the relationship among these central impulses. We know that where there is no freedom, justice

---

BOX 1

Democracy: a Continuous Search

We must consider what has not been achieved, the ruptures, tensions, limits and denials, which indirectly form part of the experience of democracy. Thus democracy poses a question that remains permanently open: it seems that it has never been possible to provide a completely satisfactory answer. Democracy presents itself as a system of government that is always characterized by the lack of fulfillment and completion.

Pierre Rosanvallon, text prepared for PRODDAL, 2002.

---

or progress, a struggle to win them will be born, and that, within that struggle, differing interests, visions and methods will be in contention.

Our search for freedom, justice and progress, and the power struggle that develops when someone tries to impose his/her interests and opinions, have given rise to different ways of organizing humankind. Democracy is one such system.

Democracy has become synonymous with freedom and justice. It is both an end and a means to that end. In essence, it is made up of a series of

---

1 This publication is an English translation of the revised second edition of the Spanish version of the Report "La democracia en América Latina" published in December 2004 (*www.democracia.undp.org*).

Democracy: an Ideal

Democracy, first and foremost, and above all, is an ideal. [...] Without an idealistic leaning a democracy is not born and, if born, will weaken rapidly. More than any other political system democracy swims against the current, against the laws of inertia that govern human groups. Despotisms, autocratic regimes and dictatorships are easy; they befall us of their own accord; democracies are difficult, they need to be nurtured and believed in.

Giovanni Sartori, 1991, p. 118.

processes designed to grant access to, and to permit the exercise of, power, but it is also, for men and women, the outcome of those processes.

Seen in this light, democracy is more than simply a method for deciding who is to rule. It is also a way of building, guaranteeing and broadening freedom, justice and progress, and of organizing the stresses and clashes that ensue from the struggle for power.

Beyond the differences expressed at the theoretical level about the scope of the idea of democracy, history shows that endeavors aimed at extending the frontiers of civic freedom and reaching higher levels of justice and progress have always been at the heart of the social and political struggles linked, in one way or another, to that idea. During periods of advance and retreat, of movement or inactivity, history shows that, where there was no freedom, it was fought for, where there was no justice, there was a struggle to acquire it, and where there was no progress, men and women searched to achieve it. Notwithstanding the lulls and relapses, the recognition of equality and the search to achieve it in society—in terms of freedom, justice and progress—constitute the historic driving force that is fundamentally linked to the idea of democracy.

This form of organization has come and gone over time. It first emerged in Greece some 2,500 years ago, only to disappear later. "Like fire, painting or the written word, democracy seems to have been invented more than once and in more than one place."[2]

Latin America has achieved electoral democracy and the basic freedoms that are part of it. Now there is a need to progress to a citizens' democracy. The first stage granted us the freedoms and the right to make our own decisions. In many countries of Latin America, it meant the difference between life and death. The second stage, far from complete, is what gives effect to the totality of our rights. It allows us to progress from voters to citizens. It uses political freedoms as a lever with which to construct civil and social citizenship.

For men and women, democracy generates expectations and hopes and leads to disappointments because of the way in which it contributes to the organization of their lives in society, safeguards their rights and allows them to enhance their quality of life. Democracy deals with life: it is much more than simply a system of government. It is more than merely a means of electing and of being elected. Its principal figure is the citizen rather than the voter.

Over the course of 200 years of independent existence, democracy in Latin America has emerged and ended on dozens of occasions. Even as it was being enshrined in Constitutions, it was being destroyed in practice. War, tyranny and short periods of stability are associated with much of this history of independence, during which even flagrant violations of democracy were committed in its name. In a global context, Latin America may well be the region that has most often proclaimed the defense of democracy over the past two centuries, although it has sometimes suspended it with the intention of reinstating it later.

After so often seeing our desire to take part in the building of democracy denied or snatched away, Latin Americans are now, finally,

2 Robert Dahl, 1999, p. 15.

taking responsibility for addressing its challenges and ensuring its development.

After two decades of differing forms of transition, democratic systems of government now extend broadly across Latin America. Some 25 years ago, of the 18 countries included in this Report, only three (Colombia, Costa Rica and Venezuela) were democracies. A quarter of a century later, all countries satisfy the basic criteria of a democratic regime, in political and electoral terms.

The freedoms we now possess are of inestimable value; this is a victory achieved through the effort and suffering of millions of people. We have witnessed the deepest and broadest advance of democracy since the independence of our Nations. But, as we shall see in this Report, what has been won is by no means secure.

Neither the preservation nor the expansion of democracy happens of its own accord. They are constructions based on free will, conceived as plans, shaped by leadership and invested with the power derived from popular support. Both require political parties that offer genuine choices, a State with the power to implement these choices, and a society capable of participating in a constructive project that goes beyond partisan claims. Policies that fail to address core problems remove meaning from the choices open to citizens; a State without power transforms an electoral mandate into a mere list of wishes without consequences; and a society without active participation leads, sooner or later, to the establishment of a dangerous autonomous power structure, which will cease to meet the needs of its citizens.

While we seem to be moving away from the threat of military coups, there are other dangers. Democracy appears to be losing its vitality; although democracy is the preferred system, people question its capacity to improve living conditions; public regard for political parties is at an all-time low;[3] the State is viewed simultaneously with both optimism and distrust and, in some respects, the democratic impetus that characterized the final decades of the twentieth century is weakening. People are protesting in the streets, but without a single purpose to unify their claims and demands.

How serious are these new fragilities? If democracy becomes irrelevant to Latin Americans, if it is divorced from their needs, will it be able to resist the new dangers, enemies and frustrations?

To analyze, as we propose, the development of democracy in Latin America we must turn our attention to the effectiveness of the rights that Latin Americans enjoy and the extent to which the hopes that they place in their representatives are satisfied. We must also investigate the sustainability of democracy—that is, its capacity to endure and improve—which hails from the legitimacy that it derives from citizens. Such analysis leads us, finally, to identify the traps and challenges confronting democracy.

How do we resolve the tensions between the expansion of democracy and the economy, between freedom and the search for equality, between growth and poverty, between public demands freely expressed and economic reforms requiring sacrifices and adjustments? What are the keys to explaining the crisis of representation, society's lack of confidence in politics? Why has the hope generated by democracy not evolved into advances in civil and social rights commensurate with the expectations that it raised? Why does the State lack the power that it needs? Why has the right to elect those who

> Democracy is a vast human experience. It is linked to the historical search for freedom, justice and material and spiritual progress. Thus it is an experience that never ends.

---

3 According to the Latinobarómetro 2002 opinion poll, only 14 percent of Latin Americans trust political parties.

> In Latin America, political reflection and debate need to be renewed and reinvigorated because they have lost vitality and content.

govern not led, in many cases, to greater freedom, justice and development?

These are dilemmas with complex solutions, as our own recent history shows. And they cannot be resolved if they are not the focus of public debate and of the choices offered by political parties. Unfortunately, there is more than one example to suggest that some types of debate are forbidden in Latin America. Some issues are considered unsuitable or, worse still, cannot be talked about. Politicians and those who set the agenda for public debate cannot continue indefinitely to ignore the clamor of hundreds of millions of people, unless they are prepared to pay the price and watch democracy in Latin America languish.

This Report deals with these issues, identifying them not through a mere intuitive exercise, but rather through theoretical analysis, empirical observation and the thoughts of intellectuals and politicians.

Grappling with these dilemmas requires that as much information as possible be available to shed light on the criteria used to formulate policies. The lack of information and debate is a serious shortcoming, because democracy—which is based on reflection and discussion among citizens and their leaders—is the only form of political organization that has the capacity to be self-correcting. This is the main advantage that makes democracy a just and effective system. The freedom that guarantees democracy is, at the same time, its principal means of self-improvement. But freedom, or, in other words, the ability to choose, requires that there is a choice to be made. In Latin America, political reflection and debate need to be renewed and reinvigorated because they have lost

vitality and content. This is happening at just the time when democracy has become most widespread and when globalization has made it increasingly urgent that, as societies and as Nations, we know what we want.

Our democracies need to rediscover their initial impetus without delay. Their deficiencies are not failures, they are challenges. The goals we have not yet achieved must now inform the policies that will make it possible to encourage the second stage of the democracy project in Latin America.

This is the main thread that should guide the reader through the rest of the Report: the search for the crucial topics that will test our ability to advance from an electoral democracy to a democracy based on citizenship. In the process, Latin America's capacity to transform democracy into a self-stabilizing, self-renewing and self-expanding system will be tested.

Our purpose is to show that, once the challenge is accepted—namely, moving from a democracy of electors to one of citizens—serious conceptual reflection will be essential. This will generate the ideas that frame our observation of reality and collection of information which, in turn, will form the empirical basis of this Report. From the sum of these two components will emerge the nucleus of issues that constitute the challenges presented in the extended agenda for the development of democracy in Latin America.

The Report marks the beginning of a task, of a debate that UNDP is seeking to foster among Latin Americans. This effort is just removing the first veil, so that the social and political actors who must re-launch and regenerate our democracies can begin to come up with alternative and specific policies.

These reflections, observations and outcomes are derived from an initial perception: the peculiar nature of democracy in Latin America. The list of challenges is new, because we are dealing with a region where democracy coexists with poverty and inequality. This triangle—electoral democracy, poverty and inequality—marks the start of our exploration.

Democracy, Poverty and Inequality: a Latin American Triangle

To understand what is required to deepen democracy in Latin America, and to comprehend its weaknesses, it is vital that one appreciate the special characteristics of democracy in the region.

Rules and institutions in Latin America are similar to those in countries where democracy is more mature, but its societies are fundamentally different.

The building and broadening of civil rights are tasks that are unfolding against a new backdrop in Latin America. In the past 20 years a number of major changes have taken place. For the first time in history, an entire developing region with profoundly unequal societies is, in its entirety, organized politically under democratic governments. Thus a new and unprecedented situation has emerged in Latin America:[4] the coexistence of democracy, poverty and inequality.

The first point of the triangle is the spread of electoral democracy in the region. All of the countries of Latin America fulfill the basic requirements of a democratic regime. Only the countries that belong to the Organisation for Economic Co-operation and Development (OECD) share that characteristic.

The second point of the triangle is poverty. In 2002 some 218 million people in the region (42.8 percent of the total population) received a level of income that was below the poverty line. Of course, the situation varies from country to country. In spite of these differences, compared with other large democratic regions of the world, Latin America is unique, in that political freedom exists alongside extreme, widespread material deprivation. Democracy and wealth, and democracy and poverty, are two combinations that give rise to different needs, problems and risks.

> For the first time in history, an entire developing region with profoundly unequal societies is, in its entirety, organized politically under democratic governments.

The third point of the triangle is inequality. Latin American societies are the most unequal in the world. This inequality has persisted throughout the past three decades.

These three factors coexist for the first time and the stability of democracy is threatened because it has to live alongside both poverty and inequality. The risks arising from this triangle are more complex than the traditional ones associated with a military coup d'etat— which, moreover, have not disappeared altogether.

Despite its unique situation, Latin America is usually placed in the same historical context as the developed democracies. But this overlooks the fact that democratic stability and expansion in Latin America differ both in terms of their content and the difficulties that they face because of their specificity. These are unequal and poor democracies, whose men and women must secure their civil and social rights while they consolidate their political rights.

Limited understanding of these special circumstances can result in two serious consequences for democracy. The first concerns lack of awareness of the fact that democracy must be economically viable. That is, to ignore the need to construct solid foundations for an economy so that it can combat poverty and inequality. For example, many Latin American citizens believe that the attainment of higher levels of development in their countries is such an important goal that they would be prepared

---

4 We do not mean that the combination of democracy, poverty and inequality does not exist in other countries or regions of the world. What we are emphasizing is that democracy in Latin America coexists with a high level of poverty and the highest level of inequality.

DEMOCRACY, POVERTY AND INEQUALITY

TABLE 1

Region	Electoral Participation (1)	Inequality (2)	Poverty	GDP per capita
Latin America	62.7	0.552 (3)	42.8 (6)	3792 (9)
Europe	73.6	0.290 (4)	15.0 (7)	22600 (10)
USA	43.3	0.344 (5)	11.7 (8)	36100

Notes:

(1) Those voting as a percentage of the population with a right to vote, 1990–2002. See Table 7.

(2) Gini coefficient. The higher the value of the Gini coefficient, the greater the degree of inequality.

(3) Simple average for the 1990s. Perry et al., 2004, p. 57.

(4) Eurostat, PCM–BDU, December 2002.

(5) OECD 2003, Social Indicators and Tables.

(6) Poverty data for 1998–2002. Average weighted by population, ECLAC, 2004.

(7) Eurostat PCM-BDU, December 2002.

(8) United States Census Bureau, 2001, Poverty in the United States, 2002.

(9) Produced for this Report based on data from ECLAC, 2004 (in constant US dollars).

(10) Western Europe (EU-15) and USA, GDP per capita, 2002. Source: OECD (in US dollars at current exchange rate).

Given the multiplicity of sources and the diverse methodologies used, we suggest that the data in this table be considered only as indicative.

to support an authoritarian regime if it met their demands for social welfare. The second concerns failure to consider the political viability of economic programs. One cannot overlook the fact that these programs are introduced in societies where citizens' demands and views on policies are freely expressed.

In fact, it is not unusual to make the mistake of thinking of economic reform as if democracy did not exist: as if the difficult and painful processes of structural adjustment were of no account in the decisions taken by the majority (which must endure the conditions of poverty and great inequality) when it comes to voting, or supporting or rejecting a government; or as if an economic plan could be implemented without the backing of the people, or, even worse, in spite of their hostility.

Thinking about democracy in Latin America independent of the economy, or vice versa, appears to be an ingenuous mistake. But this does not make it any the less recurring or worrisome for the fate of both democracy and the economies of the countries of the region.

Hence, the debate about democratic stability cannot ignore poverty and inequality. Furthermore, policies designed to stimulate growth should not ignore the fact that citizens exercise their right to accept or reject these policies. This is the reason why there is a desperate need to resolve the tensions between economics and democracy. The starting point for doing so is not to think about economics as if there were no poor democracies, nor to tackle problems concerning democratic stability independent of the need to resolve issues concerning growth. Any debate that ignores such fundamental facts will most likely end up making recommendations that are impractical.

It has been argued, therefore, that democracy in Latin America may not be viable until the problems of poverty are resolved and an acceptable minimum level of equality is attained. On more than one occasion, authoritarian regimes have taken power promising to restore democracy: "We are taking over the government in order to create the conditions in which democracy can be securely instated in the future." Supposedly, it was necessary to reach a certain wealth threshold before democracy could exist. Contrary to this view, this Report maintains that only with more and better democracy can Latin American societies achieve greater equality and development. This is because only in a democracy can those who do not enjoy a minimum level of well-being and suffer the injustices of inequality make claims and choices, and mobilize themselves in defense of their rights. For this to happen, it is essential to open up unexplored avenues and to start new debates in Latin America because—we repeat—the great challenge is to combat poverty and inequality with the instruments of democracy in order to create the social cohesion and stability which are the essential requirements for economic growth.

Political and economic reforms have already been undertaken in Latin America. Although they have led to some important developments, especially in deepening electoral democracy, there remains stark contrast between the reforms advanced over the past two decades and the current situation, which continues to exhibit major failings with regard to various aspects of citizenship, particularly social citizenship.

These were years of not only political transformation. Economics also changed profoundly, particularly in the 1990s—opening up, reform and deregulation occurred as part of a process that is known generically as *structural adjustment.* So, with a few exceptions, "the new surge of democratization in the region that began in the mid-1980s took as its own agenda economic reforms directed to expanding the sphere in which the markets held sway."[5]

As a result of these changes, Latin American countries have become developing societies, where social demands are freely expressed and the economy is organized around the markets. In this way, social demands expressed in the context of political freedom (democracy) and economic freedom (the markets) form another unique triangle, one which should be virtuous, but which, in light of the past 20 years, raises complex difficulties that require a fresh intellectual approach. The combination of political and economic freedom against a backdrop of poverty and ine-

Only with more and better democracy can Latin American societies achieve greater equality and development.

quality may not lead to stronger democracy or economic development.

The following pages offer a snapshot of the contrast between reforms and realities on the ground. They also provide a first look at Latin America's democratic deficit, underlining why frustrations exist and why it is urgent to build a citizens' democracy.

Balance Sheet of Reforms and Realities

Seven basic indicators were used to prepare this balance sheet: structural economic reforms; democratic reforms; evolution of gross domestic product (GDP) per capita; poverty; indigence; income concentration; and the employment situation.

Before presenting the table that summarizes these basic indicators (Table 2), some clarification is necessary. In the first place, the Report does not contend that a causal relationship necessarily exists among the variables. However, it does assert that Latin American citizens have experienced the effects of these variables more or less simultaneously.

Second, in a democracy citizens have expectations about how the economy should perform. These expectations have their roots in the egalitarian ideology that underlies democracy, and the discourse of national politicians, the media, international organizations and so forth. During the 1990s an economic model that promised development was placed center stage, and many now feel defrauded by it.

Third, the perception among a large num-

5 José A. Ocampo, text prepared for PRODDAL, 2003.

REFORMS AND REALITIES

TABLE 2

	Economic Reform Index (1)	Index of Electoral Democracy (1)	Growth of Real GDP per capita, Annualized % (3)	Poverty % (2)	Indigence % (2)	Gini Coefficient (2)	Urban Unemployment (1)
Southern Cone Sub-Region (Argentina, Chile, Paraguay, Uruguay)							
1981-90	0.66	0.44	-0.8%	25.6	7.1	0.502	8.8
1991-97	0.82	0.88	1.3%	21.2	5.7	0.527	8.7
1998-02	0.84	0.91	1.0%	32.3	12.9	0.558	12.1
Brazil							
1981-90	0.52	0.70	1.7%	48.0	23.4	0.603	5.2
1991-97	0.75	1.00	0.4%	40.6	17.1	0.638	5.3
1998-02	0.79	1.00	1.1%	37.5	13.1	0.640	7.1
Andean Sub-Region (Bolivia, Colombia, Ecuador, Peru, Venezuela)							
1981-90	0.53	0.83	-0.6%	52.3	22.1	0.497	8.8
1991-97	0.76	0.86	0.9%	50.4	18.1	0.544	8.3
1998-02	0.82	0.83	0.1%	52.7	25.0	0.545	12.0
Mexico							
1981-90	0.61	0.31	1.7%	47.8	18.8	0.521	4.2
1991-97	0.78	0.70	0.4%	48.6	19.1	0.539	4.0
1998-02	0.81	1.00	2.2%	42.5	15.4	0.528	2.6
Central America Sub-Region (Costa Rica, Dominican Republic, El Salvador, Guatemala, Honduras, Nicaragua, Panama)							
1981-90	0.55	0.59	4.1%	55.3	35.6	0.532	9.1
1991-97	0.80	0.89	-3.5%	52.0	27.8	0.524	9.1
1998-02	0.85	0.97	2.8%	54.0	29.7	0.546	8.8
Latin America							
1981-90	0.58	0.64	0.7%	46.0	20.4	0.551	8.4
1991-97	0.79	0.87	0.6%	42.8	18.3	0.574	8.8
1998-02	0.83	0.92	1.2%	42.8	17.7	0.577	10.4

Notes:

(1) Simple average.

(2) Weighted by population.

(3) From period to period.

The Economic Reform Index is made up of five components: international trade policies; tax policies; financial policies; privatizations; and capital accounts. The index ranges between zero, indicating lack of market-oriented reforms, and one, indicating the application of highly market-oriented reforms. The Index of Electoral Democracy ranges between zero, indicating a lack of electoral democracy, and one, indicating that the requirements of electoral democracy have been met.

The annualized rate of growth of GDP per capita was calculated in the following way: a) actual GDP values (in 1995 US dollars) were added up for the years in the period under analysis and this total was divided by the number of years in the period; b) this was then divided by the average population over the period; and c) GDP per capita for this period was divided by that of the previous period, and then the geometric root was calculated according to the number of years in the period in question. The figures for real GDP growth per capita for this period are calculated in 1995 US dollars. The figures for poverty and indigence and the Gini coefficients are averages of the data for the years available.

In the columns on poverty and indigence the data points selected are those that take in the largest geographical coverage presented in the ECLAC database. In this sense, and for certain countries, series with a different geographical coverage were used based on the criterion to employ the figure with the greatest geographical coverage. This implies that the data on poverty and indigence may be under-estimated, and that, for the countries concerned, the variation in a given series may not necessarily reflect changes in the levels of poverty and indigence. The updating of this table took advantage of the new data provided by ECLAC and the newest population data from *Latin American and Caribbean Demographic Centre* (CELADE). Drawing on decennial censuses conducted recently, CELADE re-estimated the population data for the 1990s. This affected all of the series weighted by population and the per capita data. This exercise added several million people to the official population statistics.

Sources: data for the Economic Reform Index were taken from Samuel A. Morley, Roberto Machado and Stefano Pettinato, 1999, and Eduardo Lora, 2001; information was provided by Manuel Marfán, Director of the Economic Development Division of ECLAC, 4 February 2003.

The methodology and data for the Electoral Democracy Index are presented in the Technical Note at the end of this Report and in the Statistical Compendium. The other data came from many publications produced by the Economic Commission for Latin America and the Caribbean, except for the data on the Gini coefficient prior to 1990, the source of which is Klaus Deininger and Lyn Squire, 1998.

ber of citizens is that the policies put in place 'produced' insufficient levels of growth, increasing poverty and inequality and worsening unemployment (with its consequent impact on inequality and expected future retirement income).

1. *The Economic Reform Index (ERI) points to a steady advance* in these reforms. Measured between zero and one, the ERI rose from 0.58 in the 1980s to 0.83 on average between 1998 and 2002. This index consists of five sub-indices: international trade policies; tax policies; financial policies; privatizations; and capital accounts—all related to the so-called *Washington Consensus*.

2. *Latin America today recognizes universal voting rights, without restrictions* of any significance. This is a notable achievement and is of paramount importance. The Electoral Democracy Index (EDI), prepared by the Project on Democratic Development in Latin America (PRODDAL), shows that, in electoral terms, democracy improved at a steady rate throughout the period under consideration. The processes of democratization and market reform, albeit different, moved steadily forward, resulting in high expectations that contrasted markedly with actual events.

3. *Average GDP per capita in the region* has not varied significantly over the past 20 years. In 1980, when the ERI was 0.55, GDP per capita stood at $3,734 in constant 1995 US dollars. In 2000, after 20 years of implementing reforms, the ERI was 0.83 and GDP per capita was $3,920, an almost negligible increase.

4. *Poverty levels have been reduced slightly in relative terms.* In 1990 the percentage of the poor[6] weighted by the size of each population was 46 percent for the 18 countries; between 1998 and 2002 the proportion fell to 42.8 percent. This step forward was essentially due to the relative improvement of Brazil, Chile and Mexico. In absolute terms, though, the number of people living below the poverty line increased. In 1990 some 191 million Latin Americans were poor. By 2002, this number had risen to 218 million, out of a total population of 508 million. In addition, even in relative terms, poverty throughout this period increased in the Southern Cone (from 25.6 percent to 32.3 percent) and in the Andean sub-region (from 52.3 percent to 52.7 percent).

5. *Levels of inequality have not been reduced.* In 1990 the Gini coefficient[7] (regional average weighted by population) was 0.554. In 2002 it stood at 0.576. The world average in the 1990s was 0.381, while for developed countries it was 0.337. High inequality is also demonstrated by the relationship between higher and lower income levels. In 1990 the richest ten percent of Latin Americans had 25.4 times the income of the poorest ten percent. In 2002 the correlation was 40 times.[8] Also in 2002 the richest 20 percent of Latin Americans received 54.2 percent of total income and the poorest 20 percent received only 4.7 percent. The region has the most unequal level of income distribution in the world.

6. *The labor situation has worsened throughout almost the entire region* over the past 15 years. Unemployment and the size of the

---

6 Measuring poverty using the 'Poverty Line' (PL) produced by the Economic Commission for Latin America and the Caribbean (ECLAC) involves looking at income per household and establishing the household's capacity to acquire a selection of food and non-food essentials through purchases of goods and services.

7 This measure is derived from a graphic representation of income distribution known as the Lorenz Curve. A Gini coefficient of zero represents perfect equality of distribution, while one symbolizes absolute inequality. A Gini coefficient of 0.25–0.35 can, therefore, be considered a 'reasonable' distribution; a Gini coefficient of 0.55 signifies extreme inequality.

8 The data are not exactly the same as that in the table because the measurements were taken at different times.

underground economy have increased significantly. Social protection for workers has also declined (healthcare, pensions and union membership). This is linked to a deterioration in income distribution and a rise in poverty levels, resulting in a situation that will have very negative effects in the medium and long terms.

This initial snapshot points to the immense and complex task facing Latin America. Twenty-five years ago the region faced a challenge that was both difficult and simple. To confront it required imagination and boldness, but there was no doubt as to its nature: to defeat dictatorships, end wars, and achieve democracy and peace. No one questioned what the agenda for democracy was.

Today, renewing the content of democracy and giving impetus to a new phase is a much larger and more uncertain goal. In concrete terms, what does *striving for a democracy of citizenship* really mean? What are the core issues? What conditions do we need to address them? Who are the new opponents to a deeper democracy? The choices are not as clear-cut as those of the 1970s: democracy or dictatorship; freedom or oppression; and life or death.

The challenge of awakening the imagination, stimulating the use of knowledge and mobilizing politics is a difficult, arduous and uncertain task, as the contrasts identified above make clear. The first requirement is to become aware of just how essential it is to confront that challenge. This involves getting to grips with the historical legacy of economic and technological backwardness, social fragmentation and with a disadvantageous position in the international system.

The following pages begin to explore these issues, as well as a number of subjects, such as: the nature of the challenges facing the development of democracy, the central importance of citizens' rights, the very idea of democracy and the role of the State, which are at the heart of our analysis.

This is not a theoretical exposition in the strict sense, but rather an attempt to point out some basic landmarks of the theoretical foundations of our work.

We enter into this domain not because the purpose of the Report is to conduct an academic inquiry into democracy but because the practical consequences of the different conceptions are highly relevant at the stage of drawing up policies and strategies for sustainable democracy. These differences concern the conditions for deepening democracy, the risks of it disappearing, the way in which certain public policies are formulated and perceived, the socio-cultural and gender differences, the concept of the State and all its transformations or the role of politics and political organizations. Also, depending on what views of democracy we take, there will be sharp differences with respect to what we expect from another form of social organization: the economy.

In other words, if democracy were nothing more than a system of government, we might find ourselves confronting an extremely paradoxical state of affairs: a society that is poor in terms of economic and social rights, as well as basic civil rights, but which is considered fully democratic.

Another important consequence stemming from an understanding of democracy as only a system of government is a segmentary view of public policies. Thus some policies would be designed to ensure proper conditions for the functioning of a democratic regime, others would be designed to help the economy perform adequately and still more would be designed to bring about appropriate reforms in, for example, the organization of the State.

Looking through so fragmented a lens, one might believe that it is possible to strengthen democracy simply by improving the way in which the regime operates; there might be no awareness of the impact on democracy of State reforms or of structural economic reforms, for instance.

Nor, from this standpoint, would it be obvious how policies to reform the State or the economy will ultimately be judged by the majorities that will measure results by whether their own lives have improved or the distribution of wealth has become fairer. In other words, the citizen's verdict is a substantial factor in whether reform policies will prove viable.

Democracy and the Promise of Citizens' Rights

Despite the establishment of a democratic regime, the nature and functions of the State did not change because of internal and external factors that obstruct the achievement of citizens' rights. As a result, the expectations created with respect to that regime have been frustrated because the performance of political organisms and public institutions have not matched up to the expectations of the majority of the people, who are historically subjected to 'poverty' and 'exclusion'—technocratic names that hide the social relationships that give rise to these situations. This is even more the case today, because, in the new international climate, the system of government and the State reinforce these conditions, running counter to democratic and liberal rhetoric and the promises of political leaders.

For these reasons, the disrepute of the existent democratic system gives rise to 'informal', if not illegal, arrangements established by broad sections of society, particularly the poor and those excluded from the socially diffused core of beliefs and from political action, in order to meet their individual and collective aspirations, which the State is unable to control due to a lack of material resources and public support.

The fragmentation of social interests and political representation that follows in the wake of this behavior worsens the problems concerning collective action, while, at the same time, the spread of 'free-riders,' who irresponsibly offer to resolve social demands through opportunistic short-term proposals, results in uncertainty and general unrest.

At this juncture, we should not be surprised to hear voices predicting dramatic *dénouements*; however, in spite of such dark omens, we see people who stubbornly persist in defending the validity of the democratic system, arguing that it provides the only possible framework within which to nationalize and democratize the State and society. As a Peruvian union leader said recently: "Democracy does not guarantee social justice, but it is the only arena where we can fight to achieve it."

Julio Cotler, text prepared for PRODDAL, 2002.

International Organizations and the Fostering of Democracy

The Report is inspired by the letter and the spirit of different United Nations (UN) documents:

- The Universal Declaration of Human Rights, approved by the UN in 1948, sets out a broad notion of citizenship, encompassing civil, political and social rights.
- The Vienna Declaration and Action Programme of 1993 establishes that "the international community should support the strengthening and promoting of democracy, development and respect for human rights and fundamental freedoms in the entire world."
- The United Nations Commission for Human Rights called for the promotion of democratic rights in Resolution 1999/57.

- In its Millennium Declaration of 2000, the UN General Assembly established that "we will spare no effort to promote democracy and strengthen the rule of law, as well as respect for all internationally recognized human rights and fundamental freedoms, including the right to development."

The UN, through all of its agencies and programs, promotes respect for human rights and the holding of free and fair elections. In the Millennium Declaration, the UN and other international organizations that focus on cooperation and financial assistance reinforced their call to encourage democracy, strengthen the rule of law and to strive for sustainable development. The governance programs of the United Nations Development Programme (UNDP) encourage, for example, democratic dialogue, State reform initiatives and economic development. For UNDP, democracy and human development share a common vision and

Universal Declaration of Human Rights

In its Charter, the United Nations reaffirms its belief in the fundamental rights of man, in the dignity and worth of a human being and in equal rights for men and women. The United Nations has also resolved to promote social progress and to improve living standards as part of a broader concept of freedom.

United Nations,1948.

purpose: human development is a process for strengthening our capacities as human beings, providing each person with better opportunities to live a decent and worthwhile life. This, in turn, requires a political system to ensure it: namely, democracy.

At the same time, it is important to draw attention to the role played by various regional organizations and the initiatives that they have launched that prioritize the defense and strengthening of democracy. Countries in the region have made a notable commitment to democracy through the Organization of American States (OAS). The OAS took a crucial step at its 1991 meeting in Santiago, Chile, when its member States adopted mechanisms for reacting to situations in which democracy might be threatened. Another key move by the OAS was the approval of the Inter-American Democratic Charter in 2001. Coordination by Latin American leaders of efforts to support democracy, especially through international organizations, is undoubtedly a fundamental aim in strengthening democracies throughout Latin America.

The work carried out by the Rio Group, the Ibero-American Summits of Heads of State and Government and the OAS through the Unit for the Promotion of Democracy should also be singled out. More specifically, it gives impetus to the task of defining a regional political agenda that highlights the importance of politics and political parties, civil society organizations and civic participation in the various processes of public life, democratic culture, institutions that guarantee transparency and efficient government,

Democratic Rights

The United Nations Commission on Human Rights affirms that the rights of democratic governance include, *inter alia*, the following:

a. The rights to freedom of opinion and expression, of thought, conscience and religion, and a peaceful association and of peaceful association and assembly;

b. The right to freedom to seek, receive and impart information and ideas through any media;

c. The rule of law, including legal protection of citizens' rights, interests and personal security, and fairness in the administration of justice and independence of the judiciary;

d. The right of universal and equal suffrage, as well as free voting procedures and periodic and free elections;

e. The right of political participation, including equal opportunity for all citizens to became candidates;

f. Transparent and accountable government institutions;

g. The right of citizens to choose their governmental system through constitutional or other democratic means;

h. The right to equal access to public service in one's own country.

ONU, Commission of Human Rights, 1999

Democracy means more than Holding Elections

But true democratization means more than elections. [...] Granting all people formal political equality does not create an equal desire or capacity to participate in political processes - or an equal capacity to influence outcomes. Imbalances in resources and political power often subvert the principle of one person, one voice, and the purpose of democratic institutions.

PNUD, 2002c, pp. 4 and 14.

It is by now almost a truism that elections are not isolated events but part of a holistic process.

Kofi Annan, UN Secretary General, 2003.

Free and fair elections are necessary, but they are not sufficient. We are seriously selling democracy short when we celebrate elections as proof of a democracy being in place.

Mark Malloch Brown, UNDP Administrator, 2002.

democratic governance, the rule of law, the reduction of poverty, and the impact of the new economic order on economic development.

We must emphasize that these initiatives are not limited to promoting electoral democracy alone. On the contrary, regional and international organizations include among their goals both the consolidation of the rule of law and economic development. Increasingly, the international community is moving towards adopting the broader vision of democracy that this Report proposes, and towards the idea that, in order to prevent reversals in the democratic process, it is necessary to view the democratic system as an integral part of the framework of political, civil and social citizenship. The great challenge is to consolidate this emerging consensus and to turn it into support for reforms that will strengthen the democracies of Latin America.

■ An Exploration of the Development of Democracy[9]

The more democracy, the better: this is the premise behind our exploration of the development of democracy in Latin America. But, in any case, *in dubio pro democratia* ('in doubt more democracy').

Although this criterion is widely held to be valid, it does not provide answers to the theoretical and political discussion that has been taking place regarding two points: how much democracy, and where?

To what spheres of life should democratic decision-making mechanisms and the rights of citizenship be extended? What costs, in terms of other social objectives, are we willing to pay to advance the process of democratization? Should democratic mechanisms and the rights of citizenship apply to, for example, the internal functioning of political parties and trade unions, but not to businesses, universities, international organizations and families? Is it possible for reasonably consistent and widely accepted criteria to exist on where and where not to extend the mechanisms and rights of democracy? And, perhaps even more enigmatically, who should answer this type of question, and how?

Convinced democrats from various schools and traditions will continue to debate where, how, when and by whom the limits of democracy should be set. In politics, especially democratic politics, a central question concerns the limits of politics itself, and, as a consequence, the limits of the State.[10] What social evils may be prevented? Which of them should be resolved through politics and by the State? What events are inevitable or should be left to market forces or to the goodwill of some social actors?

These questions should only be examined in the context of the specific circumstances of each country. However, in view of the focus of this Report, we cannot ignore how the realm of politics, democracy and the State has been narrowed in the recent history of Latin America.

A significant proportion of contemporary theory on democracy limits itself to characterizing democracy as a political regime. This limitation reflects, and reinforces, a general conception of what politics is about, specifically democratic politics. Such a view prohibits democ-

---

9 This section is based mainly on the documents prepared by Guillermo O'Donnell for PRODDAL: *Notes on the State of Democracy in Latin America*, 2002c; and 'The Role of the State in Contemporary Latin America: Ten Theses for Discussion', 2002. The latter is also of fundamental importance in the Third Section of the Report, most especially in the part dealing with democracy and the State.

10 S. N. Eisenstadt (2000, p. 14) makes the significant observation that one of the "central aspects of the modern political process ... [is] a continuing struggle over the definition of the realm of the political. Indeed, it is only with the coming of modernity that drawing the boundaries of the political becomes one of the major foci of open political contestation and struggle." Also see Eisenstadt, 1999.

racy—and politics in general—from taking an active stance on social injustice connected to the widespread lack of social and civil rights, as well as to the anemic condition of the State, which, as a result, loses credibility with the fluctuating majorities within society.

This reduction in the creative capacity of democracy is the result, among other things, of a conceptual failing: of judging democracy as if it was merely electoral democracy.

When citizenship is viewed as the touchstone of democracy, there is a change on how it is evaluated. In effect, a different way of thinking and acting manifests itself when democracy is measured by its capacity to guarantee and expand the role of citizens in the civil, social and political spheres.

The notion of citizenship implies that each person is a member of the community with full rights. It embraces different spheres, each with its own rights and obligations. The broadening of citizenship is one condition for the success of a society and for strengthening its capacity to fulfill people's expectations. This is the framework that we should employ to judge the quality of democracy.

Thus, the measure of the development of a democracy is its capacity to enforce the rights of its citizens and to make them the subjects of the decisions that affect them.

To sum up, when this Report talks about the extent of the development of democracy —its achievements and deficits— one is questioning the means of gaining access to public office, the system of social organization that is generated by democracy—the State, the political parties, the power structure—as well as the quality of the civil, social and political citizenship enjoyed by the men and women who make up the Nation.

An Unfinished Debate

For almost two decades, and particularly in the 1990s, public policies and agendas in Latin America have concentrated on how to strengthen democracy, the crisis of politics, reform of the State, structural economic reform and the impact of globalization on the region. However, although substantive aspects of these issues have been dealt with, the debate has side-stepped other elements, which, in light of the analysis presented in this Report, should be the central focus of the discussion.

Democracy has been seen in terms of what is essentially its electoral dimension. Politics was observed from the angle of the crisis epitomized by its parties, clientelistic structures, corruption or possible alternative electoral regimes. The problems of the State were centered on the is-

PERCEPTIONS ON WHY PEOPLE IN GOVERNMENT DO NOT KEEP THEIR ELECTORAL PROMISES, LATIN AMERICA, 2002	TABLE 3
Keeping of Promises	**People (%)**
People in government keep their electoral promises	2.3
They do not keep their promises because they are not aware of how complicated the problems are	10.1
They do not keep their promises because more urgent problems manifest themselves	9.6
They do not keep their promises because the system prevents them from doing so	11.5
They do not keep their promises because they choose to lie, in order to win the elections	64.7
None of the above	1.7

Note: n = 19.279.
Source: question P25U from the UNDP Proprietary Section of the opinion survey conducted by Latinobarómetro in 2002.

sue of balanced budgets, modernizing bureaucracy and reducing government interference in the economy. Economic debate was limited almost exclusively to the question of attaining equilibria and implementing the structural reforms that were supposedly necessary to achieve them. Lastly, globalization was seen as either the origin of inevitable evils or the source of immense benefaction, to such an extent that even the notion of the continuity of Nation States came to be questioned in a world marching towards 'the global village'.

As already noted, these debates were unavoidable at the time that they took place. Now, they are not far-reaching enough. Development of democracy means much more than how to perfect the electoral system.

The *crisis of politics* is evident not only with respect to the low credibility and prestige of political parties but also to the inefficacy of governments in dealing with key issues that are evidently deficits of citizenship: in particular, issues concerning civil and social rights. Both dimensions of the political crisis—institutional and content related—are vital, for it is politics that

> Development of democracy means much more than how to perfect the electoral system.

should frame options, represent citizens and forge links between the State and society in order to generate democratic power.

Many areas where there are crucial deficiencies are connected to the *role of the State*—by which we mean the State's capacity to fulfill functions and to meet objectives regardless of the size of its bureaucracy or the way in which it is organized. In recent times, discussion on the State has been limited to issues related to bureaucratic capacity and the structure of its expenditures and revenues—that is, the fiscal deficit. Not up for debate, it seems, was the existence of States with incomplete and ineffectual legal systems, States that are unable to establish a monopoly over the use of force, and States that lack the necessary power to implement the electoral mandate—in general States with serious problems in fulfilling their crucial role of building up democracy.[11]

11 According to George Soros (2001): "Capitalism creates wealth but cannot be relied upon to assure freedom, democracy and the rule of law. Business is motivated by profit; it is not designed to safeguard universal principles. Even the preservation of the market itself requires more than self-interest: market participants compete to win, and if they could, would eliminate competition."

Citizenship and the Community of Citizens

Citizenship is a state of inclusion within a 'community of citizens'. But the latter cannot be defined simply by the right to vote and the guarantee that a certain number of individual freedoms will be protected. Citizenship is also defined by *the existence of a common world*. In other words, it must have a societal dimension. Alexis de Tocqueville was the first to point out that democracy is characterized by a *form of society* and not just by a collection of institutions and political principles.

Pierre Rosanvallon, text prepared for PRODDAL, 2002.

The *economic question* is made up of many different options that the 'one-answer-fits-all' (*la pensée unique*) line of thought ignores. In the current debate, the relationship between the economy and democracy is appraised from the point of view of the impact of the latter on the former. Viewed in this way, democracy comes second analytically to the objective of economic growth. We must reverse these terms and ask ourselves what sort of economy we need to strengthen democracy. Then we will be able to discuss the role of the economy in the development of democracy, based on its impact on social rights, as well as the capacity of democracy to influence economic organization and to facilitate the diversity of options that the market economy offers.

Finally, although its consequences must not be overlooked, *globalization* should not lead us to draw fatalistic conclusions. Scope for democratic participation and decision-making is, first and foremost, to be found at the national level. Even if globalization imposes severe restrictions on States' capacity for action, rather than yielding to a feeling of impotence, we should focus the debate on how to create new spaces for national autonomy through regional cooperation and integration.

In order to examine the conditions needed for the development of democracy, we propose, therefore, widening the agenda that has dominated in recent years. It goes without saying that it is not the intent of this Report to propose national policies; each country has its own timeframe and its own set of conditions. But these specifics affect the type of solution to be applied in each case, not the importance of the problems to be solved. The different possible responses to these problems do not alter the common denominator among the topics that we are setting out, the most important of which is the need to establish a new democratic reform agenda for Latin America.

What are we talking about when we use the word *democracy*? What is the conceptual framework for our notion of development of democracy? What sort of democracy do Latin Americans enjoy? And, finally, what do we need to put on our agenda for debate in order to develop our democracies and to expand our citizenship?

Theoretical Groundings

We will use this section to present some of the concepts, arguments and questions for debate that constitutes the theoretical basis of the Report.[12] Our starting point is to define *the various meanings of democracy*, which also allows us to transform and enrich it.

Given the complexity of the questions at hand, when we observe new realities that cannot be dealt with intuitively we become aware of our theoretical weaknesses. We are by no

---

12 All of the statistical data and public opinion surveys presented in this Report were developed within a conceptual framework. Without that framework we could not have identified the indicators that are relevant to assessing the development of democracy. The indicators and surveys used in this Report are the product of a specific concept of democracy. This theory justifies and explains the method employed to develop them.

means saying that practicing politics should be the corollary of an appropriate theory; we are just insisting on the need for serious and sound knowledge and debate so that the practice of politics might successfully guide the future of our countries. Theory does not mean withdrawing from the practical world; it is a way of understanding where we are and where we are heading, and what needs changing most urgently.

Political theory and its subset, democratic theory, have made considerable contributions to the analysis of our reality. The world of politics, however, probably provides the most eloquent example of the distance that can exist between theory and practice. On the one hand, ideas about the complex political development of societies are discussed frequently. On the other hand, the practice of politics gives the impression that they belong to a different universe.

The manner in which theoretical analysis is often undervalued—which looks like eagerness to throw oneself immediately into the practicalities—may actually be a way of avoiding comparing decisions with their underlying reasons or even a way of covering up the true motives of those who hold public or private power. The belittling of theory is usually a means of paving the way towards magical thinking—ideas that seem so attractive they do not need to be explained.

This Report will base its descriptions, analysis and proposals on systematic and rigorous reasoning. The intention is not to embrace the whole debate on democracy, but rather to establish the foundations for the statements and proposals that the Report contains.

The Idea of Democracy

This Report is founded on a basic and general idea of democracy, without presenting a circumscribed and closed definition, but rather trying to see in the different areas of social life what it is within them that affects and is affected by democracy. In this sense, democracy is an outcome of the history of societies and not only of itself.

BOX 9

Democracy: a Work Permanently in Progress

We should remember that after its promising beginnings democratization did not evolve along an upward path right up until our times. There were rises and falls, resistance movements, rebellions, civil wars, revolutions. For several centuries [...] some of the earlier advances were reversed. Looking back over the rise and fall of democracy, it is clear that we cannot expect social forces to ensure that democracy continues to progress steadily. [...] Democracy, it seems, is a little uncertain. But its potential depends also on what we do ourselves. Also, although we cannot count on benign inclinations to promote it, we are not mere victims of blind forces over which we have no control. With sufficient understanding of what democracy requires and the will to fulfill its requirements, we can act in such a way as to satisfy democratic ideas and practice and, still more, to progress in both.

Robert Dahl, 1999, pp. 32–33.

Democracy springs from an intense and audacious social and historical experiment that evolves on a daily basis as a result of the achievements and frustrations, actions and omissions and the duties and aspirations of, as well as exchanges between, its protagonists: citizens, social groups and communities that fight for their rights and strive ceaselessly to build a common life.

Democracy implies a way of envisaging the human being and guaranteeing individual rights. Consequently, it contains a set of principles, rules and institutions that organize social relations, procedures for electing governments and mechanisms for controlling them. It is also the way society conceives of its State and intends to make it work.

But that is not all. Democracy is also a way of conceiving of and preserving collective memory and of welcoming and celebrating the different identities of local and regional communities.

Democracy is each one of these definitions

> **BOX 10**
>
> ## Democracy and Equality
>
> No theory of democracy that failed to give the egalitarian idea a central place could possibly yield a faithful representation of the extraordinary grip of democracy in the modern political imagination [...] We must keep in mind that historically a main goal of democratic movements has been to seek redress in the political sphere for the effects of inequalities in the economy and society.
>
> **Charles R. Beitz,** 1989, pp. xi and xvi. (Translated from the Spanish version of the text.)

> **BOX 11**
>
> ## Democracy and Sovereignty
>
> The exercise of democracy is an affirmation of the sovereignty of a nation: it requires a democratic framework to give back the pristine political sense to the weakened notion of sovereignty: No nation is sovereign in the international arena if it is not sovereign in the domestic arena, namely, if it does not respect the cultural and political rights of its population, conceived not as 'simple numbers' but as 'complex qualities', not in the quantity of inhabitants but rather in the quality of citizens.
>
> **Carlos Fuentes,** 1998, p. 9.

ment of both has a significant effect on the quality and sustainability of a democracy.

The distinction between an electoral democracy and a citizenship democracy centers around four basic arguments, which guide this Report:

1. The philosophical and normative foundation of democracy is to be found in the *concept of the human being as an individual with innate rights*. According to this idea, the human being emerges clearly as an autonomous, rational and responsible person. This concept underlies all notions of citizenship, including political citizenship.

2. Democracy is a *means of organizing society*, which guarantees that people can exercise their rights and work to expand their citizenship. It establishes rules for political relations, and for the organization and exercise of power, which are consistent with the aforementioned concept of the human being.

3. Free, competitive and institutionalized elections, and the rules and procedures for forming and running a government—which together we will call *electoral democracy*—are essential components of democracy and comprise its most basic sphere. But democracy is not limited to this realm either in terms of its reach or range of action.

4. The development of democracy in Latin America constitutes a *unique historical experience*, characterized by specifics that are closely linked to the processes involved in building Nations and societies, along with establishing all of their diverse cultural identities.

Social Deficits as Democratic Deficits

An important point to note in understanding democracy and its development in this way is that social inadequacies are seen as deficiencies in democracy. In this sense, poverty and inequality are not only 'social problems', but al-

and tasks, just as it is present in the variety of ways that they are embodied in rules and institutions.

We maintain that democracy is more than a set of conditions for electing and being elected, which we call *electoral democracy*. It is also, as we have pointed out, a way of organizing society with the object of assuring and expanding the rights of its people. This we define as a *citizenship democracy*.

These two dimensions of democracy are closely connected, and the degree of develop-

so democratic deficits. To solve these problems means, therefore, that we have to deal with one of the main issues of democratic sustainability. In our analysis, this is where we criticize the dangerous schism between 'economic policy', 'social policy' and the strengthening of democracy, which are often treated as separate components. The main corollary here is that the economic and social agenda cannot be divorced from the democratic agenda.

Democracy is based on mechanisms and institutions that have a certain vision of the human condition and its development: all human beings are born free and equal in dignity and rights and endowed with reason and conscience.[13]

The principles arising from this are projected throughout society. In schools, in the family, in the economy and in general, all methods of organizing society that go beyond strictly defined democratic institutions are touched by these inherent principles. The development of democracy depends on the intensity with which these principles manage to permeate different areas of life. That is why democracy is not limited to its institutional dimension; it is also a civilizing promise that establishes the expectation of increasing freedom, equality, justice and progress.

The Scope of Democracy in the Report

Viewed from this perspective, democracy presupposes a set of essential characteristics that defines its necessary conditions. These characteristics rarely exist in full but are generally combined to different degrees. It should be noted that analyzing the extent to which each of these elements has been achieved is unavoidable when evaluating how far a democracy has developed.[14] One of the core principles of democracy is that popular sovereignty should be freely delegated to a government, so that the choice of the majority may be satisfied. For this process to be effective, the set of conditions described below must prevail.

1. A necessary condition for democracy is *the existence of a political system* that manifests itself in a State and a Nation, which delimit a people, a territory and the power that is exercised within it. This system includes a set of institutions and procedures that defines the rules governing and the ways of accessing the principal State offices, the exercise of State power and the process of public decision-making.

   In contemporary political science there is consensus on the conditions that need to exist for a State government to be considered democratic:[15]

   - Elected public authorities.
   - Free and fair elections.
   - Universal suffrage.
   - The right to contest for public office.
   - Freedom of expression.
   - Access to pluralist information.
   - Freedom of association.
   - Respect for mandates, honoring periods and terms that are established under the Constitution.
   - A territory that clearly defines the voting *demos (people)*.
   - The widely held assumption that the electoral process and associated liberties will continue to exist for the foreseeable future.

2. Democracy implies *substantial access to the power of the State*, that is, there should not be any other organization on the territory (formal or otherwise) with power that is the same as, or greater than, that of the State. This defines internal sovereignty, an attribute that implies the following: a monopoly over the effective and legitimate use of force; the capacity to impart justice in an

13 Universal Declaration of Human Rights (UN, 1948).
14 The following characteristics were discussed at length with an extensive group of academics.
15 According to contributions made by Robert Dahl and Guillermo O'Donnell.

A Definition of Polyarchy

Polyarchy stems from the Greek words meaning 'many' and 'government', thus distinguishing the 'government of the many' from the government of one, or monarchy, or from the government of the few, aristocracy or oligarchy. [...] A polyarchic democracy is a political system endowed with the democratic institutions [that have been described]. Polyarchic democracy differs, then, from representative democracy with limited suffrage, such as that existing in the 19th century. It is also different from the older democracies and republics, which not only had limited suffrage but also lacked many of the other key characteristics of polyarchic democracies, such as political parties, the right to form political organizations to influence or oppose existing governments, organized special interest groups, etc. It is also different from the specific democratic practices of units small enough to permit the establishment of a direct assembly of its members and its direct decision (or recommendation) about policies or laws.

Robert Dahl, 1987, p. 105.

effective and definitive way; the ability to set standards for the behavior of individuals and organizations; and the capacity to procure the necessary means—economic and organizational—to fulfill its aims and to carry out policy decisions. In a democracy, the State's sovereign authority is derived from the renewed legitimacy accorded to it by members of society.

Access by the State to effective power also requires a certain type of relationship with other sovereign States, so that the objectives established by society (exercising its right to freedom of choice) are not substantially altered by the impositions of other powers beyond the frontiers of the Nation, unless they are a consequence of the free delegation of sovereignty to multilateral institution.

3. Democracy also implies *the enforcement of the rule of law*. This presupposes the independence of the branches of government and a legal system that is democratic in three regards: it protects political freedoms and safeguards political democracy; it protects people's civil rights; and it establishes networks of responsibility and accountability, so that the legality of the actions of public officers, even at the highest level, are subject to appropriate controls. It also presupposes that any action by the State and its branches is in line with norms that emanate from democratically designated powers.

4. Democracy presupposes *a certain form of organizing power within society*. In a democracy, power relations—between the State and citizens, among the citizens themselves, and among the State, social organizations and citizens—must be managed within a framework of political, civil and social rights in such a way that State conduct (even involving the use of force) cannot harm these rights. The essence of democracy is that power—public or private—be organized in such a way that not only does it not infringe on rights, but also that it is an essential instrument for increasing them. Any determination about the relationship between power and rights should be *objective*—that is, made by the majority of the members of society.

5. Democracy requires that the *options presented to citizens deal with substantive issues*. The rules and regulations for competing in an election try to ensure freedom of choice among candidates and government programs. These rules and regulations determine the range of options from among which the citizen may choose. This electoral topic list or public agenda goes beyond the specific regime but is fundamental for democracy—it is an integral part of its organization.

Assuming the absence of limitations on the freedom to elect, we wish to determine what the effective range of options is and how it is arrived at. This is what the public agenda is about. It is nothing less than a list of problems that society should resolve and the methods that it should employ to do so. For the citizen, the agenda identifies desirable goals for a government and specifies how they should be achieved.

But on what basis is an election held? Does it include all of the real options necessary to safeguard and expand citizenship at any given moment? Or is it that those options, subject to electoral necessity, constitute just a fraction of what is needed to advance citizenship and exclude other essential needs?

If the latter is the case, we could have flawless rules of competition and optimum conditions for the election, but electoral issues that are biased or limited in terms of content. Under these circumstances, it is possible that the main issues might be left out of the election and that marginal matters might be at the center of the debate. The regime would have a tendency, then, to lack purpose, to withdraw from broadening citizenship, to become irrelevant.

The public agenda, therefore, understood as the effective range of options available to the citizenry in accordance with the points mentioned above, constitutes a central aspect of democratic organization. The agenda consists of the most important issues on which public debate is centered, the definition of problems and the policy options on which citizens may express their views.

The agenda should detail the main challenges to individual interests, as well as to those of organizations and of society as a whole. The agenda defines the range of options including certain issues and excluding others.

But this agenda is not put together in an ideal world, independent of power politics. Should economic policy be an electoral issue? Or tax reform? Are the options for fighting poverty and inequality clear? And if these topics are not on the electoral agenda, how can democracy relate to the real need to broaden social citizenship?

This question—precisely what should be debated within a society and within a region—is one of the central concerns of this Report. Promoting a debate on our agenda in order to find out whether it is relevant to our problems, or whether there are issues that have been left off, watered down, ignored, or simply proscribed, is the first step towards utilizing our capability to dodge the obstacles and to develop our democracy. Discussing the limits of public debate, ways to start it and how to recover what has been ignored and underestimated, is an essential precondition for the democratic reforms that Latin America needs. The relevance or irrelevance of the content of the public agenda is vital to our democratic future.

Democracy, the Political Regime and the State

In a democratic system, access to the main positions in government (except those in the judiciary, the armed forces and, perhaps, the Central Bank) is achieved through *clean institutionalized elections*. By clean, we mean that the election is competitive, free, equal, decisive and inclusive and that there is complete respect for political freedoms.[16] These freedoms are essential not only during an election but also in the period in-between. Otherwise the government in power could easily manipulate or cancel future elections. Individuals who enjoy these freedoms are registered and protected with respect to the exercise of their right to participate. This means that all citizens have the right to participate in the State and in government, not only through elections, but also by making decisions, individually or collectively, which are binding throughout the land. Likewise, *inclusiveness* means that all

16 According to Robert Dahl (1989 and 1999), the most important political freedoms pertain to expression, association and access to information that contains different opinions. For a detailed list see Larry Diamond, 1999.

adults who satisfy the criteria of citizenship have the right to participate in the said elections.[17]

Moreover, elections under a democratic regime are institutionalized: most people take it for granted that clean elections will continue to be held in the future on dates pre-established by law.

There are four central aspects of democracy: 1) institutionalized and clean elections; 2) inclusiveness; 3) a legal system that recognizes and supports rights and political freedoms; and 4) a legal system that prescribes that no person or institution has the power to eliminate or suspend the implementation of the law, or to evade its effects. We see, then, that, while the first two aspects concern the regime, the latter two pertain to the State. The State is not an element that is alien or extrinsic to democracy; rather, it is one of its intrinsic components. This is why, according to the conceptual framework proposed in this Report, it is important to look into *how democratic the State is*, not just the regime.

The relationship between a democratic system of government and the State is based on the existence of a legal system that is characterized by two features: first, it recognizes and upholds the rights and freedoms implied by the democratic regime; second, all institutions and State office-holders are bound by that legal system. Seen in this way, the State is organized in line with the following principles: the separation of powers; interdependence and control of the branches of government; the existence of an independent judiciary; the preeminence of civil power over military power; and the accountability of government to citizens.

One crucial aspect of the legal system is how effective it is—the degree to which the State really does organize relations within society. In a democratic legal system, no State institution or officer may evade legal responsibility for any action taken. As for territory, the legal system is supposed to work homogenously throughout the space that is under the authority of the State.

BOX 13

Democracy and the Responsibility of Rulers

In a democracy, rulers are supposed to be subjected to three kinds of accountability.[18] One, vertical electoral accountability, results from fair and institutionalized elections, through which citizens may change the party and officers in government. Another type of vertical accountability, of a societal kind, is activated by groups and even individuals with the goal of mobilizing the legal system in order to place demands on the State and the government—aimed at preventing, redressing and/or punishing presumably illegal actions (or inaction) by public officials. Still a third kind of accountability, horizontal, results when some properly authorized State institutions act to prevent, redress and/or punish those presumably illegal actions (or inaction).

Notice, however, that there is an important difference among these types of accountability. The vertical electoral one must exist as a result of the very definition of a democratic regime; by contrast, the degree and effectiveness of societal and horizontal accountability vary depending on the case and the time. These variations are relevant in assessing the quality of democracy; for example, the lack of a vigorous and self-assertive society, or the unfeasibility or unwillingness of certain State institutions to demonstrate their authority over other State institutions (especially elected officials), are indications of a democracy that is of low quality.

Guillermo O'Donnell, text prepared for PRODDAL, 2002c.

---

17 It is only recently that urban workers, peasants, women and other minorities and sectors that were discriminated against have earned the right to inclusion.

18 This footnote applies only to the Spanish and Portuguese editions.

Likewise, the judicial system is supposed to treat similar cases in the same way, regardless of class, sex, ethnic origin or any other citizen attribute. In all of these dimensions, the legal system presupposes a State that is effective,[19] where quality depends not only on appropriate legislation but also on a network of State institutions that operates in such a way as to ensure the effective rule of a democratic legal system.

The effectiveness of the legal system depends on the combination of a set of rules and a network of institutions that should operate in a democracy according to purposes and outcomes consistent with a democratic state of law.

The Citizen: Source of, and Justification for, the Authority of the Democratic State

In a democracy, the legal system, starting with its supreme constitutional rules, establishes that, when its citizens vote in clean institutionalized elections, they themselves are the source of the authority that the State and government exercises over them. Citizens are not merely the bearers of rights and obligations; they are also the source of, and the justification for, the mandate and authority that the State and the government invoke when taking decisions that are collectively binding.

This is another of democracy's specific characteristics: all other political systems base the right to govern on foundations other than the popular sovereignty that is expressed in clean and institutionalized elections.

From what has been said, it follows that an individual is not and never should be treated as a subordinate subject, begging for the goodwill of government and State. This individual—bearer of a set of civil, social and political rights—has a legally upheld claim to be treated with all due consideration and respect.[20] Likewise, that treatment must be based on the implementation of pre-existing laws and regulations that are clear and discernible to all citizens,[21] and ratified in accordance with democratic procedures. The extent to which State institutions recognize these rights determines whether they are considered more or less democratic, or to be acting in accordance with the obligations imposed on them by the citizenry.

In fact, this aspect of direct everyday relations between citizens and the State is one of the most problematic areas concerning democracy in our region. With regard to matters relating to clean elections and the normal exercise of political rights, citizens are placed on the level of generic equals. When it comes to citizens dealing with State bureaucracies, however, extreme *de facto* inequality characterizes the relationship. Citizens tend to face bureaucracies that function in accordance with formal and informal rules—that are neither transparent nor easily understandable—and that take decisions (or cease to take them) that have significant consequences for the citizenry. This is a problem throughout the world, but it is a particularly serious one in societies that are riddled with inequality and poverty. These evils both reflect and exacerbate social authoritarianis,[22] and have repercussions in terms of the disrespectful way that State bureaucracies often treat their citizens and the even worse treatment that they dole out to immigrants and foreigners. Although this is usually ignored, it is another crucial aspect of democracy: the degree to which

---

19 Guillermo O'Donnell, 2000 and 2002a.

20 In agreement with this point, R. Dworkin (1986) states that: "a particular demand of political morality [...] requires governments to speak with one voice, to act in a principled and coherent manner toward all its citizens, [and] to extend to everyone the substantive standards of justice or fairness it uses for some."

21 Even in situations where this inequality is at its worst possible level (as in prison), the moral obligation to respect the agent remains. Nowadays, this is also a legal obligation, although it is often ignored.

22 Aristotle (1968, p. 181) was aware of this when he said: "Those who enjoy too many advantages—strength, wealth, connections, and so forth—are both unwilling to obey [the law] and ignorant [about] how to obey."

State institutions actually respect the rights of all the inhabitants of a country, whether they are citizens or not.

The Citizen: the Subject of Democracy

Democracy recognizes each individual as a legal and moral person who has rights and is responsible for exercising those rights and meeting related obligations. In this sense, the individual is seen as a human being who has the capacity to choose between different options, taking responsibility for the consequences of his/her choices, namely, as a responsible, reasonable, autonomous person.[23] This concept of the human being is not only philosophical and moral, but also legal: the individual is considered to be the bear-

er of subjective rights that are enforced and ensured by the legal system.

The potential inherent to this concept of the individual, whose rights are not derived from the position that he/she occupies in the social hierarchy, but, rather, from his/her capacity to commit himself/herself voluntarily and responsibly to fulfilling the obligations that he/she freely assumes—with the corollary right to demand that the obligations contracted be met—, has led to momentous consequences for struggles to expand citizenship.

By *citizenship* we understand a sort of basic equality to be associated with the concept of belonging to a community, which, in modern terms, is the equivalent of the rights and obligations that all individuals have just by belonging to a national State.[24] We wish to underline various attributes of citizenship when it is defined in this way:

a. its expansive character, based on the concept, morally and legally defended, of the human being as a responsible, reasonable and autonomous person;

b. its legal condition, the status that is accorded to the individual as the bearer of rights that are legally enforced and supported;

c. the social or interpersonal sense that tends to emerge as a result of awareness of social belonging;[25]

d. its egalitarian character, based on universal recognition of the rights and duties of all

---

23 According to the concept developed by Guillermo O'Donnell (2002c), democracy considers the human being to be an agent. "An agent is a being endowed with practical reason: she uses her cognitive and motivational capabilities to make choices that are reasonable in terms of her situation and of her goals, concerning which, barring conclusive proof to the contrary, she is deemed to be the best judge. This capacity makes the agent a moral one, in the sense that normally she will feel, and will be construed by relevant others as, responsible for her choices and for at least the direct consequences that ensue from these choices."

24 T.H. Marshall (1965) points out that: "modern citizenship is, by definition, national." (Translated from the Spanish version of the text.)

25 This aspect of citizenship refers to a concept of politics as common space, where we recognize each other as members of a political community aimed at building and achieving a public good in an interrelated manner. This concept has been developed extensively within the tradition of civic republicanism, which is based on Greek and Roman thought, and which has assumed a new meaning in contemporary debates between liberals and communitarians.

of the members of a democratically organized society;

e. its sense of inclusiveness, linked to the attribute of nationality implied by people's belonging to national States; and

f. its dynamic character, contingent and open-ended, which is both the product of, and the precondition for, the battles throughout history to enrich or diminish the content of democracy, and to increase or decrease the number of rights and obligations that are currently recognized.

We can identify three sets of citizens' rights[26] that govern three different aspects of society: civil; political; and social.[27]

Well before the universal expansion of political citizenship, many attempts were made—based on different religious, ethical, legal and

As we have said, the democracy of citizenship is more comprehensive than the political system and the mere exercise of political rights. Democracy must be extended into the realm of civil and social rights.

philosophical doctrines—to arrive at a legal and moral vision of the individual as the bearer of subjective rights.[28] This concept of the human being was projected into the political sphere by the theoreticians of liberalism,[29] and, subsequently, it was incorporated into the two greatest modern Constitutions: those of the United States and France.

26 This statement by no means implies that we are unaware of the current debates that propose to add 'generations' of rights others than those mentioned here. Among them we feel that it is particularly important to add an area specifically to draw attention to cultural rights—given the situation in Latin America, especially concerning indigenous peoples. However, in order to simplify this initial inquiry into an extremely complex topic, we have chosen to retain the traditional classification of rights. This does not prevent us from analyzing the subject of indigenous peoples elsewhere in this Report, nor, indeed, from revising the classification used here in future versions of the Report.

27 "I shall begin by proposing a division of citizenship into three parts. […] I shall call these three parts or elements civil, political and social. The civil element is composed of those rights relating to individual freedom: freedom of person, of expression, of thought and religion, the right to own property and conclude valid contracts, and the right to justice. This last right is of a different nature from the rest because it deals with the right to defend and uphold the set of rights of a person in conditions of equality with others, by means of the due legal procedures. By the political element I mean the right to participate in the exercise of political power as a member of a body invested with political authority or as an elector of its members. The corresponding institutions are the Parliament and units of local government. The social element includes the whole spectrum, from the right to security and a minimum of economic welfare to the right to share to the full in the social heritage and to live the life of a civilized being according to the standard prevailing in the society. The institutions directly linked are, in this case, the system of education and the social services." T.H. Marshall, 1965, pp. 22–23. (Translated from the Spanish version of the text.)

28 "The institutionalized (i.e., legally enacted and backed, and widely taken for granted) recognition of an agent carrier of subjective rights took a long and convoluted process that goes back to some of the sophists, the stoics and Cicero, runs through Roman law and medieval legists, was refined by natural law theorists, and was finally appropriated and, as it were, politicized, in spite of their differences in other respects, by the great early liberal thinkers—especially Hobbes, Locke and Kant—as well as non-liberals such as Espinoza and Rousseau." Guillermo O'Donnell, 2000.

29 Pierre Rosanvallon (1992, p. 111) notes that, before the coming of liberalism, "this vision of the autonomy of the will certainly had already seemed to be juridically formulated in civil law." This, in turn, was part of changes in the same concept of morality; like J.B. Schneewind (1998, p. 27), he notes: "During the 17th and 18th centuries the established concepts of morality as obedience began to be strongly opposed by emerging concepts of morality as self-regulation […] centered on the belief that all normal individuals are equally capable of living together in a self-regulated morality." (Translated from the Spanish version of the text.)

Citizenship consists of more than Political Rights, and so does Democracy

As we have said, the democracy of citizenship is more comprehensive than the political system and the mere exercise of political rights. Democracy must be extended into the realm of civil and social rights. This is a key point of our analysis, and from it stems the justification for thinking that democracy covers a wider, more complex field. As we have noted earlier, the practical consequences of sustaining this argument are considerable.

If the inherent rights of the human being are based on his/her capacity *qua* moral being, why, then, limit these rights to certain spheres of social and political life? If responsible autonomy means the right to choose, what are the real options or possibilities that would be reasonably consistent with the status that democracy assigns to the individual? In other words, what are the real conditions for the exercise of these rights?

These questions point to one of the central contentions of the analysis proposed in this Report: raising the matter of capabilities in the political sphere implies going beyond attributing to everyone the rights of political citizenship, and leads us to pose the question concerning the conditions under which those rights may or may not be exercised effectively.

Although, of course, under different historical circumstances, in all countries, the answers to such questions presented themselves in the numerous battles for the progressive expansion of political, civil and social rights,[30] highlighting among these the right to vote until finally it achieved its current level of inclusiveness. This is a history made up of many conflicts that eventually made it possible for marginal sectors of society to be included in democracy—that is, for them finally to obtain full political citizenship.[31]

In advanced countries these processes initially brought about an expansion of rights in the civil sphere, in the sense of widening the coverage of existing rights and granting new ones. The latter were not yet rights that pertained specifically to participation in an inclusive democracy, but, rather, *civil rights* connected to private social and economic activities.[32] With regard to these rights, it has been recognized in various ways that exercising them implies a choice, and that this choice implies the freedom to choose from among the different alternatives that each person has reason to value. This presupposes that a criterion of fairness prevails: there must be a minimum level of equality among members of society, so that everyone is presented with a reasonable range of options in order to exercise their capacity to choose and their autonomy.

In advanced countries, this criterion of fairness was also very important in the emer-

---

30 The process associated with the progressive expansion of rights, which in advanced countries saw the extension of civil citizenship prior to the expansion of political citizenship, provided a historical backdrop to the central idea of political liberalism: the government and the State must be limited and constitutionally regulated, since both exist for, and to serve individuals who have subjective rights that are enforced and supported by the same legal system that the government and State must comply with and from which they derive their authority.

31 *Political citizens* are those who, within the territory of a State that a democratic government encompasses, meet the criteria necessary to be considered a member of the Nation. Likewise, as a direct consequence of the democratic regime, political citizens possess two types of rights. The first type is freedoms like freedom of association, freedom of expression, freedom of movement and freedom to access pluralistic information sources, which, although in the final analysis are not definable ex ante, as a group permit the holding of elections that are clean, institutionalized and—currently—inclusive. The second type is of a participative nature: to elect or perhaps be elected; or named to hold State office. Political citizens, thus understood, constitute the individual side of a democratic regime, and none of them can exist without the others.

32 As T.H. Marshall (1965, p. 18) comments: "The story of civil rights in their formative period is one of the gradual addition of new rights to a status that already existed and was held to appertain to all adult members of the community." These civil rights are, according to his classic definition of civil citizenship, "The rights necessary for individual freedom—liberty of person, freedom of speech, thought and faith, the right to own property and to conclude valid contracts, and [the] right to justice."

gence of *social rights.*[33] Again, in the wake of what were often arduous struggles, different sectors that had been politically excluded ended up accepting political democracy and the benefits of the welfare State. These visions of fairness were incorporated into the legal systems, with steps forward and backward in terms of the respective power relations, through social legislation. Social rights, buttressed by corresponding legislation, joined forces with civil law to make it manifest that society, and especially the State, should not remain indifferent, at least not in situations where severe constraints are placed on human capabilities.

In sum, in advanced countries, the issue regarding the levels of development that allow people to exercise their individual freedom was challenged within the sphere of social and civil rights. The concept behind these legal constructions is that of equity in terms of human capabilities, which considers individuals to be free beings capable of choosing responsibly in the absence of coercion. This vision was inscribed on the moral conscience of humankind by the French Declaration of the Rights of Man and of the Citize.[34] It is worth pointing out that most of these rights were not simply granted, but were won, as a result of numerous struggles led by social groups that were oppressed, exploited and discriminated against.

In advanced countries the institutions and practices that we recognize today as democratic came into being in such complex ways, although they be matter-of-factly summarized here. Only three countries in Latin America (Chile, Costa Rica and Uruguay) have followed a similar route; in the rest—and even taking into account the

Democracy and its political rights have enormous importance for Latin America: they are, they must be, the main source of leverage in struggles to achieve the other rights.

significant particularities of each one—we find a situation that is very different from that described above. We have made enormous progress in the field of political rights but there is still much to be done in order to achieve for all of us a satisfactory broadening of civil and social rights. This reality underlines even more the huge importance of democracy and its political rights in Latin America: they are, and must be, the main source of leverage in struggles to achieve the other rights, which, in practice, are still very limited and unevenly distributed. These statements will be echoed in the empirical sections of the Report.

State and Citizenship

The State is a contemporary historical phenomenon, in which the struggles for power and rights converge. Its inception was marked by the expropriation, by the rulers of a nascent power center, of the means of coercion, administration and legality which until then had been controlled by other actors. The emergence of the State took place at the same time as the expansion of capitalism, which saw another expropriation, that of the means of production by direct producers. The emergence of the State also occurred at the same time as the political construction of the Nation, a privileged point of reference for State decisions. All States maintain that their authority emanates

---

33 Again according to T.H. Marshall (1965, p. 72), social rights range "from the right to a modicum of economic welfare and security to the right to share to the full in the social heritage and to live the life of a civilized being according to the standard prevailing in the society." For a useful and detailed discussion by Marshall about these rights, see José Nun, 2001.

34 We could add, for example: the Prologue and First Amendment of the Constitution of the United States; the United Nations Universal Declaration of Human Rights; the International Covenant on Civil and Political Rights; the International Covenant on Economic, Social and Cultural Rights; the Vienna Declaration of Human Rights and many other international and regional treaties and protocols, all of which have been ratified by a significant number of countries.

The Liberal State and the Democratic State

The liberal State is not only the historical but also the juridical presupposition behind the democratic State. The liberal State and the democratic State are interdependent in two ways: 1) in the thread that runs from liberalism to democracy, in the sense that certain freedoms are necessary for the correct exercise of democratic power; 2) in the thread running the opposite way, from democracy to liberalism, in the sense that democratic power is indispensable to ensure the existence and endurance of the fundamental freedoms. In other words: it is improbable that a State that is not liberal could ensure the correct functioning of democracy and, in addition, it is unlikely that a State that is not democratic could ensure fundamental freedoms. The historical proof of this interdependence lies in the fact that when the liberal State and the democratic State fall, they fall together.

Norberto Bobbio, 1992, pp. 15–16.

from being States-for-the-Nation (or, in some cases, States-for-the-people), whose mission is to promote the common good, or the general interest, of a Nation that is viewed as homogenous, to which both governed and governing supposedly owe their primary allegiance.

By State we understand a set of institutions and social relationships that covers the territory defined by it. The State normally rules supreme in respect to controlling the means of coercion within that territory. According to this definition, the State may be seen as: a) a focus of collective identity for the inhabitants of a territory—on which is based its *credibility*; b) a legal system that aspires to achieve a considerable degree of *effectiveness* in regulating social relations; and c) a set of bureaucracies whose function is supposedly to achieve *efficacy* in the carrying out of formally assigned tasks. The extent to which these dimensions have real validity in each case is contingent on history and is certainly problematic (see Guillermo O'Donnell 2002b).

Therefore, the State is:

a. an environment where the *collective identity* of all or almost all of the inhabitants of the territory is concentrated and recognized; it invites general recognition, the use of 'we', the members of the Nation;

b. a *legal system*, a network of judicial rules that aims to regulate numerous social relationships;[35] and

c. *a set of bureaucratic entities*, an administrative network with responsibilities that are formally designed to achieve and protect some aspect of the common good. Together, State bureaucracies and their legality aim to generate the great public good of order and predictability for the social relationships in which their inhabitants are involved. In this way, the State also seeks to guarantee the historical continuity of the respective territorial unit, which is usually conceived of as a Nation.

These facets of the State are tendencies that no-one has managed to put completely into practice. As for the State as a focus of collective identity, its goal of becoming a true State-

---

35 Even under a democratic system of government, the legality of the State is based on a complex mixture of equality and inequality. On the one hand, this legality ensures the enforcement of the universal rights of political and civil citizenship. On the other hand, it allows two types of inequality to exist. First, that which results from the hierarchical organization, legally regulated, of the bureaucratic institutions of the State—just as the legal system also provides backing and grants authorization to other private institutions that are also hierarchically organized. Second, the inequality that results from the fact that the same legality shapes the capitalist form of existence of society. This authorizes and supports a social order that entails in different ways the social domination of those who control the means of production, as well as (and this is increasingly important in the contemporary world) the flows of financial capital. This leads us to consider the crucial role played by the State, in its various facets, in perpetuating or correcting these inequalities at the same time as it promotes some fundamental democratic equalities.

The State: Cornerstone of Democracy

The State—as an institution in which is recognized the involuntary collective identity, based on a specific territory, sustained in the last instance by its ability to coerce, highly bureaucratized and densely legalized—is the historical and social fundament of democracy. From its earliest beginnings, contemporary political democracy implies a dual-faced citizenship: as proper to democracy, a citizenry who are (potentially) active and participative, and a second group of, as it were, adscriptive members, whose citizenship reflects only the fact that they belong to a Nation.

Guillermo O'Donnell, text prepared for PRODDAL, 2002c.

> In the past two decades the State has lost an enormous amount of power and, in some areas within our countries, has practically ceased to exist.

A Diminished Statehood and Democratic Fragility

As we have seen, for the first time in two centuries of independence, practically all of the countries of Latin America satisfy the minimum definition of democracy. They share two characteristics. First, they hold reasonably clean, institutionalized, inclusive elections, and they enforce the participative rights related to those elections. Second, they make sure that certain fundamental political freedoms—especially those concerning opinion, expression, association, movement and access to reasonably pluralist information sources—prevail, and affirm the supremacy of constitutional powers over de facto powers.

There are variations, however, in the degree to which the aforementioned characteristics are effectively applied, just as there are significant differences in the extent to which the State and its legal system cover the entire territory of the countries concerned. In this context, society's verdict on the institutional effectiveness and the level of development of our democracies is extremely critical. In general, public opinion indicates that institutions and leaders are not accomplishing all that they should be. One reason is that democratically elected governments frequently appear to be incapable of responding to, or unwilling to deal with, basic development issues, or those concerning inequality and insecurity, for instance. We believe that underlying this perception is another fact that has been over-

for-the-Nation may be considered scarcely plausible for many people. As for the legal system, it may have failings per se and may also not effectively encompass different social relationships or even cover vast areas of the country. And as far as the State as a set of bureaucracies, its performance may fall seriously short of fulfilling the responsibilities that were formally assigned to it.

Whatever the successes and failures in these three dimensions, we must underline that political democracy emerged and has continued to exist with, and operate within the framework of, the national State. It was as a result of this intersection that "democracy came into being with a sense of nationality. The two are fundamentally interconnected and neither can be properly understood outside this connection."[36] This emphasizes the importance that the State and the Nation have had, and continue to have, vis-à-vis the existence and functioning of democracy.[37]

36 L. Greenfield, 1992, p. 7. (Translated from the Spanish version of the text.)
37 R. Maíz (2002a) and M. Canovan, 1996. J. Gray (2000, p. 123) agrees: "The sovereign nation-state is the great unexamined assumption of liberal thought … The institution of the nation-state is tacitly assumed by liberal ideals of citizenship."

The State and Globalization

Economic globalization by no means necessarily translates into a diminution of state power; rather, it is transforming the conditions under which state power is exercised. [...] There are many good reasons for doubting the theoretical and empirical basis of claims that nation-states are being eclipsed by contemporary patterns of globalization. [...] [Yet it should be recognized that the] new patterns of regional and global change are transforming the context of political action, creating a system of multiple power centers and overlapping spheres of authority—a post-Westphalian order.

David Held, 1999, p. 441. (Translated from the Spanish version of the text.)

---

looked in recent discussions: in the past two decades the State has lost an enormous amount of power and, in some areas within our countries, has practically ceased to exist.

Economic crises, the impassioned anti-statism of many economic reform programs, corruption and widespread clientelism in many countries, are all factors that have contributed to the creation of an anemic State. This anemia is also apparent in the legal system. It is a fact that many of our countries have a democratic system of government that coexists with an intermittent and skewed judicial system. Quite simply, the State's legal system does not extend to immense regions within our countries—and some parts of the cities; other power entities, basically variations of Mafia-like legality structures, are in operation in these places to all practical purposes.

Likewise, even in regions where the legal system does reach, it tends to be applied in a discriminatory manner to various minorities and even to majorities, such as women, the poor and certain ethnic groups. This diminished legal system generates what has been called *low-intensity citizenship*.[38] We all have the political rights and freedoms that are part of a democratic regime; however, many lack even the most basic social rights. At the same time, to all extents and purposes, the members of these groups are denied basic civil rights: they have no protection against police violence and myriad forms of private violence; they do not enjoy equal access to the State's bureaucracies, even the courts; their homes are searched arbitrarily; and, in general, they are not only forced to live in poverty but are also subject to recurrent humiliations and the fear of violence.[39] They are poor both in a material and legal sense.

With such problems in terms of the efficacy of its institutions, the effectiveness of its legal system, and, not least, its credibility as a State-for-the-Nation, the current Latin American State, although it supports democratic government, finds it very hard to project a vision of the future that the majority of the people might at least view as attainable and worth striving for—even though, perhaps, many existing injustices and inequalities will not be addressed rapidly. Exceptions to this rule are few and far between.

---

38 See Guillermo O'Donnell (1993), who depicts a metaphorical map of "blue, green and brown zones," where the brown zones signify areas where the State's legal system is barely effective.

39 Reports from various human rights organizations have repeatedly and extensively documented the permanent threat of violence under which people live. For Brazil, see, for example, Emilio E. Dellasoppa et al. (1999), who documented the fact that the number of violent deaths in the poorest part of São Paulo is 16 times higher than that in the richest part. For data on Argentina, see, for instance, the Center for Legal and Social Studies (CELS), 2001. More generally, an investigation that analyzes several sets of data on violent crime found a positive, strong and persistent correlation in all of them between such crime, on the one hand, and poverty and income inequality, on the other (C.C. Hsieh and M.D. Pugh, 1993).

This type of low-capability State is by no means a new problem in Latin America. But it has become a more serious problem in recent years, however, and, in several instances, this has happened under democracy. The State's lack of credibility stems from the operational ineptness of its institutions and, at times, from the manifest colonization of these institutions by private interests that can hardly be argued to have the general interest of the people at heart. This lack of credibility becomes even more acute if some of those interests are in no way nationally owned; rather, if they are part of foreign entities—public and private—and linked to the relatively anonymous tendencies of economic globalization.

All of this leads us to believe in the importance of placing the discussion on the State (including why, for what purpose, and with whom to reform it) in the eminently political strategic realm of democratic development.

It must be pointed out, however, that there is no such thing as a neutral State. In all of its three aspects (sketched out above), the State is an area of complex condensation and of mediation of social forces. In fact, the neutralist view is a way of arguing in favor of a type of State that, by means of its policies and, of course, its omissions, actively reproduces inequality and is a serious obstacle to the expansion of civil and social rights.

Some have tried to explain the weakening of the State in Latin America as an inevitable consequence of globalization, in light of which the only desirable and possible reaction is passive adaptation. This is a view that is not only wrong, but also, at times, is based on self-interest. Since the winds of globalization are indeed strong, countries need States-for-their-Nations more than ever. This does not mean that it has to be a large or top-heavy State. But it must be a strong State, in the sense that it is capable of dealing with the impacts of globalization, selectively adapting to the most irresistible challenges and transposing others.

In this sense, if we observe the States of advanced countries that have institutions and democratic practices that are firmly entrenched, we

will see just how actively they try to transform, digest and redirect many of the aspects and consequences of globalization. But a necessary condition for a State to be capable of constructing democracy and achieving social equality is that it attains reasonable levels of efficiency, effectiveness and credibility. In Latin America, such a path is littered with obstacles, which, although we have referred to them above, warrant special attention.

The Specific Historical Characteristics of the Democracies of Latin America

The problems that we have considered so far are shared by many of the new and not-so-new democracies in the modern world. What does democratic theory have to say about this? Unfortunately, not a lot. To a great extent this is because most of the theories on democracy have been formulated in the context of the historical experience of European countries and the United States. These theories take it for granted that, in those countries, civil rights were in effect to a reasonable degree and were granted to most members of society before political rights became inclusive and universal.

They also presuppose that the legality of the State covers the whole territory homogenously, so that, as a result, not only national governments, but also sub-national units of government, are democratic.[40] It should be obvious by now that these assumptions coincide with neither the history of, nor the current situation in, Latin America.

The pattern of the historical evolution of democracy in Latin America is almost unique. Hence, a conception of democracy that is lim-

---

40 In fact, the United States is a partial, although important, exception to this statement. But this point is beyond the scope of this Report.

> "Human rights and human development share a common vision and a common purpose—to secure the freedom, well-being and dignity of all people everywhere."

ited to a system of government may be acceptable if it is assumed that civil and social citizenship present no problems. But when these dimensions of citizenship are fragmentary or distributed unevenly across different social sectors or even across the territory of the State, it is crucial to treat them with the utmost caution, if we truly want to understand the workings of these democracies and the main challenges to their development.

"No one ... can fully enjoy *any* right that he is supposed to have if he lacks the essentials for a reasonably healthy and active life."[41] Thus, "it would be inconsistent to recognize rights referring to life or physical integrity when the necessary means for enjoying and exercising those rights are lacking."[42] These statements refer to circumstances that facilitate or hinder the exercise of the inherent rights of citizens. Where, and based on what criteria, can we draw a firm clear line above which the quality of citizenship could be exercised reasonably fully in terms of rights and capabilities? Which rights and which capabilities are indispensable to the enjoyment of full citizenship?

These questions have given rise to extensive debate.[43] At this point it is necessary to return to one aspect of these discussions, namely, political freedoms. With regard to this topic we can make two claims: first, that the minimum sufficient set of these rights is impossible to define theoretically in a general and universal way; and second, that these freedoms (of speech, association, movement and so on) are really segments of wider and older civil rights.[44] We have already argued that all human beings are entitled to these rights, and that citizens' rights cannot easily be achieved in the political sphere if people lack 'basic' social and civil rights.[45]

By virtue of simply being citizens, people have the right to have their dignity respected, and they also have the right to be granted the social conditions necessary to engage freely in all activities related to their social existence. Subjecting individuals to physical violence or to the privation of basic material needs, or suppressing their political rights, are all acts that contradict their status as citizens, the subject-actors within a democracy. This view of the minimum conditions necessary to empower the citizen to choose between different options, while assuming responsibility for the consequences of such choices, is already clear in the origins of the tradition of human rights and has been made explicit in recent thinking about human development. As Amartya Sen states in the *Human Development Report 2000*: "Human rights and human development share a common vision and a common purpose—to secure the freedom, well-being and dignity of all people everywhere."[46]

41 H. Shue, 1996, p. 7 (original in italics).

42 R. Vázquez, 2001, p. 102.

43 See H. Shue, 1996, and Martha Nussbaum, 2000b.

44 In European countries and the United States these rights were incorporated as civil rights long before they were 'promoted' to the status of political rights. These rights are also exercised in much wider social spheres, beyond the bounds of the political system.

45 As Jurgen Habermas writes (1999, p. 332): "Without basic rights that guarantee citizens' private autonomy, there would also be no means for the legal institutionalization of conditions under which these citizens could make use of their public autonomy." The same author (1998, p. 261) affirms that: "Therefore, public and private autonomy are mutually essential in such a way that neither human rights nor popular sovereignty can gain the upper hand over the other." (Translated from the Spanish version of the text.)

46 UNDP, 2000c, p. 1.

BOX 17

Millennium Development Goals

1. **Eradicate extreme poverty and hunger**

   ■ Target for 2015: Halve the proportion of people living on less than a dollar a day and those who suffer from hunger.

2. **Achieve universal primary education**

   ■ Target for 2015: Ensure that all boys and girls complete primary school.

3. **Promote gender equality and empower women**

   ■ Target for 2005 and 2015: Eliminate gender disparities in primary and secondary education, preferably by 2005, and to all levels by 2015.

4. **Reduce child mortality**

   ■ Target for 2015: Reduce by two-thirds the mortality rate among children the under-five.

5. **Improve maternal health**

   ■ Target for 2015: Reduce by three-quarters the ratio of women dying in childbirth.

6. **Combat HIV/AIDS, malaria and other diseases**

   ■ Target for 2015: Halt and begin to reverse the spread of HIV/AIDS and the incidence of malaria and other major diseases.

7. **Ensure environmental sustainability**

   ■ Integrate the principles of sustainable development into country policies and programmes and reverse the loss of environmental resources.

   ■ By 2015, reduce by half the proportion of people without access to safe drinking water.

   ■ By 2020, achieve significant improvement in the lives of at least 100 million slum dwellers.

8. **Develop a Global Partnership for Development**

   ■ Develop further an open trading and financial system that includes a commitment to good governance, development and poverty reduction—nationally and internationally.

   ■ Address the least developed countries' special needs, and the special needs of landlocked and small island developing States.

   ■ Deal comprehensively with developing countries' debt problems.

   ■ Develop decent and productive work for youth.

   ■ In cooperation with pharmaceutical companies, provide access to affordable essential drugs in developing countries.

   ■ In cooperation with the private sector, make available the benefits of new technologies—especially information and communications.

UN, 2003b, and UNDP, 2003.

Even though Latin American Constitutions uphold the rights to education, healthcare and employment, other dimensions, such as the satisfaction of basic needs—food and shelter, social security and a clean environment—are not treated uniformly, both in real life and in terms of formal entitlement in different countries. This prioritization corresponds exactly to the development objectives set in the Millennium Declaration adopted by the United Nations General Assembly in 2000.

Achieving the Millennium Development Goals in Latin America requires the implementation of a series of particular public policies, such as investing in basic infrastructure, increasing agricultural productivity, promoting small and medium-sized businesses, fostering industry, investing in healthcare and education, and carrying out a public policy of environmental sustainability. These policies require a State that is capable of action as regards the need to achieve political consensus, maintain democracy and the rule of law, and take democracy to a deeper level with a view to creating a society in which all citizens are fully integrated, and rights and obligations are not limited to the political and civil spheres, but also apply in the social arena. These objectives imply that citizens act as individuals, as political actors who express themselves through representatives and, under predefined circumstances, directly, and as members of society, acting within their community and as part of the voluntary associations that constitute the grassroots of civil society.

This is exactly the same vision that, as we have seen, underlies our concept of democracy. All of these rights—civil rights and their connection with human rights, social rights and their connection with human development, political rights and their connection with democracy—facilitate and promote the exercise of citizenship. This is so precisely because each one of them, or any combination of them, 'pushes' for the attainment of the other, or at any rate creates favorable conditions for their realization. Likewise, as we shall see, the most important criterion for the assignation of civil, social and political rights has changed over the years. For example, even in advanced countries, people lived with tremendous inequalities for many years, justified by the argument that workers, women and others were for some reason intrinsically 'inferior'. Although many horrors and inequalities still exist, it is increasingly accepted that we are all human beings and, in some fundamental sense, equal. This is one of humanity's great achievements.

How much Citizenship does a Democracy need?

The statements made in the section above refrain from mentioning several philosophical and ethical discussions that center on the question of the balance between freedom and equality. These are extremely important issues that go beyond the scope of this Report.

In advanced countries, these discussions revolve around which principles of liberty and equity should regulate the distribution of social goods once all citizens, or a great majority of them, have obtained a basic number of rights and capabilities.[47] By contrast, in Latin America, the main discussion is about those who do not enjoy those rights or basic conditions. This raises the question of whether there are good reasons to assert a universal right to a basic set of rights and capabilities. We maintain that these reasons do exist and that they are based on the vision of citizens and of individuals in general as autonomous, reasonable and responsible human beings. These reasons refer to a primary aspect of fairness: not total equality, but basic equalization. By this we mean the right of each person to no less than two things: to be treated with the fairness and consideration owed to any human being; and to achieve, if necessary with the help of the State or social welfare, a basic minimum set of rights and conditions that eliminate at least the deprivations that prevent citizens from making responsible choices.

We recognize that, at this level, long and complex discussions will arise. However, we believe that the following questions are unavoidable: whether there is a moral obligation or not, and also whether there are legally en-

47 Partha Dasgupta (1993, p. 45, footnote) comments correctly: "A great majority of the contemporary ethics theory assumes at the start of the inquiry that these [basic] needs have been met." This assumption is explicit in the work of political philosophy, which arguably has been the most influential over the past few decades, at least in the Anglo-Saxon world (John Rawls, 1971, pp. 152 and 542–543; his theory of justice is deemed to apply to countries where "only the less urgent material wants remain to be satisfied;" for an explicit restatement of this assumption see John Rawls, 2001). Although less explicitly, the same presupposition is clearly contained in the work of Jurgen Habermas. The question that remains outstanding concerns what can be said about countries—even those with democratic governments—that do not satisfy this premise.

BOX 18

Democracy: a Tension between Facts and Values

What democracy *is* cannot be separated from what democracy *should* be ... in a democracy the tension between facts and values reaches the highest point.

Giovanni Sartori, 1967, p. 4. (Translated from the Spanish version of the text.)

forceable rights that can be appealed to in demanding the basic rights and conditions that make it easier for all citizens to exercise their citizenship. Whatever the answers to these questions, it seems undeniable that democracy provides the best possible context within which to assess it. In this regard, Amartya Sen argues that: "political and social [democratic] participation has intrinsic value for human life and welfare, [just as it also has] instrumental value when people's chances improve [...] of having their demands for political attention [including demands about economic needs] heard." Sen also sustains[48] that democracy has constructive value, since "even the idea of 'needs', including the meaning of 'economic needs', requires public discussion and the interchange of information, visions and analysis [...] Political rights, including freedom of speech and discussion, are not only fundamental in bringing about social responses to economic necessities, they are also essential for conceptualizing these very economic necessities."[49]

Thus the content of rights, their degree of specification, how far-reaching they are, the relative priority of some over others, and other issues of this sort are, and always will be, debatable. There are too many conflicting preferences, theories about what is fair or equitable, and social interests and positions for any of these questions to be resolved clearly and firmly. This is a fact of living in society, a consequence of the freedom and the diverse lifestyles, points of view and interests that it permits. Democracy and politics should honor and encourage the disputes and agreements that this plurality of different voices and interests implies. This is also why democracy is and admits to being an open space, where struggles to define and redefine rights and obligations are constantly being fought.[50]

What is the solution to these problems, limitations and doubts? Quite simply, more democ-racy. The key issues are: who takes the decision, how and on what do they base it, what rights are enforced and implemented, and to what degree and intensity, while other rights are not incorporated into the legal system or remain a dead letter. Even when demands and needs are based on universal characteristics of the human being, determining which ones should be converted into rights, to what extent they should be implemented, and what balance should be struck with other rights and obligations, is based on a social construct that emerges directly from politics, at least from politics in its highest form.

We believe that it is important to emphasize the above because, paradoxically, the very countries that most need to have a broad discussion on which needs and demands should be transformed into actionable rights are those where it is most difficult to get these questions on to the public agenda. What would be the 'decent social minimum'[51] in terms of a basic set of civil and social rights for all inhabitants? Likewise, if a country is poor and has an anemic State and an incomplete legal system, what sequences of

48 Amartya Sen, 1999a, p. 10 (original in italics). (Translated from the Spanish version of the text.)
49 Amartya Sen, 1999a, p. 11 (original in italics). (Translated from the Spanish version of the text.)
50 See Charles Tilly, 1990, 1996 and 1998b. This author (1998b, p. 55) concludes that: "rights [are] historical products, outcomes of struggle."
51 Martha Nussbaum, 2000a, p. 125.

Information:
a Basic Necessity

Even the idea of 'needs', including the understanding of 'economic needs', requires public discussion and exchange of information, views, and analyses. [...] Political rights, including freedom of expression and discussion, are not only pivotal in inducing social responses to economic needs, they are also central to the conceptualization of economic needs themselves.

Amartya Sen, 1999a. (Translated from the Spanish version of the text.)

social and political rights;[53] and the availability of political rights has prevented many famines.[54] These and many other processes show how diverse rights tend to echo and reinforce one another; there is a clear elective affinity among civil, social and political rights. The force behind these relationships is ultimately a moral one: recognition that people should not be deprived of any of the rights and conditions that normally allow them to act in a free and responsible manner.

As for Latin America, now that we have seen a remarkable expansion of political rights we should be able to utilize them not only in relation to the system of government, but also as a lever with which to achieve a much needed extension of civil and social rights.

events and paths would be adequate to achieve that minimum?[52]

The respective needs and deprivations are suffered not only by isolated individuals; these are social issues, which should be dealt with by recognizing them as duties of the State and collective responsibilities. Likewise, these are political issues, imbued by different value systems and ideologies with more or less implicit theories about the way a given society works and increasingly nowadays about how the global system operates. We must insist on these topics being included on the public agenda; that is the place to define the 'real' needs that a country faces up to, ignores or inhibits.

Throughout the history of humankind, advances in civil and social rights for the great majority of people have made it difficult to resist demands for political citizenship; the extension of political rights gave women and some minorities a significant tool with which to acquire other civil and social rights; the extension of civil rights helped the achievement of

In this analysis, the idea of developing democracy is based on a fundamental assumption: the existence of a democratic regime. Within this system of government, we discover that the citizen is supported by a legal system and is recognized as being the main subject of political democracy. Alongside this, the notion of citizenship indicates to us that 'democraticness' is also an attribute of the State. Continuing with the search, we unearth the characteristics and common roots of political, civil and social rights. This thesis is upheld in the statement that democracy implies not only political citizenship, but also civil and social citizenship. Thus we assert that the existence of a diverse and pluralist environment, backed by a legal system that reflects that reality, is another fundamental aspect of democracy, especially insofar as it upholds the liberties that are the social expression of the individual rights of citizenship.

With respect to most of these aspects we find that the democracies of contemporary Latin America have defects. However, in this Report, we underline the political and normative potential of democracy, despite the limi-

52 As M.H. Tavares de Almeida (2002) argues, even within Latin America, there are important variations on this issue, which should be taken into account when designing any plan. A detailed discussion of this question depends on a country by country evaluation, which exceeds the scope of this Report.

53 For example, Alain Touraine (1994) notes that European workers obtained their social rights while battling for general principles like liberty and justice.

54 As Amartya Sen argues in 1999a.

tations that exist at present. From this standpoint, democracy could be regarded as a set of general principles of social organization. It is also the main lever that should be utilized to try to overcome injustice and inequality. The possibility that democracy creates, with its freedoms, for fighting against that injustice and inequality makes it a boundless and evolving space. This characteristic, and the social dynamic that it allows, makes democracy, even in light of its serious shortcomings, an enormously valuable good, which it is worth making the effort to preserve and strengthen.

The next step involves empirical observation of the democratic regime, the development of citizenship and power.

Thus far we have made quite explicit the argument that guides this Report. We have explored succinctly the conceptual bases for the statement that the global challenge of re-launching democracy depends on the shift from an electoral democracy to a citizenship democracy, and we have developed the main arguments for the close connection among the ideas of democracy, citizenship and State. These ideas, in turn, have grounded our empirical investigation. Without them, the observation of data would be totally disjointed and prob-

ably would not lead us anywhere. So, trying to discover how citizens perceive democracy in their own lives, coming up with the indicators on the political regime and the development of citizenship and, finally, consulting those who are familiar with power concerning the limits of the State and governments constitute the main lines of the empirical investigation that will be developed in the following chapter. There we will find in greater detail the material that we have only sketched thus far.

The reader will find that the ideas on these first pages link up with the empirical results of the second section. The latter will be developed in the third section of this Report. There we elaborate the main ideas suggested by the two principal challenges to democracy in Latin America: ensuring freedom; and broadening the citizenship of its people.

Empirical Basis of the Report

This section investigates and analyzes the empirical correlation between the theoretical foundations of the Report presented in the first section and the specific features of democracies in Latin America. The contents of the section are set out below:

a. A look at democratic regimes in the strictest sense (rules, procedures and institutions that define the forms of access to the higher echelons of State structures). This includes an appraisal of data generated by the Electoral Democracy Index (EDI), showing that Latin America has made significant progress as regards the democratic election of its governments, as well as observations on other indicators of political citizenship.

b. An assessment of a series of civil citizenship indicators that reveals that progress as evinced by the formal recognition of rights is not necessarily matched by effective implementation of these rights. There are also social citizenship indicators that highlight relatively limited progress in certain areas and severe failings in others.

c. An analysis of the impression that Latin Americans have of their democracies, based on an opinion poll carried out in the 18 different countries and involving 19,508 people. Although the analysis reveals a clear preference for democracy, as opposed to other forms of government, it also underlines that this preference does not necessarily translate into clear and sustained support, as shown in the Democratic Support Index (DSI) and the profiles of citizenship intensity.

d. An examination of consultations on key aspects of democracy with 231 leading Latin American political and social figures, including a distinguished group of Presidents and Vice-Presidents. The consultations included discussion of subjects like political participation, controls on the exercise of power, the role of political parties, de facto powers, illegal powers, formal political powers, and setting an agenda aimed at strengthening democracy.

Democratic Development Indicators

Political, Civil and Social Citizenship

A linked series of indicators was developed for this section to depict the current state of democracy in Latin America. Their scope, meaning and employment should be understood in the context of the methodological notes to be found at the end of the Report.

Certain clarifications need to be made concerning the data presented in this section:

a. The indicators do not provide a way of rating Latin American governments. They merely aim to shed light on the sizeable arena in which elected public officials and other actors perform their duties. This does not mean that the data are to be used to level criticism at, or to rank, elected authorities. Neither is this a case of comparing one country with another.

b. They do not constitute a unified index or ranking of countries. The theoretical framework proposes as its underlying tenet that, although democracy includes the political regime, it is not limited to it. With this starting point in mind, the indicators point to various aspects or dimensions of democracy as connected to different political, civil and social rights. This complex state of affairs cannot be summed up adequately using one single index. Furthermore, given that indicators tend to reflect reality with a degree of uncertainty, no precise classifications are to be found that assume that errors are non-existent. For basic methodological reasons the data are not presented either in the form of a single index or as a ranking of countries.

c. The data represent a partial measurement of a complex situation. They attempt to capture this complexity by bringing together different kinds of indicators, some of which concern processes, while others cover politics, and still others results. Although when taken together they make up a fairly detailed picture, they nevertheless amount to only a snapshot of reality and do not provide a comprehensive interpretation of the concepts measured. Furthermore, in more than one case, the information available relates to only one specific point in time, as opposed to a long period, which would allow trends to emerge. Certain aspects, often essential for grasping the specific circumstances in which each country finds itself, are extremely difficult to portray using quantitative measurements and are better understood by employing a qualitative approach.

d. The data refer to the point in time at which the measurements were taken and should not be considered as a measure of the present situation. Given the normal lapse of time that occurs between the moment when the measurement is taken and the subsequent process of analysis and publication, it is important to take this time lag into consideration when interpreting the data. This issue becomes particularly significant when one-off or initial measurements are involved and loses importance when long-term historic or periodic measurements are involved.

e. The new indices presented in this Report represent a first quali-quantitative approximation of complex social and political phenomena. The data selected as the basis for the various indicators relate to the way in which the index has been put together. Accordingly, a change in these self-same components could affect the level of the index. The values assigned to the variables making up the indices are based on a codification process developed by analysts. Despite the care taken to ensure that similar values are assigned to similar situations, there nevertheless exists a margin of discrepancy directly linked to each analyst's individual appreciation of the situation in question. Consequently, the complicated process by which these indices were put together should be taken into account when studying the results.

Political Citizenship

Electoral Democracy Index (EDI)

The analysis of electoral regimes takes as its starting point the EDI developed for this Report. The EDI assembles measurements that correspond to the questions listed below (for a more detailed explanation, see Box 20):

- Is the right to vote recognized?
- Are the elections clean?
- Are the elections free?
- Are elections the means of gaining access to public office?

The EDI gathers together information on some of the key elements of democracy. Any violation, partial or otherwise, of any of the political rights of citizens points to the existence of major obstacles to a democratic regime. However, it is important to underline that the EDI is a relatively limited measurement of the exercise of democ-racy. The achievement of a full electoral democ-racy, measured according to EDI criteria, is certainly a significant step forward for citizens' rights. Yet the establishment of electoral democracy is only the first step towards greater rights for citizens.

The most obvious conclusion to be drawn from the EDI is that Latin America has made significant progress as regards the democratization of the regime through the provision of access to government. Never before has Latin America been able to boast of having so many democratic and durable electoral regimes as it does at the beginning of the twenty-first century.

Before the first wave of transitions, which took place towards the end of the 1970s, most countries in the region were governed by authoritarian regimes. The progress that has been made since then has been remarkable. The average value of the EDI (ranging between zero and one) for Latin America rose swiftly from 0.28 in 1977, to 0.69 in 1985, to 0.86 in 1990. It continued to improve throughout the 1990s, and by the end of 2002 stood at 0.93.

The range of experiences is extremely varied, as illustrated in Graph 1. The Mercosur countries (Argentina, Brazil and Uruguay, with the exception of Paraguay) and Chile had already abandoned their military regimes by 1990 and have lived under democratic governments ever since.

However, the story is very different in the countries of Central America and the Dominican Republic, which were still embroiled in armed conflicts during the 1990s (with the exception of Costa Rica and the Dominican Republic). The process of democratization began at the same time as the peaceful resolution of these conflicts and has steadily been gaining ground ever since. In 2002, this sub-region was judged to be the most democratic in electoral terms.

The experience of the Andean countries constitutes a third variation. By the beginning of the 1990s, some (Colombia and Venezuela)

BOX 20

The Electoral Democracy Index:
A Contribution to the Debate on Democracy

The Electoral Democracy Index (EDI) offers a new way of measuring the extent of electoral democracy. The EDI, which was created especially for this Report, has been the subject of extensive discussion in the academic world for some time. An important step forward in the debate on this methodology was taken with the publication by UNDP of its Human Development Report 2002 under the subtitle 'Deepening democracy in a fragmented world'. The EDI is based on the most recent developments in this area, as explained in the Technical Notes to the Statistical Compendium of the Report. The EDI presents a composite of four elements judged to be critical components of a democratic regime, as shown in the following conceptual tree.

Electoral Democracy Index

Right to Vote

Are all adults within a country allowed to vote in elections?

Clean Elections

Is the voting process carried out without irregularities that constrain voters from autonomously and accurately expressing their preferences for candidates?

Free Elections

Is the electorate offered a range of choices that is not constrained either by legal restrictions or as a matter of practical force?

Elected Public Officials

Are elections the means of access to government offices, that is, are the country's main political offices (i.e., the national executive and legislature) filled through elections and are the winners of elections allowed both to assume office and serve their full term in office?

Accordingly, the way in which the four elements combine is expressed in the following formula:

**Electoral Democracy Index =
Right to Vote x Clean Elections
x Free Elections x Elected
Public Officials**

The EDI is an input into the discussion on, and analysis of, the real situation in Latin America today and should not be taken as a conclusive measurement of democracy. A debate has begun recently on the possibility of including the measurement among the criteria used to identify countries eligible for funding to promote development. One example is the Millennium Challenge Account (MCA) run by the government of the United States, which uses measurements of democracy and the rule of law developed by Freedom House and the World Bank, as well as other data. PRODDAL believes that there is neither sufficient consensus nor an adequately tried and tested methodology to warrant taking such decisions on the basis of measurements of democracy.

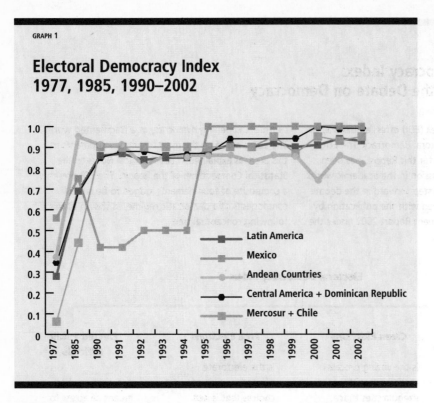

GRAPH 1

Electoral Democracy Index
1977, 1985, 1990–2002

Latin America
Mexico
Andean Countries
Central America + Dominican Republic
Mercosur + Chile

Note: the graph is based on data included in the Statistical Compendium of the Report.

were living under relatively long-established democratic regimes, while others (Bolivia, Ecuador and Peru) had been the first to make the transition away from military regimes towards the end of the 1970s and the beginning of the 1980s. However, during the 1990s, this sub-region began to confront serious problems that ultimately posed a real threat to the political systems of its members.

Finally, Mexico has made a slow but sure transition to democracy, culminating in the election of President Ernesto Zedillo in 1994.

Other more specific conclusions arise from a more detailed reading of the four indicators selected by the EDI—universal suffrage, clean elections, free elections and elections as a means of gaining access to public office.

The key condition of a democratic regime is the right to vote, as without this all other achievements become meaningless. There is little variation in this component in Latin America. Today, all countries recognize universal suffrage, although, in some cases, specific restrictions ap-

ply to the right to vote of the military, police, clergy, foreign residents and expatriate nationals.[55] Furthermore, in some countries, there are obstacles that hinder the ease with which the right to vote is exercised.[56] Nonetheless, acknowledgement of universal suffrage is without doubt a major achievement worth noting. Some of the most significant political struggles waged during the first half of the twentieth century concerned the extension of suffrage to the working class, the poor and to women.

The EDI also reflects the extent to which voters' preferences are faithfully registered by electoral processes. As shown in Table 4, a total of 70 national elections held between 1990 and 2002, and of these, 13 experienced significant problems. In two cases (the Dominican Republic in 1994 and Peru in 2000), the international community considered that the problems were so great as to undermine the democratic nature of the electoral process. In most cases, though, the irregularities do not appear to have had a decisive impact on the outcome of the polls. Further-

55 See Pamela Paxton et al., 2003.
56 See, for example, the study by Horacio Boneo and Edelberto Torres Rivas, 2001.

CLEAN ELECTIONS, 1990-2002

TABLE 4

Country	1990	1991	1992	1993	1994	1995	1996	1997	1998	1999	2000	2001	2002
Argentina		2		2		2		2		2		2	
Bolivia				2				2					2
Brazil	2				2				2				2
Chile				2				2		2		2	2-
Colombia	1	1			1				1				2-
Costa Rica	2				2				2				2
Dominican Republic	1-*				0 *		2		2		2		2
Ecuador			2		2		2		2				2
El Salvador		2			2			2		2	2		
Guatemala	1				1	1				2			
Honduras				2				2				2	
Mexico		2-			2			2			2		
Nicaragua	2						2					2	
Panama					2					2			
Paraguay				1					2				
Peru	2		2			1					0 *	2	
Uruguay					2					2			
Venezuela				2					2		2		

Number of cases of elections in which significant irregularities were detected

Latin America (**)	3	1	0	1	3	2	0	0	1	0	1	0	0

Notes: Elections are considered to be 'clean' when the electoral process does not involve any irregularities that may prevent voters from autonomously and accurately registering their preferences for a particular candidate. The EDI does not include those issues related to the competitiveness of the electoral process or to whether or not the winner of the election is allowed to take public office, or to whether all public officials are elected.

Values: 0 = major irregularities in the electoral process that have a determinative effect on the results of the elections (for example, alteration in the election for the national executive and/or the balance of power in Parliament); 1 = significant irregularities in the electoral process (such as intimidation of voters, acts of violence perpetrated against voters and electoral fraud) which do not, however, have a determinative effect on the result of elections; 2 = lack of significant irregularities in the voting process (e.g. elections that might include "technical" irregularities but not any systematic bias of considerable weight).

The signs (+ and -) are used to indicate intermediate situations. When elections are held for both the executive and the legislature in the same year and irregularities are detected only in the elections for the executive, this is indicated with an asterisk (*). In these cases, the value assigned to the legislative elections is 2.

(**) The data for the region take into account the total number of elections that took place in a given year with significant or serious irregularities, that is, they do not score either 2 or 2-.

Sources: Rodolfo Cerdas-Cruz, Juan Rial and Daniel Zovatto, 1992; Juan Rial and Daniel Zovatto, 1998; Kevin Middlebrook, 1998; Tommie Sue Montgomery, 1999; Robert A. Pastor, 1999; Jonathan Hartlyn, Jennifer McCoy and Thomas J. Mustillo, 2003; reports from the Organization of American States (OAS), the European Union (EU), the Carter Center and the National Democratic Institute; several articles published in the *Journal of Democracy*; and consultations with experts.

more, the number of problematic elections has fallen considerably: while there were ten such cases (out of a total of 35 elections) between 1990 and 1996, this fell to two (out of 35) between 1997 and 2002.

The third component of the EDI concerns free elections. This element is not completely covered by the concepts of universal suffrage and clean elections, since it concerns the voter's right to choose among alternatives. There are still a few difficulties in this area, as illustrated in Table 5. Out of a total of 70 national elections held be-

tween 1990 and 2002, there were ten examples of the ability of candidates to compete freely being significantly restricted. In spite of this, the trends make for positive reading. While major restrictions were noted in eight of the 35 elections held between 1990 and 1996, this number fell to two (out of 35) between 1997 and 2002.

Taken as a whole, the improvement is remarkable. The legal prohibitions in effect in times gone by, which affected ruling parties like the Partido Justicialista (PJ) in Argentina and the Alianza Popular Revolucionaria Americana (APRA) in

TABLE 5

FREE ELECTIONS, 1990–2002

Country	1990	1991	1992	1993	1994	1995	1996	1997	1998	1999	2000	2001	2002
Argentina		4		4		4		4		4		4	
Bolivia			4					4					4
Brazil	4				4				4				4
Chile				4				4		4		4	
Colombia	3	3			3				3				3
Costa Rica	4				4				4				4
Dominican Republic	4				4		4		4		4		4
Ecuador			4		4		4		4				4
El Salvador		3			4			4		4	4		
Guatemala	3				3	3				4			
Honduras				4				4				4	
Mexico		4			4			4			4		
Nicaragua	4						4					4-	
Panama					4					4			
Paraguay				4					4				
Peru	4		3			4					3	4	
Uruguay					4					4			
Venezuela				4					4		4		

Number of cases of elections in which significant irregularities were detected

	1990	1991	1992	1993	1994	1995	1996	1997	1998	1999	2000	2001	2002
Latin America (*)	2	2	1	0	2	1	0	0	1	0	0	0	1

Notes: Elections are considered to be 'free' when the electorate is offered a variety of options that are limited neither by legal restrictions nor by force. This measurement does not include factors that affect the ability of parties and candidates to compete on a level playing field, such as public financing, access to the media and the use of other public resources.

Values: 0 = single party system; 1 = ban on major party; 2 = ban on minor party; 3 = restrictions of a legal or practical nature that significantly affect the ability of potential candidates to run for office and/or the formation of political parties (for example, systematic assassination or intimidation of candidates, proscriptions barring popular candidates from competing and legal or practical restrictions that hinder the formation of parties or that lead certain parties to boycott the elections); 4 = essentially unrestricted conditions for the presentation of candidates and the formation of parties.

Plus and minus signs (+ and -) are used to refer to intermediate situations.

(*) The data for the region cover the total number of elections held in one year in which significant restrictions were detected, that is, they do not score either 4 or 4-.

Sources: Rodolfo Cerdas-Cruz, Juan Rial and Daniel Zovatto, 1992; Juan Rial and Daniel Zovatto, 1998; Kevin Middlebrook, 1998; Tommie Sue Montgomery, 1999; Robert A. Pastor, 1999; various articles published in the *Journal of Democracy*; and consultations with experts.

Peru, as well as other parties with less electoral weight, such as the Communist Parties in Brazil, Chile and Costa Rica, no longer exist. These restrictive practices, which were employed more or less continuously from the end of the 1940s until the 1960s in most cases—although in Brazil they continued until 1985—have been abandoned. Similarly, with the resolution of armed conflicts in Central America during the 1990s, the difficulties arising from the State's inability to guarantee the physical safety of the candidates have been overcome—with the exception of Colombia.

The fourth component of a democratic system of government concerns elections as a means of gaining access to public office. There are two issues to note here. One is whether the key public offices (presidential and parliamentary) are actually held by the winners of the elections. The other is whether those persons elected to office remain in their posts throughout the period stipulated by law, or, if they are replaced, whether this process takes place in accordance with the terms specified in the Constitution. This component complements the concept of the electoral process, as it introduces the issue of what is really at stake in elections. It has been introduced here because its violation means that the regime ceases to be democratic, even though the elections themselves may have been clean.

As shown in Table 6, the current situation in

ELECTIONS AS THE MEANS OF GAINING ACCESS TO PUBLIC OFFICE, 1990-2002   TABLE 6

Country	1990	1991	1992	1993	1994	1995	1996	1997	1998	1999	2000	2001	2002
Argentina	4	4	4	4	4	4	4	4	4	4	4	4-	4
Bolivia	4	4	4	4	4	4	4	4	4	4	4	4	4
Brazil	4	4	4	4	4	4	4	4	4	4	4	4	4
Chile	3	3	3	3	3	3	3	3	3	3	3	3	3
Colombia	4	4	4	4	4	4	4	4	4	4	4	4	4
Costa Rica	4	4	4	4	4	4	4	4	4	4	4	4	4
Dominican Republic	4	4	4	4	4	4	4	4	4	4	4	4	4
Ecuador	4	4	4	4	4	4	4	3+	4	4	3	3	3
El Salvador	4	4	4	4	4	4	4	4	4	4	4	4	4
Guatemala	4	4	4	3	4	4	4	4	4	4	4	4	4
Honduras	4	4	4	4	4	4	4	4	4	4	4	4	4
Mexico	4	4	4	4	4	4	4	4	4	4	4	4	4
Nicaragua	4	4	4	4	4	4	4	4	4	4	4	4	4
Panama	4	4	4	4	4	4	4	4	4	4	4	4	4
Paraguay	4	4	4	4	4	4	4	4	4	2+	4	4	4
Peru	4	4	2	4	4	4	4	4	4	4	4	4	4
Uruguay	4	4	4	4	4	4	4	4	4	4	4	4	4
Venezuela	4	4	4	4	4	4	4	4	4	4	4	4	3-

Number of cases of elections in which significant irregularities were detected													
Latin America (*)	1	1	2	2	1	1	1	2	1	2	2	2	3

Notes: Elections are considered to be the means of gaining access to key national public offices within the executive and legislative institutions if the winners of the elections take office and remain there throughout the periods stipulated by law. If the holders of public office are replaced, the way in which they are removed from office is analyzed, as is the selection of their replacement.

Values: 0 = none of the main political offices are filled through elections or all of the main political office holders are forcefully displaced from office and replaced by unconstitutional rulers; 1= a few political offices are filled by winners of elections or most of the main political office holders are forcefully displaced from office and replaced by unconstitutional rulers; 2 = the president or the parliament are not elected or are forcefully displaced from office and replaced by unconstitutional rulers; 3 = the president or the parliament are elected but the president is displaced from office and/or replaced by semiconstitutional means; or a significant number of parliamentarians are not elected or are forcefully displaced from office; 4 = All of the main political offices are filled by elections and none of the main political office holders are displaced from office unless their removal from power and their replacement is based on strictly constitutional grounds.

Plus and minus signs (+ and -) are used to refer to intermediate situations.

(*) The data for the region cover the total number of elections held in one year in which significant restrictions were detected, that is, they do not score either 4 or 4-.

Sources: Jorge Domínguez and Abraham Lowenthal, 1996; Jorge Domínguez, 1998; Larry Diamond et al., 1999; Thomas Walker and Ariel Armony, 2000; Aníbal Pérez-Liñán, 2001 and 2003; and consultations with experts.

Latin America is very encouraging in this regard. It is generally accepted that all of the major public offices (presidential and parliamentary) are to be filled through elections and that the authorities elected are to remain in office for the duration of their mandates. The handover of the presidency is now common practice, in contrast to the situation in Latin America between 1950 and 1980. This is one of the clearest signs of the giant strides forward that democracy has taken and the transformation it has wrought on political structures across the region.

However, there are two exceptions that deserve a closer look. In Chile, the appointment of *designated Senators* makes it very difficult for the preferences of the majority to be registered appropriately in Parliament. The other exception, which is more widespread, concerns the attempts to oust elected authorities from power in ways that do not comply completely with the rules laid down in the Constitution. Examples include: the closure of Parliament by Peruvian President Alberto Fujimori in 1992; the failed attempts by Guatemalan President Jorge Serrano to shut down Congress in 1993; the removal of Ecuadorian President Abdala Bucaram from

TABLE 7

Country	Civic Duties		Civic Participation		
	Compulsory Vote (2002)	Electoral Registration Procedure (2000)	Registered Voters (as % of Population with Right to Vote)	Voters (as % of Population with Right to Vote)	Valid Votes (as % of Population average 1990-2002)
Argentina	Yes	Automatic	98.3	78.0	70.9
Bolivia	Yes	Not automatic	76.8	55.2	51.8
Brazil	Yes	Not automatic	92.4	75.9	54.6
Chile	Yes	Not automatic	83.6	74.4	66.6
Colombia	No	Automatic	78.2	33.3	30.0
Costa Rica	Yes	Automatic	90.9	68.8	66.5
Dominican Republic	Yes	Not automatic	85.1	53.6	55.2
Ecuador	Yes	Automatic	98.1	65.8	52.5
El Salvador	Yes	Not automatic	88.3	38.7	36.6
Guatemala	Yes	Not automatic	78.0	36.2	31.5
Honduras	Yes	Automatic	101.2 (*)	68.3	63.7
Mexico	Yes	Not automatic	90.2	59.3	57.3
Nicaragua	No	Not automatic	95.8	77.9	73.7
Panama	Yes	Automatic	98.0	72.3	68.2
Paraguay	Yes	Not automatic	72.7	53.9	51.9
Peru	Yes	Not automatic	87.0	66.6	49.2
Uruguay	Yes	Not automatic	103.8 (*)	94.8	91.6
Venezuela	No	Automatic	80.9	45.7	35.6
Latin America (**)			**89.3**	**62.7**	**56.1**
Extra-Regional References					
Western Europe			96.2	73.6	
United States			69.5	43.3	

Notes:

(*) Those figures that exceed 100 percent indicate that the number of people on the electoral registers is greater than the number of those eligible to vote. This situation generally occurs when the electoral registers have not been adequately purged.

(**) The data for the region as a whole are based on the average for all the countries.

Sources: Fernández Baeza, 1998; Election Process Information Collection (EPIC), 2002; María Gratschew, 2001 and 2002; International Institute for Democracy and Electoral Assistance (IDEA), 2002b; León-Rosch, 1998; Reyes, 1998; several national Constitutions; and calculations made on the basis of information provided on CD-ROM in J. Payne et al., 2002, and data on the 2001 and 2002 elections provided by official sources.

office in 1997; the assassination of Paraguayan Vice-President Luis María Argaña in 1999; the ousting of Ecuadorian President Jamil Mahuad in 2000; the fall of Argentinean President Fernando de la Rúa in 2001; and the crisis sparked by the attempts to remove Venezuelan President Hugo Chávez from office in April 2002. These events did not, however, lead to classic military coups like those that tended to occur following the breakdown of democratic regimes not so long ago in Latin America. Nonetheless, they interrupted the exercise of power in other ways.

There are many instances of the right to democratic access to public office not being respected. Between 1990 and 2002, considerable restric-

tions of different kinds were placed on the application of this principle in six out of the region's 18 countries. This is a negative trend, as the rate of cases increased from one a year in 1990 to three a year by 2002.

Other Indicators of the Democratic Regime to ensure Access to Office

Other relevant indicators need to be taken into account, as well as the various aspects of a democratic regime included in the EDI.

Electoral Participation

Citizen participation in the electoral process in Latin America is generally of a good level, although there are significant differences among countries. At the regional level, 89.3 of the electorate is registered to vote, 62.7 actually votes, and 56.1 deposits a valid vote. These figures indicate that it is possible for a candidate to win an election without the support of the majority of the population. These percentages are below those of Western Europe but above those of the United States. Nevertheless, the general level of participation in Latin America tends to be stable over long periods.

In some Latin American countries, the level of electoral participation is very low. For instance, the percentage of voters in Venezuela (45.7), El Salvador (38.7), Guatemala (36.2) and Colombia (33.3) is very low and a cause for concern. Electoral participation in Bolivia, the Dominican Republic and Paraguay is somewhat higher, but still low. Although abstention is not a problem in the region as a whole, it is nevertheless a key issue in certain countries.

Electoral Competition and the Selection of Candidates

Other indicators cast light on the way in which candidates are selected, an issue that impacts directly on electoral competition. This is a complex process revolving around the political parties, institutions that, across the region, are the vehicle par excellence for candidates who wish to stand for public office. On this topic, it should be noted that significant differences exist among the countries of Latin America with regard to three key issues:

- the monopoly that parties have over nominees for public office and the possibility for independent candidates to stand separately;
- the rules for setting up national parties; and
- the legal requirement to hold internal elections within parties in order to nominate candidates.

As shown in Table 8, in Colombia, Costa Rica, Honduras, Mexico, Paraguay, Uruguay and Venezuela, new actors have only to over-

come minor hurdles before they can enjoy access to an electoral contest. In these countries, a certain number of internal party democratic practices or rules apply. An intermediate group consists of Argentina, Brazil, Chile, the Dominican Republic, Ecuador and Panama, where more obvious barriers to entry exist, alongside a number of legal requirements that affect the nomination of certain candidates, or where the use of primaries is limited to the election of party candidates. In a third group of countries—comprising Bolivia, El Salvador, Guatemala, Nicaragua and Peru—the power to select candidates is highly concentrated in the hands of the party elite.

The problems of barriers to entry and of internal party democratic rules and practices are certainly complex. Before a comprehensive analysis can be presented, it is necessary to obtain more detailed information than that which is currently available about independent candidates, the setting up of parties, the procedures they follow in order to select their own candidates, the conditions under which candidates compete in primaries and the way that the primaries are controlled.

One relevant point that has a bearing on electoral competition is the existence of legislation that opens up the political arena to women by reserving for them a certain number of places on the party lists for the national legislature. This kind of legislation has been adopted by many countries in the region over the past ten years. Between 1991 and 2003, 11 of Latin America's 18 countries introduced quota laws that, by and large, require that 20–40 percent of the places on party legislative lists be assigned to women. This instrument

TABLE 8

POLITICAL PARTIES AND INTERNAL DEMOCRACY, 1990-2001 (*)

Country	Party Control of Candidate Selection Process, 1990–2002			Legal Requirements for nominating Presidential Candidates, 1990–2002 (2)		Use of Primaries to nominate Presidential Candidates for Main Parties, Elections in 2001 or Preceding Year (4)
	Party Monopoly on Candidacies	Independent Candidates allowed to Stand	Restrictions on forming National Parties, 2002	None	Some	
Argentina	1990-01		Moderately restrictive	1990-01		At least once
Bolivia	1990-01		Moderately restrictive	1990-99		None
Brazil	1990-01		Few restrictions		1999-01 (3)	None
Chile		1990-01	Moderately restrictive		1990-01	At least once
Colombia		1990-01	Few restrictions	1990-01	1990-01	At least once
Costa Rica	1990-01		Few restrictions		1990-01	All
Dominican Republic	1990-01 (1)		Moderately restrictive		1990-01	All
Ecuador	1990-95	1995-01	Moderately restrictive	1990-01	1990-01	None
El Salvador	1990-01		Very restrictive	1990-01		At least once
Guatemala	1990-01		Moderately restrictive		1990-01	None
Honduras		1990-01	Few restrictions		1990-01	All
Mexico	1990-01		Few restrictions	1990-01		All
Nicaragua	1990-01		Very restrictive	1990-01	1990-01	At least once
Panama	1990-01		Very restrictive			All
Paraguay		1990-01	Few restrictions	1990-01	1990-01	All
Peru		1990-01	Moderately restrictive	1990-01		All
Uruguay	1990-01		Few restrictions	1990-1997	1997-01	None
Venezuela		1990-01	Few restrictions	1990-1999	1999-01	None

Notes:

(*) Relevant reforms introduced since the end of 2001 include: Law Nº 25.611 passed in Argentina in June 2002, and the Law on Political Parties passed in Peru in November 2003.

(1) Although legislation in the Dominican Republic allows independent candidates to stand, the requirements for doing so are similar in nature to those covering the setting up of a political party.

(2) This category also takes into account whether the Constitution or electoral legislation requires candidates to be nominated through primaries or a party political convention.

(3) The Law on Political Party Reform passed in June 1999 in Bolivia has still not been implemented.

(4) Primaries are defined as a process in which presidential candidates are elected freely and directly by means of a secret ballot, either by party members or by those citizens registered to vote in national elections.

Sources: Manuel Alcántara Sáez, 2002, pp. 20–34; J. Payne et al., 2002, pp. 156–166; and national Constitutions and legislation on political parties, as well as consultations with experts associated either now or in the past with electoral tribunals in each country.

QUOTAS FOR FEMALE CANDIDATES TO THE LEGISLATURE, 2003 (% OF TOTAL) TABLE 9

Country	Lower or Single Chamber	Senate	Year adopted
Argentina	30	30	1991
Bolivia	30	25	1997
Brazil	30	0	1997
Chile	0	0	-
Colombia	0	0	-
Costa Rica	40	-	1996
Dominican Republic	25	-	1997
Ecuador	20	-	1997
El Salvador	0	-	-
Guatemala	0	-	-
Honduras	30	-	2000
Mexico	30	30	2002
Nicaragua	0	-	-
Panama	30	-	1997
Paraguay	20	20	1996
Peru	30	-	1997
Uruguay	0	0	-
Venezuela	0	-	-

Notes: these figures represent the minimum percentage of women candidates that each party must propose for the parliament. The information only includes the quotas stipulated in the legislation on political parties and legislatures; it does not refer to the quotas set out in internal party regulations. The minus sign indicates that the information is not applicable.

Sources: Economic Commission for Latin America and the Caribbean (ECLAC), 1999, p. 69; Myriam Méndez-Montalvo and Julie Ballington, 2002; OAS Inter-American Commission of Women, 2002; and the International Institute for Democracy and Electoral Assistance (IDEA), 2003.

undoubtedly represents a vast improvement, as it enshrines in law formal recognition of the need to create greater opportunities for women. However, it is only a first step towards overcoming the many obstacles that still lie in the way of women who want to compete in the political arena on equal terms with men.

Another relevant issue that has a bearing on the electoral contest concerns the rules on political funding. Its impact is increasingly evident with respect to the nature of the elec-

toral contest itself, as the matter is directly related not only to whether the elections are free and fair, but also to whether everybody has the same opportunity to run.

Information on State financing of elections and parties reveals a broad range of situations. In order to ensure that the issue of financing does not undermine the electoral process, some countries use public funds to finance part of an election campaign, assigning funding in proportion to votes or facilitating advertising in the media, largely television spots. Most countries resort to a mixed funding system, although there is a trend towards assuming greater control, as its implementation still presents difficulties.

Electoral Representation

It is also important to take into account certain features of the people and the parties elected to public office. The number of female members of national legislatures in Latin America has increased from eight percent at the end of the 1980s to 15.5 percent at the time of the last election, although there are considerable differences among countries.

The number of indigenous peoples in the lower or single chamber of the legislature in 2001–2002 stood at: around 0.8 percent in Peru (one out of 120); 3.3 percent (four out of 121) in Ecuador; 12.4 percent (14 out of 113) in Guatemala; and 26.2 percent (34 out of 130) in Bolivia.[57] These statistics are in stark contrast to the percentage of the population of these countries that native communities comprise (43, 34, 60 and 61 percent respectively).[58]

Finally, the number of descendants of African peoples in the lower chamber of the legislature in Brazil stood at: 0.8 percent (four out of a total of 479) between 1983 and 1987; 2.1 percent (ten out of 487) between 1987 and 1991; 3.2 percent (16 out of 503) between

57 These figures may change even during the period indicated, according to the criteria used by the observers consulted. Personal communication from L.E. López Hurtado, 2002, and Simón Pachano, FLACSO-Ecuador, 2003; and US Department of State, 2001.
58 These figures are the average of the highest and lowest estimates provided by José Matos Mar, 1993, pp. 232–233. Also see Angela Meentzen, 2002, p. 12.

FINANCING FOR PARTIES AND ELECTORAL CAMPAIGNS, 2003

TABLE 10

Country	Direct Public Funding	Access to Private Funding Sources				Access to Television	
		Limits on Private Donations to Parties	Limits on Anonymous Donations to Parties	Limits on Donations by State Contractors to Parties	Laws on Public Disclosure	Access to Free Television	Party Spending on Private Television
Argentina	Yes, low threshold	Yes	Yes	Yes	Moderately strict	Yes	Limited
Bolivia	Yes, high threshold	Yes	Yes	Yes	Moderately strict	Yes	Limited
Brazil	Yes, low threshold	Yes	Yes	Yes	Strict	Yes	Prohibited
Chile	Yes, low threshold	Yes	Yes	Yes	Moderately strict	Yes	Prohibited
Colombia	Yes, high threshold	No	No	No	Moderately strict	Yes	Limited
Costa Rica	Yes, high threshold	Yes	Yes	No	Weak	No	Unlimited
Dominican Republic	Yes, low threshold	No	No	No	None	No	Unlimited
Ecuador	Yes, low threshold	No	Yes	Yes	Very weak	No	Unlimited
El Salvador	Yes, low threshold	No	No	No	None	No	Unlimited
Guatemala	Yes, high threshold	No	No	No	None	Yes	Unlimited
Honduras	Yes, low threshold	No	Yes	Yes	None	No	Limited
Mexico	Yes, low threshold	Yes	Yes	Yes	Very weak	Yes	Limited
Nicaragua	Yes, high threshold	No	Yes	No	Weak	Yes	Limited
Panama	Yes, low threshold	No	No	No	None	Yes	Unlimited
Paraguay	Yes, low threshold	Yes	Yes	Yes	Very weak	Yes	Limited
Peru	Yes, low threshold	Yes	No	No	Weak	Yes	Limited
Uruguay (*)	Yes, low threshold	No	No	No	None	Yes	Unlimited
Venezuela	No	Yes	Yes	Yes	None	No	Limited

Notes: the term 'direct public financing' refers to the direct provision of financial resources to political parties, as opposed usually to indirect forms of support, such as the provision of services and tax benefits.

(*) Public funding has been legislated in Uruguay since 1928 through ad hoc laws passed before each election.

Sources: Pilar Del Castillo and Daniel G. Zovatto, 1998; J. Payne et al., 2002, pp. 169–172; Michael Pinto-Duschinsky, 2002a, pp. 76–77, and 2002b; Gene Ward, 2002; Daniel G. Zovatto, 2003; and consultations with experts associated either currently or in the past with electoral tribunals in each country, as well as various Constitutions and pieces of national electoral legislation.

SEATS IN CONGRESS WON BY WOMEN, 1990-2003

TABLE 11

Country	End of 1980s		Middle of 1990s		Last Elections	
	Year	% Women	Year	% Women	Year	% Women
Argentina	1989	6.3	1995	21.8	2003	34.1
Bolivia	1989	9.2	1997	11.5	2002	18.5
Brazil	1986	5.3	1994	7.0	2002	8.6
Chile	1989	5.8	1997	10.8	2001	12.5
Colombia	1986	4.5	1994	10.8	2002	12.0
Costa Rica	1986	10.5	1994	14.0	2002	35.1
Dominican Republic	1986	7.5	1994	11.7	2002	17.3
Ecuador	1988	4.5	1994	4.5	2002	16.0
El Salvador	1988	11.7	1994	10.7	2003	10.7
Guatemala	1985	7.0	1994	7.5	2003	8.2
Honduras	1989	10.2	1997	9.4	2001	5.5
Mexico	1988	12.0	1994	14.2	2003	22.6
Nicaragua	1984	14.8	1996	9.7	2001	20.7
Panama	1989	7.5	1994	8.3	1999	9.9
Paraguay	1989	5.6	1993	2.5	2003	8.8
Peru	1985	5.6	1995	10.0	2001	17.5
Uruguay	1989	6.1	1994	7.1	1999	12.1
Venezuela	1988	10.0	1993	5.9	2000	9.7
Latin America (*)		**8.0**		**9.9**		**15.5**

Notes: the numbers refer to the percentage of seats won by women in the lower or single chamber of the national legislature. The data refer to the results of the elections held in the year indicated and may vary from poll to poll.

(*) The data for the region as a whole are based on the average for all countries.

Source: Inter-Parliamentary Union (IPU), 1995 and 2003.

1991 and 1995; and 2.8 percent (15 out of 511) between 1995 and 1999.[59] Afro-descendants represent approximately 44 percent of the population of Brazil.[60]

Various relevant indicators also consider the issue of representation from the perspective of the political parties. One relatively simple measurement takes into account the percentage of votes received by those political parties that do not enjoy representation in the lower or single chamber of the national legislature. The regional average of 4.3 percent is relatively low, and in some countries—Brazil, Honduras, Paraguay and Uruguay—the percentage of valid votes won by parties that do not enjoy representation is extremely low. However, in other countries—Chile, Costa Rica and Guatemala—this number is high,

varying between 7.8 and 12.3 percent. Similarly, the index of disproportionate representation—a more complex measurement that refers to the relationship between the votes cast for specific parties and the seats won by them in the lower or single chamber of the national legislature—paints a fairly positive picture. The regional average of 5.6 percent is reasonably moderate, indicating that there is a considerable degree of correlation between the number of votes received and the seats won by each party. Furthermore, in various countries—Colombia, Honduras, Nicaragua and Uruguay—this index is particularly low, although in others, such as Guatemala and Panama, it is high, fluctuating between 11.9 and 13.9 percent.

59 Ollie A. Johnson III, 1998, pp. 103–105.
60 Cristina Torres, 2001, p. 94.

PROPORTIONALITY OF REPRESENTATION VIA POLITICAL PARTIES, 1990-2002

TABLE 12

Country	Percentage of Votes won by Parties without Parliamentary Representation (average 1990–2002)	Index of Electoral Disproportionality (average 1990–2002)
Argentina	3.8	6.7
Bolivia	4.2	5.0
Brazil	1.4	3.8
Chile	8.9	7.2
Colombia	4.8	3.0
Costa Rica	7.8	5.0
Dominican Republic	5.4	6.3
Ecuador	4.2	5.9
El Salvador	2.2	4.7
Guatemala	12.3	11.9
Honduras	0.4	2.5
Mexico	3.7	5.7
Nicaragua	2.4	2.7
Panama	4.9	13.9
Paraguay	0.7	6.1
Peru	3.5	5.2
Uruguay	0.5	0.6
Venezuela	6.2	5.3
Latin America (*)	**4.3**	**5.6**

Notes: the term 'percentage of votes won by parties without parliamentary representation' refers to votes cast during elections for seats in the lower or single chamber of the legislature. The term 'electoral disproportionality' refers to the deviation of a party's share of the seats from its share of the votes. The measure of electoral disproportionality for the lower house or single chamber, in this table, is the least squares index, which is calculated by squaring the vote seat share difference for each party, adding up all of these figures, dividing the total by two and taking the square root of the resulting value. A low figure can be interpreted as an indication that parties receive a number of seats that is closely proportional to their share of the votes, while higher numbers indicate that the relationship between these two variables is more disproportional.

(*) The data for the region as a whole is based on the average for all countries.

Sources: calculations made on the basis of data on the CD-ROM in J. Payne et al., 2002, and data on the 2001 and 2002 elections obtained from official sources.

Evaluation of the Democratic Regime to ensure Access to Office

According to the components of the EDI, we may observe that, in Latin America:

- every citizen enjoys the right to vote without restriction;
- clean elections have become common practice, and there has been marked progress towards free elections. There have been a few isolated cases of electoral fraud and other irregularities, as well as of voters being intimidated; and
- significant improvements have been made with respect to gaining access to public office through elections. Generally, the key posts within the executive and the legislative branches of the State at the national level are held by elected candidates and the transition between governments takes place in accordance with constitutional rules, even in times of political or socio-political crisis (after the head of a government has resigned). There are a few exceptions, including, most notably, isolated attempts to topple elected rulers using unconstitutional means.

The following observations can be made about those aspects of a democratic regime that are not included in the EDI:

- The level of citizen participation in electoral processes is fairly high in Latin America, although we have detected a shift towards a lower level of electoral participation in some countries.
- There are no marked trends as regards obstacles to participation in the electoral contest, nor concerning citizen participation in the selection of candidates. However, in several countries, the party elite has centralized decision-making with regard to the nomination of candidates.
- There is a tendency to introduce legal regulations designed to create greater opportunities for citizen involvement. This is

BOX 21

Handling of Citizens' requests by Public Authorities

Although they may refuse a citizen's request, public officials must nevertheless ensure that the treatment they provide meets two conditions: that their decisions respect the rights and dignity of people and that they are backed by a legal mandate approved by democratic means. Otherwise, the citizen is being abused. A certain percentage of cases of abuse may be due to circumstance, but circumstance does not explain satisfactorily the existence of recurring patterns of abuse in exchanges between the State and its citizens. Accordingly, the Report examines whether patterns of abuse exist in order to see whether this is due to structural reasons, such as the persistent presence of undemocratic practices in the way the State is organized and run. One of the first findings of the Report is that, in 2002, a small proportion of persons declared that they had contacted a public body in connection with formal procedure (39.9 percent). A very high percentage of these persons stated that they had suffered some form of abuse at the hands of the public officials (78 percent). In most cases, these abuses were relatively minor (long queues, the observance of unnecessary formalities, and information being refused or obtained with difficulty). Other factors also have a bearing on the situation, such as the lack of appropriate facilities and the fact that demands on services may be at an optimum. However, a major concern is the extensive reference to experiences of serious abuse: almost one in four persons who had had dealings with public authorities claimed to have been humiliated, treated with disrespect or asked for a bribe (22.3 percent). In these cases, the interviewees felt that their right to fair treatment and to respect for personal dignity had been violated by public officials.

EXPERIENCES OF TREATMENT AMONG PEOPLE WHO HAVE PRESENTED THEMSELVES AT A PUBLIC INSTITUTION OVER THE PAST 12 MONTHS, 2002   TABLE 13

Status	Experience of Treatment (1)	Percentage of Total	Percentage of Those Involved
Contact with a public entity	Bad experiences: severe and minor	6.1	15.4
	Bad experiences: severe	2.8	6.9
	Bad experiences: minor	22.2	55.7
	No bad experiences (2)	8.8	22.0
	Total	**39.9**	**100.0**
No contact with a public entity		60.1	
Total		**100.0**	

Notes: the column 'percentage of total' is based on interviews with 19,536 people who stated whether or not they had presented themselves at a public institution in the past 12 months. The column 'percentage of those involved' is based only on the views of 7,790 interviewees who stated that they had presented themselves at a public institution over the past 12 months and who therefore had experience of receiving treatment.

(1) Minor bad experiences: long queues, the observance of unnecessary formalities, and information being refused or obtained with difficulty. Severe bad experiences: the interviewee was asked for a bribe or felt humiliated, or the officials were disrespectful or rude.

(2) It is supposed that the interviewees did not have bad experiences if the answer to question p12u was that they had presented themselves at a public institution and if they did not answer question p13u, which only allows for negative replies.

Source: results of processing answers to question p13u in the UNDP Proprietary Section of Latinobarómetro 2002.

OVERALL PRESIDENTIAL POWERS, 2002

TABLE 14

Country	Non-Legislative Powers (1)		Legislative Powers (2)		Index of Formal Presidential Powers (3)	
Argentina	0.38	Medium low (*)	0.44	Medium high (*)	0.41	Medium high (*)
Bolivia	0.50	Medium high	0.23	Medium low	0.37	Medium low
Brazil	0.50	Medium high	0.62	Very high	0.56	Very high
Chile	0.50	Medium high	0.66	Very high	0.58	Very high
Colombia	0.00	Very low	0.59	Very high	0.29	Very low
Costa Rica	0.50	Medium high	0.23	Medium low	0.36	Medium low
Dominican Republic	0.50	Medium high	0.37	Medium low	0.44	Medium high
Ecuador	0.50	Medium high	0.59	Very high	0.55	Very high
El Salvador	0.50	Medium high	0.33	Medium low	0.42	Medium high
Guatemala	0.25	Medium low	0.29	Medium low	0.27	Very low
Honduras	0.50	Medium high	0.25	Medium low	0.38	Medium low
Mexico	0.50	Medium high	0.24	Medium low	0.37	Medium high
Nicaragua	0.50	Medium high	0.25	Medium low	0.38	Medium low
Panama	0.50	Medium high	0.43	Medium high	0.46	Medium high
Paraguay	0.50	Medium high	0.19	Very low	0.34	Medium low
Peru	0.13	Very low	0.50	Medium high	0.31	Medium low
Uruguay	0.38	Medium low	0.38	Medium	0.38	Medium low
Venezuela	0.19	Very low	0.30	Medium low	0.25	Very low
Latin America	**0.41**		**0.38**		**0.40**	
Extra-regional references						
United States	0.48	Medium high	0.15	Very low	0.31	Medium low

Notes:

(1) This figure is the average of the points assigned according to the capacity of the legislature to cast a vote of censorship to the Cabinet and the capacity of the executive power to dissolve the national legislature. The scales were standardized between zero and one to allow comparison.

(2) The weighted average of the legislative powers of the President.

(3) The general index of the formal powers vested in the President is an average of the legislative and non-legislative presidential powers.

(*) The level of any of these powers is assessed from a comparative regional perspective. A 'very high' level in any of the power dimensions signifies that the country's record is above one standard deviation from the regional average. 'Medium high' means that its score falls between the regional average and one positive standard deviation. This same method is used to grade the 'medium low' and 'very low' levels.

Sources: Matthew Sobert Shugart and John Carey, 1992; Scott Mainwaring and Matthew Sobert Shugart, 1997; John M. Carey and Matthew Sobert Shugart, 1998; David Samuels, 2000; David Altman, 2001 and 2002; J. Payne et al., 2002; and Georgetown University and the Organization of American States (OAS), 2002.

the case with respect to those laws promulgated in most Latin American countries that set quotas on the number of women to be included on legislative lists.

- Between the end of the 1980s and today, the number of women in the legislatures of Latin America has risen, although it falls far short of their demographic representation. Such a shortcoming is even more marked when it comes to the legislative representation of indigenous communities and Afro-descendants.

- The electoral systems permit a considerable degree of proportionality be-

tween the level of electoral support and the level of representation enjoyed by political parties in legislative institutions.

- Few countries have as yet passed legislation on the financing of political parties and electoral campaigns, which facilitates access to public funding and effective regulation of money in politics.

Other Dimensions of Political Citizenship

Political citizenship is not merely about the relationship between voters and decisionmakers, but also extends to the particular orientation of those self-same decision-makers—elected or not—towards public welfare or personal gain. Therefore, a key aspect to be taken into consideration is accountability and control over how public officials perform their duties. In this section we will analyze firstly the classic constitutional powers (executive, legislative and judicial), then the public bodies charged with overseeing State activities at the horizontal level, and finally, a few direct democracy instruments that may offer opportunities for citizen participation in policymaking.

Classic Constitutional Powers

The first characteristic to take note of with respect to the issue of political oversight concerns the relationship that exists among the classic constitutional powers. Political oversight is rendered more effective when there is a genuine division of powers, each of which is legally empowered to control the others and to sanction their conduct.

The relationship between the executive and the legislature is perhaps the most important factor in the association between the branches of government. This is particularly the case in Latin America, given its presidential tradition—whether overtly authoritarian or not—as well as the tendency of the executive to overrule the legislature.

We should note here that the formal powers vested in Latin American Presidents is relatively great compared with the classic style of presidential rule as seen in the United States.

Another key point concerns the power held by the judiciary and its degree of independence from the other branches. Many Latin American countries have undertaken constitutional and legal reforms aimed at reinforcing the independence of the judiciary. Despite such reforms, in several countries, the executive still reserves for itself significant powers vis-à-vis the nomination of Supreme Court judges. However, pri-

> **Political oversight is rendered more effective when there is a genuine division of powers, each of which is legally empowered to control the others and to sanction their conduct.**

or vetting of judges by some sort of council of jurists or magistrates is becoming more widespread, as it is an instrument that has the potential—although this has not yet been proven definitely—to reduce the level of political influence over the selection process, as well as to enhance the independence and professional status of the judicial branch. In nearly all of the countries of the region, another entity, generally connected with the legislature, is responsible for selecting candidates from a list of nominations and ratifying their selection based on an overall or qualified majority.

To sum up, the indicators shown in Table 14 suggest that, at least formally speaking, the judicial branch of government avails itself of a considerable degree of autonomy and authority in the exercise of its functions. There is not enough information currently available, though, to allow us to draw any definitive conclusions about the true independence of the judicial authorities in Latin America, as the indicators only refer to matters of form and frequently ignore some fundamental realities. We still do not have a reliable and broadly accepted method of measuring the degree of independence of the judiciary. According to several surveys and the opinions of experts, there has been marked improvement in the level of independence of the judicial branch, but serious problems still exist in the region as a whole.[61]

Another issue that needs to be examined once there is enough information available is

---

61 Edmundo Jarquín and Fernando Carrillo, 1998; P. Domingo, 1999; William C. Prillaman, 2000; Margaret Popkin, 2001; and Linn Hammergren, 2002.

TABLE 15

Country	Constitutional Texts	Conditions for the Appointment of Judges			Control of Constitutionality
		Initial Selection of Candidates	Selection and Appointment	Period of Appointment	
Argentina	1853 Constitution, 1994 reform	Executive nominates candidates (*)	Senate appoints (2/3 vote)	Life tenure (obligatory retirement at 75)	Supreme Court
Bolivia	1967 Constitution, 1994 reform	Judicial Council presents shortlist	Congress in plenary session selects from list and appoints (2/3 vote)	Ten years, option to re-elect after a period	Constitutional Tribunal
Brazil	1988 Constitution, 1998 reform	Executive nominates candidates	Senate appoints (absolute majority)	Life tenure (obligatory retirement at 70)	Federal Supreme Tribunal
Chile	1980 Constitution, 1997 reform	Supreme Court presents shortlist	President selects from list and Senate appoints (2/3 vote)	Life tenure (obligatory retirement at 75)	Constitutional Tribunal
Colombia	1991 Constitution, 1997 reform	Higher Council of Jurists presents list	Supreme Court selects from list and appoints (absolute majority)	Eight years, without re-election	Constitutional Court
Costa Rica	1949 Constitution, reformed in 1954 and 1993	Congress identifies candidates	Congress selects candidates from list and appoints	Eight years, re-election permitted	Special chamber of Supreme Court
Dominican Republic	1966 Constitution, 1995 reform	National Council of Jurists identifies candidates	National Council of Jurists appoints (absolute majority)	Life tenure (obligatory retirement at 75)	Supreme Court
Ecuador	1978 Constitution, reformed in 1986, 1993, 1996 and 1997	Supreme Court nominates candidates	Supreme Court appoints (2/3 vote)	Life tenure	Constitutional Tribunal
El Salvador	1983 Constitution, 1996 reform	National Council of Jurists and lawyers' associations of El Salvador present list	Congress selects from list and appoints (2/3 vote)	Nine years, successive re-election	Special chamber of Supreme Court
Guatemala	1985 Constitution, 1994 reform	Applications Commission made up of governmental and non-govern-mental members presents list	Congress selects from list and appoints (2/3 vote)	Five years, re-election permitted	Constitutional Court
Honduras	1982 Constitution, 2000 reform	Nomination Comittee, with non-governmental membership, presents list	Congress selects from list and appoints (2/3 vote)	Seven years, successive re-election	Constitutional chamber
Mexico	1917 Constitution, reformed in 1992, 1993 and 1994	Executive presents list	Senate selects from list and appoints (2/3 of those present)	15 years, without re-election	Supreme Court

(CONT. IN P. 95)

TABLE 15 *(CONT. OF P. 94)*

| Country | Constitutional Texts | Conditions for the Appointment of Judges | | | Control of Constitutionality |
		Initial Selection of Candidates	Selection and Appointment	Period of Appointment	
Nicaragua	1987 Constitution, 1995 reform	Executive and Congress present list	Congress selects from list and appoints (6/10 vote)	Five years, re-election permitted	Supreme Court
Panama	1972 Constitution, reformed in 1978, 1983 and 1984	President and Cabinet present list	Congress appoints (absolute majority)	Ten years, re-election permitted	Supreme Court
Paraguay	1992 Constitution	Council of Magistrates presents list	Senate appoints, with approval of executive	Five years, re-election implies life tenure (obligatory retirement at 75)	Supreme Court
Peru	1993 Constitution	National Council of Magistrates identify candidates	National Council of Magistrates appoints (2/3 vote)	Obligatory retirement at 70	Constitutional Tribunal
Uruguay	1967 Constitution	Congress identify candidates	Congress (both chambers) in plenary session approves (2/3 vote)	Ten years, re-election permitted at alternate five-year periods thereafter (obligatory retirement at 75)	Supreme Court
Venezuela	1999 Constitution	National Applications Judicial Committee presents list	Congress selects from list and appoints	12 years, without re-election	Supreme Justice Tribunal

Note:
(*) In Argentina, the process of appointing judges to the Supreme Court has been modified by Decree No. 222 of 19 June 2003.
Sources: State of the Nation Project 1999, p. 199; Elin Skaar, 2001, Appendix 1; UNDP, 2002b, pp. 78 and 81; OEA-CIDH (Organization of American States-Inter American Commission of Human Rights), 2003; Institute of Comparative Public Law, 2003; Andean Commission of Jurists, 2003; and various national Constitutions.

the use that the judiciary makes of its growing autonomy, at least in some countries. In itself, such independence does not preclude (and might even facilitate) the corruption of the judiciary and entanglement with particular corporate interests. We hope that the huge amount of effort being invested in reforming the judicial branch, not to mention the considerable amount of international financial assistance that has been provided, will result in greater heed being paid to this issue than has hitherto been the case. The independence, growing professionalism and appropriate authority vested in this branch of the State become fully justified only when they are put wholeheartedly at the service of not just a rule of law, but a democratic rule of law.

Mandated Oversight Agencies

Other State entities that contribute to political control are those specialize in horizontal oversight of the activities of the State.[62] These agencies are distinct from the classic constitutional powers as their sphere of activity is limited to some more specific functions.

The first kind of entity is that which is in

62 Enrique Peruzzotti and Catalina Smulovitz, 2002a.

TABLE 16

MANDATED OVERSIGHT AGENCIES, 2002

Country	General Comptrollers (1)			Offices of Public Prosecutor (2)			Ombudsmen (3)	
	Appointment (4)	Dismissal (4)	Level of Authority (5)	Appointment (4)	Dismissal (4)	Established	Appointment (4)	Dismissal (4)
Argentina	Legislature	..	Weak	Executive++	Undefined	1993	Legislature+	Legislature+
Bolivia	Executive+	Legislature++	Weak	Legislature	Legislature	1994	Legislature	Legislature
Brazil	Legislature-	Judiciary	Strong	Executive++	Legislature	-	-	-
Chile	Executive++	Legislature+	Strong	Executive++	Legislature++	-	-	-
Colombia	Legislature++	Judiciary	Strong	Legislature-	Supreme Court	1991	Legislature-	Unspecified
Costa Rica	Legislature	Legislature	Moderate	Supreme Court	Undefined	1992	Legislature	Legislature
Dominican Republic	Legislature-	..	Weak	Executive	Executive	2001	Legislature	Supreme Court
Ecuador	Executive+	Legislature	Weak	Legislature-	Legislature	1998	Legislature++	Legislature
El Salvador	Legislature	Legislature	Strong	Legislature	Legislature	1991	Legislature	Legislature
Guatemala	Legislature	Legislature	Strong	Executive	Executive	1985	Legislature++	Legislature
Honduras	Legislature	Legislature	Weak	Legislature	Legislature	1992	Legislature	Unspecified
Mexico	Legislature-	Legislature-	Weak	Executive ++	Executive	1990	Legislature	Legislature
Nicaragua	Legislature-	Legislature++	Moderate	Legislature-	Legislature	1995	Legislature++	Legislature
Panama	Legislature	Judiciary	Strong	Executive++	Supreme Court	1997	Executive+	Supreme Court
Paraguay	Legislature+	Executive++	Moderate	Executive++	Legislature+	1992	Legislature	Legislature+
Peru	Legislature-	Legislature	Weak	Board of Higher Prosecutors	Legislature	1993	Legislature	Legislature
Uruguay	Legislature	Legislature	Moderate	Executive++	Executive++	-	-	-
Venezuela	Legislature++	Legislature++	Weak	Legislature++	Legislature++	1999	Legislature++	Legislature+

Notes: two consecutive dots (..) indicate that information is not available. (1) Includes those bodies in charge of overseeing public spending: the General Accounting Office, audit bureaux and General Comptrollers of the Republic. (2) Includes those bodies responsible for pressing criminal charges on behalf of the State: prosecutors, attorneys and public ministries. (3) Includes those bodies responsible for defending citizen's rights against the State: defense counsels and human rights prosecutors. (4) Executive: appointment or dismissal is undertaken exclusively by the executive. Executive+: appointment or dismissal is undertaken by the executive based on the list of candidates put forward by the legislature. Executive++: appointment or dismissal is undertaken by the executive but requires legislative approval or ratification. Legislative-: appointments are made by the legislature on the basis of a list sent by the executive; alternatively, there is a mixed system for appointing and dismissing officials, involving both the executive and legislative powers. Legislative: appointment or dismissal is the exclusive responsibility of the lower or single chamber. Legislative+: appointment or dismissal is within the remit of the legislature but requires the involvement of both chambers. Legislative++: appointment or dismissal is undertaken by the legislature together with civil society bodies or judicial entities. (5) Weak: decisions are not binding. Moderate: decisions are binding but lack the legal weight to ensure their implementation. Strong: decisions are binding and also carry the legal weight necessary to ensure that they are enforced.

Sources: Enrique Groisman and Emilia Lerner, 2000, Jorge Luis Maiorano, 2000; J. Payne et al., chapter 9; Georgetown University and the Organization of American States (OAS), 2002; and Fredrik Uggla, 2003.

Experience of Participation in Local Government

The 1990s saw the emergence of a process of decentralization that opened up new opportunities for citizen participation. Some of the most outstanding examples are popular participation in Bolivia, participative budgeting in Porto Alegre and Villa El Salvador, and the promotion of civic culture in Bogotá. Certain features are common to all of these experiences. They are each the work of a strong social movement. They aim to improve the quality of life, the capabilities and the independence of those taking part. Despite the fact that they occur in a 'patrimonialist' culture, they represent a clear break from populist mechanisms of distribution, a common practice in Latin America that favors political co-option. Many of the successful experiences of participation in local governance have been documented as part of the UNDP project that is seeking to develop an agenda for local governance in Latin America. They can be found at www.logos.undp.org.

charge of public finance, whose duty is to ensure that public funds are used according to the rules and procedures set out in law: *comptroller's offices, auditing offices or general accounting offices*. All of the countries of Latin America have institutions that perform these functions. Nevertheless, there are significant variations in the degree of independence of these bodies from the executive (the branch of State that is their main target) and the real weight that their oversight decisions carry in practice. In most countries of the region, the highest audit agencies are appointed by the legislature subject to specific conditions, such as a qualified vote, prior recommendation by the Supreme Court, and, in certain cases, recommendations from non-governmental organizations (NGOs). However, in three countries—Bolivia, Chile and Ecuador—the executive appoints these authorities directly. In 12 of the 18 countries, the authority wielded by these audit agencies is weak to moderate and their decisions are not binding or, if they are, they lack the legal backing to guarantee compliance.

A second kind of entity is the *Office of the Attorney General or Public Prosecutor*. These bodies are responsible for the legal representation of the State and, in several countries, have the capacity to take public penal action. Less information is available on them. Unlike auditing offices, not all countries have an Attorney General. The executive may intervene both to appoint and remove the head of this kind of entity.

Lastly, since 1990, most countries in Latin America have established the post of *Ombudsman*, with the exception of Brazil, Chile and Uruguay. This office is distinct from those mentioned above in that it is open to citizens who wish to make an accusation or formal complaint. Effectively, the office operates as an agent with a horizontal and vertical line of accountability. Generally speaking, the legislature is responsible for appointing and removing its directors. The rate of consolidation and the success of the Ombudsman's office in Latin America are, however, extremely varied.[63]

The existence of these organisms reveals a positive trend. Their tasks include overseeing and, in some cases, punishing public officials. They offer another alternative to classic constitutional power in the area of political governance accountability, although in some countries they lack the resources necessary to carry out their tasks effectively or their activities are, in practice, controlled by the executive—or both conditions prevail. This is why the existence of these bodies in itself cannot necessarily be taken as evidence of greater and more effective political governance accountability.

63 Fredrik Uggla, 2003.

'TOP-DOWN' MECHANISMS OF DIRECT DEMOCRACY, 1978-2002

TABLE 17

Country	Plebiscite				Non-Binding Plebiscite			
	In Existence	In Use	Times Used	Success in Use	In Existence	In Use	Times Used	Success in Use
Argentina	Yes	No	-	-	Yes	Yes	1	1
Bolivia	No	-	-	-	No	-	-	-
Brazil	Yes	Yes	2	0	..	..	..	..
Chile	Yes	No	-	-	..	..	..	..
Colombia	Yes	Yes	1	1	..	..	..	..
Costa Rica	Yes	No	-	-	..	..	..	..
Dominican Republic	No	-	-	-	..	..	..	..
Ecuador	Yes	Yes	17 (2)	14	Yes	Yes	16 (3)	6
El Salvador	Yes (1)	No	-	-	..	..	..	..
Guatemala	Yes	Yes	5	1	..	..	..	..
Honduras	No	-	-	-	..	..	..	..
Mexico	No	-	-	-	..	..	..	..
Nicaragua	Yes	No	-	-	..	..	..	..
Panama		Yes	2	0	..	..	..	..
Paraguay	Yes	No	-	-	..	..	..	..
Peru	Yes	Yes	1	1	..	..	..	..
Uruguay	Yes	Yes	2	1	No	-	-	-
Venezuela	Yes	Yes	3	3	..	..	..	..
Latin America (*)	**14**	**8**	**33**	**21**	**2**	**2**	**17**	**7**

Notes: the information only refers to official mechanisms of direct democracy that function nationwide. The periods of time referred to cover from 1978 onwards or since the moment that these instruments were established. However, it only takes account of their use within the context of democratic systems of government. The hyphen (-) indicates that the information is not relevant. The two consecutive dots (..) indicate that the information is not available.

(1) Only as regards Central American integration.

(2) Fourteen of these were held on the same date, in May 1997.

(3) Fifteen of these were held twice, in August 1994 and November 1995.

(*) The data for the region refer to all of the countries that permit the use of mechanisms of direct democracy and to the total number of times that these mechanisms were employed.

Sources: David Altman, 2002, p. 8; and various Constitutions and national electoral laws.

Mechanisms of Direct Democracy

The mechanisms of direct democracy offer citizens opportunities to contribute to the control and management of political affairs.[64] They can be divided into two categories. The first includes processes that are set in motion on a 'top-down' basis, that is to say, initiated by State agents, such as binding and non-binding plebiscites. The second type involves processes that are activated from the bottom up by citizens themselves, such as binding and non-binding initiatives, referenda and petitions calling for mandates to be revoked.

As regards the legal existence and use of these instruments, the data show that there are three distinct groups of countries:

- those in which the mechanisms of direct democracy simply do not exist—Bolivia, the Dominican Republic, Honduras and Mexico;
- those where some of the mechanisms are present but have hitherto not been employed—Chile, Costa Rica, El Salvador, Nicaragua and Paraguay; and

64 As mentioned earlier, citizens may also contribute in a more indirect fashion to the control of political governance. For example, when they make a formal complaint concerning the conduct of State agents, leading to the launch of an investigation by the respective entities involved.

TABLE 18

'BOTTOM-UP' MECHANISMS OF DIRECT DEMOCRACY, 1978-2002

Country	Binding Initiative				Non-Binding Initiative				Referendum				Revocation of Mandate			
	Exis-tence	Use	Times Used	Suc-cess in Use	Exis-tence	Use	Times Used	Suc-cess in Use	Exis-tence	Use	Times in Use	Suc-cess in Use	Exis-tence	Use	Times used	Suc-cess in Use
Argentina	Yes	No	-	-	Yes	No	-	-	No	-	-	-	No	-	-	-
Bolivia	No	-	-	-	..	..	..	..	No	-	-	-	No	-	-	-
Brazil	Yes	No	-	-	..	..	..	..	Yes	No	-	-	No	-	-	-
Chile	No	-	-	-	..	..	..	..	No	-	-	-	No	-	-	-
Colombia	Yes	No	-	-	Yes	Yes	2	2	Yes	No	-	-	Yes	No	-	-
Costa Rica	Yes	No	-	-	..	..	..	..	Yes	No	-	-	No	-	-	-
Dominican Republic	No	-	-	-	..	..	..	..	No	-	-	-	No	-	-	-
Ecuador	Yes	No	-	-	..	..	..	..	No	-	-	-	No	-	-	-
El Salvador	No	-	-	-	..	..	..	..	No	-	-	-	No	-	-	-
Guatemala	Yes	No	-	-	..	..	..	..	No	-	-	-	No	-	-	-
Honduras	No	-	-	-	..	..	..	..	No	-	-	-	No	-	-	-
Mexico	No	-	-	-	..	..	..	..	No	-	-	-	No	-	-	-
Nicaragua	Yes	No	-	-	..	..	..	..	Yes	No	-	-	No	-	-	-
Panama	No	-	-	-	..	..	..	..	No	-	-	-	No	-	-	-
Paraguay	Yes	No	-	-	..	..	..	..	Yes	No	-	-	No	-	-	-
Peru	Yes	No	-	-	..	..	..	..	Yes	No	-	-	Yes	No	-	-
Uruguay	Yes	Yes	5	2	No	-	-	-	Yes	Yes	6	2	No	-	-	-
Venezuela	Yes	No	-	-	Yes	No	-	-	Yes	No	-	-	Yes	No	-	-
Latin America (*)	11	1	5	2	3	1	2	2	8	1	6	2	3	0	0	0

Notes: the information only refers to official mechanisms of direct democracy that function nationwide. The periods of time referred to cover from 1978 onwards or since the moment that these instruments were established. However, it only takes account of their use within the context of democratic systems of government. The hyphen (-) indicates that the information is not relevant. The two consecutive dots (..) indicate that the information is not available.

(*) The data for the region refer to all of the countries that permit the use of mechanisms of direct democracy and to the total number of times that these mechanisms were employed.

Sources: David Altman, 2002, p. 8; and various Constitutions and national electoral laws.

■ those in which these mechanisms are not only legally recognized but also have been employed. There are nine countries; the majority—Brazil, Ecuador, Guatemala, Panama, Peru and Venezuela—has only utilized the top-down mechanisms of direct democracy.

Corruption in Public Office

A key issue with respect to political oversight is control of corruption in public office. The paucity of information available makes it difficult to appreciate its actual magnitude, but it does provide some proof of the gravity of the problem.

There are two complementary sources of information on perceptions of the levels of corruption (Table 19).

The persistent and widespread corruption in public office extends uninhibited when citizens either resign themselves to living with it or contribute to spreading it further. A strong rejection of corrupt practices by the citizens themselves is a valuable tool for greater control and improves the efficiency of those instruments aimed at preventing and eradicating it.

In the 18 countries of Latin America, 41.9 percent of those consulted agree that it is worth paying the price of having a certain amount of corruption if this guarantees that 'things work'. An analysis of the social and political profiles of those who tolerate corruption indicates that this attitude is prevalent among all social and demographic groups throughout the region as a whole (Table 20).

INDICATORS OF PERCEPTIONS OF CORRUPTION, 2002

TABLE 19

Country	Transparency International		World Economic Forum	
	1999-2001	2002	2001	2002
Argentina	3.5	2.8	4.28	4.42
Bolivia	2.0	2.2	4.26	3.56
Brazil	4.0	4.0	4.45	4.82
Chile	7.5	7.5	6.35	6.34
Colombia	3.8	3.6	4.73	5.14
Costa Rica	4.5	4.5	4.60	4.41
Dominican Republic	3.1	3.5	4.46	4.43
Ecuador	2.3	2.2	3.91	3.67
El Salvador	3.6	3.4	4.47	5.16
Guatemala	2.9	2.5	4.12	3.81
Honduras	2.7	2.7	3.64	3.84
Mexico	3.7	3.6	4.40	4.82
Nicaragua	2.4	2.5	3.76	4.31
Panama	3.7	3.0	4.26	4.52
Paraguay	..	1.7	2.77	3.55
Peru	4.1	4.0	2.31	5.21
Uruguay	5.1	5.1	4.78	5.88
Venezuela	2.8	2.5	4.05	3.85
Region				
Latin America	**3.6**	**3.4**	**4.37**	**4.52**
Western Europe	7.1	7.8	6.07	6.08

Notes: two consecutive dots (..) indicate that information is not available. Both organizations constructed their indices on the basis of interviews with panels of experts selected by each entity. Obviously, the results do not have any statistical significance numerically speaking. The data of Transparency International are based on a scale of 11 points, with the higher numbers indicating a correspondingly lower level of corruption. The scale used by the World Economic Forum has seven points, again with the higher numbers indicating a correspondingly lower level of corruption.

Sources: Johann Graf Lambsdorff, 2001, pp. 234–236; and Transparency International, 2002.

Cronyism

Cronyism, or patronage, creates privileges and implies the discretional handling of public resources. In the survey carried out by Latinobarómetro in 2002, the interviewees were asked if they knew of people who had received privileges in return for supporting the ruling party. Of these, 31.4 percent stated that they knew of one or more cases of cronyism (Table 21).

Conclusions on Political Citizenship: Achievements and Failings

■ The information that we have presented on political citizenship, beyond the issue of electoral processes, shows that there have been some significant achievements in Latin America.

■ The institutional bases for the independence and professional conduct of the judicial branch have been strengthened following a series of recent reforms. However, the contribution that these reforms will make to the full restoration of the democratic rule of law is not yet clear.

■ The competent bodies responsible for controlling the performance of elected or other public officials—some of which have been created in the past decade—constitute alternative channels for monitoring the activities of the classic constitutional powers. Nevertheless, there are still some failings that impact on some of the progress that has been made. Specifically, we have observed that the various monitoring bodies are experiencing difficulties in performing their functions and,

TABLE 20

PROFILE OF PERSONS WITH DIFFERENT ATTITUDES TOWARDS CORRUPTION, 2002

Categories		Structure of Sample	The Price of a certain Level of Corruption in the Government is worth paying as long as the Country's Problems are solved				Significance (3)
			Very much in Agreement	Agree	Disagree	Very much in Disagreement	
Central America and Mexico (1)	% of people	n=7,424	16.1	31.4	31.5	21.0	..
Andean sub-region	% of people	n=5,238	11.3	32.2	37.6	18.9	..
Mercosur and Chile	% of people	n=5,351	6.8	25.5	39.4	28.3	..
Latin America	% of people	n=18,013	12.0	29.9	35.6	22.6	..
Gender	% Men	49.6	50.3	49.9	49.0	49.9	ns
	% Women	50.4	49.7	50.1	51.0	50.1	
Age group	% 16–29 years	37.0	43.0	38.5	35.7	34.0	**
	% 30–64 years	54.6	50.2	53.7	55.4	56.7	
	% 65–99 years	8.4	6.7	7.9	8.9	9.3	
	Average of age groups	38.43	36.17	37.71	39.03	39.63	**
Years studied	% No schooling	8.1	11.9	8.4	7.2	7.2	**
	% 1–6 years	33.8	34.7	35.8	31.8	33.8	
	% 7–12 years	41.6	38.4	42.0	43.3	40.3	
	% Higher education, completed or incomplete	16.4	14.9	13.7	17.7	18.7	
	Average of years studied	89.04	8.52	8.79	9.31	9.22	**
Income bracket (2)	% Low	43.9	50.7	46.6	40.1	42.9	**
	% Middle	47.5	41.5	46.1	50.7	47.4	
	% High	8.6	7.8	7.3	9.2	9.7	
	Average income bracket	83.92	3.68	3.8	4.04	4.0	**
Democratic leanings	% Pro-democracy	42.8	29.7	31.9	48.8	55.0	**
	% Ambivalent	30.5	47.9	38.6	23.8	21.1	
	% Not pro-democracy	26.7	22.4	29.5	27.4	23.8	

Notes:

(1) Includes the Dominican Republic.

(2) Based on the economic index developed on the basis of information on the family's socio-economic level and the level of studies of the head of the family. This index may vary between zero and ten. If the index registers a number between zero and 3.33, this is considered to be indicative of a low-income bracket; if the number is between 3.34 and 6.66, this is considered to be indicative of a middle-income bracket; and if the number is between 6.67 and ten, this is considered to be indicative of a high-income bracket.

(3) The symbol '**' indicates that the measurement used, or the Analysis of Variance (ANOVA) between groups, is significant to the order of five percent. The symbol '*' indicates that the result is significant to the order of one percent. The reference 'ns' means that the test was not significant either to the order of one percent or five percent. Two consecutive dots (..) indicate that the measurement used or ANOVA is not relevant. Please consult the Statistical Compendium for more details on the tests carried out in each case.

Sources: results of processing question p23uf in the UNDP Proprietary Section of the Latinobarómetro 2002, as well as other questions of a socio-economic nature.

CRONYISM NETWORKS, 2002

TABLE 21

Level of Awareness (1)	Country (2)
Low level of awareness of examples of cronyism	Brazil (23.9), Chile (16.0), Colombia (16.3), Ecuador (24.4), El Salvador (23.3)
Moderate level of awareness of examples of cronyism	Argentina (32.4), Bolivia (33.9), Costa Rica (27.2), Honduras (36.7), Nicaragua (35.2), Panama (27.4), Paraguay (34.0), Peru (32.2), Uruguay (32.3), Venezuela (31.8)
High level of awareness of examples of cronyism	Dominican Republic (53.1), Guatemala (42.3), Mexico (43.4)
Democratic tradition	Proportion of people who are aware of one or more cases of cronyism
Oldest democracies (3)	24.7
Newest democracies	34.0
Average of Latin America	31.4

Notes: n = 19.366.

(1) Low level of awareness: 25 percent or less of those consulted declared that they knew of one or more cases of privileged treatment. Moderate level of awareness: between 25 and 40 percent. High level of awareness: over 40 percent.

(2) The figures in brackets after the country name indicate the proportion of people who said that they were aware of one or more cases of privileged treatment.

(3) The oldest democracies include Colombia, Costa Rica and Venezuela.

Sources: results of the processing of question p7u in the UNDP Proprietary Section of Latinobarómetro 2002.

in some cases, in punishing abuses perpetrated by other State entities.

■ Employment of the mechanisms of direct democracy is still limited.

■ Even where certain control mechanisms are to be found, the information available suggests that corrupt practices and cronyism continue to play a part in the management of public affairs.

Civil Citizenship

Civil citizenship is the aspect of citizenship that has seen the greatest development in terms of doctrine and legal definition. In general terms, its underlying principles are seemingly contradictory. On the one hand, they try to put limits on the actions of the State, while on the other, they seek to establish a State guarantee of equality under the law and personal freedom.

In order to analyze the development of civil rights, we have taken into account four different components: equality under the law and protection against discrimination; the right to life, personal inviolability and security; the administration of justice; and freedom of the press and the right to information.

Equality under the Law and Protection against Discrimination

A starting point for the analysis of citizens' equality under the law and protection against discrimination are the constitutionally or legally established guarantees of this legal equality and, in particular, the acceptance by countries of international legal norms on this matter. When they ratify international treaties, States take on the obligation of safeguarding certain rights, not only vis-à-vis their own populations but also vis-à-vis the international community. It is a positive sign that most countries in Latin America have ratified the principal international treaties on rights under the sponsorship of the United Nations, the

TABLE 22

TREATIES OF THE UN, ILO AND OAS: GENERAL RIGHTS AND THE RIGHTS OF DIFFERENT CATEGORIES OF CITIZENS, 2002

Rights	Treaty	Year	Number of Non-Ratifying Countries	Non-Ratifying Countries
General rights	UN International Covenant on Civil and Political Rights	1966	0	–
	UN International Covenant on Economic, Social and Cultural Rights	1966	0	–
	American Convention on Human Rights, 'Pact of San Jose, Costa Rica'	1969	0	–
Labor rights	ILO Convention 29: Convention Concerning Forced or Compulsory Labor	1930	1	Bolivia
	ILO Convention 87: Convention Concerning Freedom of Association and Protection of the Right to Organize	1948	2	Brazil, El Salvador
	ILO Convention 98: Convention Concerning the Application of the Principles of the Right to Organize and to Bargain Collectively	1949	2	El Salvador, Mexico
	ILO Convention 105: Convention Concerning the Abolition of Forced Labor	1957	0	–
Women's rights	ILO Convention 100: Convention Concerning Equal Remuneration for Men and Women Workers for Work of Equal Value	1951	0	–
	ILO Convention 111: Convention Concerning Discrimination in Respect of Employment and Occupation	1958	0	–
	UN Convention on the Elimination of All Forms of Discrimination against Women	1979	0	
	Inter-American Convention on the Prevention, Punishment and Eradication of Violence against Women 'Convention of Belém do Pará'	1994	0	–
Rights of indigenous peoples and ethnic groups	International Convention on the Elimination of All Forms of Racial Discrimination	1965	1	Panama
	ILO Convention 169: Convention Concerning Indigenous and Tribal Peoples in Independent Countries	1989	6	Chile, Dominican Republic, El Salvador, Nicaragua, Panama, Uruguay
Children's rights	ILO Convention 138: Convention Concerning the Minimum Age for Admission to Employment	1973	2	Mexico, Paraguay
	UN Convention on the Rights of the Child	1989	0	–
	ILO Convention 182: Convention Concerning the Prohibition and Immediate Action for the Elimination of the Worst Forms of Child Labor	1999	3	Bolivia, Colombia, Venezuela

Notes: the en dash (–) indicates that the information is not relevant. Information on the rights of indigenous and peoples ethnic minorities was correct as of 24 November 2002. The rest of the information was correct as of 1 April 2003.

Sources: United Nations Organization (UNO), 2003a; International Labor Organization (ILO), 2003; and Organization of American States (OAS), 2003.

BOX 23

Dimensions of Civil Citizenship

Dimension	Outstanding Issues
Legal equality and protection against discrimination	International treaty commitments, legislation and application of legislation related to general rights and the situation of the workforce, women, indigenous peoples and minors.
Right to life, personal inviolability and security	International treaty commitments, legislation and application of legislation related to basic civil rights.
Administration of justice	Allocation of financial resources to the judicial system and measures designed to defend the rights of the accused and of those in jail.
Freedom of the press and the right to information	Legal, political and economic restrictions on freedom of the press, violence against journalists, access to public information and *habeas data*.

International Labor Organization (ILO) and the Organization of American States.

The most important advances in terms of recognition of rights have occurred in the field of general rights, with all of the countries of Latin America ratifying three of the four treaties, and in the sphere of women's rights, with all of the countries of the region ratifying the main treaties. In other areas, the shift towards the recognition of rights is almost complete, as is the case for international instruments dealing with labor rights and the rights of children. The most important delay is over the Convention Concerning Indigenous and Tribal Peoples in Independent Countries (Convention No. 169 of the ILO), which has yet to be ratified by six countries.

A second aspect of the study on discrimination has to do with national laws that countries have promulgated to protect civil rights, either by incorporating into national legislation clauses from international treaties that they have ratified or those drafted on their own initiative. It is important to emphasize the fact that, over the past decade, there has been intense activity in relation to the development of legal rules in two areas: women's rights; and the rights of indigenous peoples. With regard to the former, every country has passed laws aimed at protecting women from discriminatory treatment, as well as at asserting certain rights proactively. The protection of women against domestic violence has been a particularly active area in this respect.

Notable progress has also been made in the protection of the rights of indigenous peoples. Several Constitutions—especially those of countries with large indigenous populations, such as Bolivia, Ecuador, Guatemala and Peru—have recognized the multinational and pluri-ethnic nature of their societies. In other cases, like Brazil and Colombia, there has also been an expansion of the rights of indigenous peoples. In most countries, however, the constitutional rights that indigenous peoples are recognized as having are far from being adequately implemented through proper legislation and jurisprudence, and indigenous languages are yet to be recognized as official languages by respective States (Table 23).

A third aspect of the analysis of equality under the law concerns the effectiveness of constitutional or legal protection of civil rights. With respect to this issue, the available information suggests the existence of serious and, at times, increasingly severe inequalities among people who belong to different sectors of the population.

In the workplace, a growing disparity was seen throughout the 1990s between the protection of the rights of business executives (the general business environment) and those of employ-

BOX 24

Legislation on Violence against Women, 2002

Country	Legislation on Domestic Violence and Violence against Women
Argentina	Law 24.417 on protection against family violence, December 1994.
	Act 25.087 modifying the Penal Code, 1999.
Bolivia	Law 1.674 against domestic and family violence, 1995.
	Law 1.678, which modifies the Penal Code with respect to sexual offenses, 1995.
Brazil	Legislative Decree 107, giving legal force to the Inter-American Convention on the Prevention, Punishment and Eradication of Violence Against Women, 1995.
	Article 226 of the Federal Constitution of 1988, and several Penal Code articles.
Chile	Act 19.325, which establishes standard procedures and penalties for acts of violence within the family, 1994.
	Law 19.617 on sexual crimes, 1999.
Colombia	Law 294 to prevent, punish and remedy domestic violence, 1996 (partially modified by Law 575, 2000).
	Law 360 on offenses against sexual freedom and human dignity, 1997.
	Law 599 of the Penal Code, which refers to violence within families, 2000.
Costa Rica	Act 7.142, which promotes the social equality of women; includes Chapter 4 on family violence, 1990.
	Law 7.586 against domestic violence, 1996.
Dominican Republic	Law 24-97, which defines the offenses of domestic violence, sexual harassment and incest, 1997.
Ecuador	Law 103 on violence against women and the family, 1995.
El Salvador	Decree-Law 902 on family violence, 1996.
Guatemala	Decree-Law 97-96, to prevent, punish and eliminate family violence, 1996.
	Law on the dignity and integral promotion of women, 1999.
Honduras	Decree 132-97, to prevent, punish and eliminate violence against women, 1997.
Mexico	Law referring to and preventing domestic violence, 1996.
	Decree to reform the Civil and Penal Codes in reference to domestic violence and rape cases, 1997.
Nicaragua	Law containing amendments and additions to the 1996 Penal Code; and a law creating a police service for women and children, included in the legislation establishing the National Police Force, 1996.
	Law 230, which establishes protection for women victims of domestic violence, 1996.
Panama	Act 27, 1995.
	Law 4 on equal opportunities for women, 1999.
	Law 38 on domestic violence, 2001.
Paraguay	Law 1600/00 against domestic violence, 2000.
Peru	Law 26.260 establishing the legal status of, and social policy on, family violence, 1993 (modified as a result of Law 27.306 of 2000).
	Law 26.763 establishing mechanisms to provide more protection for victims, 1997.
	Law 26.770, which reforms the Penal Code; establishing that marriage does not vitiate grounds for prosecution of crimes against sexual freedom, 1997.
	Act 27.115, which establishes public penal action for offenses against sexual liberty, 1999.
Uruguay	Act 16.707 on citizens' security adds a new article to the Penal Code, defines domestic violence and establishes penalties, 1995.
	Law 17.514 on domestic violence, 2002
Venezuela	Law on equal opportunities for women, 1993.
	Law on violence against women and the family, 1998.

Note: information correct as of 24 October 2002.

Sources: Economic Commission for Latin America and the Caribbean (ECLAC), 2000, pp. 50–51; and the Organization of American States (OAS), 2003.

TABLE 23

Country	Constitution	Constitutional Rights	
		Multicultural Rights	Existence of Rights Related to the Use of Language
Argentina	1853/1994	Weak	No, but there is no official language
Bolivia	1967/94	Yes	No, but there is no official language
Brazil	1988	No	No, Portuguese is the official language
Chile (*)	1980	No	No, but there is no official language
Colombia	1991	Yes	Yes, Spanish is the official language, but indigenous languages and dialects have official status in their territories
Costa Rica	1949	No	No, Spanish is the official language
Dominican Republic	..	..	..
Ecuador	1998	Yes	Yes, Spanish is the official language, but restricted official use of indigenous languages is permitted
El Salvador	1983/92	No	No, but 'autochthonous languages' are respected
Guatemala	1985	Yes	Yes, indigenous languages are officially recognized in the areas where they are spoken
Honduras	1982	No	No, Spanish is the official language
Mexico	1917/92	Yes	No, but indigenous languages are promoted
Nicaragua	1987/95	Yes	Yes, the languages of the Atlantic coast communities are official in those regions
Panama	1972/78/83/93/94	Yes	No, but 'aboriginal languages' are conserved and spread
Paraguay	1992	Yes	Yes, but Guaraní is an official language
Peru	1993	Yes	Yes, Spanish is the official language, but indigenous languages are also officially used in the areas where they are dominant
Uruguay	1967/97	No	No
Venezuela	1999	Yes	Yes, indigenous languages are used officially by indigenous peoples and must be respected throughout the country

Notes: the dates of the Constitutions refer to the original documents and to the last instance of reform or amendment. Multicultural rights refer to whether multiple ethnic identities are recognized by the State. The rights referred to in this table are sometimes considered to be collective rights and are not, strictly speaking, civil rights.

(*) In Chile, Indigenous Law No. 19.253 of October 1993 permitted the promotion of indigenous cultures and languages, as well as bilingual inter-cultural educational systems (Article 39), and guaranteed the use of indigenous languages in trials (Article 74).

Sources: International Labour Organization (ILO), 2002b; Cletus Gregor Barié, 2000, pp. 42 and 572–574; Donna Lee Van Cott, 2003; and George-town University and the Organization of American States (OAS), 2002.

ees. On the one hand, the trend shows sustained growth in the rights of business executives, attaining levels close to those of Western Europe (Graph 2). On the other hand, the steadily worsening rights of workers has resulted in a considerable widening of the gap between Latin America and Western Europe (Graph 3).

With respect to women, throughout the region there has been a generalized process of women slowly drawing abreast of men. The gradual incorporation of women into the labor force is apparent—from 28.81 percent in 1990 to 33.93 percent in 2000—as is a reduction in wage disparities between women and men. But this same data indicate that women's participation in the workforce remains relatively low and that women, on average, suffer substantially higher income differentials (Table 24).

Lastly, the laws to protect children in the workplace are frequently violated. In particular, there is a high rate of employment of children aged between five and 14 years and of some forms of abuse, such as trafficking in children and child pornography (Table 25).

Indigenous Peoples and Citizenship

Although it might sound obvious, this relationship is fundamental to understanding the specific features and the historical background of Latin America's political system, which distinguish it from that of Northwest Europe. To review the facts, the second wave of colonial expansion, together with the 'scientific' redefinition of racial concepts and the engrained racist treatment of 'indigenous peoples' and 'Africans', led to the emergence of the alliance of the 'criollos'—white men—with the interests represented by the economic and political agents of the countries to the Northwest. These factors also encouraged them to identify with the official culture of the metropolitan countries, formally adopting their values and institutions, which, paradoxically, contradicted the subsisting and strengthened hereditary social hierarchy, which then gave rise to the presence of imaginary citizens.

It is widely known that, as a consequence, 'dualism' and social and cultural polarization were renewed and revitalized, all of which projected itself on to the 'internal colonialism' of the 'indigenous' and African population, a process that would frequently be justified by liberal principles. The social fragmentation and dislocations generated by the wave of metropolitan expansion provoked intermittent social conflict and constant repression imbued with a strong ethnic flavor, which responded to the pulse of 'the heart of darkness'.

However, in spite of the many and profound changes that Latin American countries have undergone as their relationships with the Northwest have altered over the course of time, it is significant that, whatever degree of political and economic development was attained, the national integration of the majority of the population and the consolidation of the rule of law are still pending, while dualism and socio-ethnic polarization at various levels of intensity still persist, with rare exceptions. For example, in Peru and Brazil, approximately 60 percent of the indigenous and black peoples, respectively, live below the poverty line, a proportion that must certainly be similar in other Latin American nations with a similar ethnic composition. Likewise, it is equally significant that, under any political system, democratic or authoritarian, different economic policies, orthodox and heterodox, have contributed to supporting and, frequently, strengthening this structural reality.

Julio Cotler, text prepared for PRODDAL, 2002.

Ethnic Democracy and Multiculturalism

Speaking as a Mayan woman and as a citizen who has been engaged in the processes associated with building a multicultural society, I fully understand what democracy means, that it is conceived by the people for the people. The main problem of our 'democracies', at least in Latin America, is that they are incomplete. They seem to be what they are not, due to the fact that they were conceived within mono-cultural States, excluding some, and granting privileges to a few, to the detriment of the majority. We, indigenous men and women, are peaceful and respectful persons and seek harmony, not only among human beings but also with other forms of life and natural elements.

For indigenous peoples, consultation, participation and consensus are of the utmost importance in relation to decision-making—in order that the decision of the majority will prevail as a democratic principle. This process is based on recognition that all human beings are equal and have the same rights and obligations. Consequently, we sincerely wish that our political systems might change for the benefit of all, so that there is equality of opportunity without exclusion of any kind. Indigenous peoples place their trust in the future. They want democracy to be inclusive, representative, inter-cultural, in other words, respectful of differences.

The unity of Guatemala and that of other similar countries must be based on such a rich source of diversity, which, in turn, must be reflected in an 'ethnic democracy'.

Otilia Lux de Cojti, former Minister of Culture, Guatemala. text prepared for PRODDAL, 2004.

GRAPH 2

Business Environment:
Latin America and Western Europe, 1990-2000

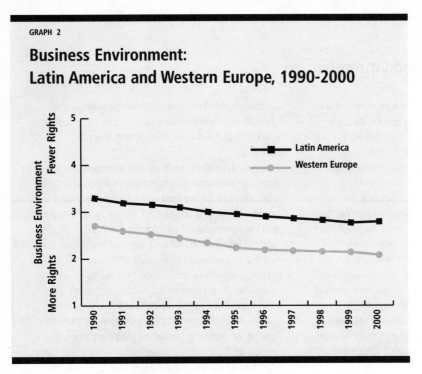

Note: the scores correspond to a five-point scale: a lower score implies that the government has succeeded in securing a propitious environment for business. This index was created from a set of variables that includes: tax pressure; governmental intervention in the economy; and the law and regulations concerning property. The data for 1994–2000 were taken from the Heritage Foundation's Index of Economic Freedom; the score for 1990 was generated by transforming data obtained from the Fraser Institute and applying it to the scale used by the Heritage Foundation. The scores for years in which data were lacking were extrapolated by linear regression. The data for 1994–2000 cover July–June. Thus data for 2000 pertain to the period between July 1999 and June 2000.

Sources: for 1990, James Gwartney et al., 2002; for 1994–2000, Gerald O'Driscoll, Jr., et al., 2002, pp. 14 and 18; and Gerald O'Driscoll, Jr., et al., 2003, pp. 13 and 17.

GRAPH 3

Labour Standards
Latin America and Western Europe, 1990-2000

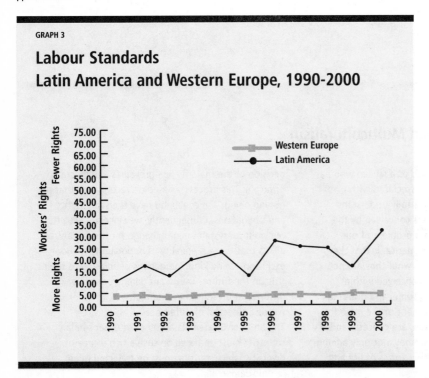

Note: the data are a measurement built on multiple indicators, such as the right of workers to organize, to bargain collectively and to strike. The scores range from zero, which indicates a high degree of respect for workers' rights, to 76.5, which indicates an extremely high degree of infringement of those rights. These scores capture the range of rights that are infringed but do not reflect the frequency of infringement or the number of workers affected by such infringements.

Source: Layna Mosley and Saika Uno, 2002.

WOMEN IN THE WORKFORCE, 1990-2000

TABLE 24

Percentage of the Economically Active Population (EAP)

1990			1995			2000		
Total	Men	Women	Total	Men	Women	Total	Men	Women
49.37	70.30	28.81	50.77	70.55	31.32	52.23	70.86	33.93

Gender Wage Disparity
(Based on Average Incomes in Urban Areas)

Beginning of 1990s		Mid-1990s		Late 1990s	
EAP	Salary Earners	EAP	Salary Earners	EAP	Salary Earners
61.99	70.89	64.90	72.23	67.34	77.89

Note: the data on income disparities according to gender represent the percentage of male income earned by women. The EAP column compares differences in income between men and women in the context of the global economically active population. The salary earners column compares income differences between men and women in the context of only the wage-earning population. Regional numbers are the average of all cases for which data are available for any year.

Sources: Economic Commission for Latin America and the Caribbean (ECLAC), 2001a, pp. 201–202, Table 8; ECLAC, 2002b, pp. 201–202, Table 8; and ECLAC, 2003, pp. 20–21, Table 15.

INCIDENCE OF CHILD ABUSE IN DIFFERENT REGIONS OF THE WORLD, 2000

TABLE 25

Region	Economically Active Children (five to 14 years of age)		Children involved in Worst Type of Child Labor				
	Number of Children (millions)	Proportion Who Work (%)	Trafficking (thousands)	Forced and Servile Work (thousands)	Armed Conflict (thousands)	Prostitution and Pornography (thousands)	Illicit Activities (thousands)
Developed economies	2.5	2	..	..	1	420	110
Asia and the Pacific	127.3	19	250	5.500	120	590	220
Sub-Saharan Africa	48.0	29	..	..	..	..	..
Middle East and North Africa	13.4	15	..	..	..	..	..
Africa	..	..	200	210	120	50	..
Latin America and the Caribbean	17.4	16	550	3	30	750	260

Notes: the proportion who work refers to the number of children who work in proportion to the total number of children. Statistics on children implicated in 'the worst types of labor' are estimates.

Sources: the International Programme on the Elimination of Child Labor (IPEC)–Statistical Information and Monitoring Programme on Child Labor (SIMPOC), 2002, p. 17, Table 2, and p. 27, Table 10.

BOX 27

Citizen's Perception of Equality under the Law

Despite the progress made in Latin America in approving constitutional and legal rules for recognizing and safeguarding the rights of people who belong to underprivileged groups, citizens' perceptions on this matter suggest that there is still much to be done to attain a reasonable amount of equality under the law.

According to data obtained from Latinobarómetro 2002, most people believe that the rich always or almost always manage to have their rights respected, with only a few variations among sub-regions and countries. At the same time, similar majorities are of the opinion that the poor, immigrants and indigenous peoples suffer severe legal disadvantages. This situation exists both in countries with long democratic traditions and in those that have recently undergone a transition to democracy, as well as in nations that have recorded different levels of achievement on the Index of Human Development. Citizens' perceptions of the legal situation of women are considerably better. In every country most people believe that today women always or almost always manage to have their rights respected. This majority fluctuates between a minimum of 54.8 percent in Bolivia and Mexico and a maximum of 78.4 percent in Uruguay.

In order to examine coherently the views of people belonging to vulnerable groups, an indicator of perception of equality under the law was created (see www.democracia.undp.org). In every Latin American country, only a minority believes that vulnerable groups always or almost always manage to have their rights respected (the proportion does not exceed 31 percent in any country). The average value on the index of perception of equality under the law in Latin American countries tends to be low (2.19 points out of five possible points; the minimum is one point).

PERCEPTIONS OF SPECIFIC GROUPS REGARDING EQUALITY BEFORE THE LAW, 2002

TABLE 26

Country	Always or Almost Always have their Rights Respected (1)			
	Women	Indigenous People	Poor People	Immigrants
Argentina	69.7	9.1	7.9	21.4
Bolivia	54.8	21.2	13.9	38.5
Brazil	78.3	34.3	20.1	47.6
Chile	68.9	33.5	19.9	27.2
Colombia	70.3	22.1	18.1	24.1
Costa Rica	59.8	23.2	13.7	21.3
Dominican Republic	76.4	11.5	22.2	40.2
Ecuador	60.4	40.2	25.2	30.6
El Salvador	72.0	32.3	32.4	30.9
Guatemala	65.3	38.7	24.8	18.7
Honduras	69.8	34.6	23.5	25.1
Mexico	54.8	7.5	5.6	9.9
Nicaragua	60.3	23.5	17.7	21.5
Panama	65.6	10.5	10.7	21.0
Paraguay	71.5	15.0	10.9	54.1
Peru	61.9	16.0	11.6	55.4
Uruguay	78.4	17.1	21.8	39.3
Venezuela	73.7	28.2	26.1	30.3
Central America and Mexico (2)	66.4	22.2	18.9	23.3
Andean sub-region	63.8	27.8	19.2	36.2
Mercosur and Chile	71.2	19.2	14.6	36.2
Region				
Latin America	**67.0**	**23.1**	**17.8**	**30.8**

Notes: the number of women, indigenous people, poor people and immigrants varies between 18,040 and 19,596.

(1) Includes the answers to both options ('always' and 'almost always').

(2) Includes the Dominican Republic.

Source: results of processing answers to question p24u in the UNDP Proprietary Section of the Latinobarómetro 2002.

In short, citizens' equality under the law and protection against discrimination is still not applied with due force nor is it widespread in Latin America. Notable progress has been achieved in the realm of rules and standards, but the gaps are still notorious and affect those sectors of the population that are larger and weaker and hence in need of protection.

UN AND OAS TREATIES ON FUNDAMENTAL CIVIL RIGHTS, 2003

TABLE 27

Treaty	Year	Number of Countries Non-Ratifying Countries	Non-Ratifying Countries
UN Convention against Torture and Other Cruel, Inhuman or Degrading Treatment or Punishment	1984	2	Dominican Republic, Nicaragua
OAS Inter-American Convention to Prevent and Punish Torture	1995	3	Bolivia, Honduras, Nicaragua
Protocol to the Inter-American Convention on Human Rights to Abolish the Death Penalty	1990	10	Argentina, Bolivia, Chile, Colombia, Dominican Republic, El Salvador, Guatemala, Honduras, Mexico, Peru
Inter-American Convention on the Forced Disappearance of Persons	1994	9	Brazil, Colombia, Dominican Republic, Ecuador, El Salvador, Honduras, Mexico, Nicaragua, Peru

Note: information correct as of 1 April 2003.

Sources: United Nations Organization (UNO), 2003; and the Organization of American States (OAS), 2003.

Right to Life, Physical Integrity and Security

A second component of civil rights concerns effective protection of the right to life, personal inviolability and security. A significant number of countries have yet to agree to international obligations in this respect and postponements in the ratification of the respective treaties are evident.

The situation is particularly worrying where the Protocol to the Inter-American Convention on Human Rights to Abolish the Death Penalty is concerned, because ten of Latin America's 18 countries have not yet ratified it and in Guatemala the death sentence is still employed as a punishment for ordinary criminal offenses. Few countries have ratified the Inter-American Convention on the Forced Disappearance of Persons as well. Notorious examples are Nicaragua, which has not ratified any of the four relevant treaties, and the Dominican Republic and Honduras, which to date have ratified only one of them.

More positively, the situation in Latin America contrasts very favorably with that in other parts of the world as far as military violence is concerned. At the beginning of the twenty-first century, the number of deaths in Latin America is notably less than in Africa, Europe and Asia.[65] Today, Colombia is the only Latin American country where military conflict continues to exist.

Unfortunately, other types of social and political violence are still common phenomena in the region, despite the advent of democratic governments. One of the central issues is the capacity of States to guarantee human rights. In this area, the data highlight an improvement when compared with the non-democratic period. However, given that these are basic rights that should be guaranteed under the democratic rule of law, a warning light has flashed on to alert us to this situation in Latin America.

There is no doubt that, since the end of

65 E.G. Krug et al., 2002, p. 282.

MORTALITY CAUSED BY INTENTIONAL INJURY IN LATIN AMERICA AND OTHER PARTS OF THE WORLD, C. 2000

TABLE 28

Country	Year	Number of Deaths	Number of Deaths per 100.000 Inhabitants
Argentina	2001	3,048	8.2
Bolivia	2000	2,558	32.0
Brazil	2001	39,618	23.0
Chile	2001	699	4.5
Colombia	2000	29,555	70.0
Costa Rica	1999	245	6.2
Dominican Republic	1998	1,121	15.8
Ecuador	1999	3,217	25.9
El Salvador	2001	2,196	34.3
Guatemala	1994	3,239	33.3
Honduras	1998	9,241	154.0
Mexico	2000	13,829	14.0
Nicaragua	1998	1,157	24.1
Panama	1998	54	2.0
Paraguay	2001	890	15.6
Peru	2001	1,298	5.0
Uruguay	2000	154	4.6
Venezuela	2000	8,022	33.2
Latin America	**c. 1997**	**109,135**	**25.1**
Extra-regional comparisons			
Western Europe	c. 2000	4,519	1.4
East Mediterranean	c. 1995-99	31,000	7.1
South Asia and East Asia	c. 1995-99	78,000	5.8
Africa	c. 1995-99	116,000	22.2
Western Pacific	c. 1995-99	59,000	5.1
World	**c. 1995-99**	**521,000**	**8.8**

Note: regional figures are the sum of all cases for which data exist and reflect an unweighted average. The figure for Latin America is for 1997. The number of homicides in El Salvador and Honduras is an estimate. Western Europe does not include Luxemburg and the United Kingdom.
Sources: Interpol, 2004; United Nations Office on Drugs and Crime (UNODC), 2002; United Nations Organization (UNO), Population Division, Department of Economic and Social Affairs, 2001 and 2002; and E.G. Krug et al., 2002, pp. 274 and 308–312.

military rule in the Southern Cone in the 1980s and the resolution of armed conflicts in Central America during the 1990s, progress has been made with respect to unjustified deprivation of freedom, torture and political assassinations. Nevertheless, the progress achieved is not as great as could have been expected after the elimination of totalitarian regimes and the end of nearly all wars in the region. There is one substantial reservation: the vast majority of the violations are not the consequence of deliberate and planned action by the State, but, rather, of its inability (or sometimes unwillingness) to enforce the effective rule of law and to ensure that it enjoys a monopoly of force.

Another relevant issue concerns citizens' security and the State's ability to provide this public good. A serious defect is that, in many democracies in Latin America, the State does not ensure the physical security of wide sectors of the population. One indicator of this is the high rate of mortality caused by intentional injury. With 25.1 homicides per 100,000 inhabitants, the region has the highest average in the world.

In short, even though military violence has

FINANCIAL AND HUMAN RESOURCES DEVOTED TO THE JUDICIAL SYSTEM, 2001

TABLE 29

Country	Financial Resources		Number of Judges		Number of Public Defenders		
	Year	% of National Budget	Year	Number of Judges per 100,000 Inhabitants	Year	Number of Public Defenders	Number of Public Defenders per 100,000 Inhabitants
Argentina	2000	3.2	2000	11.1	2001	857	2.3
Bolivia	2001	1.5	2002	9.1	2001	82	0.9
Brazil	2000	2.1	2000	3.6	2001	3,000	1.7
Chile	2002	0.9	2002	5.0	2004	417	2.7
Colombia	2002	1.2	2002	7.4	2000	1,126	2.7
Costa Rica	2001	5.2	2001	16.0	2001	128	3.2
Dominican Republic	2001	1.4	2001	7.0	2001	39	0.5
Ecuador	2001	1.5	2002	5.6	2001	33	0.3
El Salvador	2002	4.5	2002	9.2	2001	274	4.3
Guatemala	2002	3.4	2002	6.0	2001	92	0.8
Honduras	2002	7.2	2002	8.2	2002	200	3.0
Mexico	2000	1.0	2000	0.7	2001	686	0.7
Nicaragua	2001	2.9	2001	6.0	2001	15	0.3
Panama	2000	2.6	2002	8.0	2001	48	1.7
Paraguay	2001	1.6	2001	10.5	2001	200	3.6
Peru	2002	1.5	2002	6.0	2001	263	1.0
Uruguay	2001	1.6	2000	15.5	2001	74	2.2
Venezuela	2002	1.4	2000	6.1	1998	159	0.7
Latin America		**2.5**		**4.9**			**1.5**

Notes: the number of judges for Mexico refers only to the federal level. The data on public lawyers in Argentina refer to the total number of staff and for Brazil are estimates. Regional data for the percentage of the national budget are unweighted; the number of judges and public defenders is the weighted average in every case.

Sources: Justice Studies Center of the Americas (JSCA), 2003a and 2003b; and World Bank, Legal and Judicial Reform Practice Group, 2003.

been significantly reduced, the notable progress achieved in democratizing regimes has not been accompanied by similar advances with respect to the right to life, physical inviolability, protection against discrimination and security. Existing information from different sources on the development of human rights and the differing circumstances surrounding social violence in the region merits careful study. We will confine ourselves here to indicating that, beyond the information that is available and the methodologies according to which it was elaborated, there is undoubtedly a situation that centers on basic human rights that gives cause for concern. This poses a challenge to our institutions, to the governments that are part of the system and to the future of the democracies of Latin America.

Administration of Justice

The judicial system, a third component of civil citizenship, is a key element in the protection of people's rights. The resources, financial and human, allocated to the judicial system are a significant indicator of the extent to which States in Latin America defend citizens' rights.

As the data in Table 29 reveal, the regional average in terms of resources allocated to the judicial system amounts to 2.5 percent of national budgets—obviously, in some cases, it is even less. In eight of the fourteen countries for which information is available, though, there is less than one public defender for every 100,000 inhabitants. Given that the possibility of defense in the event of a legal case depends for the vast majority of people on the existence of public legal representation, this in-

BOX 28

Citizens' Dealings with the Judicial System

Citizens' expectations with regard to the judicial system in their respective country are favorable. Two-thirds of them (66.5 percent) expect that, should they have a problem that requires that they appeal to the judicial system, the latter will act positively in at least one of the dimensions of prompt justice and effective justice. The experience of those who have actually come into contact with the judicial system, 20 percent of the total, is different. Fewer than half of them were able to bring an action or complete the process (40.3 percent). The main reasons for dropping their claims relate to lack of money, slow judgments or distant courts. One-third of them state that they were not treated fairly or fast enough, and that there was a widespread incidence of 'soft mistreatment' (long queues, inadequate information and unnecessary red tape). Only a minority of people with experience of the judicial system, however, report having been victims of 'hard mistreatment' (for example, bribes and discrimination). Finally, four out of ten said that they had to pull strings or borrow money to pay for their judicial proceedings.

CITIZENS' EXPERIENCE OF THE JUDICIAL SYSTEM, 2002

TABLE 30

	Circumstances	Percent
Need for the system (1)	Had to turn to the judicial system	20.0
	Had no problems that required a claim	80.0
Obtained a result (2)	Could not bring an action or conclude the lawsuit	59.7
	Brought an action and concluded the lawsuit	40.3
Reasons for dropping the action (3)	Barriers to access (8)	49.8
	No confidence in justice	11.3
	Others (9)	38.9
Presence at court (4)	Has been present at a court hearing	17.4
	Has never been present	82.6
Evaluation of process (5)	They did not act fairly or quickly	33.0
	They acted quickly	9.7
	They acted fairly	24.7
	They acted fairly and quickly	32.5
Evaluation of treatment (6)	Bad experiences, minor and serious	12.4
	Bad experiences, serious (10)	12.1
	Bad experiences, minor (11)	40.5
	No bad experiences (12)	35.0
Things that had to be done (7)	Pull strings or borrow money	39.1
	No need to pull strings or borrow money	60.9

Notes: n = 14,035 (need for the system); n = 19.533 (presence at court).
(1) According to question p15u. All of those polled were asked this question. (2) According to question p15u. Based only on those who turned to the judicial system. (3) According to question p16u. Based only on those who in response to question p15u said that 'They could not bring an action or complete the lawsuit'. (4) According to question p17u. All of those polled were asked this question. (5) According to question p18u. Based only on those who turned to the courts. (6) According to question p19u. Based only on those who turned to the courts. (7) According to question p20u. Based only on those who turned to the courts. (8) Combines the answers 'No money', 'The decision took a long time', 'The court was a long way away' and 'I didn't know how to do it'. (9) Combines the answers 'Better to sort it out privately', 'Several of the above' and 'None of the above'. (10) Combines the answers 'They asked for a tip' and 'He felt discriminated against, humiliated or they were discourteous and disrespectful in their treatment of him'. (11) Combines the answers 'He had to queue for a long time', 'They made him undertake unnecessary formalities' and 'They failed to give him information, or he had to work hard to get it'. (12) The experience is assumed to be positive when the person polled failed to select any of the answers to the question.
Source: elaboration of answers to questions included in the UNDP Proprietary Section of Latinobarómetro 2002.

PRISON POPULATIONS, PRE-TRIAL DETAINEES OR THOSE WHO HAVE NOT BEEN SENTENCED, EXISTING PRISON CAPACITY AND OVERCROWDING, 2002

TABLE 31

Country	Year	Prison Population Total (includes Pre-Trial Detainees and Detainees who have not been sentenced)	Prison Population Rate (per 100,000 of National Population)	Pre-Trial Detainees/Detainees who have not been sentenced (Percentage of Prison Population)	Occupancy Level (based on Official Capacity)
Argentina	1999	38,604	107	55.2	119.9
Bolivia	1999	8,315	102	36.0	162.5
Brazil	2002	240,107	137	33.7	132.0
Chile	2002	33,098	204	40.4	134.3
Colombia	2001	54,034	126	41.1	136.5
Costa Rica	1999	8,526	229	39.5	109.6
Dominican Republic	2001	15,341	178	64.5	175.3
Ecuador	2002	7,716	59	69.9	115.0
El Salvador	2002	10,278	158	49.7	167.5
Guatemala	1999	8,460	71	60.9	112.9
Honduras	2002	11,502	172	78.5	207.6
Mexico	2000	154,765	156	41.2	127.8
Nicaragua	1999	7,198	143	30.8	113.0
Panama	2002	10,423	359	55.3	136.5
Paraguay	1999	4,088	75	92.7	151.0
Peru	2002	27,493	104	67.2	137.8
Uruguay	2002	5,629	166	72.5	150.8
Venezuela	2000	15,107	62	57.5	97.2
Latin America	**c. 2002**	**36,705**	**145**	**54.8**	**138.2**
Extraregional Comparison					
United States	2001	1,962,220	686	18.8	106.4

Note: regional figures are the average of all cases. The total prison population for Latin America is 660,684 with a regional population in 2002 of 508 million.

Sources: International Center for Prison Studies, 2003; data on occupancy levels in Argentina are taken from the Center for Legal and Social Studies (CELS 2001, Chapter 2, Figure 2.4, and correspond to 2000.

dicator is of concern and points to a certain limitation on the right to an effective defense.

The seriousness of the deficiencies in the administration of justice in Latin America becomes more apparent when one analyzes indicators on prison populations, pre-trial detainees or those who have not been sentenced and existing prison capacity. The number of people who have been deprived of their freedom varies considerably from country to country. Some nations stand out for their relatively small prison population— Ecuador, Guatemala, Paraguay and Venezuela— while others stand out for being at the other end of the spectrum—Chile, Costa Rica and Panama.

The average number of prisoners in Latin America is 145 per 100,000 inhabitants, much lower than the 686 prisoners per 100,000 inhabitants in the United States. Even so, Latin American countries do much less to respect the rights of the accused and of prisoners. The number of prisoners in Latin American jails who are pre-trial detainees or are being held on remand is simply outrageous—54.8 percent of the prison population—whereas the comparable figure for the United States is 18.8 percent. In several countries—Honduras, Paraguay and Uruguay—the proportion is over 70 percent.

The living conditions of those who are de-

FREEDOM OF THE PRESS, 2001-2002		TABLE 32
Country	Freedom House 2002	Reporters Without Borders 2001-2002
Argentina	39	12.0
Bolivia	30	14.5
Brazil	38	18.8
Chile	22	6.5
Colombia	63	40.8
Costa Rica	14	4.3
Dominican Republic	33	..
Ecuador	41	5.5
El Salvador	38	8.8
Guatemala	58	27.3
Honduras	51	..
Mexico	38	24.8
Nicaragua	40	..
Panama	34	15.5
Paraguay	55	8.5
Peru	35	9.5
Uruguay	30	6.0
Venezuela	68	25.0
Latin America	**40.4**	**15.2**

Notes: the scales measuring freedom of the press produced by Freedom House and Reporters Without Borders range between zero and 100. Lower figures indicate greater amounts of freedom. The information from Reporters Without Borders covers the period between September 2001 and October 2002. The two dots (..) indicate that information is not available.
Sources: Karin Deutsch Karlekar, 2003; and Reporters Without Borders, 2003.

DEATHS OF JOURNALISTS, 1993-2002		TABLE 33
Country	1993-1997	1998-2002
Argentina	1	1
Bolivia	0	1
Brazil	6	4
Chile	0	0
Colombia	13	18
Costa Rica	0	1
Dominican Republic	1	0
Ecuador	0	0
El Salvador	1	0
Guatemala	2	2
Honduras	1	0
Mexico	5	3
Nicaragua	0	0
Panama	0	0
Paraguay	0	1
Peru	1	0
Uruguay	0	1
Venezuela	1	1
Region		
Latin America	32	33
Western Europe	1	2

Note: the measure records only confirmed cases of journalists killed in the line of duty, either in direct reprisal for their work or as a result of being caught in crossfire.
Source: Committee to Protect Journalists (CPJ), 2003.

prived of their freedom in Latin America are also noticeably worse than in the United States. A basic indicator, overcrowding, shows that, in Latin America, the prison population exceeds existing capacity by 38.2 percent, six times the figure in the United States.

Freedom of the Press and the Right to Information

Freedom of the press and the right to information, the fourth component of civil citizenship, are classic civil rights, important in themselves but also inasmuch as they strongly affect people's ability to exercise other civil rights. For example, democratic theory emphasizes freedom of the press as an essential condition if the electoral process is to be democratic and, in particular, if it is to be truly competitive. Freedom of the press and the right to information are necessary conditions for a society to be able to control the State and the government, as well as to be able to participate in public matters in general. The situation in the region has improved remarkably in recent decades, notwithstanding the fact that there are some unfavorable perceptions in some cases.

A first approach to the problem, utilizing data from Freedom House on freedom of the press, leads to certain important conclusions. On a scale of 100 points—which was constructed after consulting panels of experts designated by that organization and takes into account perceptions and opinions—the average for Latin America points to stagnation over the past decade. The contrast between Latin America and Western Europe is significant and indicates that freedom of the press in Latin America still faces serious shortcomings.

The situation varies among countries. In this

RIGHT OF ACCESS TO PUBLIC INFORMATION AND *HABEAS DATA*, 2002

TABLE 34

Country	Right of Access to Public Information	Right of Access to *Habeas Data*	
		Legal Remedy	Year Adopted
Argentina	Yes	Yes	1994
Bolivia	No	No	-
Brazil	Yes	Yes	1988
Chile	Yes, but ambiguous	No	-
Colombia	Yes	Yes	1997
Costa Rica	No	No	-
Dominican Republic	Yes	No	-
Ecuador	No	Yes	1996
El Salvador	No	No	-
Guatemala	Yes	Yes	1995
Honduras	Yes	No	-
Mexico	Yes	Yes	2002
Nicaragua	Yes, but ambiguous	Yes	1995
Panama	Yes	Yes	2002
Paraguay	No	Yes	1992
Peru	Yes	Yes	1993
Uruguay	No	No	-
Venezuela	Yes	Yes	1999

Note: the 'right of access to public information' refers to the right of individuals to gain access to information in the hands of the State that pertains to the conduct of public affairs. 'Habeas data' refers to an action that guarantees an individual access to information contained in public or private databases or to records that make reference to his/her or his/her property, and, when necessary, provides him/her with the ability to update, correct, remove or reserve such information for the purpose of protecting certain fundamental rights.

Sources: Organization of American States (OAS)–Inter-American Commission on Human Rights (ICHR), Office of the Special Rapporteur for Freedom of Expression, 2001, Chapter 3, Table 1; and Andrés Guadamuz, 2000 and 2001.

regard it is important to mention that, even with the obvious difficulties of measuring freedom of the press, a considerable amount of consensus exists between the data produced by Freedom House and that by Reporters Without Borders—another acknowledged source of information on this subject—at least with respect to the most favorable and the most problematic cases.

One important feature is how safe the lives of the journalists themselves are. There are only four countries in the region in which not one journalist has lost his/her life in the past ten years. The contrast with Western Europe is once again striking.

The right of access to public information is legally recognized throughout the region, with the exception of five countries.

In particular, in recent years, progress has been made with respect to recognition of *habeas data* held in public and private databases. Today there are only seven countries in Latin America where this right does not exist.

A more complete analysis of this subject, with the aim of gaining a more precise idea about the conditions under which people acquire access to this type of information, would require data that are currently lacking.

Conclusions on Civil Citizenship: Achievements and Deficiencies

- The data point to certain significant achievements, especially concerning legal recognition of civil rights in general, as well as of the rights of women and of indigenous peoples in particular.
- Progress has also been made with regard to respect for human rights and freedom of the press.
- Equality under the law and protection against discrimination are affected by

disparities in their application among different categories of citizens.

- The right to life, personal inviolability and security is limited by the high levels of public insecurity in the region.
- In general, the way in which the judicial system works does not prevent violations of the rights of those who have been prosecuted and of prisoners.

Social Citizenship

Social citizenship refers to those aspects of citizens' lives that affect their potential to develop their basic capabilities. Unlike other types of citizenship, social citizenship does not always have a clear legal basis in national Constitutions and legislation, and the extent of international acceptance of social citizenship through the adoption of agreements and treaties is even less extensive.[66] Steady action by civil society, however, has encouraged progress not only with regard to this debate, but also in terms of permanent mobilization, so that social citizenship may be an effective component of integral citizenship.

Debates are taking place in academic and political circles about how to define the content of social citizenship. These debates have achieved a degree of consensus as to the basic components of that citizenship. The reports on human development have made a great contribution in this respect.[67]

The rights to health and education are regarded as basic components of social citizenship. Likewise, unemployment, poverty and inequality have been widely recognized as elements that hinder the integration of individuals into society. A key assumption of democracy—that individuals are full citizens who function within a public sphere in which equality prevails—is not able to work to full effect in conditions of extreme poverty and inequality.

BOX 29

Poor and Unequal Citizens

This is a problem everywhere. We know that it is inherent to the bureaucratic dimension of the State; and it is more serious, and systematic, when the 'subject' of the relationship is afflicted by severe and prolonged poverty and inequality. Such ills breed social authoritarianism, practiced extensively in Latin America by the rich and powerful, and reverberate in the ways in which State bureaucracies treat many individuals, citizens and, even more so, migrants and foreigners. This is, to my mind, another crucial dimension of the quality of democracy.

Guillermo O'Donnell, text prepared for PRODDAL, 2002c.

In the following pages we present some crucial indicators of social citizenship, health, education, employment, poverty and inequality, which are grouped into the two categories indicated in Box 30. These indicators provide us with an approximation of how effectively citizenship is being exercised in Latin America.

Data on social citizenship reveal that most

BOX 30

Dimensions of Social Citizenship

Dimensions	Relevant Issues
Basic needs	Health and education
Social integration	Employment, poverty and inequality

---

66 For example, the Additional Protocol to the Inter-American Convention on Human Rights (covering economic, social and cultural rights)—the 'Protocol of San Salvador'—was only signed in 1988.

67 On the impact of inequality and poverty on the capacities of citizens, see Amartya Sen, 1999b, pp. 20–24, and Chapter 4. On health and education as two basic needs, see UNDP, 2002c, pp. 252–253.

CHILD MALNUTRITION, 1985-2000

TABLE 35

Country	Last Year		Recent Trend	
	Year	Percentage	Years Compared	Change in Percentage
Argentina	1995/96	12.4	1994-95/96	7.7
Bolivia	1998	26.8	1989-98	-10.9
Brazil	1996	10.5	1989-96	-15.4
Chile	1999	1.9	1986-99	-7.7
Colombia	2000	13.5	1989-00	-3.1
Costa Rica	1996	6.1	1989-96	-3.1
Dominican Republic	1996	10.7	1991-96	-5.8
Ecuador	1998	26.4	1986-98	-7.6
El Salvador	1998	23.3	1993-98	0.2
Guatemala	1999	46.4	1987-99	-11.3
Honduras	1996	38.9	1991/92-96	2.6
Mexico	1999	17.7	1988-99	-5.1
Nicaragua	1998	24.9	1993-98	2.4
Panama	1997	18.2	1985-97	-0.6
Paraguay	1990	13.9	..	..
Peru	2000	25.4	1991/92-00	-6.4
Uruguay	1992/93	9.5	1987-92/93	-6.4
Venezuela	2000	12.8	1990-00	-1.0
Latin America		**18.9**		**-4.2**

Notes: small size for age is a measure that compares the height of a child at a certain age to that of the average for members of the relevant population. This indicator shows poor accumulated growth and constitutes a measure of insufficient previous physical growth. It is associated with a set of long-term factors, such as chronically insufficient food intake, frequent infections, persistent bad eating habits and a low household economic level.

Source: calculations based on data from the World Health Organization (WHO), Department of Nutrition for Health and Development, 2002.

Latin American countries have acute shortcomings that affect large segments, and, at times, the majority, of the population. All of the countries of the region have a level of inequality that is greater than the world average; 16 of the 18 can be classified as severely unequal. For the year 2002, In 15 cases, more than 25 percent of the population lives below the poverty line, and, in seven, the proportion of poor people is over 50 percent.

Basic Needs

Some progress has been made in this respect, although the indicators are still far from satisfactory. Indicators on child malnutrition and illiteracy point to some improvement in the region. Three countries—Chile, Costa Rica and Uruguay—stand out for their relatively satisfactory performance in these problem areas.

Specifically, child malnutrition has decreased in 13 countries, most notably in Bolivia, Brazil and Guatemala. Nevertheless, this problem still affects more than five percent of children in 16 of the 18 countries, and, in seven of these, at least one in five children suffers from malnutrition.

The rate of illiteracy has fallen in all of the countries of the region, with the greatest improvements coming in Bolivia, El Salvador, Guatemala and Honduras. However, in 14 of the 18 countries, illiteracy still affects more than five percent of the population over 15 years of age, and, in four of them, it is as high as 21.3 percent or more.

Other indicators, such as infant mortality, life expectancy and schooling also show some improvements, although, on occasion, the level of improvement is insufficient in light of the breadth and depth of existing deficits.

A positive general trend is also evident in

ILLITERACY IN ADULTS OVER 15 YEARS OF AGE, 1970-2000 — TABLE 36				
Country	1970	1980	1990	2000
Argentina	7.0	5.6	4.3	3.2
Bolivia	42.3	31.2	21.8	14.5
Brazil	31.9	24.5	19.1	14.8
Chile	12.2	8.5	5.9	4.2
Colombia	22.1	15.9	11.5	8.3
Costa Rica	11.8	8.3	6.1	4.4
Dominican Republic	32.8	26.1	20.6	16.4
Ecuador	25.7	18.1	12.3	8.4
El Salvador	42.0	34.1	27.5	21.3
Guatemala	54.8	46.9	38.9	31.4
Honduras	46.7	38.6	31.5	25.4
Mexico	25.1	17.7	12.1	8.6
Nicaragua	45.5	41.2	37.2	33.5
Panama	20.8	15.2	11.0	8.1
Paraguay	20.2	14.1	9.7	6.7
Peru	28.5	20.5	14.5	10.1
Uruguay	7.0	5.1	3.4	2.3
Venezuela	23.6	16.0	11.0	7.4
Latin America	**27.8**	**21.5**	**16.6**	**12.7**

Note: the data represent the proportion of the adult population that is illiterate. It refers to a population over 15 years of age that is unable to read or write a short phrase in an everyday situation. The data for the region are the average of all cases.

Source: United Nations Educational, Scientific and Cultural Organization (UNESCO), Institute of Statistics, 2002a.

the areas of health and education. We must be cautious when evaluating these indicators, though. Other available data challenge some of the claims made in the research that we have drawn on here. In this respect, the report entitled *Literacy Skills for the World of Tomorrow*, produced by the Organisation for Economic Co-operation and Development (OECD) and the United Nations Educational, Scientific and Cultural Organization (UNESCO), and including 41 countries, revealed that a very sizeable proportion (more than 50 percent) of pupils in Latin America, although literate, have effectively no real reading and comprehension skills (Table 40). The six Latin American countries included in this report occupy the lowest positions with respect to quality of education and student performance.

Social Integration

The greatest deprivations with regard to social citizenship in Latin America are to be found in this category. Problems of unemployment, poverty and inequality are very marked. This is so much the case that even where a degree of improvement can be noted, as in the case of poverty, it is not sufficient to classify the situation as anything other than extremely serious. The unemployment situation has worsened and levels of inequality have remained the same or have increased. The unemployment rate in Latin America is one of the highest in the world and the level of inequality is the greatest in the world.

Inasmuch as social citizenship contains an economic component, for most people, employment constitutes a basic pillar of their citizenship. Employment is the way in which citizens contribute to the generation of wealth in society and through which they secure the means to exercise their rights. For the vast majority of Latin Americans, employment is the way to escape poverty. Often, however, this aspiration proves impossible to satisfy, constituting a tremendous challenge to politics and democracy in the region.

Everything indicates that, in Latin America, the quality of employment as well as its influence as a means of social insertion have diminished. As the Economic Commission for Latin America

BOX 31

Genuine Insertion for the 'Supernumeraries'

Nearly everybody openly condemns the model of 'dual society'. But many welcome any accomplishment—from the development of a sector of 'social utility' to the opening of 'new sources of employment'—as long as it provides some activity to the supernumeraries. Now, if one focuses on the issue of social integration, it is not only a matter of finding jobs for everyone, but of also providing a legal status.

Robert Castel, 1995, pp. 454–455.

INFANT MORTALITY, 1970-2000

TABLE 37

Country	1970-75	1975-80	1980-85	1985-90	1990-95	1995-2000
Argentina	48.1	39.1	32.2	27.1	24.3	21.8
Bolivia	151.3	131.2	109.2	90.1	75.1	65.6
Brazil	90.5	78.8	65.3	55.3	46.8	42.1
Chile	68.6	45.2	23.7	18.4	14.0	12.8
Colombia	73.0	56.7	48.4	41.4	35.2	30.0
Costa Rica	52.5	30.4	19.2	16.0	13.7	12.1
Dominican Republic	93.5	84.3	63.9	54.6	46.5	40.6
Ecuador	95.0	82.4	68.4	57.1	49.7	45.6
El Salvador	105.0	95.0	77.0	54.0	40.2	32.0
Guatemala	102.5	90.9	78.8	65.0	51.1	46.0
Honduras	103.7	81.0	65.5	53.3	45.4	37.1
Mexico	69.0	56.8	47.0	39.5	34.0	31.0
Nicaragua	97.9	90.1	79.8	65.0	48.0	39.5
Panama	43.4	35.4	30.4	28.4	25.1	21.4
Paraguay	53.1	51.0	48.9	46.7	43.3	39.2
Peru	110.3	99.1	81.6	68.0	55.5	45.0
Uruguay	46.3	42.4	33.5	22.6	20.1	17.5
Venezuela	48.7	39.3	33.6	26.9	23.2	20.9
Latin America	**80.69**	**68.28**	**55.91**	**46.08**	**38.40**	**33.34**

Note: infant mortality is measured in terms of the probability of death between birth and the first year of life and is expressed in terms of deaths per 1,000 births. The data for the region are the average of all cases.
Source: United Nations, Department of Social and Economic Affairs, Population Division, 2001.

LIFE EXPECTANCY AT BIRTH, 1970-2000

TABLE 38

Country	1970-75	1975-80	1980-85	1985-90	1990-95	1995-2000
Argentina	67.1	68.5	70.0	70.8	71.9	72.9
Bolivia	46.7	50.0	53.7	56.8	59.3	61.4
Brazil	59.5	61.5	63.1	64.6	66.0	67.2
Chile	63.4	67.1	70.6	72.5	74.2	74.9
Colombia	61.6	63.8	66.6	67.6	68.2	70.4
Costa Rica	67.9	70.8	73.5	74.5	75.3	76.0
Dominican Republic	59.7	61.8	62.8	64.7	66.5	67.3
Ecuador	58.8	61.3	64.3	66.8	68.5	69.5
El Salvador	58.2	56.7	56.6	63.2	66.8	69.1
Guatemala	53.7	56.0	58.0	59.6	62.5	64.0
Honduras	53.8	57.3	60.9	64.3	65.0	65.6
Mexico	62.4	65.1	67.5	69.6	71.2	72.2
Nicaragua	55.1	57.5	59.3	62.0	65.9	67.7
Panama	66.2	68.8	70.5	71.4	72.5	73.6
Paraguay	65.9	66.5	67.1	67.6	68.5	69.6
Peru	55.4	58.4	61.4	64.1	66.5	68.0
Uruguay	68.7	69.5	70.8	71.9	72.8	73.9
Venezuela	65.7	67.5	68.6	70.3	71.4	72.4
Latin America	**60.54**	**62.67**	**64.74**	**66.79**	**68.50**	**69.76**

Note: this indicator shows life expectancy at birth in years. The data for the region are the average of all cases.
Source: United Nations, Department of Economic and Social Affairs, Population Division, 2001.

PRIMARY, SECONDARY AND TERTIARY SCHOOLING, 1999

TABLE 39

Country	Net Rate of Primary Schooling	Net Rate of Secondary Schooling	Rate of Tertiary Schooling
Argentina	100.0	76.0	48.0
Bolivia	99.1	..	32.9
Brazil	96.5	68.5	14.8
Chile	88.9	71.8	37.5
Colombia	88.1	54.3	22.2
Costa Rica	91.3	43.4	..
Dominican Republic	90.6	40.0	..
Ecuador	97.7	46.9	..
El Salvador	80.6	..	18.2
Guatemala	81.0	18.4	..
Honduras	..	..	13.0
Mexico	100.0	57.4	19.8
Nicaragua	79.4	..	..
Panama	98.0	60.9	..
Paraguay	91.5	45.0	..
Peru	100.0	61.5	28.8
Uruguay	93.6	77.4	33.6
Venezuela	88.0	50.4	29.2
Latin America	**92.0**	**55.1**	**27.1**

Notes: the two dots (..) indicate that the information is unavailable. The net rate of primary and secondary schooling is the percentage of children of school age (according to each country's definition) effectively enrolled in school. The net rates of tertiary schooling are unavailable. The data for El Salvador (in all categories) and Peru (secondary and tertiary) are for 1998–1999; the rest are based on information for 1999–2000. The data for the region are the average of all available cases.
Source: United Nations Educational, Scientific and Cultural Organization (UNESCO), Institute of Statistics, 2002b, 2002c and 2002d.

QUALITY OF EDUCATION AND STUDENT PERFORMANCE, 2002

TABLE 40

Country	Percentage of Students at each Level		
	Low	Medium	High
Argentina	43.9	45.8	10.3
Brazil	55.8	40.6	4.7
Chile	48.2	46.6	5.3
Mexico	44.2	48.8	6.9
Peru	79.6	19.4	1.1
Finland	6.9	43.0	50.1
South Korea	5.7	55.4	36.8
United States	17.9	48.4	33.7

Notes: percentage of students at each performance level on the combined scale of reading skills. The concept of literacy employed by the Programme for International Student Assessment (PISA) is broader than the traditional one, that is, 'able to read and write'. Here, literacy is measured along a continuum, not in terms of whether a student is literate or is not literate, even when it may be necessary or advisable for some purpose to define a point within the band below which performance levels are considered inadequate. In fact, there is no dividing line between a totally literate person and someone who is not. The PISA test—reading skills test—was carried out with 15-year-old students. The students were required to look up information, understand and interpret written material, and evaluate and reflect on the content.
Source: Organisation for Economic Co-operation and Development (OECD) and the United Nations Educational, Scientific and Cultural Organization (UNESCO), 2003, p. 274.

and the Caribbean (ECLAC) has pointed out: "Employment is the most important link between economic development and social development, since it is the main source of family income (producing 80% of the total). The exclusion and segmentation derived from lack of access to quality employment are therefore determining factors of poverty and social inequality which are self-perpetuating, expressed in the high and persistent income concentration that prevails in the region."[68]

As we have already pointed out, the employment situation has worsened in Latin America.[69] The weighted rate of open unemployment in 2002 was 10.8 percent, the highest since reliable figures have been available.

The urban unemployment rate fell in Colombia, Ecuador, and, to a lesser degree, in Chile and El Salvador. But it increased in Argentina, Bolivia, Costa Rica, Dominican Republic, Mexico, Nicaragua, Panama, Paraguay, Peru, Uruguay and Venezuela.

Among Latin American youth, the unem-

68 J. A. Ocampo, 'Globalization and Social Development', presentation by the Executive Secretary of the Economic Commission of Latin American and the Caribbean at the Second Meeting of former Latin American Presidents, Santiago, Chile, 22–23 April 2002.
69 International Labour Organization, Regional Office for the Americas, 2002.

OFFICIAL URBAN UNEMPLOYMENT (AVERAGE ANNUAL RATES), 1985-2002

TABLE 41

Country	1985	1990	1995	2000	2002
Argentina	6.1	6.1	16.4	15.1	19.7
Bolivia	5.7	7.2	3.6	7.5	8.7
Brazil	5.3	4.3	4.6	7.1	7.1
Chile	17.0	7.4	6.6	9.2	9.0
Colombia	13.8	10.5	8.8	20.2	16.2
Costa Rica	7.2	5.4	5.2	5.2	6.8
Dominican Republic	..	..	15.8	13.9	17.2
Ecuador	10.4	6.1	7.7	9.7	6.3
El Salvador	..	10.0	7.0	6.5	6.2
Honduras	11.7	6.9	6.6	..	5.9
Mexico	4.4	2.8	6.2	2.2	2.7
Nicaragua	3.2	7.6	16.9	9.8	12.1
Panama	15.7	20.0	16.4	15.3	16.4
Paraguay	5.1	6.6	5.3	10.0	14.7
Peru	10.1	8.3	7.9	7.0	9.4
Uruguay	13.1	9.2	10.8	13.6	17.0
Venezuela	14.3	11.0	10.3	13.9	15.9
Latin America	**8.3**	**5.7**	**7.4**	**8.5**	**10.8**

Notes: the two dots (..) indicate that the information is unavailable. The survey covers urban areas throughout the country in Argentina, Bolivia, Costa Rica, El Salvador, Honduras, Nicaragua, Panama, Uruguay and Venezuela. In Brazil, six metropolitan regions are considered (a new series for Brazil is not included here). In Chile, the whole country is covered. For Colombia, only seven metropolitan areas are taken into account; since 2000, the universe of the survey was expanded to include 13 metropolitan areas. In Ecuador the whole country is covered until 1997; from 1998 only Cuenca, Guayaquil and Quito are included. In Mexico, 39 urban areas are surveyed. The International Labour Organization's overview contains no data for Guatemala. In Paraguay, the survey was carried out only in Asunción. The data for the Dominican Republic include hidden unemployment. Finally, for Peru, from 1996–2000, the survey covered the national urban population; from 2001, the figures refer to metropolitan Lima. The averages for Latin America were weighted by the ILO.

Source: based on information from Household Surveys conducted in each country, International Labour Organization, *Labour Overview 2003*, Statistical Annex. Note that the data for this table do not necessarily coincide with that presented in Table 2, which used information from the Economic Commission for Latin America and the Caribbean (ECLAC), 2003.

ployment rate, in most countries, is double or almost double the national average.

At the same time, social security coverage for workers has narrowed and informal employment has increased: seven out of every ten new jobs created in the region since 1990 have been in the informal sector. In addition, only six out of every ten new jobs generated since 1990 in the formal sector include some kind of social security provision. This situation sounds a serious alarm about the future of our societies: many Latin Americans, in addition to the deficiencies they

are experiencing at present, are in danger of lacking coverage at retirement.

The growth in the proportion of informal employment is an eloquent indicator of the crisis. Moreover, it is an inappropriate means of reducing unemployment, since it creates jobs of low quality and low social usefulness that do not guarantee minimum welfare thresholds and social integration.

According to data from the International Labor Organization, in 1990, the primary deficit in 'decent work'[70] affected 49.5 percent of the

70 The primary deficit in decent employment is an indicator that was developed and calculated by the ILO. To create it, the evolution of gaps in employment and social security coverage were examined. Two components are used to estimate the *employment gap*: unemployment; and informality. The former corresponds to the difference between the current unemployment rate and the average over a 30-year period (1950–1980), which provides a so-called historical unemployment rate. The latter component records those who hold low-quality informal positions (characterized

YOUTH UNEMPLOYMENT(ANNUAL RATES), 1990-2002

TABLA 42

Country	Age	1990	1995	2000	2002
Argentina	15-19	21.7	46.8	39.5	45.4
	15-24	15.2	30.1	..	..
Bolivia	10-19	13.3	5.0	14.7	20.0
	20-29	9.5	5.4	10.8	10.7
Brazil	15-17	..	11.0	17.8	34.5
	18-24	..	9.3	14.7	21.4
Chile	15-19	15.9	15.8	26.1	28.4
	20-24	12.0	10.1	20.1	20.0
Colombia	12-17	..	21.0	33.3	32.7
	18-24	..	16.6	32.4	32.0
Costa Rica	12-24	10.4	13.5	10.9	16.3
Ecuador	15-24	13.5	15.3	17.4	17.4
El Salvador	15-24	18.6	13.3	14.3	..
Honduras	10-24	10.7	10.2	..	8.8
Mexico	12-19	7.0	13.1	5.4	6.5
	20-24	..	9.9	4.0	5.2
Panama	15-24	..	31.9	32.6	34.1
Paraguay	15-19	18.4	10.8	..	20.6
	20-24	14.1	7.8	..	16.7
Peru	14-24	15.4	11.2	17.1	15.1
Uruguay	14-24	26.6	25.5	31.7	40.0
Venezuela	15-24	18.0	19.9	25.3	27.2

Notes: the two dots (..) indicate that the information is unavailable. In Argentina, the Household Survey is carried out in Greater Buenos Aires; in Bolivia, in national urban areas 1996 (15–25 years); in Brazil, in six metropolitan areas (new series from 2001); in Chile, it is the national total; and in Colombia, in seven metropolitan areas in September of each year—from 2001 in 13 metropolitan areas. In Costa Rica, Ecuador, El Salvador and Honduras the data cover the national total (urban). In Mexico, the survey is carried out in 41 urban areas; in Panama, in the metropolitan region; and in Paraguay, in Asunción. For Peru, from 1996, the data cover the national total (urban); from 2001, the data cover metropolitan Lima. In Uruguay the survey covers Montevideo; and in Venezuela it is the national total (urban). No data are provided for the Dominican Republic, Guatemala or Nicaragua.

Source: based on information from Household Surveys in each country, International Labour Organization, *Labour Overview 2003*, Statistical Annex, 2003.

urban workforce in Latin America. By 2002 the proportion had risen to 50.5 percent. The increase has raised the figure to 15.7 percent of the entire workforce. In 2002, the primary deficit in decent work affected 93 million workers in the region, 30 million more than in 1990. The employment gap widened, affecting 21 million workers, including the unemployed and informal workers, and the gap in social coverage widened, affecting nine million newly employed workers (basically in the informal sector).[71]

Between 1990 and 2002, the level of poverty fell in 12 countries in Latin America, particularly in Brazil, Chile, Ecuador, Mexico and Panama. But in 15 of the 18 countries under consideration, one-quarter of the population lives below the poverty line, and in seven of these, more than 50 percent of the population is poor.

But, as José Nun maintains, "the issue is not reduced to the marginal access of the 'structurally poor' to the rights of citizenship." In the more modernized areas of Latin America, many

by low productivity, income levels that are volatile and close to the poverty line and employment instability). In order to calculate the gap in social protection, the ILO takes into account employees in both the formal and informal sectors who do not contribute to social security. The summation of the employment gap and the social protection gap define the *primary deficit in decent employment*. International Labour Organization, Regional Office for the Americas, 2002, pp. 30–31.

71 International Labour Organization, Regional Office for the Americas, 2002, pp. 31–32.

LATIN AMERICA: STRUCTURE OF NON-AGRICULTURAL EMPLOYMENT (PERCENTAGES), 1990-2002				TABLA 43
		Informal Sector	Formal Sector
Year		Total	Total
1990	Total	42.8	57.2
	Men	39.4	60.6
	Women	47.4	52.6
1995	Total	46.1	53.9
	Men	42.7	57.3
	Women	51.0	49.0
2000	Total	46.9	53.1
	Men	44.5	55.5
	Women	50.3	49.7
2002	Total	46.5	53.5
	Men	44.3	55.7
	Women	49.4	50.6

Notes: Household Surveys cover the following: Argentina (national urban), Brazil (urban area), Chile (whole country), Colombia (ten metropolitan areas), Costa Rica (whole country), Ecuador (urban area), Mexico (urban area), Panama (whole country), Peru (Metropolitan Lima), Uruguay (whole country) and Venezuela (urban area).

Source: based on information from Household Surveys carried out in each country, International Labour Organization, Regional Office for the Americas, 2003.

LATIN AMERICA: WAGE EARNERS WITH SOCIAL SECURITY (PERCENTAGES), 1990-2002					TABLA 44
		Informal Sector	Formal Sector	Total
Year				
1990	Total	29.2	80.6	66.6
	Men	32.5	79.1	68.4
	Women	27.0	82.8	65.1
1995	Total	24.2	79.3	65.2
	Men	25.4	78.2	66.6
	Women	24.0	81.1	65.7
2000	Total	27.2	79.6	64.6
	Men	26.6	78.4	66.0
	Women	27.9	81.5	62.9
2002	Total	26.2	78.9	63.7
	Men	25.5	77.9	64.9
	Women	27.0	80.6	62.3

Notes: Household Surveys cover the following: Argentina (national urban), Brazil (urban area), Chile (whole country), Colombia (ten metropolitan areas), Costa Rica (whole country), Ecuador (urban area), Mexico (urban area), Panama (whole country), Peru (Metropolitan Lima), Uruguay (whole country) and Venezuela (urban area).

Source: based on information from Household Surveys carried out in each country, International Labour Organization, Regional Office for the Americas, 2003

profound changes have occurred in the areas of production and employment, leading to an increase in unemployment and underemployment and to a widespread crisis of the social and political fabric. This gives rise to another class of problem of low quality, brought about mainly by a kind of 'citizenship de-linking' by people who were previously integrated into society: the class of the 'new poor'.[72]

Between 1991 and 2002, 15 of the 18 countries made progress in terms of economic growth per capita. And 12 achieved a slight reduction in poverty levels (in fact, only in Argentina, Bolivia, Dominican Republic Paraguay, Peru and Venezuela did poverty worsen). However, in 2002 only in Guatemala, Honduras, Mexico, Nicaragua, Panama and Uruguay, however, was there a decrease in inequality.[73] Reasons exist that permit us to maintain that only if inequality is reduced will it be possible to continue to address poverty, and that the decrease in inequality tends to better the prospects for acceptable rates of economic growth.

The possibility of greater equality is linked to the strength of democracy. Satisfaction of the social objectives of development, especially human development, cannot be achieved through market forces alone. The drive for equality does not come from the markets but from the promise implicit in democracy. Equality among citizens strengthens and consolidates democracy.

72 J. Nun, text prepared for PRODDAL, 2002.
73 *To reduce the level of poverty* means to lower the percentage of the population with income below the poverty line (based on the household survey measurement). Inequality is measured using the Gini coefficient. Both measurements are based on data for 1991 (or the nearest possible year) and are contrasted with figures for 2002.

BOX 32

The Role of Civil Society

The invisible in Latin American societies are those who are not part of civil society, simply because they have no identity, project, method of social organization or way of struggling to maintain themselves, to defend themselves, in order to obtain their rights and public recognition. They are politically destitute of any real power. In all honesty, it is necessary to recognize the progress made in formal citizenship, which carries with it the right to vote, particularly in the recent period of democratization. But having the right to vote is not the same as being a citizen ... as far as social inclusion and the practical guarantee of fundamental rights, not only civil and political rights, but also the right to work, the right to an income, food, housing, health, education and so forth, are concerned. Between 30 percent and 60 percent of the people in our countries suffer from some form of social exclusion that denies them their citizenship. When these people are unable to organize and fight, with a view to reinserting themselves politically and having some expectation of change in the circumstances that produced the inequality, poverty and social exclusion, they constitute the enormous contingent of invisible men and women in our societies. Civil societies lose in this process, as does democracy. But, if for some reason, the groups of invisible people should organize themselves, civil society would win and so too would democracy, since their presence as real players is the indispensable condition for their sustained inclusion among the citizenry. [...]

Consolidating democracy ... necessarily implicates civil society, above all because of the possibility of making those who are invisible visible. This is so simply because the rights of citizenship cannot exist unless they exist for all men and women. Rights for some people, however numerous, are not rights but privileges. Citizenship is the expression of a social relationship that is based on the inclusion of everyone, without exception. How does one include oneself in the relationship among citizens? Taking our current situation, in which millions of people still remain outside of the system without their citizenship being recognized, it is a question of seeing how and under what conditions they can be transformed into historical subjects of their own social inclusion, initiating a virtuous process of rupture and of reformulation of social, economic, political and cultural structures in a democratic and sustained manner. It is especially worth remembering that these groups of people in situations of poverty and inequality, and virtual social exclusion, are not ontologically or necessarily democratic. Like all social subjects they need to become democratic by the same process through which they become active subjects. The crux of the matter is the fabric of social organization based on which a group—of *favela* dwellers or landless farmers, for example—develops its identity, designs its vision of the world, becomes aware of its rights and of the importance of participation, formulates proposals and strategies. In the process, literally, the members of the group acquire the power of citizenship even though they are far from changing effectively the set of relationships that exclude them.

If we understand *empowering* as achieving power as a citizen—of securing visibility for the people who until this point had been invisible in the building of power relationships—then we are talking about gains for the group, civil society and democracy. The process of 'empowering' brings with it new types of organization, a democratic culture of rights and a real capacity to influence the political struggle. What is apparent in Latin America is that the subjugation of democratization by neo-liberal globalization stalled and even reversed the continuing emergence of new subjects. The struggle against this process of globalization, on the contrary, is unveiling the contradictions that are again allowing these groups to develop. However, this is a new turn of events, and it depends on how the greater segmentation produced between included and excluded people is seen and experienced in different societies. The large cities in Latin America are not just fragmented—as with Rio de Janeiro, with its highways and favelas—but one part can actually turn its back on the other, ignoring and despising it.

Cândido Grzybowski, text prepared for PRODDAL, 2002.

SOCIAL CITIZENSHIP: INEQUALITY AND POVERTY, C. 2002

TABLA 45

Country	Inequality: Gini Coefficient, c. 2002	Poverty: Percentage below Poverty Line, c. 2002
Argentina	0.590	45.4
Bolivia	0.614	62.4
Brazil	0.639	37.5
Chile	0.559	20.6
Colombia	0.575	50.6
Costa Rica	0.488	20.3
Dominican Republic	0.544	44.9
Ecuador	0.513	49.0
El Salvador	0.525	48.9
Guatemala	0.543	59.9
Honduras	0.588	77.3
Mexico	0.514	39.4
Nicaragua	0.579	69.3
Panama	0.515	34.0
Paraguay	0.570	61.0
Peru	0.525	54.8
Uruguay	0.455	15.4
Venezuela	0.500	48.6

Note: the higher the Gini coefficient the greater the degree of inequality. Information for Argentina, Bolivia, Ecuador, Paraguay and Uruguay covers urban areas. The values for the remaining countries correspond to the national average. In 1999, the world average in terms of the Gini coefficient was 0.381. Poverty: the figures indicate the percentage of people living below the poverty line. The poor are those whose income is less than double the cost of the basic food basket. Sources: Economic Commission for Latin America and the Caribbean (ECLAC), 2004.

Civil Society as the Promoter of Social Citizenship

The problems and difficulties encountered by welfare States in pressing ahead with initiatives to protect their citizens, as well as the activities of large non-governmental organizations involved in poverty relief, initially encouraged the expansion of voluntary organizations and gradually extended their scope of action to a large number of other fields concerned with citizens' welfare.

The growth of civil society was most dynamic in countries with dictatorial regimes, where political parties could not articulate the demands of the citizenry, and in areas, urban and rural, where the State ceased to provide adequately basic necessities, such as healthcare, education and support for vulnerable sectors.

A large number of organizations have also sprung up that are dedicated to promoting civic values, which ensure that citizens are registered and that clean elections take place, and to improving the performance of political parties, political movements and representative institutions.

In the sphere of practical action to reduce poverty, many NGOs (technically, we should say *non-State* organizations) take taken on functions that, until this point, were seen as the responsibility of the State. At present, a significant portion of public social policies are implemented by NGOs in accord with State institutions.

The work of these organizations has resulted in an increase in the rate of participation by the people. In many cases, the civil society organization aims to promote existing democratic values and also to affect the way in which decisions are made.

Although vigorous State action is needed to recover universal social policies that involve all citizens and provide for the meeting of people's basic needs, these should be implemented whith the inclusion and participation of different civil society organizations that promote transparency and prevent bureaucratic abuses.

Conclusions about Social Citizenship: its Achievements and Shortcomings

Shortcomings in the field of social citizenship constitute one of the most important challenges to the region. No other kind of citizenship sees democracy being as compromised as that of social citizenship.

There are good reasons to maintain that the citizens who suffer exclusion in one area of citizenship are the same ones who suffer exclusion in another. Physical poverty has a negative impact on education opportunities, on health and nutrition, on employment prospects, and on the ability to exercise effectively civil, political and social rights. Education, health and employment depend on food, housing and clothing. All of these, in turn, make it easier to achieve liberty, progress and justice. Below a certain minimum threshold with respect to social rights the very concept of citizenship is called into question by reality. The picture becomes even more

GRAPH 4

Income Distribution in Latin America, c. 2002

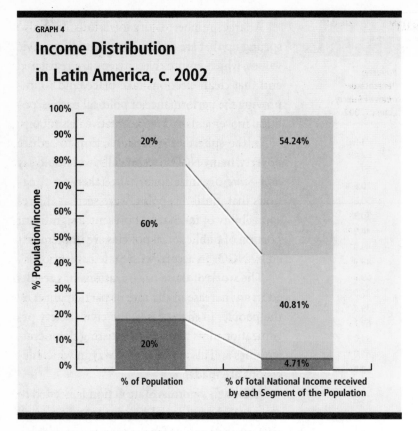

% of Population

% of Total National Income received by each Segment of the Population

Note: the data are weighted by population and calculated using the most recent statistics available on income distribution among urban households, divided into quintiles and deciles and shown as percentages of total national income. The information on Argentina, Bolivia, Colombia, Costa Rica, the Dominican Republic, Ecuador, Guatemala, Honduras, Mexico, Panama, Uruguay and Venezuela are for 2002. For Brazil, El Salvador, Nicaragua and Paraguay, the data are for 2001. Finally, the data on Chile are for 2000, while data for Peru are for 1999. The sum of the figures in the column on income distribution does not equal 100 percent because the distribution of income divided into quintiles and deciles in some countries does not add up to 100 percent either.

Source: Economic Commission of Latin America and the Caribbean (ECLAC), Social Statistics Unit, Division of Statistics and Economic Projections.

BOX 33

Decency as a Collective Value

What I am going to suggest is linking the defeat of poverty and inequality with something that we could argue constitutes a general public interest: democracy. Now, why should democracy be of any interest to the privileged? [...] The valid moral and political argument is that democracy is founded in values that require respectful consideration of the dignity and autonomy of every human being; no more and no less [...] the principal cementing force can only be an ethical reason: the decent treatment deserved by every human being. An additional reason is in the public interest: improving the quality of our democracies is equivalent to advancing towards achieving that decency as a collective value in society as a whole.

Guillermo O'Donnell, 1999c, p. 82.

BOX 34

Dysfunctions in the World Economy

If capitalism by excluding politics should become totalitarian, it would run the risk of crumbling [...] Because in no other period of our history— with the very brief exception of the 1930s— were the dysfunctional aspects of the world economy as severe as they are today: massive unemployment; formidable increases in inequality and poverty in rich countries; unsustainable misery and recurrent crises in many developing countries; and the deepening inequality of income per capita among countries. Democracy cannot remain indifferent to all of this.

Jean-Paul Fitoussi, text prepared for PRODDAL, 2003.

BOX 35

Poverty and Inequality: Little Significant Change

The relationships that exist between economic inequality and poverty, on the one hand, and the quality of democracy, on the other, have often been noted. In this respect it is worth looking carefully at the findings of research, such as those of an econometric report that has just been released: "The most important conclusion which it is possible to derive from the present report is that the main obstacle hindering the success of efforts to reduce poverty in Latin America and the Caribbean is rooted in the fact that the best remedy for treating the poverty that afflicts the region—the reduction of inequality—seems to be one that is very difficult to prescribe. A slight decrease in inequality would contribute significantly to reducing the extreme deprivation in the region. However, apparently only a very few economies in the region have been able to achieve this even in small measure."[74]

José Nun, text prepared for PRODDAL, 2002.

complicated if we take into account the fact that hopes for, and expectations of, improvement in some of these areas are generally linked to the evolution of one or more of the other aspects of citizenship.

To summarize, the development of democracy in Latin America demands that the problems that hinder the enforcement and the expansion of social citizenship be tackled decisively. To this end, it seems necessary to concentrate on attacking poverty and creating high-quality jobs, bearing in mind that this will be very difficult to achieve without also reducing inequality in the region.

Deficiencies in the field of social citizenship are one of the most urgent challenges confronting the region.

■ Most of the data reveal a serious situation. Latin America is known to have widespread needs in multiple areas of social citizenship. The improvements achieved in some countries in this respect, although significant in themselves, are minor in comparison with the scale of the problem.

■ There are overlapping types of social exclusion. Deprivation in one sphere of social citizenship often coincides with deprivation in another. This situation suggests that there may be structural deficits where social citizenship is concerned.

■ The social outlook for the region is therefore bleak; the search for an extended and better kind of social citizenship, starting with the fulfillment of people's basic needs, represents a key challenge for Latin America.

74 Economic Commission for Latin America and the Caribbean (ECLAC), International Institute for Democracy and Electoral Assistance (IDEA) and UNDP, 2003, p. 49.

■ How Latin Americans see their Democracy

The support of citizens is key to democratic sustainability. History shows that democracies were overthrown by political forces that relied on the support (or at least the passivity) of an important segment and, on occasion, the bulk of the citizenry. Democracies become vulnerable when, among other factors, authoritarian political forces find fertile ground for their activities in the attitudes of citizens. Hence the importance of understanding and analyzing the support that democracy can count on in Latin America.

A survey of citizens' perceptions of democracy was carried out in May 2002 with that very purpose in mind. It took into account the views of 19,508 people, covering more than 400 million inhabitants in the 18 countries included in the Report.

An initial look at people's perceptions identified in previous surveys by Latinobarómetro indicates that, in 1996, 61 percent of those interviewed in the region preferred democracy to any other kind of regime; in 2002, the proportion was 57 percent. That preference for democracy, though, does not necessarily imply strong support. In fact, many people who profess a preference for democracy vis-à-vis other regimes have highly undemocratic attitudes to-

WEAKNESSES IN THE PREFERENCE FOR DEMOCRACY   TABLA 46
COMPARED WITH OTHER SYSTEMS OF GOVERNMENT, 2002

Specific Attitudes related to the Relevance and Importance of Democracy	Percentage of the Total Sample of all 18 Countries	Percentage of those who prefer Democracy to any other Form of Government
Believe that economic development is more important than democracy.	56.3	48.1
Would support an authoritarian government if it resolved economic problems.	54.7	44.9
Do not believe that democracy solves a country's problems.	43.9	35.8
Agree that the President should be above the law.	42.8	38.6
Believe that democracy can exist without political parties.	40.0	34.2
Believe that democracy can exist without a national legislature.	38.2	32.2
Agree that the President should impose order by force.	37.2	32.3
Agree that the President should control media.	36.1	32.4
Agree that the President should ignore the national legislature and parties.	38.1	32.9
Do not believe that democracy is essential to development.	25.1	14.2

Note: n varies between 16,183 (democracy may exist without a national legislature) and 17,194 (democracy versus economic development).
Source: calculation by PRODDAL based on data from Latinobarómetro 2002.

wards various social issues. In 2002, almost one-half (48.1 percent) of those surveyed who said that they preferred democracy to any other regime had an equal preference for economic development over democracy, and a similar percentage (44.9) who said that they preferred democracy were willing to support an authoritarian government if it could solve the country's economic problems.

A fair number of people who expressed a preference for democracy oppose some of its basic rules. Approximately one in three believe that democracy can function without institutions like a legislature and political parties.

These responses amount to a sort of 'wake-up call': a substantial proportion of Latin Americans value economic development more than democracy and would be willing to put democracy to one side if a non-democratic government could help to solve their economic problems.

In an attempt to scratch beneath the surface with regard to this situation, we analyzed the answers to 11 questions that reflect not only a preference for democracy but also attitudes concerning the way in which power is exercised in a democratic system, the basic institutions of democracy and various social matters.[75]

Three Orientations towards Democracy: Democratic, Ambivalent and Non-Democratic

We have identified three categories into which we group the opinions and attitudes of Latin Americans towards democracy: democratic; ambivalent; and non-democratic (Graph 5).

The *democrats* are those whose replies to all of the questions were in favor of democracy. They prefer democracy over any 'other form of government' and they support the implementation of democratic rules with respect to government even at the most difficult of times. Asked to choose between democracy and development, the democrats said that they preferred the former or that both were equally important objectives. Moreover, they believe that "it is essential for a country to be democratic in order to be developed." Democrats disagree with *delegative*[76] approaches to solving national problems: they oppose the President acting without the consent of the legislature, controlling the media and imposing order by force, even in times of crisis.

The *non-democrats* are those who gave non-democratic responses to all of the questions

75 See the methodology used to construct the Democratic Support Index. Below are the key questions that guide this part of the research (the original survey questions were in Spanish, and have been translated by PRODDAL). Support for democracy: (1) Which one of the following sentences are you most in agreement with? a) Democracy is preferable to all other forms of government. b) Under some circumstances, an authoritarian government can be preferable to a democratic one. c) For people like me, it doesn't matter whether we have a democratic or a nondemocratic regime. (2) If you had to choose between democracy and economic development, which would you say is more important? a) Economic development is most important. b) Democracy is most important. c) Both are equally important. (3) In order for (country) to become a developed country, do you believe democracy is indispensable as a system of government? Or do you think it is possible to become a developed country with a system of government other than democracy? a) Democracy is indispensable for a country to become developed. b) It is not indispensable; it is possible to become a developed country with another system of government. (4) I would not mind a non democratic government in power if it could solve the economic problem: a) very much in agreement; b) in agreement; c) in disagreement; d) very much in disagreement. (5) Some people say that democracy permits us to find solutions to the problems that we have in (country). Others say that democracy does not help with solving problems. Which statement best expresses your viewpoint?: a) Democracy solves problems; b) Democracy doesn't solve problems. *Support for democratic institutions* (6) a) You can't have democracy without a National Congress; b) Democracy can function without a National Congress. (7) a) You can't have democracy without political parties; b) Democracy can function without parties. *The delegative dimension* If the country has serious dificulties, are you very much in agreement, in agreement, in disagreement or very much in disagreement that the president should?: (8) a) Not be limited by what the laws say; (9) b) Secure order by force; (10) c) Control the media; (11) d) Bypass Congress and the parties.
76 The concept of delegative democracy was coined by Guillermo O'Donnell (1994) and refers to countries where elections are free and clean, but where those who govern (especially Presidents) believe that they are authorized to act without

GRAPH 5

Profile of Orientations towards Democracy, Latin America 2002 [1]

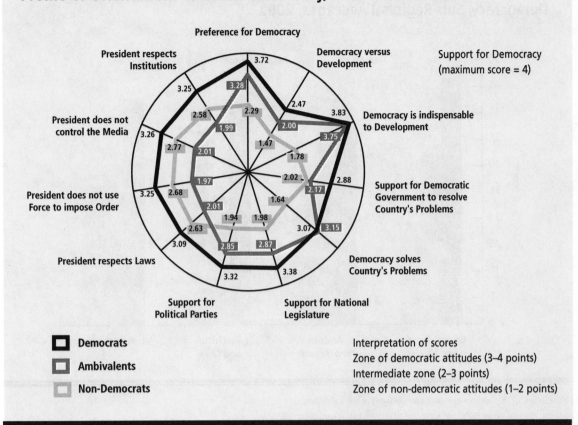

Notes: n = 15,216

(1) Each question was codified so that its score could fit within a range of one to four, so that the score of four would always be equated with a pro-democratic attitude. All averages are based on valid samples of different sizes. For Latin America the general valid sample varies between 14,532 and 15,216 people.

Source: calculation by PRODDAL based on data from Latinobarómetro 2002.

asked. They prefer an authoritarian regime to a democratic one. They believe that a country's development is more important than preserving democracy and they do not believe that democ-

racy is essential for development. Asked to choose between the two, they opt for the latter. They agree that "a non-democratic government might take power if it could resolve the coun-

---

institutional restrictions. With regard to this strongly majoritarian and consultative concept of political power, the person in power is still democratic in the sense that there are free and clean elections and there is no intention to limit them in the future. But those in power feel no obligation to accept the restrictions and controls put in place by the other constitutional institutions (the legislature and the judiciary) or by the various State or social supervisory organisms; on the contrary, they normally ignore, annul or co-opt these entities. The basic idea behind this concept is that the voters see the President as the exclusive embodiment of democratic legitimacy, and, as a result, they entrust him/her with the right and obligation to resolve all of the country's problems as he/she sees fits. This idea—which does not exclude the notion of clean, free elections in future, which can lead to a change in the executive and the party—accords the President the authority to engage in anti-institutional acts, including, as we shall see, the taking of decisions ('to put things in order' or 'to resolve crises') that are totally authoritarian. This does not, of course, imply that the delegative President is omnipotent, as that would conflict with the remaining working elements of public institutions, with various de facto relations of power and, depending on the circumstances, with opposition movements, especially when it comes to accountability to the whole of society.

GRAPH 6

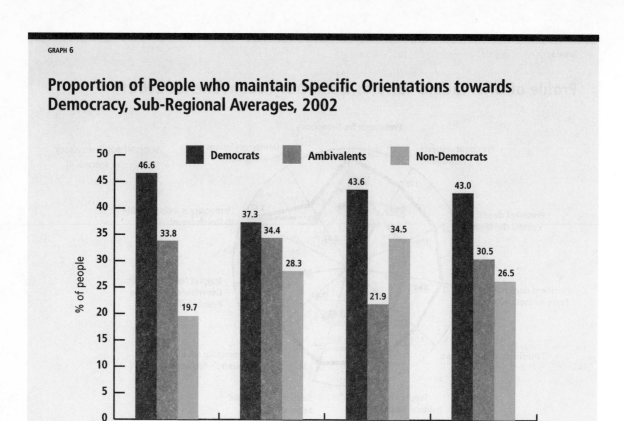

Proportion of People who maintain Specific Orientations towards Democracy, Sub-Regional Averages, 2002

Legend: ■ Democrats ■ Ambivalents ■ Non-Democrats

Central America and Mexico: 46.6, 33.8, 19.7
Andean Sub-Region: 37.3, 34.4, 28.3
Mercosur and Chile: 43.6, 21.9, 34.5
Latin America: 43.0, 30.5, 26.5

Note: n = 15,216. The figures indicate percentages of the valid sample.
Source: calculation by PRODDAL based on data from Latinobarómetro 2002.

try's economic problems." They agree that "the President should not have to consult Congress and political parties if the country has serious difficulties." Finally, they do not seem to rate very highly the likelihood of a country's problems being solved under a democratic system, even when it is a delegative sort of democracy. In short, they prefer to substitute any other system of government for democracy.

Those who belong to the *ambivalent* group have ambiguous opinions, if not contradictory ones. The views that they express are broadly consistent with delegative notions of democracy. In principle they support democracy, but they believe that it is valid to take anti-democratic decisions when running the government if circumstances so demand. As a consequence, on some topics, they share the opinions of the democrats and on others they share those of the non-democrats. Like the democrats, they say that they prefer a democratic government

to an authoritarian one, they believe that "democracy solves problems" and they are convinced that democracy is essential for development. But, like the non-democrats, they believe that it is more important to develop a country than to preserve democracy and they would not object if a non-democratic government came to power if it managed to resolve the country's economic problems. Moreover, ambivalents distinguish themselves from the other two groups by accepting that, in times of crisis, the President may impose order through force, control the media and ignore the national legislative body and the parties.

It may seem paradoxical that the ambivalent, who say that they prefer democracy, express agreement with government measures that are clearly authoritarian. We believe that these opinions are derived from the delegative concept of democracy held by these interviewees. This is an important finding: the preference of those who are ambivalent towards a democratic leadership, yet at the same time support authoritarian features in order to make it more efficient, could possibly be capitalized on by adversaries of democracy.

Scope of the Orientations towards Democracy

In 2002, those with democratic attitudes constituted the largest group in Latin America. However, they were not strong enough to form a majority (Graph 6), comprising 43 percent of the consultees in the 18 countries. To achieve a majority the democrats require the support of the ambivalent—the second largest group (30.5 percent). Finally, the non-democrats make up the smallest group in the region (26.5 percent).

Each sub-region is different: in some, democrats prevail numerically, in others, there is equilibrium, and, in still others, there is polarization. In Central America and Mexico, democrats make up almost one-half of the population, more than twice as many people as are in the non-democrat category and significantly more than in the ambivalent grouping. In the Mercosur countries (Argentina, Brazil, Paraguay and Uruguay) and Chile, the situation is polarized: the most extensive orientation groups are those that are completely opposed to each other, the democrats and non-democrats. Also the difference in size between the two groups is narrow. Finally, in the Andean sub-region, there is virtually equilibrium among the three orientations: the difference between the democrats and the ambivalent is small, and neither enjoys much of an advantage over the non-democrats.

Distance between the Different Orientations towards Democracy

Which profile (democrats or non-democrats) are the ambivalents closest to? In most Latin American countries, the existence of a majority that supports democracy depends on the ability of democrats to attract the backing of the ambivalent. The distance between the two is relevant when considering the effect of the size of the democratic orientation.

When it comes to support for representational institutions (the national legislature and political parties), preference for democracy, and whether democracy is essential to a country's development and to resolving its problems, the opinions of the ambivalent and the democrats are substantially closer than those of the ambivalent and the non-democrats. On two topics in particular—'Democracy solves problems' and 'Democracy is essential for a country's development'—there is practically no difference between the ambivalent and the democrats. Moreover, in all of these cases those who are ambivalent fall within the democratic attitude zone, achieving a high score on the respective scales.

When it comes to delegative attitudes and the tendency to support a non-democratic government if "that is the way to solve the country's problems," however, the situation is inverted. The distance between the non-democrats and the ambivalent is substantially less than that between the democrats and the ambivalent. On two questions in particular the distance between the ambivalent and the democrats is remarkable: support for a President who ignores the legislature and political parties; and support for a possible non-democratic government.

Finally, with respect to the choice between democracy and development, we note that all three orientations have moved 'down the scale': democrats are in the intermediate attitude range (the average score is 2.47), the ambivalent are edging towards the non-democratic attitude range (the average score is 2.0) and non-democrats have moved into a completely closed position (the average score is 1.47).

Even though the differences among these orientations remain true to type, the fact that

> In most Latin American countries, the existence of a majority that supports democracy depends on the ability of democrats to attract the backing of the ambivalent.

BOX 36

How many 'Pure' Democrats and Non-Democrats are there in Latin America?

Of all the people interviewed in the 18 countries of Latin America, only 142 'pure' democrats and seven 'pure' non-democrats were identified (together constituting just one out of every 100 persons). A 'pure' non-democrat is a person who with regard to all aspects of the study of orientations towards democracy always chose the answer most hostile to democracy. Since the scale used ranges between one (attitude most hostile to democracy) and four (most in favor of democracy), these non-democrats achieved an average of one. A 'pure' democrat, meanwhile, is a person who in all cases chose the answer most favorable to democracy. The average score of the pure democrats was thus the highest possible (four).

The vast majority of those interviewed have points of view that are more mixed and less extreme, although these people also have clearly discernible leanings. As has been pointed out, the democrats tend to score at the higher end of the scale with respect to all of the topics under consideration: 70 percent of those so classified have an average score of between 3.01 and four—9.8 percent of ambivalents also achieved this

score (no non-democrats did so). In the zone reflecting non-democratic attitudes, however, where the average is between one and two points, non-democrats predominate, constituting 75 percent of the people situated in this range.

In the intermediate zone (average score of between two and three points), a less defined situation is evident, as significant proportions of all three orientations co-exist there. It is still possible, nonetheless, to identify tendencies. First, nearly all of the ambivalents are to be found in this range (84.2 percent). Second, there is a significant non-democratic presence in the zone between 2.01 and 2.50, below the median point on the scale, and there is a degree of concentration of democrats in the area between 2.51 and 3, above the median point. In both cases, these zones are adjacent to their respective 'natural ranges'.

In short, even though in reality there are few 'pure types', the study managed to group people in orientation clusters according to their support for democracy.

GRAPH 7

Democrats, Ambivalents and Non-Democrats according to their Position on the Democratic Attitude Scales, Latin America, 2002

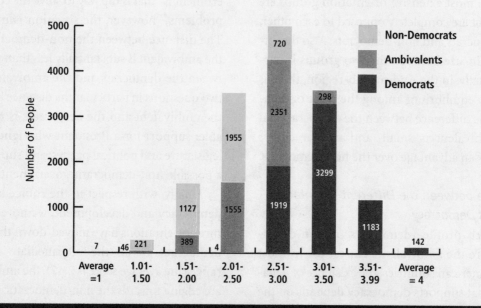

Note: n = 15,216 people. Figures represent the average score on the scales measuring attitudes towards the 11 variables under consideration for the study of orientations towards democracy. The scales have a range of between one and four, where one is the response that is most hostile to democracy and four is the response that is most favorable.

Source: calculation by PRODDAL based on data from Latinobarómetro 2002.

DISTANCE BETWEEN THE ORIENTATIONS TOWARDS DEMOCRACY

TABLE 47

ON THE DIFFERENT TOPICS STUDIED LATIN AMERICA, 2002

Score on the Scale of Democratic Attitudes (1)	Distance between Orientations (2)			
	Less Distance between Democrats and Ambivalents	Di	Less Distance between Non-Democrats and Ambivalents	Di
Zone of democratic attitudes (3–4 points)	Prefer democracy	0.45		
	Democracy essential to development	0.04		
	Democracy solves problems	0.05		
	Support national legislature	0.57		
	Support parties	0.52		
Intermediate zone (2–3 points)	Democracy versus development	0.90	Support democratic government to resolve problems	4.61
			President respects the law	1.76
			President does not use force	1.80
			President does not control the media	1.65
			President ignores the legislature and parties	2.13
Zone of non-democratic attitudes (1–2 points)				

Notes: values for n = between 14.532 (p41st) and 15.216 (p39st and p40st).

(1) The range of variation in the scales used to measure democratic attitudes in response to the questions asked in the survey of orientations towards democracy was standardized. A value of four was assigned to attitudes most favorable towards democracy, and a value of one to most negative attitudes towards democracy.

(2) See the explanation of the concept of distance and its respective indicator under the title 'Third dimension: distance between orientations' in the DSI Technical Note in the Annexes.

Source: calculation by PRODDAL based on data from Latinobarómetro 2002.

the average score is lower than for previous questions in all three cases is worthy of mention: the choice between economic development and democracy is where there is the greatest tension among the preferences of Latin Americans.

From a general standpoint, the distance between the attitudes of the ambivalent and the democrats is almost the same as that between the ambivalent and the non-democrats. For now, the ambivalent do not lean in either direction.

In sum, the relatively similar distance between the democrats and the ambivalent, and between the ambivalent and the non-democrats, seems to be the result of an underlying strain: the greater degree of sympathy between ambivalents and democrats with regard to the subject of support for democracy and its institutions compensates for the greater degree of sympathy between ambivalents and non-democrats with respect to delegative attitudes.

Social Profile of People with Different Orientations towards Democracy

The social origin of those with a particular attitude towards democracy is heterogeneous: people who hold a certain view do not for the most part belong to a specific group or social class. In particular, the social composition of democrats shows that support for democracy is fairly evenly distributed across the different sectors of society. Even so, the following relationships are apparent:

■ People with higher education (complete or incomplete) are most likely to be democratic.

SOCIO-ECONOMIC PROFILE OF PEOPLE ACCORDING TO THEIR

ORIENTATION TOWARDS DEMOCRACY, 2002

TABLE 48

Categories		Structure of the Sample	Orientation towards Democracy			Significance (5)
			Democrats	Ambivalents	Non-Democrats	
Central America and Mexico (1)	% of people	n=6,402	46.6	33.8	19.7	..
Andean sub-region	% of people	n=4,377	37.3	34.4	28.3	..
Mercosur and Chile	% of people	n=4,438	43.6	21.9	34.5	..
Latin America	% of people	n=15,217	43.0	30.5	26.5	..
Sex	% men	51.5	52.9	50.8	50.0	**
	% women	48.5	47.1	49.2	50.0	
Age	% 16-29 years	37.6	35.1	38.5	40.8	**
	% 30-64 years	54.3	56.3	53.3	52.2	
	% 65-99 years	8.0	8.6	8.1	7.0	
	Average age	38.16	39.24	37.83	46.8	**
Level of education	% no schooling	7.2	6.3	8.5	7.2	**
	% 1-6 years	32.0	30.4	34.2	31.8	
	% 7-12 years	43.1	41.9	43.2	45.0	
	% enrolled in or completed higher education	17.7	21.4	14.1	16.0	
	Average number of years of schooling	9.33	9.69	8.84	9.29	**
Economic level (2)	% low	41.5	40.0	44.8	40.2	*
	% medium	49.2	49.5	47.3	50.9	
	% high	9.3	10.5	7.9	8.9	
	Average according to economic index	4.01	4.12	3.84	4.05	**
	Average according to index of socio-economic mobility (4)	-0.44	-0.42	-0.38	-0.52	**
Cohort (3)	% socialized under an authoritarian regime	51.8	48.8	53.3	55.1	**
	% socialized during a transition period	11.6	11.9	11.0	11.9	
	% socialized under democracy	36.6	39.4	35.7	33.0	
	Average number of years of socialization in a non-democracy	6.36	6.04	6.49	6.74	**

Notes:

(1) Includes the Dominican Republic.

(2) Based on an economic index put together using information on possession of electrical appliances in the home and the education of the head of the household. This index can vary between 0 and 10. If the index is between 0 and 3.33, the economic level is considered low; if it is between 3.34 and 6.66, the economic level is considered medium; and if it is between 6.67 and 10, the economic level is considered high.

(3) By looking at the number of years that a person spent being socialized under a democratic regime, it can be determined whether he/she was socialized under a democracy, during a transition period or under an authoritarian regime. The period of socialization is judged to be 11 years (between the ages of seven and 17).

(4) The index of socio-economic mobility is based on interviewees' evaluations of their parents' economic situation and comparisons with their own circumstances.

(5) An asterisk (*) indicates that the measure of association used or the Analysis of Variance (ANOVA) is significant at five percent. Two asterisks (**) mean that the result is significant at one percent. When the degree of association or ANOVA is not relevant, this is indicated by two consecutive dots (..). For the tests carried out in each case, please consult the Statistical Compendium.

Source: calculations based on data processed by PRODDAL from Latinobarómetro 2002.

- There is little difference, though, between people with primary and secondary education.
- Democrats have received more education than their parents.
- The young figure relatively more among non-democrats.
- Non-democrats are, on average, people who believe that their economic position has worsened relative to that of their parents and more than has that of other groups.
- Non-democrats least expect their children to experience an improvement in their economic circumstances.

A little over one-half of the people in Latin America grew up and were socialized under an authoritarian regime (51.8 percent). When we look at democrats the proportion falls to 48.8 percent; among non-democrats, it rises to 55.1 percent.

Heterogeneity

Our opinion study also allows us to explore whether, apart from sharing opinions on democracy, people with the same orientation also have the same attitudes regarding what a country should be doing and who should receive support at election time.

The data gathered reveal that these orientations are politically heterogeneous. In particular, people who share a positive attitude towards democracy are not concentrated in any particular political group, nor do they hold opinions that differ significantly from other consultees. However, they do reveal some interesting differences:

- Non-democrats tend to think more than others that the main problem for them is not being solved or even that the country is going backwards.
- Non-democrats tend to perceive more frequently that the political sector they belong to does not have an equal chance of coming to power as others.
- Non-democrats tend to be less satisfied with democracy than democrats and am-

bivalents (only 19 percent of them are satisfied, compared with 40 percent and 43.9 percent, respectively).
- Non-democrats tend to trust institutions and public figures less than other groups do.
- Non-democrats believe more often than the rest that politicians lie in order to be elected.
- Democrats tend to want the State to play a more proactive role in developing the country than the non-democrats or the ambivalent do.
- There are no major differences of opinion on the primary national problems in need of resolution: democrats, ambivalents and non-democrats all agree that poverty and unemployment are the most serious problems.

From the analysis of the profile of non-democrats and their perceptions of political and economic realities it is possible also to prove that this orientation is associated with less education, socialization under authoritarian regimes, low social mobility in comparison with their parents, less positive perspectives regarding their children's future and the likely resolution of public problems, and significant lack of trust in institutions and politicians.

Ways in which Citizens participate in Political Life

Although it is not possible to determine in general the optimum level of participation that should exist in a democracy, any democracy requires a certain degree of citizen participation. In the most dynamic democracies people find numerous ways of exercising this right.

By looking at citizen participation we can determine which of the orientations already examined is the most active and thus add a new element with which to judge how much support for democracy there is in the region, as well as how vulnerable it is.

Most people in Latin America are not disconnected from the political and social lives

POLITICAL PROFILE OF PEOPLE ACCORDING TO THEIR
ORIENTATION TOWARDS DEMOCRACY, 2002

TABLE 49

	Categories	Structure of the Sample	Orientation towards Democracy			Significance (2)
			Democrats	Ambivalents	Non-Democrats	
Central America and Mexico (1)	% of people	n=6,402	46.6	33.8	19.7	..
Andean sub-region	% of people	n=4,377	37.3	34.4	28.3	..
Mercosur and Chile	% of people	n=4,438	43.6	21.9	34.5	..
Latin America	% of people	n=15,217	43.0	30.5	26.5	..
Vote	% that voted at last election	78.3	82.3	76.9	73.6	**
	% that did not vote out of disillusionment or disinterest	8.9	7.2	10.2	10.2	**
	% that indicates they belong to a political party	47.5	51.7	46.6	41.7	**
	Average according to index of voting efficiency	3.01	3.03	3.13	2.84	**
Democracy	% that gives negative meaning to democracy	5.4	2.4	3.8	12.8	**
	% that is satisfied with the way democracy works	35.6	40.0	43.9	19.0	**
Other political attitudes	% that profess not to have equal political chances	32.5	29.5	31.0	39.3	**
	% that say that others should be treated with consideration	80.7	79.0	78.9	85.5	
	Average on scale from left to right	5.93	5.77	6.33	5.75	**
	Average according to index of confidence in institutions and public figures	1.93	1.97	2.03	1.77	**
Strategies for development	% that believes that public institutions offer no solutions or should be privatized	5.0	3.8	5.1	6.8	**
	% in favor of administrative reform measure	42.0	41.8	43.6	40.7	
	% in favor of improving State accountability	53.0	54.4	51.3	52.6	
	Average according to index of economic intervention by the State	3.82	4.05	3.55	3.76	**

(CONT. IN P. 141)

	Categories	Structure of the Sample	Orientation towards Democracy			Significance (2)
			Democrats	Ambivalents	Non-Democrats	
Most urgent problems	% that mentions unemployment, poverty, inequality and insufficient income	60.2	62.6	58.2	58.6	**
	% that mentions corruption	12.0	12.3	11.6	12.0	ns
	% that mentions political violence	7.4	5.7	7.8	9.6	**
Answer to most urgent problems	% that thinks the country is going backward in trying to solve problems or that there is no solution	32.0	31.9	27.4	37.8	**
	% that thinks that the most urgent problem is being solved	7.5	6.9	9.5	6.3	**
	% that mentions an urgent problem not raised in the campaign	82.9	84.2	80.3	83.6	ns
	% that thinks politicians do not fulfill campaign promises because they are liars	64.4	65.3	58.3	69.7	**

Notes:

(1) Includes the Dominican Republic.

(2) An asterisk (*) indicates that the degree of association used or the Analysis of Variance (ANOVA) is significant at five percent. Two asterisks (**) mean that the result is significant at one percent. The notation 'ns' is used when the test is non-significant, neither at one percent nor at five percent. When the measure of association or ANOVA is not relevant, this is indicated by two consecutive dots (..). For the tests carried out in each case, consult the Statistical Compendium.

Source: calculations based on data processed by PRODDAL from Latinobarómetro 2002.

of their countries. Only a small minority of those consulted (7.3 percent of the total) had not engaged in any act of citizen participation in the past few years. Another 22.1 percent said that their only act of civic participation was to have voted in the previous presidential election. All in all, around 30 percent of these people may be categorized as 'unmobilized citizens': either they do not exercise their right to participate or they do so only intermittently, via the action that requires least personal effort: voting.

Almost four out of every ten persons interviewed (37.6) intervene in the public life of their country in ways that go beyond participation in elections. In addition to voting, they contact public authorities when there are problems that affect their community, they take part in public demonstrations, and they donate their time, labor or money to initiatives to resolve community problems. These are all citizens who exercise their rights actively.

Two groups stand out among them. First, there is a very active sector composed of people who literally 'do a bit of everything'. They are active with respect to all of the aforementioned acts of citizen participation. In Latin America, these citizens make up approximately 25 percent of the total, a figure that is only slightly below that of unmobilized citizens.

TABLE 50

SOCIO-ECONOMIC PROFILE OF PEOPLE ACCORDING TO TYPES OF CITIZEN PARTICIPATION, 2002

Categories		Structure of Sample	Methods of Citizen Participation						Significance (2)	
			Does not participate	Only votes	Participates with or without voting	Politically Active with or without voting	Participates and is Politically Active without voting	Participates, is Politically Active and votes	(Tests carried out by comparing People who Participate via these six Methods)	(Tests carried out by comparing People who do not do anything or only vote or by comparing People who are only Politically Active or who combine this with some other form of Participation)
Central America and Mexico (1)	% of people	n=7,387	7.3	20.2	35.2	6.9	5.0	25.4	...	...
Andean sub-region	% of people	n=5,178	7.9	23.1	34.3	8.0	4.3	22.6	...	...
Mercosur and Chile	% of people	n=5,330	6.6	23.8	29.2	11.1	5.2	24.0	...	...
Latin America	% of people	n=17,895	7.3	22.1	33.2	8.5	4.8	24.2	...	...
Sex	% men	48.5	41.8	45.5	46.3	49.0	52.1	55.4	**	**
	% women	51.5	58.2	54.5	53.7	51.0	47.9	44.6		
Age	% 16-29 years	33.1	51.0	28.3	34.9	31.7	49.7	26.8	**	ns
	% 30-64 years	57.8	38.4	59.8	57.3	58.4	44.6	65.1		
	% 65-99 years	9.0	10.6	11.9	7.8	9.8	5.8	8.1		
	Average age	39.68	35.78	42.06	38.72	40.58	33.96	40.83	**	*
Level of education	% no schooling	9.2	14.1	11.7	9.3	6.9	9.2	6.3	**	**
	% 1-6 years	35.4	38.5	37.4	37.6	33.2	30.6	31.2		
	% 7-12 years	39.5	39.8	38.4	39.9	43.2	43.7	37.7		
	% enrolled in or completed higher education	15.9	7.6	12.6	13.2	16.6	16.5	24.8		
	Average number of years of schooling	8.79	7.64	8.23	8.58	9.18	8.97	9.77	**	**

(CONT. IN P. 143)

TABLE 50 (CONT. DE P. 142).

SOCIO-ECONOMIC PROFILE OF PEOPLE ACCORDING TO TYPES OF CITIZEN PARTICIPATION, 2002

Categories	Structure of Sample	Methods of Citizen Participation						Significance (2)	
		Does not participate	Only votes	Participates with or without voting	Politically Active with or without voting	Participates and is Politically Active without voting	Participates, is Politically Active and votes	(Tests carried out by comparing People who Participate via these six Methods)	(Tests carried out by comparing People who do not do anything or only vote or by comparing People who are only Politically Active or who combine this with some other form of Participation)
Economic level (3)									
% low	45.4	52.8	51.3	47.6	42.9	44.1	35.8		
% medium	46.5	43.2	42.7	45.7	49.3	45.8	51.3	**	**
% high	8.1	4.0	6.0	6.7	7.8	10.2	12.9		
Average according to economic index	3.85	3.45	3.60	3.73	3.95	4.02	4.29	**	**
Issue not on the agenda (4)									
% that mentions an issue not on the agend	18.4	31.4	27.2	14.5	21.7	11.2	13.8		
% that does not mention an issue not on the agenda	81.6	68.6	72.8	85.5	78.3	88.8	86.2		
Confidence (5)									
Average level of confidence in institutions and public figures	1.91	1.84	1.88	1.90	1.96	1.89	1.97	**	**

Notes:

(1) Includes the Dominican Republic.

(2) An asterisk (*) indicates that the measure of association used or the Analysis of Variance (ANOVA) is significant at five percent. Two asterisks (**) mean that the result is significant at one percent. The notation 'ns' is used when the test is non-significant, neither at one percent nor at five percent. When the degree of association or ANOVA is not relevant, this is indicated by two consecutive dots (..). For the tests carried out in each case, consult the Statistical Compendium.

(3) Based on an economic index put together using information on possession of electrical appliances in the home and the education of the head of the household. This index can vary between zero and ten. If the index is between zero and 3.33, the economic level is considered low; if it is between 3.34 and 6.66, the economic level is considered medium; and if it is between 6.67 and ten, the economic level is considered high.

(4) Based on question p27u in the UNDP Proprietary Section of Latinobarómetro 2002: "What issue interests you which you feel that candidates at the last election did not dare to deal with?"

(5) Based on the index of confidence in institutions and public figures, constructed using answers to questions about trust in 'the legal system', 'the government', 'local government', 'the national legislature', 'political parties' and 'the people who run the country'.

☐ Unmobilized citizen—does not participate politically or only takes part in action that is sporadic and requires the least effort, that is, voting. May engage in social activities.

Active citizen—contacts the authorities and attends public demonstrations but is not active in all areas of citizen participation.

Highly participative citizen: active in all areas of citizen participation.

Source: calculations based on data processed by PRODDAL from Latinobarómetro 2002

A second sector, comprising around one in eight people (13.3 percent), also engages in political participative activities that go beyond voting, but they do not extend as far as those that the former are involved in. These people combine voting with at least one other kind of political participation: they vote and contact the authorities; they vote and participate in public demonstrations; and, in some cases, they may also collaborate with their communities. Among their number is one group of citizens that participates politically but not in elections: its members abstain from voting but they do contact public authorities and take part in public demonstrations (4.9 percent).

Finally, one-third (33.2 percent) of Latin Americans are socially active people, most of whom involve themselves in politics intermittently through voting. Members of this group are in an intermediate position between unmobilized citizens and politically active ones. On the one hand, they collaborate in community-based organizations and in this sense do exercise their right to participate in those activities that interest them. On the other hand, that action takes place mainly in a non-political sphere.

Citizen Participation and Orientations towards Democracy

A final aspect of the analysis of participation is its connection with different orientations towards democracy. In Latin America democrats tend to participate slightly more actively in the political life of their country than ambivalents or non-democrats. Some 43 percent of democrats engage in other political activities, such as contacting authorities and public officials and taking part in public demonstrations, as well as in almost all cases voting; 37 percent of non-democrats may be classified as active, as may 39 percent of the ambivalent. It is particularly important to appreciate that democrats are not always the most participative citizens.

Profiles of Citizenship Intensity

An integrated analysis of the size of the different orientations towards democracy, as well as the distance between them and the different levels of activism, gives us an idea of the extent to which citizens support democracy. This is the rationale behind the Democratic Support Index.

The DSI helps us to evaluate the current balance of forces and the potential for creating broad-based citizen coalitions to support democracy, including sectors with ambivalent views. It is a tool that distinguishes favorable political situations from unfavorable, high-risk ones. In favorable situations there is a balance of forces that is positive for democracy—since democrats are in the majority, they are the most politically active, and the views of the ambivalent are relatively close to those of the democrats. In the opposite situation, when the balance of forces is negative, the non-democrats are in the majority, they are more active and they are closest to the ambivalents. When applying the DSI in the future, therefore, we may be able to analyse changes in the political situation and assess the bases of democratic stability by looking at the strength of citizens' support.

The sources of information for the DSI may also be used to study *citizenship intensity*—that is to say, how people exercise their status as citizens, if they do at all.

The concept of citizen intensity is derived from the term *low-intensity citizenship*, coined by Guillermo O'Donnell.[77] Citizenship intensity means the free and active exercise of rights and the fulfillment of the duties that are inherent to the status of citizen. In order to approach this topic we utilize a typology of profiles of citizenship intensity that enables us to classify people according to the way in which they exercise their status as citizens.

With the information based on the different attitudes towards democracy and the ways that citizens participate in Latin America, people can be classified according to four profiles of citizenship intensity:

77 Guillermo O'Donnell, 1993.

- Participative democrats.
- Unmobilized democrats.
- Unmobilized ambivalents and non-democrats.
- Participative ambivalents and non-democrats.

The first two groups share a democratic orientation but differ in terms of their level of participation in political life. The latter two groups both demonstrate a lack of commitment towards democracy and also differ with respect to their level of political participation.

Approximately one in five people in Latin America (18.9 percent) may be classified as participative democrats, while a little more than one-third of those consulted (34.9 percent) are ambivalent or unmobilized non-democrats. People in the latter category have doubts about democracy or oppose it, but they are not involved in political life. Those who are ambivalent or participative non-democrats are of roughly equal number to those who are participative democrats. According to our data, in Latin America, ap-

proximately one in five people (21.6 percent) may be classified as fitting this profile: persons who have doubts about democracy or are opposed to it, and are politically active.

The social characteristics of the people in each category of citizenship intensity are similar to those described above as regards to the social origin of groups with different attitudes towards democracy. In general terms, two conclusions can be drawn: the two groups that are most similar socially are, paradoxically, those that might well confront each other in the event of a crisis that threatens the stability of democracy: participative democrats, on the one hand, and ambivalents or participative non-democrats, on the other. With regard to age, education and economic status, members of these broad groupings have more in common with other members of the same group than with members of other groups.

The second conclusion is that unmobilized ambivalents or non-democrats seem to attract younger people of a lower economic status to a greater extent than the other three categories. The young are more numerous in this group than among participative democrats (38.4 per-

BOX 37

Low-Intensity Citizenship

In 1993 Guillermo O'Donnell came up with the theory that recognized that, in Latin America, a considerable proportion of citizens cannot exercise their civil rights and are discriminated against despite the fact that their political rights are reasonably well protected. He named this phenomenon 'low-intensity citizenship', and attributed it to objective barriers like the weak state of the democratic rule of law and the effect of extreme social inequality. A study of low-intensity citizenship therefore requires that different sources of information are drawn on, including both perceptions and official statistics.

As well as these obstacles, the intensity with which people exercise their citizenship may be affected by the degree to which they feel obliged to fulfill their duties and to exercise their rights. This is precisely the aspect examined in this chapter, using information derived from Latinobarómetro. Although this perspective is inspired by O'Donnell's thinking, it differs somewhat as it is centered

on the study of the activities and the behavior of individuals.

A democracy in which a significant number of citizens decide not to exercise their rights or to fulfill their duties is a democracy that is in trouble.

To develop this topic, a typology of profiles of citizen intensity has been constructed, classifying people according to the criteria set out below:

- In the context of citizens' duties, the obligation to accept the validity of democratic norms. We used the study of orientations towards democracy for this purpose.

- In the context of citizens' rights, the degree to which people participate in political life. Here we used the study on the ways in which citizens participate.

cent of the first two groups and 30 percent of the latter two groups). People with no education or with primary schooling that is either complete or incomplete (one to six years of schooling) are distributed in a similar way: proportionally, they tend to be found more often among unmobilized ambivalents or non-democrats. Yet people with complete or incomplete higher education are more numerous among participative democrats.

The Democratic Support Index

The results of the DSI for the region are positive for democracy. Democrats, in terms of the correlation of forces, are in a better position than their opponents, the non-democrats. In effect, democrats are the largest group in terms of basic orientation towards democracy and have tended (although only slightly) to participate more in the political and social life of their country than people with other profiles. Likewise, the ambivalent were slightly closer to the position of the democrats than the non-democrats (Graph 8). The aggregate regional DSI was 2.03.

In any case, the group to watch is the ambivalent one, as most democratic countries require the support of its members to form a majority of citizens. The factors most strongly associated with non-democrats should also be noted, as they are related to deficiencies in social citizenship and to poor prospects for economic and educational mobility, areas where we know the region still has serious shortcomings.

In summing up the results of this analysis, we find that:

- 43 percent of interviewees have a pro-democracy orientation, and thus comprise the largest group (based on the processing of data from the 2002 survey by Latinobarómetro);
- an obvious tension manifests itself when people are asked to choose between economic development and democracy—many seem to prefer the former;
- interviewees from countries where there are lower levels of social inequality tend to be more in favor of democracy;
- non-democrats tend to be people who have less education, were socialized un-

---

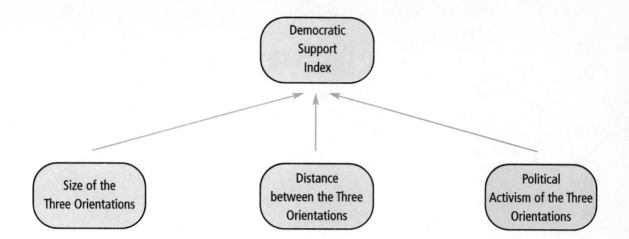

der an authoritarian regime, believe that they have less social mobility than their parents, have low expectations regarding the likelihood of a better future for their children, and have the least confidence in institutions;

- most citizens are not disconnected from political and social life in their respective country; and
- on average, democrats tend to participate slightly more actively in the political life of their country.

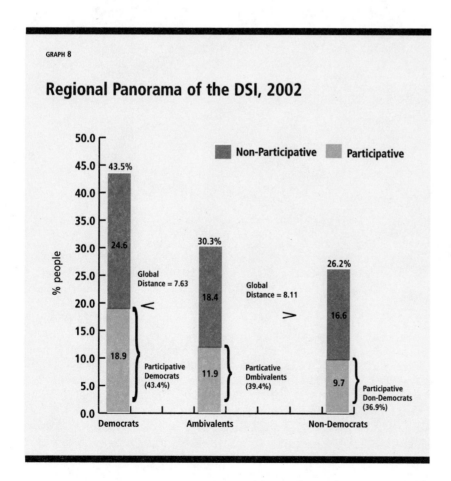

GRAPH 8

Regional Panorama of the DSI, 2002

Note: the percentages of people within each orientation do not exactly correlate with those shown in previous graphs because when information on orientation is combined with information on participation the absence of answers increases and causes variations.
Source: calculation by PRODDAL based on data from Latinobarómetro 2002.

◼ The Perceptions of Latin American Leaders

An exploration of the development of democracy in Latin America is enriched by the perceptions and views of the decision- makers who have had the greatest impact on political life in the region.

This section sets out and systematizes opinions expressed in the round of consultations with 231 leading Latin American figures, including 41 current and former Presidents and Vice-Presidents.

Here we analyze their views on the extent of development in our democracies, emphasizing citizen participation, the limits of democratic power, confidence in institutions, especially political parties, and relations with de facto powers, new and traditional. The consultees also pointed to tension among the variables of poverty, inequality and democracy, and highlighted problems encountered in elaborating the public agenda and challenges facing Latin America's democracies.

We would like to thank the 231 individuals who generously helped us and we regret that we were unable to speak to as many as we wished. Hence important leaders may have been omitted.

Profile of the Actors Consulted

There are two important factors to note with regard to these consultations, which took place between July 2002 and June 2003. First, we undertook no fewer than six interviews in each country, and we carried out more consultations in the larger countries (specifically Brazil and Mexico, where 34 and 25 leaders were consulted respectively).

Second, *this is not a random sample and therefore the data are not statistically representative.* The goal was to collate basic judgments on democracy in the region through interviews with a relevant group of influential leaders. The participants were not made aware of the interview agenda in advance.

At the end of the Report we provide more information on the methodology and the procedural criteria used. It is important to bear in mind that this study does not aspire to be a substitute for other opinion polls (but rather to complement them).

The interviewees are key players in the political, economic, social and cultural spheres of Latin America, whose importance arises from the outstanding nature of their careers: a) political leaders who hold, or have held, office at the highest institutional level, leaders of political parties, legislators, senior civil servants or mayors; b) labor leaders, business executives, academics, journalists, religious leaders and the heads of social movements or organizations, among other primary actors in society; and c) members of the armed forces.

Politicians make up 51 percent of those consulted. The remainder consists of a substantial proportion of business leaders (11 percent) and intellectuals (14 percent). The other categories are as follows: trade unionists (seven percent),

> There is also general agreement that more participation through political parties is good for democracy.

journalists (six percent), civil society leaders (seven percent), and members of the church (2.5 percent) and military (1.5 percent).

The Conceptual Point of Departure

One thing the statements have in common is that they emphasize a diagnosis that can be summarized as follows: never before has there been so much democracy in Latin America nor has the threat of a coup d'état been so controlled. And yet democracy has various weaknesses, such as those deriving from the low esteem in which political parties are held and the so-called *crisis of political society*.[78] Today, all of the region's countries satisfy the requirements associated with a democratic form of government and these are especially valued by those consulted, in contrast with the authoritarian past. From this perspective, the realization and consolidation of the basic attributes of democracy are considered to amount to a fundamental success and a key advancement for the region. This view leaves open a range of issues to be tackled and a host of unfulfilled objectives. There is widespread agreement that the construction of democracy in Latin America is incomplete, even in those countries where the process has been going on for longer.

Necessary Conditions for Democracy

Although they do not share a common understanding, Latin American leaders believe that political participation and controlling the exercise of power are two fundamental conditions for democracy, and that both have been strengthened in the past decade.

The Growth of Political Participation

Although the word 'participation' has different political meanings, a narrow interpretation usually restricts its scope to electoral participation. In its broader sense, it assumes a stable degree of connection with the area of public decision-making, principally through political parties or civil society organizations. Some intermediate definitions allude to more or less active forms of exercising citizenship, such as involvement in public consultations or in deliberative circles at the local level.

Consultees were almost unanimous in their view that greater involvement in whatever form tends to strengthen the workings of democratic institutions. In this broad sense, more participation generally appears to be preferable to less. As shown below, however, this generic opinion breaks down when a large number of interviewees refer to more specific forms of participation. There is also general agreement that more participation through political parties is good for democracy. The leaders consulted tend to share this view, even when they are skeptical as to whether the parties are functioning properly as channels for citizen participation, or whether they can once again play an active role in this area.

At the same time, the vast majority of those consulted concurred that participation of the population in the broad sense (that is, in terms of electing governments and defining their policies) has increased significantly over the past decade.

Two trends can be identified in interpreting the electoral act as an expression of political participation. In countries with a weaker democratic tradition, voting is seen as an act of participation because it permits the leveling of criticism at the old patrimonial structures, and, in any case, rewards or punishes those who govern.

78 M. A. Garretón, text prepared for PRODDAL, 2003.

The rise in voter turnout is associated with the increase in participation. In contrast, in democracies with greater continuity, the act of voting is seen as something ordinary, of no particular significance in evaluating the level of participation. For those interviewed in these countries participation implies more active forms of exercising citizens' rights.

In almost all of Latin America, the increase in participation is seen as one of the most visible characteristics of the democracy-building process. However, the reduction in, or the stagnation of, participation highlighted by leaders from Chile, Costa Rica and Uruguay seems to be common to democracies that see themselves as having a system of democracy that has deep historic roots. This does not mean that these countries are free of difficulties—in fact, two of them suffered the harsh experience of authoritarian rule; still, this is a different problem to the ones that confront countries where democracy has a more shallow foundation or has more recently taken root.

A leader consulted in Chile spelt this out: "The participation that democracy implies was more institutionalized [from the middle of the last century until the coup d'etat in 1973], fundamentally though political and social organizations. [...] Today, the reality in Chile is very worrying: [...] in ballots and elections the interest of citizens has been progressively diminishing and electoral abstention has increased. [...] [Now] there exists a more disorganized kind of participation, more circumstantial [...]. The political parties have lost presence and representativeness."

> **In almost all of Latin America, the increase in participation is seen as one of the most visible characteristics of the democracy-building process.**

A Brazilian leader, furthermore, put emphasis on the expansion of participation: "Poverty is diffuse, not organized [...]. As democratic power is perfected, so the bottom-up pressures increase [so that the problems of the poor are taken into account]. And this is what happens [...], [there are] more democratic organizations, more social organizations and more pressure from those at the bottom. This is the test we will now have to pass."

An important difference between countries with more established democracies and the rest are the channels through which participation is exercised. Those consulted in the first category tended to presuppose that parties are one of the natural conduits (not the only one but certainly one of the most important). By contrast, in a number of countries with less established democracies, some of those consulted were of the opinion that greater participation results when citizens are involved outside of the parties, either because they distance themselves sufficiently to cast their votes independently (for example, by supporting independent candidates) or because they join civil society organi-

---

HAS VOTER PARTICIPATION INCREASED IN LATIN AMERICA?	TABLE 51
Participation has increased	Honduras, Mexico, Bolivia, Brazil, Paraguay, Colombia, Dominican Republic, Venezuela, El Salvador, Panama, Ecuador, Guatemala, Nicaragua, Peru, Argentina
Participation has neither increased nor decreased	Costa Rica
Participation has decreased	Uruguay, Chile

Note: the countries are arranged according to 'balances of opinion', that is, the difference between those who say that participation increased and those who say that it decreased. The first country is the one with the most positive net assessment, that is, the one where the difference is most in favor of those who think that participation has increased. The other countries are then arranged in descending order.
Source: PRODDAL, round of consultations with Latin American leaders, 2002.

HAVE CONTROLS ON POWER INCREASED IN LATIN AMERICA?

TABLE 52

Controls have increased	El Salvador, Mexico, Peru, Brazil, Colombia, Dominican Republic, Guatemala, Chile, Honduras, Costa Rica, Bolivia, Paraguay
Controls have neither increased nor decreased	Uruguay, Nicaragua
Controls have decreased	Ecuador, Panamá, Argentina, Venezuela

Note: the countries are arranged according to 'balances of opinion', that is, the difference between those who say that controls on power have increased and those who say that they have decreased. The first country is the one with the most positive net assessment, that is, the one where the difference is most in favor of those who think that controls on power have increased. The other countries are then arranged in descending order. Source: PRODDAL, round of consultations with Latin American leaders, 2002.

zations that present themselves as alternatives to the parties. According to those consulted, this reality is connected not just to the fact that the parties have a bad image, but that they are seen as an obstacle to participation.

Again according to those interviewed, this phenomenon of greater participation through channels other than party structures often seems to be linked to another strong trend: the strengthening of deliberation and decision-making forums at the local level. This is the level—village, rural district, city and province—where we are beginning to see the emergence of leaders capable of attracting significant amounts of support and where civil society organizations may be better managed, which, in turn, makes it easier to involve citizens. This is how one of the leaders consulted in Colombia described it: "In Bogotá […] successive governments […] brought about a radical transformation of the city: […] public politics became a vital essence, […] what was public took a front seat to what was private, which was not as things had been seen before, […] the results for the citizens generated political conviction and continuity, [but] almost not at all for the parties, because the last three candidates to be elected have been independents."

A heterogeneous perception of social participation exists among those consulted. The new social movements and the rise in participation outside of the parties have meant that the former are seen by more than a few interviewees as a threat to governability. There is also disagreement about the institutionalization of social involvement. Some countries have institutional channels through which they can make demands viable and negotiate them. For some of those consulted, resistance to the development of institutional participation mechanisms has a negative effect on the expansion of democracy; others object to these processes for their single issue focus and for generating specific agreements that limit pluralism.

Increased Controls on the Exercise of Power

In most Latin American countries, the primary view is that governments are more controlled and restricted than in the past. In general, this is seen as something positive, because it implies the presence of a citizenry that is more alert and determined to exercise its rights (consistent with the perception of greater participation). That controls on the exercise of power have been significantly enhanced is the predominant belief of the leaders of 12 of the 18 countries studied, notably politicians and civil servants.

Various leaders consulted also mentioned the existence of traditions that militate against controlling the exercise of power in some Central American countries, where the absence of efficient restrictions seems to be linked to longstanding problems.

However, those consulted link such control with the strengthening of civil society (starting, above all, with the role played by NGOs) and of the media. The media is considered to be both a control mechanism and a pressure group, which allows us to understand the paradox of how the media is perceived: as a condition *sine qua non* for democracy and at the same time as a tool of power groups that have undue influence over public decision-making.

In general, the existence of an independent media is seen as a factor that has contributed decisively to the increase in controls. Many of the leaders consulted emphasize the capacity of the media to detect irregularities and excesses (or simple mistakes and difficulties) and to publicize them. But this very same weight of the media is seen as a danger by most of the leaders consulted. Supported by the popularity that results from muckraking, certain elements of the media end up creating their own agenda and following their own interests (consistent with those of the economic group to which they belong or the power sectors with which they are associated). For many consultees, a serious problem is that there are no effective mechanisms to control these potential excesses, at least if one does not wish to endanger the freedom of the press. In both its best and its worst manifestations, though, the media is seen by leaders as one of the main counterweights to political power.

Opinions on the Nature of Democracy

Latin American leaders believe that the political conditions necessary for democracy improved significantly over the past decade. Consider the definition of democracy offered by an interviewee in Guatemala: "If we had asked Guatemalans in 1986 what democracy meant to them they would have said 'that there should be a civilian government and that it should be voted in by a popular vote', and that is basically what should happen in all of Latin America." Assuming that this definition is correct, there is no doubt that most consultees would agree that their countries are democratic.

The interview guidelines stated that, after an extensive conversation, participants would be invited to respond to the question regarding the presence or absence of democracy in their particular country ("Taking everything into account, would you say that your country today is a democracy?"). Only 14 percent gave an un-

equivocal answer (six percent said yes, eight percent said no). The remainder wanted to clarify and redefine the concept.

Consequently, we need to explore the meaning of these expressed qualifications and reservations. For six percent, as noted above, there is a 'full democracy' in their particular country, while for 66 percent there is a democracy with some limitations. Seventeen percent believes that numerous limitations exist in their democracy, while a further eight percent thinks that their country is not a democracy.

At least as a first approximation, therefore, the bulk of those interviewed (almost nine out of ten) accept the use of the term 'democracy' to describe their respective national situation, although they do so with a number of qualifications.

This observation may appear trivial, but it confirms the progress that has been made in recent years. For the first time in the history of the continent, the leaders of all of the nations included in the study believe that their countries meet at least the most basic definition of democracy —that is, there is genuine competition for power and there are at least some limits on the exercise of power by government. However, 25 percent of interviewees underscored that there is still "a long way to go" before they can say that there is democracy in their countries.

In some cases, consultees insisted that the weakness of democracy has less to do with political blockages, problems of legitimacy or questions of institutional design (although these problems were mentioned), and more to do with the living conditions of the population. "From the economic and social point of view, we really have grave problems in wealth distribution, of participation among Panamanians

> **For the first time in the history of the continent, the leaders of all of the nations included in the study believe that their countries meet at least the most basic definition of democracy.**

[...]. How can there be democracy in these conditions?" That inequality and social segmentation are impediments to full-blown democracy building is a view frequently associated with the more pessimistic camp. In all of the consultations, the comment most often linked to a skeptical judgment on how strong or how developed democracy really is was the one that usually made reference to the living conditions of the population.

A Nicaraguan leader said, for example: "It has been a great effort for us to get as far as we have: deaths, internal struggles [...]. We have progressed more than many countries in terms of consolidating democracy but there is much more to do, because complete democracy in poverty and misery is inconceivable. When the only liberty one seems to have is that of dying [...] it is difficult." The same idea runs through this summary provided by a Peruvian leader: "Some 54% of the population live below the extreme poverty line and 23% are under the extreme-extreme poverty line [...]. Those people participate in politics in the sense that they vote on election day, because it is obligatory and they have to pay a fine if they don't, but this is not democracy. Democracy is not a political electoral act. Someone who goes to sleep not knowing whether tomorrow he will have something to eat is not free."

At the other extreme, the most positive answers are delivered in particular by those who come from the most deep-rooted democracies and the larger countries. As pointed out by a Brazilian leader, recent elections have contributed to the building of confidence in democracy: "We are living at a time when a person [Luiz Inácio Lula da Silva] has emerged

from extreme poverty in the northeast and reached the most powerful position in the country; [...] social mobility is one of the ingredients of democracy: [...] the more chance there is to cross the barriers [between social classes], the more democracy there is."

These cases demonstrate that, in Latin America, the link between socio-economic conditions and attitudes towards democracy is not automatic or necessarily a determinant. What distinguishes the attitudes of those in power in these countries does not rest, therefore, on 'objective' socio-economic conditions at home but on the degree of confidence in the capacity of democratic institutions to live with, and, in the medium term, to alter, these situations of poverty and exclusion. For those who see things this way, poverty and exclusion are problems that must be solved through a political system that is unequivocally democratic.

According to one former President, "We have achieved a republic and we must still build the democracy. The republic protects our individual freedoms, prevents us from being killed by a despotic government, or from being made prisoners by it [...], but in addition to these liberties which are sometimes called negative there are other liberties, the positive ones of democracy, concentrated in social rights."

Reasons for the Limitations of Latin America's Democracies

Institutional Powers and De Facto Powers

A traditional problem in the countries of Latin America has been the divorce of institutional powers from de facto powers: although written Constitutions give great weight to the executive branch and provide the legislative branch and the judiciary with significant scope for action, real power tends to reside with institutions to which the law assigns other functions (as was the case, in the recent past, with the armed forces) or with groups that do not form part of the political-institutional order (traditional families, economic groups and others).

The tension between institutional and de

facto powers remains a reality in Latin America. There is information to suggest, and the interviews confirm this, that, over the past few decades, despite the strengthening of democratic institutions, de facto powers continue to play a very important role in the region.

The armed forces are seen as the most important power center by some of those consulted in the Dominican Republic and Guatemala, and, to a lesser extent, in Chile, Ecuador and Venezuela. But the armed forces are not mentioned in the other countries, including those that have recently experienced acute political crises (Argentina, Colombia and Paraguay). This weakening of the armed forces as a major political force is an important new development for democracy in Latin America.

Some consultees, however, identified three main risks that could threaten the smooth running of the democratic order:

1. The first risk, according to leaders in the largest countries and those with more established democracies, are limitations stemming from two sources. On the internal front, they

The tension between institutional and de facto powers remains a reality in Latin America.

arise from the proliferation of inappropriate institutional controls, such as the multiplication of the number of interest groups (especially business entities) that function as powerful lobbies. On the external front, they arise basically from the behavior of the international markets (especially, but not exclusively, the financial ones), the surveillance carried out by risk assessors and the role of the international lending organizations.

Interviewees from the smaller countries or those with less established democracies also highlight external and internal limitations, but they describe them differently. On the internal front, they mention special interest groups (particularly businesses and landowners), but the methods used comprise not only *lobbying* but also practices like buying votes and 'fabricating' candidates. On the external

WHO EXERCISES POWER IN LATIN AMERICA?

ACCORDING TO THE NUMBER OF MENTIONS BY THE LEADERS CONSULTED

TABLE 53

		Number of Mentions	% of Interviewees who Mentioned it
De facto powers	Economic groups/business executives/financial sector	150	(79.8%)
	Communications media	122	(64.9%)
Constitutional powers	Executive branch	68	(36.2%)
	Legislative branch	24	(12.8%)
	Judicial branch	16	(8.5%)
Security forces	Armed forces	40	(21.3%)
	Police	5	(2.7%)
Political institutions and political leaders	Political parties	56	(29.8%)
	Politicians/political operators/political leaders	13	(6.9%)
Foreign factors	USA/Embassy of the United States of America	43	(22.9%)
	Multilateral lending organizations	31	(16.5%)
	International factors/external factors	13	(6.9%)
	Transnational companies/multinationals	9	(4.8%)

Note: n = 188. The total does not add up to 100 percent because multiple answers were permitted.

Source: PRODDAL, round of consultations with Latin American leaders, 2002.

front, they emphasize dependence on international lending organizations, to which they add the disproportionate influence exerted by foreign companies set up in their countries.

2. The second risk concerns the *threat of drug trafficking*. Naturally, the importance that Latin American leaders accord to this factor is directly linked to how developed the phenomenon is in their respective country. Almost all of them agree, though, that drug trafficking constitutes a double challenge. It is a direct challenge because it attempts to control part of the State apparatus and significant parts of the national territory, while simultaneously creating strong incentives to encourage movement from the formal to the informal economy. Drug trafficking also presents a number of indirect challenges, of which consultees drew attention to two. First, given that the issue has attracted the attention of the government of the United States, new external pressures are being generated that further limit scope for action by national authorities. The second has to do with corruption: 'dirty money' has devastating effects on the behavior of some political leaders and on the functioning of institutions.

3. The third risk that limits the power of political institutions are attributed to the communications media. The great influence of the media is seen as part of the rise in controls that have allowed the exercise of government to be democratized. However, based primarily on the perceptions of the politicians consulted, it is also seen as a restriction on the democratic process. The media has the capacity to generate an agenda, to prompt public opinion to be in favor or against different initiatives and to erode the image of public figures through the manipulation of exposés.

There was broad consensus among those consulted that the great influence of the media limits the power of political institutions.

In fact, it has always enjoyed significant influence and politicians have always attempted to exploit this fact. What is new, apart from the greater exposure of the public to the views of the media, is that the latter has come out of a period in which most media bodies were linked to political parties—in some cases, political parties exercised a certain amount of control over them. Many media organizations have gained independence from party structures and now form part of economic groupings that are not subordinate to political power centers and have extremely diverse interests.

The Role of Political Parties

According to the leaders consulted, political parties, key players in today's democracies, are in serious state of crisis. A revealing fact is that not only do most of the leaders consulted believe that parties are not fulfilling their function properly but also that 59 percent of the politicians consulted agree with them. In this case, only 18 percent expressed agreement ('clearly yes' and 'agree') and 16 percent expressed neutral opinions ('partly yes, partly no').

There are major differences from country to country. In some cases (Argentina and Ecuador), the political parties have suffered an extreme loss of prestige. In others (Honduras, Uruguay and, to a lesser extent, Chile), the parties seem to be in substantially better shape. In general it can be said that, with few exceptions, skepticism towards the parties is widespread and the willingness of the public to be linked with them is tending to decline throughout the region. (It is important to note that these opinions refer to the political situation that existed in 2002 and early 2003, and that hence a new round of consultations would likely yield new results.)

What are the reasons for this? The most common accusation relates to personalistic leadership and the absence of internal democracy. In the words of a leading Costa Rican: "For the past 40 years it's been the same faces, the same people recycling the same ingredients; the legislator today is ambassador tomorrow, and on another occasion he'll get a ministry [and later] it's his turn again."

This rejection of *party oligarchies* may result in part from the modernization of the expectations of citizens (the old caudillo-style government and the old paternalistic style are not so easily accepted). Also, the sharp deterioration in the power of the State in many of our countries (due to a variety of factors) has led to the weakening of one of the biggest attractions that political parties had in the past: the parties are no longer able, through their influence over different sections of the State, "to resolve the people's problems", at least in the eyes of a large majority of citizens. Yet, while this clientelistic appeal has weakened, the parties have not been able to modernize themselves enough to stand out based on the strength of their proposals or the capacity of their governing teams. In the words of a Peruvian interviewee: "Political parties have been unable to take the pulse of Latin America."

The political parties are going through a serious crisis of representation that has had a negative impact on the level of electoral participation, and has also resulted in citizens looking for alternative channels of participation (generally towards civil society organizations). However, nearly all of the leaders consulted recognize the importance of political parties and the need for them to play a more responsible part. According to one President, "Our societies have been through a rapid transformation under the table and we politicians have not monitored this closely, so therefore there is a great gap." According to a business executive, "People want to be involved and feel that the formality of voting at the ballot box, however transparent the elec-

tions, does not give them the feeling of involvement [...]. Democracy needs political parties, but I cannot be involved in one because each party has an owner."

The interviewees link this crisis of representation with the absence of internal democracy within the parties, the use of clientelistic practices to manage the electorate, encouraging caudillo-style personal favors, the abandonment of party political platforms (the lack of ideological differences and the absence of programs), the creation of schisms along personal (not ideological) lines, the connections between the parties and de facto power bases, and the building of alliances in which political identities become unclear.

For these reasons, most of the consultees believe that the parties, particularly the long-established ones, have not been successful conduits for the channeling of citizens' demands. At the same time, the opposition appears fragmented and speeches by opposition politicians tend to focus on attacking controversial political figures rather than on presenting solid proposals. Far from expressing the will of the majority of the people, according to the opinions of the interviewees, parties generally reflect spe-

---

ARE THE POLITICAL PARTIES FULFILLING THEIR ROLE?   TABLE 54

Yes, or more or less 'yes'	Uruguay, Honduras
No, or more or less 'no'	Chile, Peru, Mexico, Dominican Republic, El Salvador, Bolivia, Panama, Brazil, Guatemala, Paraguay, Venezuela, Argentina, Colombia, Ecuador, Nicaragua, Costa Rica

Note: the countries are arranged according to 'balances of opinion', that is, the difference between those who say that party participation increased and those who say that it decreased. The first country is the one with the most positive net assessment, that is, the one where the difference is most in favor of those who think that parties fulfill their role adequately. The other countries are then arranged in descending order.
Source: PRODDAL, round of consultations with Latin American leaders, 2002.

> **The political parties are going through a serious crisis of representation that has had a negative impact on the level of electoral participation, and has also resulted in citizens looking for alternative channels of participation.**

cial interests and are influenced too much by powerful pressure groups, legal and illegal.

One academic noted: "[The parties] have great difficulty being in touch with people's needs because a political career depends above all on the party leaders and not so much on citizens. Curiously, there is more or less a solid party oligarchy and the parties have a good proportion of the votes although people do not have a good opinion of them."

Certain actors, particularly journalists, see the political parties as fragile institutions, detached from the needs of citizens, subject to the rule of personalist leaders ('caudillos'), concerned only with the included sectors of society and increasingly out of touch with their social bases—sometimes they behave like a mafia. Academics, for their part, tend to link the crisis of political party representativeness with the institutional deficit in each country. It is clear that various dimensions: the system of proportional representation in some countries; the balance of forces represented in the national legislature; and the mechanisms for selecting candidates both within parties and outside of them. According to this viewpoint, the problems associated with political representation may be connected more to the way in which the representational system operates than the credibility of the political parties vis-à-vis citizens.

According to the interviewees, people's lack of faith in political parties has tended to encourage the spread and diversification of civil society organizations—just as these bodies have strengthened their ability to get people's de-

mands to be taken seriously. The imbalance between the levels of participation achieved by parties and by civil society organizations invites a critical examination of the role that each performs in the democratic process.

The interviewees who belong to NGOs criticize political parties strongly, attacking basically their corrupt activities, the way in which they distance themselves from the interests of society and their pursuit of power in order to satisfy their private interests.

However, for some consultees who are closer to the parties, the problem is not so much that the parties have not fully modernized but that they have not managed to demonstrate to the people that they have done so. One Chilean leader put it as follows: "I believe that here we have to make a mea culpa. I think the parties have not been able to make their proposals clear to the public, the alternatives they represent, the way forward that they offer." Explanations of this sort do not go far enough for those consulted in countries that face quite severe crises. Among these countries, a recurring theme is that it is not the citizens who turned their backs on the parties, but rather the parties who turned their backs on the people. In the words of one interviewee from Argentina: "Politicians talk more about candidates, internal elections, elections, electoral mechanisms and speak little about unemployment, poverty, marginalization, lack of public safety, which are the subjects that most concern people. [...] In essence, this crisis arises from a political leadership that declined to accept any responsibility or make any effort. The only objective was to stay in office for as long as possible."

The consultations also generated criteria for analyzing the health of other democratic institutions. The leaders interviewed are aware of citizens' lack of confidence in these institutions (see the third section). Some point out that the representative capacity is being exhausted and link this to the increased influence of unelected powerful groups. While those consulted recognize, to differing degrees, the central importance of political parties as instruments of representation in a good-quality democracy, they note that parties suffer in special ways as a result of the influence of de facto powers.

There was broad agreement among consultees regarding the power accumulated by important business leaders, the financial sector and the media in the past decade. In their view, these are the main power centers in the democracies of the region. They also stress the influence exerted by the multilateral lending organizations. There is wide consensus that government agendas are essentially determined by the interests of these players.

De Facto Powers

Corporations

Of those consulted in Latin America, 80 percent drew attention to the power that has been amassed by business leaders, the financial sector and the media[79] in the past decade. They comprise the principal power group that limits the decision-making authority of governments.

The influence exerted by de facto powers gives the impression that governments and political parties cannot respond to the needs of citizens. According to one former President, "The great de facto power of an incipient democracy is private economic power. It is comprised of pressure groups that dictate the behavior of the President, legislators, judges and other government officials as well as public servants." According to a politician, "We have a democracy that is disconnected from the public interest and, basically, linked to de facto powers that end up turning the country's economy into an oligarchy and changing democratic government into plutocratic government."

The leaders underline the fact that the importance of the business sector is based on its ability to lobby governments, defending and promoting its interests and guiding political actions for its own benefit. According to one church leader, "The government is at the service of private business and of those who make decisions [...] the multimillionaires are the ones who decide what does and does not get done in the country." A President stated, "The power of money is rapidly turned into political power, with the ability to limit democratic political power." A politician said, "Their influence is based [...] on the fact that they finance electoral campaigns." According to another politician, "The business world has a great deal of power. As the business leaders take investment decisions, and without investment there is no development and no growth, they have there the power to veto. [...] The power of business bosses with their capital and their veto power which can lead to unemployment, is undoubtedly very strong."

Some of the Presidents consulted expressed concern about the level of corporate pressure in the Southern Cone, which appears to be an obstacle to the establishment of broader democracy, because privileges are granted to some groups within the context of weak parties and a State that should be more republican. In smaller countries, such as those in Central America, they highlighted the pressure placed by the private sector—linked to an oligarchic power structure—on the President and the co-opting of senior officials, leading some of the consultees to speak of the *capturing of the State*.

Most of the interviewees singled out for mention the close links between economic groups and the media. Business executives acquire even more power through the media, either as their owners or because they impose conditions to the media through the manipulation of advertising inguidelines. This alliance affords them great capacity to shape opinion, to set the agenda and to manipulate the public image of officials, political parties and institutions.

The Media

The media sector is defined as a means of control that is itself uncontrolled, fulfilling functions that go beyond the right to informa-

---

79 In contrast with the rest of Latin America, no one in Brazil mentioned the link between the financial and economic sectors and the media. However, they do recognize the great impact that they have on public opinion.

tion. According to one politician, "They form public opinion, they decide what will be investigated and, as a result, they have the most influence on governability." Another politician stated: "They act like supra-powers, [...] they have taken on a power that exceeds that of the executive and the legitimately constituted powers, [...] they have completely replaced political parties."

Most of the journalists consulted see the economic and financial sectors and the media as the main power centers. The media sector is peculiar because it functions as a mechanism for overseeing or constraining the actions of the three constitutional branches of government and of the political parties, irrespective of who are its owners. One journalist said, "The real scrutiny is carried out by the press." At the same time, journalists recognize that they act like a corporation that determines the public agenda and even delineates the presidential agenda.

Generally, those consulted consider the relationship between the media and politicians to be problematic. A trade union leader noted: "Here they are feared by the political class. Because they can undo a public figure at any moment." A politician added: "The way the concessions were set up and the interests that bound together the whole structure of the media have turned them into a power."

For some, however, the influence of the media is a positive factor. According to a business leader, "Thanks to the media we can still talk about democracy." Advocates value the monitoring role played by the media. One journalist noted, "Clearly, if it were not for the vigilance of the press, things would be much worse." Another said, "[The press] makes the modes of deception more sophisticated, but on the other hand it operates as a restraint."

Foreign Factors

The role played by the government of the United States and the multilateral lending organizations—the Inter-American Development Bank (IADB), the International Monetary Fund (IMF) and the World Bank (WB)—was highlighted by approximately one-half of those questioned as a factor of great significance. These people stressed the influence that these entities have on internal issues and the resulting loss of autonomy. This dependency is evident in the priorities of the public agenda, particularly in the coincidence between the suggestions made by these bodies and the guidelines on economic, tax and State reform, in both the short and the medium terms.

One journalist said, "The direction, the control, and the rhythm of things are predetermined by outside conditioning [...] with the Fund, with the banks, with the IADB." A politician added, "The seal of approval of the US government in dealing with all these multilateral organizations is essential. Without a favorable view from the IMF, the World Bank and the IADB, the economy of a country would collapse quickly, because of the debt situation [...]. North American help is vital for the correlation of internal forces at this time."

According to a senior official, "Economic policy is not democratically managed [...]. There is only one model for the region. And anyone who wants to do things differently has to face the fact that it cannot be done, or if he does it, he does it at his own risk. [This is the] constraint imposed by the international and global nature of economic forces." A journalist noted, "People vote and the institutions that result from that vote are facilitators for decisions that are taken somewhere else [...]. Gradually the frontiers between powers are smoothed in line with these de facto powers who fix it so that the decisions taken in parliament, the executive, the judiciary and in each jurisdiction all look just about the same."

While recognizing the influence of these forces, some interviewees believe that the democratic political powers retain an autonomous capability. A politician stated, "The challenge is how to adapt democratic institutions to the existence of de facto powers. Perhaps there is no way of institutionalizing them, but one must be aware that they exist, that they have influence and that these influences carry weight."

In this context and looking towards the future, one President pointed to the difficult task of breaking the link between foreign factors and national priorities, including overcoming poverty and thereby strengthening democracy: "This situation presents us with a huge challenge, which is whether or not the governments of the region are capable of ensuring responsible management of economic policies which function in an efficient and forward-looking manner."

Churches

One-half of those consulted said that churches still have influence, although less so than in the past. These people noted that the expansion of evangelical churches is undermining the influence of the Catholic Church. A civil society leader said, "I believe that the Catholic Church is still dominant. [...] The more conservative sectors became stronger, [...] those making the greatest advances are some Pentecostal groups, evangelicals who now have great influence because they control some of the media, [...] speak in a way that attracts people as a solution to their problems and this is extremely alienating from the point of view of democratic awareness [...]. People do not need to participate in building democracy, they have to go pray and God knows what they do. Besides, these churches are turning into an extraordinary economic force."

Mention was also made of authorities in the Catholic Church who, during electoral campaigns, make political points in their sermons. A politician said, "Those are the ones who, during the electoral campaign, will influence or imply whom to vote for from the pulpit." A high-ranking official added, "This has meant that the Catholic Church exerts not only a strictly pastoral influence but also a real influence on the process of taking political decisions."

Labor Unions

Approximately one-third of those interviewed see the trade unions as a power factor, particularly in terms of their ability to veto decisions through the application of pressure and the holding of demonstrations, as well as through their influence over the setting of the public agenda (as far as labor issues are concerned). Consultees pointed in particular to public sector unions, emphasizing their link with political power, while at the same time highlighting the declining power of private sector unions.

Illegal Powers

The weight of powerful illegal groups is a matter of especial concern in some countries. Such entities are involved in all kinds of illicit activities, such as drug trafficking, the shipment of contraband, prostitution and unlawful gambling.

One business executive stated, "Some sectors of organized crime are a growing power. In large urban centers closely linked to drug trafficking, they benefit from the support of the police and from other resources such as abundant financial assets. So this power is a real threat to democracy."

According to a Mayor, "At the next election we will have, for the first time officially, direct representatives of these Mafiosi groups. Before they had their contacts with politicians, now they have their own representatives. In the lists of candidates for senators and representatives we can pick out, for example, the son, the son-in-law, the brother-in-law and in some cases the Mafioso group leader himself [...]. They are the groups with the greatest influence and greatest ability to maneuver in marginally-illegal operations involving the falsification of documents, that is, all cross-border trade and the most profitable kinds of activities in our country today."

The influence of these groups over the institutions of the State and over legitimate businesses was underlined. A President commented, "[In some areas] where a lot of coca is produced, drug trafficking has influence, of course murky and secretive, by corrupting the authorities." A high-ranking official said, "We are deal-

> **The influence of these illegal groups has been strengthened by changes in the economy and by the weakness of the State, which they can permeate.**

ing with an aggressive force, anti-democratic and terrible [...]: they buy everything, judges, border guards, police, whole institutions."

The influence of these illegal groups has been strengthened by changes in the economy and by the weakness of the State, which they can permeate. A trade union leader noted, "These extra-legal groups have the power they do because the State is weak, and institutions such as the Congress are discredited [...]. In a large proportion of cases, drug trafficking was able to corrupt them, and they continue to be corrupt [...]. There are still people in Congress who are in the pay of drug traffickers [who] were able to corrupt the top leadership of traditional parties [...]. They provide finance for insurgency and for paramilitaries."

Formal Political Powers

The Executive

Strong presidential rule characterizes most of the democratic regimes in Latin America. It is interesting to note that Central American and Caribbean Presidents and executives are included when the most powerful groups are identified.

Around one-third of consultees believe that the executive has a great deal of power in Latin America. However, there are different ways of looking at this. On the one hand, the executive is considered to be a benign power, helping to reach agreements and making governance possible. On the other hand, despite the executive's capacity to take the initiative, he/she is conditioned by, and subordinate to, de facto and foreign influences.

Presidents attempt to maintain supremacy over the legislature and the judiciary beyond their constitutional attributes and restrictions. A President said, "They have tried to gain more influence over the Courts and National Assembly [...]. This is a presidential regime and we have to do what the President says [...]. He has power which goes well beyond the already very strong powers granted him by the Constitution." The same President added, "When there is strong leadership and he sweeps the board at election time [...], there is no way for Congress to control the President."

The Armed Forces

Around one-fifth of those interviewed believe that the armed forces still have significant influence. But these people tend to believe that the armed forces have lost importance, because they are going through a process of institutionalization and also because, in some cases, internal disputes remain unresolved, which have undermined the extensive power that they enjoyed in the past. In only two countries—Ecuador and Venezuela—are the armed forces reported to play a supervisory role with respect to democracy, to be held in high regard by the public, to have established bases of support that are linked to social organizations and policies, and to be associated with the indigenous movement. In this sense, the armed forces appear to be politicized. A point that is worthy of note concerns the militarization of public administration as a result of the involvement of active military personnel. A journalist underlined, "When there is any threat, the military take to the street."

The Views of Presidents and Vice-Presidents

The evidence provided by those who hold or held the position of President or Vice-President (henceforth 'heads of government') in Latin America is of particular importance. This is because their reflections are informed by the actual exercise of political power at the highest institutional level.

As has already been noted, there is general agreement that a strong President symbolizes the democratic governments of Latin America. According to one member of the executive branch, "The presidency still retains a great deal of power [that is seen in] the President's attitudes, in his mission, his behavior and his way of seeing things."

In some countries presidential performance is criticized: personalist political practices are widespread resulting in party identities becoming mixed up with the presidential figure. Other elected heads acknowledge the extent of presidential power but they do not see it as incontestable, identifying certain cracks in the structure; the decay worries them.

Other heads of government note that the electoral regime distorts the executive's political power base. Similarly, the context in which power is exercised also imposes conditions. Some heads of government from the Southern Cone see a gap between formal presidential power and the capacity to exercise it. According to them, the image of the President as a caudillo or '*criollo* monarch' is very far from the truth: "The President is a fellow fairly limited in what he can do, as a general rule."

A head of government of a Mercosur country added that the increase in the number of controls arising from the mechanisms of direct democracy and from the creation of new institutions as a result of constitutional reforms is generating greater legitimacy for the exercise of the presidential power and hence the consequent strengthening of democracy. He stated, "I governed in an institutional framework that allowed me to legislate." The main challenge revolves around whether or not the President has the power to lead the political process: "The danger is when one cannot propose a way forward."

Pressure put on the President by De Facto Powers

The leaders consulted analyzed how the President carries out his/her duties when under pressure from diverse de facto power centers. In addressing this subject, they made personal references, reflecting on their capacity to impose decisions.

One said, "In the exercise of the presidency I did not feel particularly under pressure. Perhaps because we were just starting out, or because the power base of the democratic government was very strong; perhaps because, without false modesty, the people know me, and they knew that I wasn't going to be put under pressure."

However, all of these elected leaders spoke of coming under pressure from foreign powers, primarily the government of the United States and the multilateral lending organizations.

In all cases, pressure that undermines the autonomy of presidential decisions is seen as negative. Below are some of the views of various heads of government: "It is a power that is exercised negatively, it is the power to arouse rather than of decision-making;" "We are totally constrained, they set the rules [...]. Sovereign governments depend on the analysis of a private risk-assessment agency, on the decision of an international organization, 'I'll help you or I won't help you';" "Governments have more constraints on the exercise of power. We have lost the capacity to make national decisions because international lending organizations set conditions that work against growth and, in the end, against democracy, when fundamental human rights are impaired;" "Thus you have a President of the Republic, under brutal bilateral pressure and subject to the influence of international cooperation which I wouldn't say is brutal, but is very significant;" and "Bilateral organizations, with their demands to follow set models and programs and under politically non-viable conditions, are not responsible for the political results brought about by these demands which they impose on you [...]. That is, an international bureaucrat arrives and, following instructions from his organization, he draws a line and afterwards the gentleman has carried out his mission and leaves."

> **"This situation presents us with a huge challenge, which is whether or not the governments of the region are capable of ensuring responsible management of economic policies which function in an efficient and forward-looking manner."**

The Role of the Communications Media

The heads of government described constant intervention by media organizations as a counterbalance to the exercise of their power—in the sense that public opinion tends to be guided by media reporting and its analyses of government actions. One said, "The media informs, opines, judges and condemns [...]. It is a power factor that can be exercised well or badly, and which is influenced by economic interests, passions, feelings and ideas, and at the same time is under no control. [...] Therefore, this is why the person running the country feels harried by the press [...]. No matter what political color the government is, its leader will always feel harried."

Likewise, it is generally acknowledged that the media has enormous capacity to affect the fate of a government. One leader remarked, "The influence of the media can make a strong institutional set-up useless if it undergoes attacks or confrontation from that sector." Another commented, "The press has a decisive influence over Congress [...]. If the press moves against a law, it is very difficult to pass it."

Although elected leaders value the role of the media as a check on power, they are very concerned about the fact that, free of all control themselves, media organizations have become a means for the expression of the interests of economic groups. One said, "In this landscape we cannot ignore the role the more developed, more professional media organiza-tions have performed in terms of exposés and surveillance. [...] but there is also more interference in the free flow of democratic life. [...] Big capital is a much more real power factor today because it is taking over the media's tools, which means that not only do they have power, they can also exercise it."

Heads of government think that the lack of State controls on the press, which, as we have seen, are a vital element of democracy, can threaten their ability to fulfill their duties. They criticize media outlets for the irresponsible way in which they disseminate news, made possible by the position that they occupy in the power structure of each country. One noted, "The media has an enormous influence, perhaps the strongest and most solid. [...] They fall into the strategy of easy sensationalism and they hamper governability and consistent administration. [...] I do not believe that society understands clearly the implication of this. I was speaking to elected leaders from the region and we are all aware of the same problem."

The pressure exerted by the media is also reflected in the influence it enjoys over the setting of the public agenda. One leader pointed out, "The media are going through a process of evolution in which there is a confusion of power the like of which has never been seen in their history: total power and zero responsibility [...]. The media today have a power which can topple a minister, which can influence policy and which is setting the agenda, sometimes in an unfair and excessive way."

One leader summed up the views of many Latin American heads of government when he said, "The media have become superpowers [...], linked to economic sectors, of course, they have more power than the military, the executive, even the Catholic Church and the political parties. They have totally replaced political parties. They are established at the center of society, which is good for controlling the other powers, but at the same time if there is no control over them, that power could turn into a disquieting perversion."

*Appraisal of Social Organizations
in the Political Life of a Country*

When it comes to assessing the role of social organizations, a number of heads of government point to competition and even opposition among political parties and different civil society entities. One elected leader said, "Many NGOs have been formed that are useful and stimulate participation, organizing meetings and listening to people, increasing representative democracy insofar as that is possible [...], but generally there exists a certain 'anti-politics' position and this is bad, just as in politics there is a certain tension with NGOs. This must be overcome by thrusting ahead on a common cause that will require great effort to push forward."

Another spoke more strongly, "We are confronted with a phenomenon common to all America, which is dangerous if we do not know how to organize it, which is that of the NGOs and the wrongly termed civil society. [...] The parties are facing competition from NGOs and from intermediate organizations that do not have the legitimacy of parties. We have therefore to strengthen that legitimacy because the parties are the only organizations that, through the exercise of power, can pass laws, acts, rules, that are obligatory for society."

Together, social organizations comprise a wide and diverse grouping, which is not clearly defined, according to those interviewed. Consequently, some heads of government are inclined to consider them sources of power that are a cause for concern. "Civil society is growing in importance. Nobody is yet very clear who they are and what they represent and this is one of the worries."

For another elected leader, the power of social organizations is linked to globalization. "There was one wave from the great powers and another wave consisting of the demands of the world power; government had to be minimized, the State had to be limited and the NGOs had to be strengthened."

NGOs are also called into question with respect to whether they truly represent people's interests, as they claim. "The NGOs are privileged but do not see themselves as such. They speak in the name of the people, but they speak against reforms that are for the good of the people."

According to these heads of government, the controversies surrounding political parties and civil society organizations are projections of the concepts of representative and participative democracy. Mixed up with these are arguments about the extent of democracy in the institutional sense and/or the strengthening of democracy through improvements in social equality. One leader said, "If one wants to recover the democratic base, not only do we have to tell people to get organized, get involved, but we also have to include them, and that inclusion is not only a problem of channeling people's protests and allowing them to speak or protest, but it is also connected to the concept of liberty on the basis of meeting needs [...], it is social investment, broadening protection, the quality of education [...]. Participation means that people consider themselves a part of the State." Another added, "The great secret in promoting participation is to get as close as possible to people's problems, which are basically health, education, culture and sport."

Strengthening Democracy

Having presented the various views of heads of government, we now return to the consultees as a whole. We asked them: what steps should be taken to strengthen democracy in the coming years? This question gave rise to a relatively broad spectrum of answers. However, two-thirds of interviewees delivered the same set of answers, which can be grouped into three large categories.

The first category brings together answers concerning the *need to undertake political reforms in order to strengthen institutions*, including political parties. The characteristics of such a reform effort vary from country to country: some consultees spoke of electoral reform, others of reforming the national legislature, and still others of reforming the State or strengthening institutions in general. But the common

PROBLEMS THAT NEED TO BE ADDRESSED IN ORDER TO STRENGTHEN DEMOCRACY	TABLE 55

	% of Leaders Consulted
Political reform	45
Increased participation	13
Institutional and political party reform	32
Fight inequality	18
Social policies	8
Economic policies	10
Democracy education	11
Fight corruption	9
Others	17
Total	100

Note: the values reflect the proportion of the leaders consulted who mentioned this problem at first.

Source: PRODDAL, round of consultations with Latin American leaders, 2002.

denominator is that better designed institutional mechanisms and incentives could greatly improve the functioning of democracy. A significant proportion of respondents said that political reform should involve the construction of new channels to facilitate the participation of civil society organizations. Many of the leaders consulted said that improvements to participatory channels, as well as an increase in their number and a broadening of their scope, lead to reversals in popular apathy and citizen mistrust of institutions.

This first category of answers suggests that, in contrast to a few decades ago, institutions are not seen as a reflection of something essential, but rather they are viewed as something essential in themselves. The same is true of political parties. Although many consultees agreed that the parties are not fulfilling their role properly, a similar number highlighted the need to strengthen them. The interesting point here is that, despite all of the evidence pertaining to the problems that the parties face, there is no general move to reject them or to seek out alternatives.

The second category of answers emphasizes the need to adopt substantive (not 'pure-

ly institutional') measures to help tackle the deep inequalities that exist in Latin American societies. These inequalities conspire against the strengthening of democracy and are evident both in economic terms (extreme poverty and lack of basic resources, such as food) and in cultural terms (marginalization of rural and urban sectors and of indigenous people). Genuinely to include the whole of the population in a democracy requires the eradication of such forms of exclusion. To do so, it is necessary to develop social and economic policies that will lead to a general improvement in living standards.

The third category focuses on the need to strengthen education in general (not just access to education, but also the quality of education) and the democratic culture in particular. At least some elements of the political problems facing Latin American societies are the result of poor understanding of the rules of the democratic game or, more often, superficial understanding of these rules, which is not associated with a sufficiently firm commitment to democratic values. Those interviewed believe that a concerted effort to strengthen education, particularly education relating to democracy, could improve this situation.

A final point on which a number of consultees agree concerns the need to step up the fight against corruption. If corruption is one of the problems that most affects democracy and discredits it in the eyes of the people, the fight against it must be a fundamental priority.

It is worth adding that the views of those consulted on the main problems that must be addressed in order to strengthen democracy differ according to their view of events in their respective country. Those who maintain that there is democracy in their country, or democracy with few limitations, underline the need for institutional and party reform. This emphasis diminishes among those who perceive there to be various limitations, and it lessens even more among those who see many limitations to democracy at home (or simply think that there is no democracy). Where people stress the need for greater participation the reverse occurs: this is more frequent where democracy is not seen to exist, or is thought to be very limited, and much less frequent at the opposite extreme.

Constructing Public Agendas in Latin America

Consultees' opinions on the current political agenda vary significantly. Corruption is the topic mentioned most often (36 percent). By contrast, 20 percent of interviewees referred to the inadequate role played by political parties and the need to reform them.

As for the economic agenda, recovery—including the use of productive resources, privatizations and financial reforms—is the subject mentioned most often (53 percent). Twenty-three percent of leaders pointed to foreign debt and regional integration.

Unemployment and violence (34 percent) were defined as the main priorities on the social agenda.

Perceptions appear to be similar with respect to influential groups and topics on the agenda. Those consulted broadly agree that corporate groups (80 percent) and the media (65 percent) have the greatest capacity to formulate and influence the agenda. Consensus is strongest on the need to reactivate the economy.

The priorities of non-political leaders do not

> **Many of the leaders consulted said that improvements to participatory channels, as well as an increase in their number and a broadening of their scope, lead to reversals in popular apathy and citizen mistrust of institutions.**

differ from those of the consulted group as a whole. For them, recovery is also the central issue on the economic agenda (57 percent), although other economic questions scarcely received mention. With regard to the social agenda, matters like violence and public insecurity, as well as reforms in the healthcare and education sectors, are highlighted mostly by academics, while unemployment and poverty are key issues for journalists.

For women leaders, fiscal reform is as important as economic recovery (45 percent). As regards to the social agenda, poverty is considered a higher priority (it ranks second with 27 percent) and fewer people are concerned about violence (21 percent). The same proportion of women leaders (21 percent) point to healthcare and education reforms. How-

PROBLEMS THAT NEED TO BE ADDRESSED IN ORDER TO STRENGTHEN DEMOCRACY ACCORDING TO THE OPINION OF KEY LATIN AMERICAN FIGURES ON THE STATE OF DEMOCRACY IN THEIR COUNTRY OF ORIGIN

TABLE 56

	Full Democracy or Democracy with few Limitations	Democracy with some Limitations	Democracy with many Limitations or not a Democracy
Political reform	45	46	45
Increased participation	3	14	19
Institutional and political parties reform	42	32	26
Fight inequality	22	16	20
Democracy education	12	13	7
Fight corruption	10	8	10
Others	11	17	18
Total	100	100	100

Note: the values reflect the proportion of the leaders consulted who mentioned this problem at first.
Source: PRODDAL, round of consultations with Latin American leaders, 2002.

CURRENT AGENDA BY ISSUE

TABLE 57

Issues	Number of Interviewees who mentioned it	
Economic agenda		
Economic recovery (debate on the use of productive resources: gas, oil, coca; privatizations, financial reform)	80	(53%)
Fiscal issues	24	(16%)
External debt	9	(6%)
Regional integration (Andean/Mercosur/ALCA)	9	(6%)
Free trade treaties	8	(5%)
Agreement with the IMF	3	(2%)
Social agenda		
Unemployment	52	(34%)
Violence, delinquency, citizen security	51	(34%)
Educational reform/healthcare	40	(26%)
Poverty	37	(24%)
Political agenda		
Corruption	55	(36%)
Political reform/role of parties/decentralization	30	(20%)
State reform (openness, modernization)	23	(15%)
Resolution of political institutional conflict/ institutional reconstruction/institutional weakness	12	(8%)
Money laundering and drug trafficking (coca)	12	(8%)
Reform of judicial system/rule of law/judicial security	11	(7%)
Constitutional reform	9	(6%)
Government–society relationship, national conciliation	6	(4%)

Note: the table was prepared using the responses of 152 interviewees. The total does not add up to 100 percent because multiple answers were permitted.

Source: PRODDAL, round of consultations with leading Latin American figures, 2002.

ever, the political agenda is as important for women leaders as it is for the consulted group as a whole, although women leaders mention corruption less often (22 percent).

The Agenda for the Future

The future agenda, based on the interests and concerns of those interviewed, does not vary significantly from the current agenda. As for economic topics, 42 percent of respondents focused on recovery and 24 percent on problems linked to regional integration.

As for the social agenda, the spread of opinions is maintained, although greater priority is accorded to sectoral reforms in the health and education spheres and to the issues of poverty and inequality, which are highlighted by approximately one-third of leaders.

Unemployment and violence were granted less importance.

The political agenda is constructed around a wide range of subjects. Political reform is the main priority, but this was mentioned by only 35 percent of consultees. Only ten percent of respondents considered the defense of human rights and freedom to be agenda items. It is interesting to note that, while people stress the need for reforms, social and political, they do not offer any thoughts on what they should involve in terms of content.

Academics mostly agreed with general opinion on the future agenda. However, while 32 percent of all consultees think that education and healthcare reforms should be on the future agenda, only 17 percent of academics agree. The latter tend to give priority to a reform strategy

FUTURE AGENDA BY ISSUE

TABLE 58

Issues	Number of Interviewees who mentioned it	
Economic agenda		
Economic recovery: debate on the use of productive resources: (gas, oil, coca; privatizations, financial reform)	66	(42.3%)
Fiscal issues	28	(17.9%)
Regional integration (Andean Region/Mercosur/ALCA)	22	(14.1%)
External debt	13	(8.3%)
Free trade treaties	4	(2.5%)
Role of the IMF, World Bank, IADB	1	(0.6%)
Social agenda		
Educational reform/healthcare	45	(28.8%)
Poverty and inequality	44	(28.2%)
Unemployment	26	(16.6%)
Violence, delinquency, citizen security	13	(8.3%)
Political agenda		
Political reform/role of parties/decentralization	55	(35.2%)
State reform (openness, modernization, administrative reform)	33	(21.1%)
Reform of justice system/rule of law/judicial security	15	(9.6%)
Democratic security (defense of democratic freedoms, human rights, peace)	15	(9.6%)
Corruption	10	(6.4%)
Constitutional reform	9	(5.8%)
Resolution of political institutional conflict/institutional reconstruction/ institutional weakness	9	(5.8%)
Money laundering and drug trafficking (coca)	5	(3.2%)
Government–society relationship, national conciliation	2	(1.2%)

Note: the table was prepared using the responses of 156 interviewees. The total does not add up to 100 percent because multiple answers were permitted.

Sources: PRODDAL, round of consultations with leading Latin American figures, 2002.

linked to the stability of the democratic system and its institutions. Therefore, political reform, redefining the role of political parties and decentralization are their main focus (48 percent of academics compared to 36 percent of interviewees in general). A similar situation exists with respect to judicial reform, the functioning of the rule of law and legal security (22 percent of academics compared to 15 percent of interviewees as a whole).

For Presidents and former Presidents, economic recovery in the region is the prominent issue on both the current and the future agenda. Other subjects, such as unemployment and violence, which are important features of the current agenda, are accorded slightly less importance on the future agenda. Based on the number of times that the political agenda is mentioned in responses, heads of government judge it to be the least important of the three.

The Challenges

What steps should be taken to strengthen the development of democracy in the coming years? One set of answers, divided into three categories, was mentioned by two-thirds of those consulted. What follows is a summary of their opinions on the steps to be taken in the future; this means that there will be some repetition in terms of their comments on the current state of democracy.

The first category focuses on the need to undertake political reforms that fortify institutions, including political parties. The characteristics of the proposed reforms vary from country to country: some refer to the electoral system, others to the national legislature and still others to the State. But the general idea is that a better design with respect to institutional mechanisms and incentives should improve the functioning of democracy. Once again, institutions are not seen as something of secondary importance, but rather as an essential part of democracy.

The second category includes the need to strengthen education in general and the democratic culture in particular, as well as the need to confront the profound social injustices that exist in Latin America. The first aspect should be addressed through civic education and, more generally, by raising the educational level of the people. It is believed that a concerted effort to develop education, especially education for democracy, could improve this situation. The lack of fairness conspires against the strengthening of democracy: this can be seen both in economic terms (extreme poverty and an absence of basic resources, such as food) and in cultural terms (marginalization of urban and rural sectors and of indigenous groups). Educational inequality, in particular, is one of the most visible and important aspects of this problem. In order to integrate the whole population genuinely into society and to engage all people in the defense of democracy it is necessary to confront these inequalities.

The third category highlights the need to construct new channels that facilitate the participation of organized civil society. For many of the leaders consulted, citizens' apathy and their lack of confidence in institutions would be reversed by improving the channels of participation and increasing their number and scope.

A last point on which all agree, more specific than those above, is the need to intensify and prioritize the struggle against corruption in order to strengthen the democratic order.

Taking Stock of Democracy in Latin America

What is the prevailing view of democracy? All of those consulted place a high premium on the sustainability and deepening of democracy in Latin America. They see the safeguarding of liberties and the holding of regular elections (in some cases with power shifting between the incumbent government and the opposition) as great achievements of democratic processes. Also acknowledged are the constitutional reforms that have permitted mechanisms of direct democracy to be established and control mechanisms to be reformulated and/or created.

However, there is significant tension when it comes to the scope of democracy and levels of poverty and social exclusion. Among consultees it is possible to pinpoint a central theme: the ability (or inability) of democracies to achieve acceptable levels of social inclusion.

The difficulties involved in attaining an acceptable level of social integration are evident when one examines the opinions of consultees on the functioning and weaknesses of democracy on the one hand, and the topics that are currently on the public agenda on the other. Restrictions on the formulation of a long-term agenda account for the difficulties involved in drafting a 'national plan' (as well as a regional one) that could provide programmatic answers to serious existing problems. Likewise, limitations on the formulation of a socially constructed agenda pose the risk that these democracies could become 'irrelevant'.

How is Power exercised in these Democracies?

As shown, in the view of many interviewees, the power of the executive tends to be limited primarily as a result of the interference of de facto powers. It cannot rely on strong political parties to sustain it or on an opposition that contributes to the strengthening of democratic institutions.

On the power map that consultees drew for us, the strong influence of de facto powers, particularly those in the economic and financial sectors and in the media, stands out. Those interviewed agree that the restrictions imposed by these powers seriously hamper the ability of governments to respond to citizens' demands. They also reiterate that the parties are not formulating collective programs that would allow them to become an authentic expression of citizenship, as well as noting the influence of foreign powers that, for example, is evident in the relatively low importance accorded to regional integration on the public agenda.

However, the institutionalization of the processes of social participation is seen as weak or embryonic. Many of those consulted stressed the importance of strengthening social participation processes; few people, though, drew attention to the benefits that can be derived when such strengthening occurs. This seems to be linked to the dearth of appropriate institutional channels for social participation.

Synthesis of the Round of Consultations

The summary we have provided allows some conclusions to be drawn on the predominant opinions held by Latin American leaders about the development of democracy in the region.

1. Latin America has taken very important strides along the road towards democratization. Increased participation and institutional control are seen as decisive steps in this direction.

2. The whole region is at least formally democratic. This second conclusion highlights a new development in the region and one that is associated with a very important notion: although Latin American leaders agree for the most part that institutional characteristics are not enough to claim that democracy exists, they realize that they are necessary. The institutional dimension is not seen as something that is incidental to what really matters, but rather as a fundamental element of democracy.

3. Some of the traditional threats to Latin American democracies have disappeared or have been weakened considerably. Most important, the risk of military insubordination has almost completely vanished. It is also notable, though, that paternalistic practices and cults of personality also enjoy less significance.

4. Although traditional threats have disappeared or have been weakened considerably, others have appeared that call into question the continuity and deepening of democracy. The most obvious is drug trafficking, engendering the creation of parallel extralegal power bases, violence, corruption and the destruction of the formal economy.

5. Other threats to the democracies of Latin America are political. The most important ones are inter-related: the reduced autonomy of institutional powers vis-à-vis decision-making and the weakening of political parties.

6. The crisis of the parties is not the result of citizens' reluctance to participate; in fact, it is playing itself out against a background of increased participation. Latin American parties are not in the midst of a regional version of a more general problem (such as the flight to the private sector that is happening in other regions). Rather, they face a new and in one sense specific problem, which combines three distinct elements: the desire for greater participation and control over political power; general rejection of parties as channels for participation; and a shift of participation and social control towards other types of organizations, generally from civil society.

7. Although the leaders consulted see these problems clearly, they are looking for solutions within rather than outside of politics. They are convinced that what is important is to have strong parties and governments that are capable of making decisions.

8. These general results do not mask the fact that there are some differences among countries. For instance, the judgments of leaders in the region's older nations (Brazil and Mexico) differ from those in the young democracies. In Brazil and Mexico there is a greater degree of optimism about the progress that has been made with respect to the conditions necessary for democracy and

greater satisfaction with regard to the successes that have been achieved to date.

9. In light of the above, we may conclude that the initial challenge facing the democracies of Latin America is to find political solutions to their political problems. This implies identifying new ways of channeling participation, controlling public policies and institutions, managing agendas and reaching political agreement within a framework that is characterized by the growing tendency towards the 'globalization of influences' and the 'transnationalization of problems'. In part, this is a universal problem, but it raises specific issues with respect to Latin America.

10. A second challenge is to find solutions to inequality and poverty and to address the fact that most people now find it impossible to attain the levels of well-being that are necessary for them to enjoy their rights fully. In the past, these problems were used to justify the search for solutions other than democracy. Today they are seen as major obstacles that democracy itself must overcome.

Towards a Citizens' Democracy

For almost two decades, but particularly during the 1990s, the focus of the Latin America agenda has been on the strengthening of democracy, the crisis of politics, State reform, structural reform of the economy, and the impact of globalization on the region. However, despite the fact that many of the substantive aspects of these issues have been addressed, others have remained absent from the debate. In light of the present analysis, these need to be placed in the spotlight.

The Report concludes that the development of democracy is intimately linked to the search for greater social equality, an effective struggle against poverty and the expansion of citizens' rights. It is necessary, therefore, to review the policies introduced and the action taken to date, to learn from recent historical events, to pay very close attention to emerging social realities and to explore new paths. This will make it possible to open the doors to prescriptions for re-launching the debate on politics and its role in Latin America. This debate could be structured, for example, under the following headings:

- The need for a new understanding of the role of the State ('stateness')—what is the role of the State in strengthening democracy?

- The economy as perceived from the standpoint of democracy—which economic policies favor the development of democracy?

- Latin American democracies in the context of globalization—what degree of autonomy do they require in order to achieve growth?

■ Four Issues on the Agenda for Debate

In this section we will review the factors that need to be taken into account in putting together an extensive *agenda* for the development of democracy. In the context of this Report, the term agenda refers to the presentation of topics that need to be debated. Thus it is not a list of public policies or measures.

The implications and scope of these contributions are the result of three converging elements: a specific understanding of democracy; awareness of the unique reality of Latin America; and the data generated by our own empirical research.

These are all topics that concern people throughout the region. However, the particular policies that may arise as a result of these discussions must take account of the specific and special situation of each country.

In the previous section we looked at how citizenship is faring in the region. Different formulae, technical principles and ambitious reform programs have been proposed on many occasions to deal with the situation. Some have been implemented with a certain degree of success and have led to significant achievements. After a decade of reforms, though, deficiencies in citizenship have not been corrected. Other criteria for action must be developed in order to move closer to the solutions that our societies demand.

Every democracy holds out the promise of freedom, justice and progress for its citizens, and, as Pierre Rosanvallon states, "We must consider what has not been achieved, the ruptures, tensions, limits and denials which indirectly form part of the experience of democracy."

In the gap between that promise and the reality described in the second section of this Report lie the great topics that comprise the agenda for the development of democracy in Latin America.

But what would remain of the freedom to elect governments democratically, which, in theory, we enjoy, if key social issues that relate to the most basic rights of citizens are not subject to public debate and citizen determination, if governments cannot implement policies that have been formulated democratically? Or what if, even with efficient and effective governments and States, the electoral mandate cannot be fulfilled because other internal or external forces prevent it?

To confront the deficits within our democracies we need *democratic power*. That is, the capacity to act effectively when faced with problems in terms of broadening citizenship. This democratic power is impossible to acquire with-

> To confront the deficits within our democracies we need *democratic power*. That is, the capacity to act effectively when faced with problems in terms of broadening citizenship.

> **In sum, it is about entwining society and politics and consequently about integrating the needs of society into politics.**

out politics. However, politics needs to be relevant, that is, it must be able to propose ways of addressing issues that are important for society, it must be capable of implementing them with the firm commitment of leaders and citizens, and it must be prepared to sustain them using suitable instruments of collective action, of which political parties are the main, although not the only, type.

Political parties' proposals for action are carried out through representative institutions and the government of the State. Democratic power is also increased through a functioning State. At the same time, civil society, which is constantly creating new voluntary organizations that increase the level of participation, represents another important mechanism through which citizenship, and therefore democracy, is expanded.

Behind each and every right there is a State that guarantees it. And, conversely, behind each and every right that has been curtailed there is a State that did not uphold it. This abdication of responsibility by the State is linked to the quality of its institutions, and basically to the power that flows through them, as well as to the ensuing capacity, or lack thereof, of the State to fulfill its objectives.

Hence, the problems associated with developing democracy that have been addressed in the preceding sections reveal themselves as an array in which are interfused the limitations of the State along with the demands of economic growth and the inequalities that it often generates. These problems are further compounded by the impotence of politics when addressing citizens' aspirations to acquire democratic power, the tensions within fractured societies, the existence of de facto forces that break the law, peddle influence and infiltrate the highest echelons of decision-making, and signs that globalization is shrinking still further the democratic space, removing from the domain of civic determination the key issues concerning the future of society.

In other words, the agenda at issue here concerns to the complex variables that help or hinder the expansion of citizenship and the reconstruction of political society within the framework of Latin American democracy. The task at hand is, therefore, to discuss the necessary preconditions that will allow our democracies to create the solutions to the problems we have described, by expanding the set of tools provided by democracy itself.

In summary, these clearly delineated problems—constituting the challenges to the development of democracy in Latin America—manifest themselves within four key areas of interest (politics, the State, the economy and globalization). Each sphere is influenced by the power question, a feature that cannot be ignored if the will of the majority is to be translated into policies that will effectively modify the existing reality.

The criteria presented here are meant to be a starting point for triggering debate: as such, they are a beginning not an end. We propose that the agenda include: how to change from a democracy whose subject is the voter to one whose subject is the citizen endowed with increased rights and responsibilities in the political, civil and social realms; how to transit from a State with a deficient legal system to a State with universal reach throughout its territory and whose main objective is to guarantee and promote rights—a State both of and for a Nation of citizens; how to move from an economy conceived in terms of single option dogmatic thinking (*la pensée unique*) to one with a diverse set of options; and how to create an autonomous space in the age of globalization. In sum, it is about entwining society and politics and consequently about integrating the needs of society into politics.

Politics, the First Condition

Politics plays a vital role in the democratic process: it produces public policies to tackle central problems and turns them into comprehensive projects for society; it provides the politicians needed to implement them; it groups together the goals of millions of citizens into common objectives, allowing them to choose from among a reasonable number of electoral alternatives; and, finally, it develops the public power necessary to carry forward the projects presented to society.

Ultimately, *politics embodies options, unites common aspirations and creates power.* These are three sine qua non conditions for the development of democracy. A form of politics that does not fulfill them puts democratic sustainability at risk. In Latin America, politics is in a state of crisis and so too is representation, because these three conditions are only partially being satisfied, and, in some cases, they are not being satisfied at all. The debate on politics must focus on how to correct this situation, from which stems not only the crisis of representation but also the threat to democracy itself.

What are needed are effective institutions, as well as transparent and responsible political parties and practices. These conditions are far from being met in many countries in the region, which, in turn, dangerously weakens the effectiveness of political parties as the main architects of democratic politics.

In the past, public debate on politics has concentrated primarily on this notorious and widespread deficiency. However, even though it was crucial, the debate focused on other matters that seemed more significant than institutional weaknesses—ignoring the fact that the crisis has to do with the content of politics and the struggle to build democratic power.

Even with optimal institutional tools, if politics does not recover the capacity to establish substantive options and power, both *electoral democracy and citizenship democracy* will become unsustainable and irrelevant for citizens. If politics does not provide society with options and power, it will have failed in terms of being representative. In the analysis presented in the second section of this Report, it is striking that the different empirical instruments are in agreement with respect to the deficits that beleaguer our democracies. These should be at the center of efforts to renew the content of politics. In this regard, the following issues stand out:

- Problems with exercising political citizenship are the least prevalent. Although in some countries voter turnout is still low, mechanisms are being developed to address the issue, such as improving the methods used to register voters and providing assistance to polling sites. Hardly any cases of flagrant fraud exist, and voter intimidation has decreased remarkably. As in any country, though, there is always scope for manipulating a certain number of voters. In many cases, furthermore, top party members continue to exert close control over the candidate selection process. The rules permitting positive discrimination in representative office in favor of women have improved. And slowly, measures are being approved to control the impact of private contributions on political action, although in many cases there is a long way to go before these initiatives have any practical relevance.

- Throughout Latin America, the political formula centers on the constitutional President. While the presidency usually enjoys a significant degree of formal power, this does not necessarily translate into effective governance, creating another source of dissatisfaction among citizens and frustration among politicians. The national legislature, for its part, lacks prestige among most people and is considered to be an inefficacious means of representing and defending the interests of the majority. Although the judicial branch of government is seen to enjoy formal independence, in several countries severe limitations hinder its ability to fulfill its daily tasks in a thorough manner. Organizations that specialize in monitoring government agencies, such as treasury comptrollers or citizens' rights advocates, along with gen-

> **Politics, particularly democratic politics, is the realm where different alternatives and projects for a society gestate.**

eral accounting offices or public defenders, sometimes lack the necessary independence or, at other times, the power to carry out their duties. It is well known that public defenders cannot have their own power base in the judicial or administrative spheres because this would trespass on areas reserved for other State authorities. Mechanisms of direct democracy have managed to widen the space for political participation by citizens, yet, at the same time, they have also, on more than one occasion, contributed to political destabilization. The jury is still out on whether they are an effective tool for the development of democracy.

- Beyond the fundamental advances achieved with respect to human rights, which were subject to systematic violation during the period of authoritarian rule and civil war in the region, the right to life continues to be infringed, as does the right to personal inviolability, both of which result especially from the ineffectiveness of the State in controlling violence and overseeing the activities of the security forces. Freedom of the press has improved markedly, and although the first steps are being taken towards ensuring that access to State information, this is a challenge that still needs to be pursued.

- Deficits in social citizenship linked to the ineffectiveness of the State (in fulfilling its role) and to the economy are the most obvious—high levels of inequality and poverty persist, and, in many countries, social inequalities have not only not been reduced, but they have actually increased. Basic needs are still not being met in a considerable number of countries.

These affirmations coincide with citizens' perceptions. In the opinion study, they said that the main problems are unemployment, poverty, inequality and insufficient income, crime and drug abuse, corruption, and inadequate service infrastructure.

Likewise, the leaders consulted highlighted reactivation of the economy, corruption, unemployment, violence and crime, healthcare and education.

To give politics meaning involves not only making the perceived deficits 'visible', but also creating a set of substantive options to resolve the deficits effectively and to place them at the core of the public debate. Some of the topics for debate are summarized in the points below:

1. Politics, particularly democratic politics, is the realm where different alternatives and projects for a society gestate. Politics is about representation, about staking social claims, about the collective search for meaning. Today, however, we must point out that politics is seriously unable to assemble collective projects. Politics has become almost entirely an activity that has little connection with the identities, interests or aspirations of society.

Civil Society, Politics and Participation

People who become organized through independent civil society groups overcome the dichotomy between public and private autonomy. They are exercising civic citizenship, not just to protect their own interests but also to expand the possibilities of protecting the interests of others who are less fortunate. They are also exercising political citizenship, not just through voting or making decisions based on their personal interests but also by increasing the possibility of access and participation for those who are left out of the political system. For this reason, they themselves embody all of the potential of human beings as agents, because they encompass both the personal and the social dimension of citizenship.

Latin America has seen a huge increase in the number of independent civil society organizations. Particularly in the field of human rights, the democratic transition has resulted in a generational renewal of organizations founded to counter illegal repression under dictatorships, as well as in the creation of new entities dedicated to advancing the rights of women, children, indigenous peoples, African-Americans and various excluded minority groups. [...] Society interprets politics in a much wider and richer sense than that pertaining simply to electoral competition.

Juan Méndez, text prepared for PRODDAL, 2002.

2. The crisis of politics is connected to the rupture that exists between the problems that citizens demand to have solved and the capacity that politics has to address them. Politics thus tends to lack validity, so it cannot develop the power and the tools it needs to respond to the main challenges facing our countries. This is the source of a significant proportion of the problems of confidence and legitimacy that confront democracy and politics, as well as basic institutions and leaders throughout Latin America.

3. It is necessary, therefore, to ask what should be the role of politics in Latin America, where, while the important right to free, frequent and fair elections has been achieved, at the same time, globalization has pervaded politics, severe social problems prevail and existing States lack the ability to guarantee and expand citizenship. May politics embody the aspirations of citizens to reduce poverty and inequality, and increase employment and solidarity? Can it help to generate the prospect of progress for our countries and our citizens?

4. Many topics that used to pertain to politics and to Nation States are being addressed and decided today in other domains and by other entities, notably the economy, de facto powers and the media. In this regard, there are three inter-related factors to be aware of:

- Nation States are losing internal sovereignty. On the one hand, they are losing out to de facto and illegal power structures. On the other, they are suffering as a consequence of deficits that limit State capabilities due to inefficiency and inefficacy in bureaucratic institutions.

- There is an imbalance in the relationship between politics and the market, which tends to trap the former and relegate it to less relevant areas, removing, for example, important economic problems from deliberation and political decision-making. This displacement is inconsistent with democracy and with the rights of citizenship that are implicit within it.

- An international order is limiting the capacity of States to act with a reasonable degree of autonomy and, as a result, is restricting national options.

  These problems undermine the purpose of politics, which is to transform reality—a particularly serious situation in Latin America. In this context, a certain loss of the desire for progress, of the very possibility of viable collective projects, is added to existing material deprivation. The ap-

The Associative Dimension of Democracy

The quality of democracy is determined as much by those who are involved in associative practices as by those who are excluded from them. Throughout Latin America a Hobbesian world of completely disorganized groups of people coexists with a much smaller world inspired by Alexis de Tocqueville. This gives rise to two problems. The first is related to the definition of the public sphere, through the silent daily work of those who control access to the apparatus of the State. This explains the need to democratize elite cultures and the resulting links that facilitate the appropriation of the public domain by organized special interests. The second problem requires an evaluation of the nature of associative patterns themselves, both as to how widespread they are and as to their content and quality. In the event that positive institutional consequences emerge out of social capital, the dynamics of association must be considered an essential ingredient of democracy.

Renato Boschi, text prepared for PRODDAL, 2002.

nance. Most Latin Americans, though, think that democracy cannot exist without political parties and a legislature, but are dissatisfied with their performance.

6. The media appears at times to fill the void in representation that stems from the crisis of politics and its institutions. This void will continue to exist as long as politics does not assume its proper powers to deal with important issues, and political parties show themselves unable to develop collective projects and to administer the State.

7. When politics is drained of content, that is, when the State ignores the big issues confronting citizens, it is up to society to recover it. In recent years, in parallel with the crisis of representation and the desertion of the State, organizations from within society, from the most diverse sources, have increasingly emerged to address the demands that have been ignored or left unresolved. They are a collection of intermediate groups that have organized themselves spontaneously and are relatively independent of the State and private enterprise. They are able to discuss and implement collective forms of action to defend or promote their own interests, within the framework of the prevailing legal and civil structure.[80]

8. Citizens and civil society organizations play a key role in building democracy, keeping an eye on the management of government, voicing the demands of the people and strengthening the pluralist base that every democracy promotes and needs. They are important actors in a citizens' democracy. Their role is complementary to that of traditional political actors in a democracy. De-

parent impotence of politics seriously weakens democracy, not only with respect to its prospects for growth, but also, perhaps, in terms of its sustainability.

5. Basic democratic institutions in Latin America, especially political parties and the national legislature, are held in low regard. Thirty-six percent of Latin Americans (Latinobarómetro 2002) agree that, if necessary, a President should ignore political parties and the legislature when it comes to gover-

---

80 As a result, these intermediate groups cannot include organizations that favour illegal means to achieve their objectives, whether they are 'mafias' or subversive political groups, or actors with more specific ends that are part of society, such as trade unions, the media—insofar as it comprises bodies focussed on the provision of information and entertainment—political parties, households or mainstream churches. But they do include related entities that come under the definition adopted.

Politics, Parties and Democracy in Latin America

When we speak of transforming the relations between State and society, we are talking about transforming politics. If the whole of society believes itself to be affected by this crisis of politics, which, in turn, affects the quality and importance of new democracies, even more affected are the main political participants, that is, the political parties, which are very harshly judged by public opinion.

In the new scenario created by the social, structural and cultural changes of recent decades, which are destroying the unity of the *society-polis,* the importance of politics as the sole expression of collective action tends to disappear. But politics is acquiring a new significance, more abstract in nature, because it must necessarily approach and combine the different spheres of societal life, without destroying its autonomy. Thus there is less room for policies that are highly ideological, reflect simple rhetorical declamation or tend towards globalization. Instead there is a demand for politics to have social and ethical meaning, something that sheer market forces, the media, special interest groups or mere calculations of individual or corporate self-interest cannot deliver.

The great task for the future is to reconstruct the institutional domain, the *polis,* within which politics can regain its purpose as a valid link between strong and autonomous social actors and a State that can resume its role as the agent of development in a world that threatens to destroy all national communities.

The option is reinforcement, autonomy and complementarity among the State, the government, political parties and the independent social actors: in other words, a new socio-political matrix.

Manuel Antonio Garretón, text prepared for PRODDAL, 2003.

spite the difficulties and obstacles linked to the acceptance of civil society as an arena for participation in democracy and strengthening it, the importance of civil society in spreading democracy throughout Latin America must be clearly recognized. In this sense, politics should not only recover its key content in order to make the transition to a citizens' democracy feasible, but should also examine its unaccomplished task, taking onboard the demands made by a society that has organized itself to entreat, control and make proposals.

9. In Latin America, the invading of public areas by civil society organizations has been a key factor in opening up political channels that previously were closed, restricting the building of democracy. In this manner, civil society widens the parameters of the public arena by participating, expressing identities and demands, and organizing citizens. At the moment, alternative forms of representation are necessary. Without replacing traditional representatives (political parties and legislatures, for instance), these alternatives complement and strengthen them, responding to new needs, to the particular circumstances of marginal or under-represented sectors, to the need for political consensus to encompass the healthy and growing manifestation of diversity, and to the essential need for citizens to recapture the areas in which the democratic will can be strengthened.

10. This issue is linked to certain powerful circles where decisions are made that affect a society profoundly without giving its members a chance to participate. These closed circles of economic decision-making, together with de facto legal and illegal power groups, national and foreign, all contribute to making politics void of meaning. Democracy paves the way for citizens to participate in decision-making and invites them to do so; however, if the arenas in which that participation occurs have little weight when it comes to important national decisions, the consequences tend to take the form of generalized apathy and lack of trust.

Democracy as the Organizational Principle of Society

The social order can no longer rest exclusively upon the regulation by the State of its co-existence, nor can it operate like a self-regulating system. The heart of the problem lies in refounding social co-ordination in a society in which the State and politics have ceased to be its mainstays.

In my opinion, it is in this context that the discussion on 'the democratic question' in Latin America should be seen. Whereas the current trend is to aim for 'electoral democracy', it is worth asking about the role of democracy as a privileged arena for co-ordinating social issues. Instead of restricting democracy to a question of legitimacy, its potential as an organizing principle should be explored. As a matter of fact, democratic institutions and procedures have always acted as mediators among pluralist interests and opinions with the intent of deciding 'where we are heading'.

Norbert Lechner, 1996.

The Need for a New Concept of the Functioning State ('Stateness')

The debate on the State in Latin America must be widened. While the emphasis over the past 20 years has been on matters like privatization, the size of the State and its spending levels and the modernization of State bureaucracies, two important topics have been sidelined: the effectiveness of the State in implementing the electorate mandate; and the democratizing potential of the State, that is, its capacity to reach out universally to all social classes. This latter topic relates to a necessary precondition for ensuring that both rights and responsibilities apply fully to everyone, everywhere. If these conditions are not met, a deficit in stateness will result: serious failings in enforcing the rule of law would directly affect the sustainability and development of democracy.

Under the pretext of initiating institutional reforms to improve the functioning of the markets, these matters have been ignored or hidden. A State that favors democracy attempts to enforce rights and responsibilities equally, which will inevitably cause a change in power relations, particularly in regions like Latin America where the strong concentration of income leads to the concentration of power.

This debate is urgent, because in Latin America, stateness, or State functionality—by which we mean the State's capacity to fulfill its functions and to satisfy its objectives independent of the size of its bureaucracy and the way in which it is organized — is in crisis. In many cases, Latin American States have lost the ability to make legitimate, efficient and effective decisions to address the problems that society deems to be important.

It is imperative that this capacity be restored in order to promote democracy. Democracy cannot exist without a State, and democracy cannot develop without a State that is able to assure and foster citizenship for all. If this condition is not fulfilled, democracy ceases to be a way of organizing power, capable of resolving relationships based on cooperation and conflict. Power slips away, and democracy becomes void of substance.

Recovering the State for its citizens is a crucial challenge for the development of democracy in Latin America. With weak and minimalist States the most one can hope for is to hold on to electoral democracy. Citizenship democracy requires a State that guarantees the universality of rights.[81]

The State must be able to direct society down the general pathway, process conflicts according to democratic principles, make sure that the legal system functions efficiently (protecting both property rights and citizenship rights simultaneously), regulate the markets, establish macroeco-

---

81 Whatever the definition of citizenship we adopt, the link between citizenship and democracy always implies the concept of universality.

nomic equilibria, set up systems of social protection based on the tenet of universal citizenship and make the pre-eminence of democracy the principle for organizing society.

A fully functioning State is a mandatory precondition for a democracy that wants to develop beyond the electoral level, to be able to confront the challenges of democracy effectively. On the basis of this assumption, we can enumerate the topics that we believe an extended agenda to expand the democratic functionality of the State should consider:

1. The agenda for democratic reform must consider all three dimensions of the State: as a set of bureaucratic entities; as a legal system; and as a focus for collective identity. These three dimensions vary historically, and in most of Latin America they are deficient. State bureaucracies often lack power and efficacy, the effectiveness of the legal system is limited socially and territorially, and claims to being a State-for-the Nation, dedicated to pursuing the public interest, are simply not credible in the eyes of many citizens. These shortcomings go a long way towards explaining why Latin American governments have so little power to democratize.

2. Each country in the region is particular in this regard, but, in almost all of them, a large proportion of people live below the minimum threshold of human development, not only with respect to material goods and access to public services but also with respect to basic rights. The solution to these regrettable problems obviously requires both the implementation of appropriate economic and social policies and simultaneously the establishment of an all-encompassing, inclusive and compassionate State, one that is also reasonably efficient, effective and credible. It also requires a vibrant civil society, which through active participation aims to complement the implementation of public policies.

3. The problem of the State in Latin America concerns not just the size of its bureaucra-

cies, but also the inefficiency and inefficacy of these bureaucracies, the ineffectiveness of their legal systems and the low credibility of the State and of government. This is in total contrast to the strong demand by citizens for a State presence, which is apparent, for example, in the survey presented in the second section of this Report.

4. Although, of course, unnecessary bureaucracy should be eliminated and all administrative processes rationalized, one problem that some Latin American States confront is excessive fragmentation and frequently the existence of a blurred boundary between public and private interests. When this manifests itself, the State is sapped and becomes a series of disconnected agencies with civil servants and politicians busily involved in rent-seeking.

5. There is one particularly disturbing problem: the existence of large and, in some cases, growing areas where the State's legal authority does not reach, or does so only intermittently. It is striking that such an important issue is disregarded in State reform programs. The main problem for the State in Latin America is how to deal with a State that is incomplete and weak, with little capacity to be effective universally.

6. Another dimension of this problem is the presence of various kinds of effective 'legality', which are informal, patrimonial and illicit. On occasion, these 'legalities' are found on discretionary sub-national regimes, which coexist with democratic regimes at the national level. The actors operate on the basis of informal institutions such as personalism, nepotism, prebendalism and

Perverse Privatization of the State

A detailed examination of development in the region reveals a chronic democratic deficit, which has often resulted in authoritarianism, clientelism, cronyism and, in extreme cases, nepotism, the expression at the government level of institutions and public policy 'captured' by special interest groups (associated with a given political party, a union, a business organization, a family or local or regional interests). This sort of 'perverse privatization' of the State, which has underpinned the phenomenon of corruption, has led to various interventions by the State that have undermined the efficient working of the market and promoted rent-seeking and speculation.

Enrique V. Iglesias, text prepared for PRODDAL, 2003.

'*caudillismo*'. These power structures rely on the destruction of the boundary between public and private affairs, and on the curtailing of the legality of the State. Furthermore, clientelism—a network of connections that allows a 'boss' to secure support from others in exchange for certain benefits—generates privileges and exclusions, and usually implies discretionary manipulation of public resources.

7. A basic function of the State is to protect people against private acts of violence. Democracy assumes the existence of a State that has violence under control throughout its territory. This is not the case for some regions of Latin America, however. Terrorist groups, criminal and paramilitary organizations and others operate within them. Such entities have their own legal codes, impose their own 'tax' systems and sometimes achieve what is virtually a monopoly over coercion in what they perceive as 'their' territory. This type of private violence, which the State does not control, is one of the principal sources of abuse of basic rights.

8. The protection of citizens by a democratic State is also endangered by the violence associated with crime against people or property. Its level and degree of persistence highlight the weakness of a State that is unable to fulfill its mandate across the board. This situation is even more serious given the prevailing social climate in the region, engrained with poverty and inequality, where the poorest suffer violence most frequently.

9. Among the other consequences of what we have just described, the acute reduction in the State's autonomy is worthy of mention. In fact, a very limited set of policies can actually be designed and implemented outside of the de facto, local and international power structure that effectively influences the State apparatus.

10. An agenda of a State that is in favor of democracy should be structured according to the idea of the Nation on behalf of which the State is supposed to act. It should consider the State to be the center for legitimate decision-making, as well as to be an effective and efficient entity that is focused on addressing the most important problems facing society.

11. For this reason it is essential to debate the issues that in Latin America cast doubt on the efficiency and efficacy of the region's bureaucracies, the effectiveness of its legal system and the very credibility of the State, namely:

- The operational inefficiency of the State and the reduction in its autonomy, stemming from its colonization by special interests (corruption).
- The ineffectiveness of the legal system as a result of patrimonial legal systems.
- The incapacity of some States to govern their entire territory and population, leading to a truncated legal system (lack

of equality under the law and asymmetric enforcement of citizens' rights).

- In the case of some States, the lack of an effective monopoly over the use of force, resulting, for example, in persistent human rights violations.
- The State's inability to represent a diverse society.
- The loss of credibility by the State due to a lack of transparency and a lack of accountability to citizens.
- The capacity of the State to build its own power base, so that it can implement with autonomy the mandate granted to it by the people.

The State is one of the faces of democracy: a State without power is a democracy without power.

An Economy for Democracy

Problems of social citizenship directly affect the durability of democracy in Latin America. Democratic sustainability depends in large measure, therefore, on resolving these problems. In order to do so, the debate on the economy and the diverse ways in which the markets can be organized must become part of the public agenda and be included among the alternative choices available to citizens —for it is within the economy that the solution to significant aspects of the deficits of social citizenship is to be found.

At the beginning of this Report it was stated that a unique trait in Latin America is that it is the first entirely democratic region to be made up of societies with very high levels of poverty and the highest level of social inequality in the world. Thus we referred to the triangle made up of electoral democracy, poverty and inequality, in order to synthesize the nature of these democracies and to underline the need to establish a way of thinking that takes this reality into account. We cannot garner useful answers to questions about the sustainability of democracy in Latin America if the particular chal-

lenges arising from the coexistence of these three phenomena are ignored.

When we described the results of empirical research in the second section of the Report, the poor living conditions of many Latin Americans emerged clearly as the greatest deficit in 'citizenship democracy'. The sheer scale of the problems of social citizenship is such that we keep repeating a crucial question: how much poverty can freedom bear?

Yet the debate on democracy tends to set the economic issue aside, and frequently presents it only in terms of the institutional limitations on economic growth that are implied by democracy. The debate on economics, dodged on the grounds that it is technically complex, is increasingly removed from the arena of public discussion and such issues do not feature among the real options open to citizens when it comes time to vote. In light of these realities it would appear that the well known phrase 'technical issues are not voted on' should be countered by 'the people's well-being in society is not decided by technicians in a laboratory', however enlightened they might be.

This is a problem that is not restricted to our region. The growing trend in certain countries in the developed world to create economic institutions that are almost totally autonomous directly affects their transparency and, there-

BOX 46

An Economy for Democracy

Classical political economy has created a nonexistent economic world, a *Guterwelt*, an isolated world that is always the same and in which the conflicts between purely individual forces are resolved in accordance with unchangeable economic laws. In reality, it is within communities that are quite different from one another that individuals try to acquire wealth, and both the nature and the success of these efforts change, depending on the nature of the community in which they arise [...], this makes State action indispensable for organizing the markets, guaranteeing the sanctity of contracts and establishing currency and credit standards, as well as for the supply of manpower, labor relations, foreign trade, income distribution norms, the tax burden and so forth.

José Nun, text prepared for PRODDAL, 2002.

fore, their accountability to society, with an ensuing loss of credibility in the eyes of the people. Substantive economic decisions removed from the popular will presages, as Jean-Paul Fitoussi sees it, a century in which the crisis of democracy will be dominant.[82] In Latin America, where the deficits in social citizenship reach the levels described, this matter takes on even greater relevance and urgency, to the point where issues such as the rate of democratic development, the sustainability of the system and the resolution of the crisis of political representation depend on our capacity to incorporate the economy and its options into the public agenda, involving both democracy and society.

The economy is a key issue for democracy. This statement, though, does not mean that one should confuse two clearly differentiated forms of social organization: democracy, which organizes relations between power structures; and economics, which organizes relations between production, reproduction and exchange. Nevertheless, the outcome of how the economy is organized is a decisive factor for democracy, especially for *citizens' democracy*, as defined in this Report.

The economy is an issue for democracy because the development of social citizenship depends on it, and because economics both creates and alters power relations. Therefore, the agenda for democratic sustainability must include debate on the diversity of policies and types of market organization that is possible, as well as on the regulatory role of the State.

That the State cannot manage the economy in a frivolous fashion is a lesson that has been learned in Latin America: the (democratic) State has an unavoidable role to play in guiding the economy, which implies a strong capacity to influence economic policy.

Following the suggestion of Dani Rodrik, there are "five functions that public institutions must serve in order for markets to work adequately: protection of property rights, market regulation, macroeconomic stabilization, social insurance, and conflict management."[83] The State and the markets are susceptible to being combined in many different ways, giving rise to the diverse forms that market economies can adopt.

The concept of the markets as a set of institutions 'given by nature' leads to acceptance of the notion that the economy functions completely independently of decisions that are taken democratically. From a democratic viewpoint, however, economic policies are one of the instruments available to a society to achieve full citizenship. For this reason, the economy must be a topic for political debate and must not be excluded on the basis that it 'contextualizes' the organization of the State. This is because:

■ The eventual elimination of inequality is not a marginal economic problem, resulting

82 See Jean-Paul Fitoussi, 2002.
83 Dani Rodrik, 2000.

Democracy and the Market

The advance of democracy and the establishment of clear and strong macroeconomic rules should not be considered as antagonistic but as complementary situations.

José Antonio Ocampo, text prepared for PRODDAL, 2003.

> The economy is an issue for democracy because the development of social citizenship depends on it, and because economics both creates and alters power relations.

from (or a residual of) good economic policy. Rather, distribution affects the efficiency and the very survival of the economic system itself.

- The State plays a highly significant part in income distribution through its fiscal role, through market regulation, and through the provision of subsidies or other means of promotion of certain sectors or long-term policies. This implies the existence of a strong and able State, not a feeble one. To role back the State, the dominant refrain during the 1990s, with the implication that its responsibilities did not go beyond maintaining economic stability and providing some public goods, was a serious mistake, the results of which are now evident.

- If this State role is not filled, democracy becomes irrelevant and is not a credible force for the development of social citizenship.

- Democracy offers the best guarantee of good governance, both in the economic and the political spheres. Civil rights, political freedom and participative processes are key variables for ensuring labor standards, environmental sustainability and economic stability. The performance of democracies in all of these areas has been superior to that of regimes that restrict political participation

- The wider the domain in which market discipline prevails, the broader will be the space for democratic governance. In principle, and to the extent to which market discipline is based on *economic fundamentals* and long-term considerations, there is no reason for conflict to arise between markets and democratic governance. But reality is far from this ideal. The *trade-off* does exist, not just because today the driving force behind the markets is purely financial, but also because they are excessively volatile, dominated by short-term considerations. In this situation, the primacy of democratic discipline over market discipline should be reaffirmed on a frequent basis.

- Markets need both governance and rules. Functioning governance can only be as-

Single Development Model

The 'fetishism' of the reforms introduced by 'market fundamentalism', one expression of which was the 'Washington Consensus', refuses to recognize the diversity implicit in democracy [...]. Behind the argument of the Washington Consensus lies the assumption that a single developmental model exists, applicable to each and every country regardless of local conditions, and a vision of the 'market economy' as the direct opponent of State interventionism. This notion is 'ahistoric', harmful and contrary to democracy.

José Antonio Ocampo, text prepared for PRODDAL, 2003.

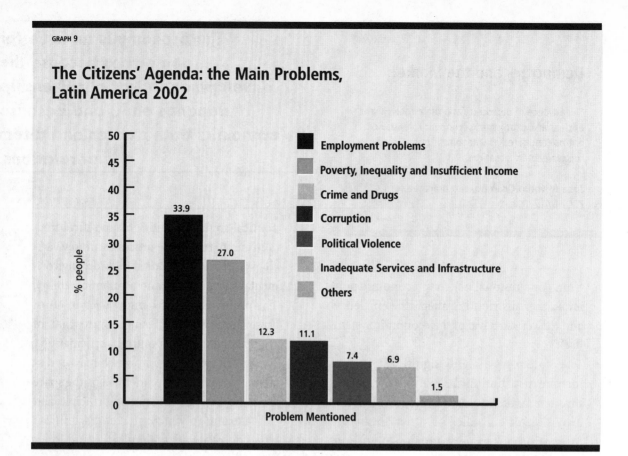

GRAPH 9

The Citizens' Agenda: the Main Problems, Latin America 2002

Note: valid sample n = 18,843 based on the answers to the question p4st in the questionnaire. The category 'Employment Problems' clusters the answers: 'instability in the employment', 'unemployment' and 'lack of opportunities for the youth'. The category 'Poverty, Inequality and Insufficient Income' clusters the answers: 'low salaries', 'inflation/increase of prices' and 'poverty'. The category 'Crime and Drugs' clusters the answers: 'drug trafficking', 'public delinquency/security' and 'drugs consumption'. The category 'Political Violence' clusters the answers: 'terrorism/political violence/guerrilla warfare' and 'violation of human rights'. The category 'Inadequate Services and Infrastructure' clusters the answers: 'transportation', 'education problems', 'housing problems' and 'health problems'. The category 'Others' clusters the answers: 'environmental problems', 'racial discrimination' and 'other'.

Source: calculation by PRODDAL based on data from Latinobarómetro 2002. Result of processing question p4st from Latinobarómetro 2002.

sured through democracy. And democracy continues to be coterminous with the Nation State.[84]

The agenda for democratic sustainability must include these issues concerning the economy and the diverse set of options open to it; otherwise democracy risks becoming devoid of content.

These diverse economic options must form part of the renewed content of politics, for they are a substantial component of the public agenda, just as the debate on diversity is an absolute must in order to put together the best possible combination in terms of the role of the market, the State and the historic context in each of our countries. Conversely, single option dogmatic orthodoxy (*la pensée unique*), universal and timeless prescription, hampers democratic and even economic development.

We single out below the topics that should be part of an agenda centered on a vision of economics that is based on the needs of democratic development in Latin America, from the viewpoint adopted in this Report:

1. Never before in world history—except for the transitory period in the 1930s—were the problems concerning the world economy as serious as they are today: massive unemployment; rising inequality and poverty in rich countries;

84 For these citations, see Dani Rodrik, 2001.

widespread extreme poverty and recurrent crises in numerous developing nations; and increasing inequality among countries.

2. Democracy cannot remain indifferent to all of this. We should remember that we live simultaneously in democracies and market economies. Inevitably, therefore, tension exists between these two dimensions: on the one hand, the individualism and inequality resulting from the functioning of the market, and, on the other, the equality prized by democratic citizenship and the ensuing need for a public arena for collective rather than individual decision-making. There must be reconciliation between the two spheres.

3. The tension that exists between these two dimensions is dynamic in nature, because it allows the system to adapt instead of breaking apart, as generally occurs in systems that are governed according to a single organizing principle (the Soviet regime, for example). Only dynamic systems manage to survive: the rest succumb to sclerosis. In other words, capitalism has survived as the dominant form of economic organization not in spite of democracy but because of it.

4. Two opposing currents are evident in the debate on the relationship between the market and democracy. According to the first, currently dominant, the extension of the market's domain would require limiting democracy's field of action. The second postulates that constant tension between the market and democracy and the latter's desire for equality should be resolved through a search for complementarity.

5. Quite a number of theories prevailing today hold that State intervention usually decreases economic efficacy. The argument of those who favor more of the market is clearly anti-State: "The State is a necessary evil; its ca-

> ### BOX 49
>
> ## Four Economic Advantages of Democracy
>
> Furthermore, those who sustain the first position tend to think that the existing political system is always indifferent as far as the economy is concerned. Nevertheless [...] democracy has at least four advantages over authoritarian regimes: the volatility of growth is less over time; short- and medium-term macroeconomic stability is greater; exogenous crises are better controlled; and salary levels (and their share of national income) are higher.
>
> **Dani Rodrik,** 1997, p. 15. (Translated from the Spanish version of the text).

pacity to intervene should be radically restricted." This Report, however, maintains that a State that adjusts to democracy—efficacious, efficient and credible—is an indispensable aspect of development.

6. Democracy assumes a hierarchical relationship between politics and the economic system, and therefore presupposes that society has the autonomy to choose the manner in which it organizes its market.

7. Democracy, in its quest to curb the exclusion caused by the market, enhances the legitimacy of the economic system; the market, by limiting the power that politics and the State have over the lives of citizens, encourages a greater adherence to democracy. Collective freedom needs to be based on individual freedoms, and vice versa. Both are in an iterative relationship, proving that democracy is a form in movement. "History shows that democracy achieved is never more than a moment in the democratic movement. A movement that never stops."[85]

85 Georges Burdeau, 1985. (Translated from the Spanish version of the text.)

How Democracy and the Market complement Each Other

Relations between democracy and the market are thus more complementary than confrontational. Because democracy prevents exclusion by the market, it increases the legitimacy of the economic system, and the market, by limiting the power that politics has over people's lives, encourages greater adherence to democracy. Thus each of the principles governing politics and economics finds its limitations, as well as its legitimacy, in the other.

Jean-Paul Fitoussi, text prepared for PRODDAL, 2003.

8. National societies, of course, including those in developed countries, do not enjoy the same types of social equality; there is in fact an enormous amount of diversity within these systems. This should not surprise us: democracy implies diversity; there exist different 'varieties of capitalism', different ways of combining the State and the market, and different modes of State action. This is an important truth, which, despite all of the evidence, dogmatic orthodoxy (*la pensée unique*) denies.

9. Opening up economies favors the more mobile factors, not only financial capital, but also some forms of knowledge. The increased mobility of these factors transfers to the less mobile factors—especially to labor—the weight of economic insecurity. Inherent to this process is the risk of reducing popular adherence both to democracy and to the market itself.

10. In light of this situation, it is appropriate to review some criteria for economic policies and their relationship to democracy in line with Latin American experiences in recent decades:

- A debate is needed to identify policies that redistribute income without severely distorting the workings of the market, thus avoiding the 'populism' or 'quick fixes' so prevalent in Latin America.

- The achievement of greater levels of welfare for people requires sustained economic growth, but the latter is insufficient when it is accompanied by unfavorable redistributive consequences.

- International experience shows that competitive advantages based on low wages are fragile and unstable. To compete in the world today, efficient production, process innovation, product design and differentiation and the development of an adequate support service are mandatory. Qualified human capital is essential in this regard. Social policies must in turn be guided by four basic principles: universality; solidarity; efficiency; and inclusiveness.

- Limits on the scale of extensive property ownership and private enterprise are related to the levels of inequality that any given society is inclined to tolerate, as well as to its forms of taxation. A second type of restriction concerns potential abuse of market power by top business executives and large companies. The third one has to do with the capacity of these business executives and companies to extend their influence beyond the market as a result of their significant ability to lobby and their capacity to tap into other spheres of power that are typical in contemporary society—especially the media.

- A political agreement among the different social sectors on what the State should do helps to legitimate the level, composition and pattern of public expenditure, as well as the amount of tax required to finance the public sector.

Finally, we wish to highlight that that our data show two things of great practical importance. The first is that many Latin Americans

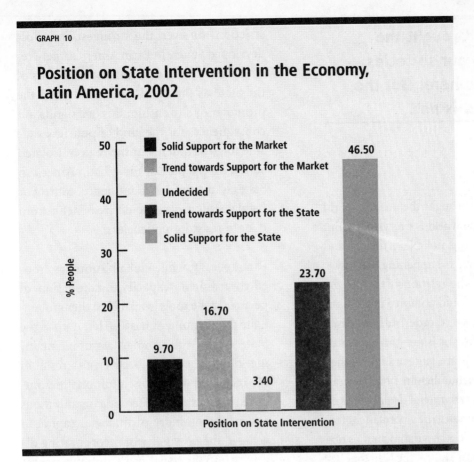

GRAPH 10

Position on State Intervention in the Economy, Latin America, 2002

Notes: valid sample, n = 17,646. For the construction of this variable, questions p21no2, p22sta, p22stb, p22essd and p22esse of Latinobarómetro 2002 were recodified. For more information, see the note to the Table 142 in the Statistical Compendium of the Report.
Source: calculation by PRODDAL, based on data from Latinobarómetro 2002.

share a highly critical view of the functioning of market economies. The second aspect—surely the counterpart of the frustration just described—is that the majority looks favorably on State intervention in the economy.

Power and Democratic Policies in the Era of Globalization

An extended agenda on globalization should include a debate on its political and military nature, its restrictions on diversity and the strong limitations on State power. Globalization crudely posits questions about the power of Nation States and about the domestic power of the States. The key problem of democracy manifests itself once again, but in a different way: the presence or absence of power to satisfy the will of the majority.

The debate that has developed naturally up until now has emphasized the financial and commercial aspects of globalization, and has left more or less to one side its principal characteristic: that external forces have ceased to be external. They are now as internal as are local powers. They condition or determine the decisions of the State and their field of action is not limited to finance or trade. Increasingly they encompass political questions, security and internal organization, the social welfare, education and healthcare systems

It is necessary, therefore, to broaden the debate on globalization to take account of the following two factors: first, the real impact of globalization on States' internal sovereignty; and second, how to implement strategies in order to increase national and regional capacity so that a national power is not extinguished in the name of an uncontrollable global force.

Globalization has brought the outside world into our societies. The world is everywhere. But the power of the world is not.

Globalization has brought the outside world into our societies. The world is everywhere. But the power of the world is not. Nevertheless, and at the same time as this is happening, acknowledging the nature of the relations that rule the world that we live in should not force us to abandon the concept of a world order ruled by laws. The reality surrounding us is one thing, yet our dreams and aspirations are quite another—they may indeed be utopian, but they are not chimeras. The struggle for an *international democratic system of law* should not cease to be a permanent feature of a civilization that boasts democracy as one of its conquests, and nor should the idea that behavior is determined by rules designed to protect equal rights for all, individuals and States.

In effect, in the world that has come into being since the end of the post-Cold War (on 11 September 2001), existing power relationships, mainly military and economic, regulate the international system. Under these conditions, the most urgent priority to emerge is the need to address the contradiction between diversity—which demands a large degree of autonomy for countries as well as for a world system based on clear, shared norms—and a world homogenized by power relations that grant national actors the capacity to establish normative rules concerning only relatively marginal issues. What substantive choices with respect to significant issues remain open to citizens under such circumstances? And what are the chances that what they decide will be put into practice?

The Report offers the following thoughts and ideas in order to foster debate on globalization and the development of democracy:

1. At the same time that it has promoted democracy, globalization has imposed restrictions on even the strongest and most developed States. In Latin America, these restrictions call into question the credibility of the State as the builder of society and the promoter of citizenship; this has significant consequences for the kind of policies available to governments in the region. Isolated action on the part of most Latin American States is not enough to influence, control or regulate this process, to derive benefits from it, or to resist its tendencies.

2. Paradoxically, while globalization has eroded governments' capacity to take action, in particular the tools available to them to regulate the economy, it has also left it up to the State to fulfill the complex task of maintaining social cohesion. Moreover, as a result of the increased weight of conditionalities imposed by international lending organizations and of the mobility of financial capital in general, the possibility of incorporating diversity into the social and economic organization models implied by democracy has been progressively reduced.

3. Nevertheless, there is significant distance between this affirmation and government passivity. Recognizing existing restrictions does not necessarily imply accepting the status quo. Building an autonomous space for national States that confront globalization is a challenge that is inherent to democratic politics, which, as we have asserted throughout this Report, should have as its central objective the construction and expansion of the diverse forms of citizenship.

4. It is dangerous to become fatalistic when faced with globalization, arguing that the asymmetry of forces is such that there is no room for political autonomy. This fatalism, which unfortunately is quite widespread, overlooks the fact that real areas for negotiation exist in the world, as well as the fact that these spaces may be expanded if there is consistent and sustained political will to establish regional entities.

BOX 51

Globalization and the Impotence of Politics

Globalization not only increases the role of the market in the system of equity and reduces that of democracy, but also it does so in the name of market efficiency and of an order that is higher than that of democracy. This is what they call political impotence.

Jean-Paul Fitoussi, text prepared for PRODDAL, 2003.

5. The institutional spaces where political citizenship may be perfected remain basically national. This means recognizing that democracy as a universal value only assumes its full meaning if national processes of representation, participation and decision-making are allowed to determine strategies for economic and social development, providing effective forms of mediation to respond to the tensions that are innate to globalization.

6. From the perspective of democratic development itself, it is also necessary to discuss how to build the autonomous spaces mentioned above; they are needed so that Latin American democracies may develop a solid basis on which to grow.

7. Democracy is severely affected by the increasing tendency to shift responsibility for making important decisions to circles that are beyond the control of citizens. This tends to cast doubt on the relevance that democracy really has for citizens, which, in turn, has considerable implications for the loyalty that they show towards it. This concern must be underlined, because we may be heading towards a form of politics limited only to restricted agendas, which sooner or later may lead us to be caught up in irrelevant agendas or ones that prevent the development of the diverse approaches needed to deal with the specific characteristics of each of our countries.

8. From the above, it can be deduced that the question of how to increase autonomous capacity with regard to defining and solving the important problems that affect us concerns not only each individual country but also the region as a whole.

9. This implies a debate on regional policies, too, to make it possible to achieve a shared increase in autonomy. To this end, the political renascence of regional activities takes on new meaning and urgency, going beyond purely commercial efforts to recreate and widen the political spaces in which countries and citizens make their own decisions.

10. This does not necessarily require the creation of new organizations to take on these tasks, nor, even less, that they should be supranational. The key factor is that the States in the region decide to tackle these issues at the political level. Current regional and sub-regional institutions offer a reasonable platform from which to do this, after making essential adjustments to their agendas and structures.

11. Presented in this fashion, the challenge facing political integration centers around construction of the Nation and construction of the region, a region of Nations that complement and strengthen one another. In other words: a political association of sovereign States.

12. The international order should respect the diversity that exists between and within countries, within the limits of interdependence. But power practices in current international relations do not tend to take this requirement into consideration.

13. The capacity to establish autonomy in a globalized world with one single hegemonic

power implies new challenges. At issue here are not only the classic problems concerning relations between the center and the periphery, the empire and its zones of control, but also those concerning relations in the current era of globalization, in which exterior phenomena are as immediate and common as those that manifest themselves within a Nation's own borders.

14. The post-Cold War era ended on 11 September 2001, the day the United States of America came under attack by terrorists. Security returned to center stage, becoming the number one issue in world politics. In turn, subsequent events have signaled an important change in world relations, with a significant impact on multilateral collective defense systems.

15. The prominence of security on the international agenda has created tension with democracy and freedom. First World countries have better mechanisms than our own to resolve this tension.

16. The Latin American experience in the decades prior to the end of the Cold War is a good example of what happens when security issues become the only prism through which politics and international relations are observed.

17. For its part, the region has a long history when it comes to this matter. It has been the target of several brutal terrorist attacks in the recent past. Also, for several decades some Latin American countries suffered tremendous violence at the hands of both insurgents and of the State itself. Therefore, the threat of terrorist violence is no abstract premise for the region.

18. Recently, military power relationships have shaped world ties decisively. The notion that globalization was responsible for shifting the focus of international relations from military and security issues to financial ones, and that economics was replacing politics, vanished completely. The prominence of the terrorist theme puts under the microscope the impact that a potential terrorist attack would have on State capabilities on the one hand, and on the other the impact of inappropriate responses on those capabilities and on democracy itself. An appropriate response is one where the State reacts effectively to the threat of aggression while simultaneously preventing that response from weakening its ability to foster democracy or from reducing the quality of that democracy.

19. It is fundamental for democracy that security problems do not arise as a result of an agenda imposed by outside actors but rather that a country comes up with its own solutions. In this regard, the security issue acquires central importance. Passivity on this matter could make us extremely vulnerable to external strategies, which are formulated without taking into account important regional interests.

20. In light of the events of 11 September 2001 and their ramifications, and as a result of the singular nature of their democracies, the countries of Latin America must devise their own criteria to inspire the creation of options for responding to the threat of terrorism.

In Summary

This Report has argued that the right to vote regularly in order to elect individuals to govern in accordance with the rule of law is not merely important but is a sine qua non if a system of government is to qualify as a democracy. However, it goes beyond this narrow definition of democracy to assert that the horizon for democracy should be extended. This process entails not only perfecting existing institutional political mechanisms and ensuring efficient implementation of civil rights for all citizens, but also effectively broadening social citizenship.

The discussion focuses on how to advance towards an integral form of citizenship, which must have politics at its heart—the way in which the citizen, and more specifically the community of citizens, can participate in important decision-making. Globalization is a fact, but this does not mean that everything that arises as a consequence of technological transformation and market expansion must be accepted without reflection and without answer. We must understand the constant and rapid transformation that is going on in the world today, and we must live with uncertainties, but we must also work to modify these macro-trends in accordance with the specific situation in each country. The challenge is to cope with globalization at the local and regional levels, utilizing a proactive and not a passive approach. Thus, the economy is not a given that is to be viewed passively either; there is not just one way to think and to make the market work. It is already known that there are different ways of organizing economies, which have proved successful over time in different cultural contexts.

This community of citizens should, therefore, promote a new legitimacy for the State, that entity that must not only supply the administrative bureaucratic machinery in each country but must also respect and extend the reach of political institutions and the rule of law, and lay the foundations to ensure equity in order to implement social policies to broaden social citizenship. Creating an inclusive vision of citizenship, harnessing the functioning of the economy with the political decisions of the citizens, are just some of the issues that arise from this Report, written to provoke a new kind of approach to the discussion of democracy in Latin America.

Final Reflections

The Unending Challenge

In one of his famous essays Isaiah Berlin reminds us that "more than 100 years ago the German poet Heine warned the French that they should not underestimate the power of ideas: philosophical concepts nurtured in the silence of an academic's study could destroy an entire civilization."

Latin America was the product of an idea, and that idea remains at the heart of its vision of the future: the building of a democratic society. The process via which the continent attained its independence was indissolubly linked to the republican ideal, and its liberators devoted themselves to the realization of that dream. The historical outcome, however, has involved a strange journey of discovery, full of contradictions, interruptions and reconnections, of evenings and dawns. At times, events—social, economic and military— have overflowed the boundaries of principles. But ideas have also fallen into their own traps, because whenever freedom and justice go their separate ways, both are at risk. That is what happened, unfortunately, when we dreamed of going beyond the core of the democratic idea, that is, of assuring freedom and organizing a government that is representative, and that is able to reconcile freedom with the greatest possible amount of equality among people.

To what extent has this ideal been achieved in reality? What must be done to consolidate that which has been achieved and to keep moving forward? In response to these crucial questions, this project was launched two years ago—involving consulting, inquiring, stirring things up, awakening interest and trying to find some objective means of measuring situations that are always more complex than any statistic. Ideas and reality are in a state of constant tension. If we confine ourselves to the realm of ideas, we may betray them with facts. If we lose sight of ideas in the eager struggle against unjust realities, we risk falling into a dangerous and disjunctive empiricism. It is essential, therefore, to define concepts and to compare them as closely as possible with reality.

We should remember that UNDP is able to do this today because the region has achieved a higher level of democratic development than ever before. In the 1970s, the map of Latin America was overshadowed by so many dictatorships that the conditions did not exist that would permit an international organization to attempt to engage in serious reflection on the issue. The encouraging assumption of renewed democratic development allowed work to begin, which has enjoyed the collaboration, without exception, of governments and parties, of political and civil figures and of economic and academic leaders. Meetings, seminars, interviews, reports, studies and statistical research contributed to a growing body of work, which, quite apart from its intrinsic value, aroused interest in the subject throughout the region. People began to understand that it was essential—and possible—to act on our situation in order to change it.

Today we present this Report on democracy, hoping that, despite its inevitable limitations and necessary imperfections, it puts at the disposal of all Latin Americans a tool with which to work. This is not a tomographic scan of a particular State. Nor is it a specific analysis of some known pathology. What is offered here is a general impression of democratic health, an approximate description of current areas of concern and some instruments designed for continuous monitoring so that we may all carry on building.

As Pierre Rosanvallon told us, "democracy poses a question that remains permanently open: it seems that it has never been possible to give a completely satisfactory answer to it." This irritating feeling that nothing is ever finished is the very essence of freedom, and we must live with it. Each time we try out, in the name of democracy, some system that has all of the answers, totalitarianism ensues. The past century was the period, perhaps, in which this search for answers led to the greatest tragedies. Heirs to that experience, today, we accept that reality will never fulfill us completely because compared with pure abstraction it will always be unsatisfactory; but we also know that, since democracy is "first and foremost an ideal," as Giovanni Sartori tells us, we should try, at all times, slowly but surely, to continue to perfect it.

Poverty, social inequality, ethnic conflict and the gap between expectations and reality introduce an element of instability—at a point in history when a scientific revolution is altering our daily lives. From this stems the incessant need to think ahead. If this Report helps to raise positive awareness of this need among all of the main players it will have succeeded in its fundamental purpose, which is not to judge anybody but rather to wake everybody up. UNDP achieved this with the *Index of Human Development*, which went beyond the provision of partial and insufficient figures on gross domestic product. In that same innovative vein, we are trying today to make sure that the betterment of democracy is not simply a rhetorical expression, always open to question, but instead a reality that can be acted on, involving steps forward and steps backwards, which can be observed objectively. Those advances, those quests, conform to the notion that democracy and human development are two sides of the same coin.

If we underestimate the progress that has been made, while accumulating deficits and deficiencies, we will discourage society from its task of necessary and constant improvement. If we allow ourselves to be complacent, rejoicing in a goal achieved, we will put everything at risk. With this Report, a new stage of the journey begins.

The effort of the past two decades has been remarkable, and what it has achieved should be flaunted to the full extent possible. That effort must be maintained, and a continuous process of observation and analysis, of publicizing experiences and of warning about risks, could well start here. An alert sense of awareness is the only possible state of mind if democracy is to advance, adapting itself to the times. Democracy remains, after all, the most revolutionary of ideas and, because it is always unfinished, the most challenging. There are no definitive answers to the questions that it raises but there will always be, as with respect to the broader destiny of humankind, opportunities to do good on behalf of one's fellow men and women.

Julio María Sanguinetti

Former President of Uruguay
President of the Fundación Círculo de Montevideo

■ Acknowledgements

This Report could not have been prepared without the generous collaboration of many people and organizations.

We wish to extend particular thanks to the European Union, especially Chris Patten, the Commissioner for External Relations of the European Commission, Eneko Landaburu, Fernando Valenzuela and Thomas Dupla del Moral, Director-General, Assistant Director-General and Director for Latin America, respectively, of the Directorate of External Relations, and Fernando Cardesa, Director for Latin America of EUROPEAID, as well as to all of the officials of the General Directorate of External Relations and EUROPEAID's Office of Co-operation who helped with this project, and assisted in the publication and dissemination of this Report.

Institutions that helped with the Preparation of the Report

The Economic Commission for Latin America and the Caribbean (ECLAC), the Inter-American Development Bank (IADB), the Organization of American States (OAS), the Club de Madrid, the Círculo de Montevideo, the Latinobarómetro Corporation, Fundación Chile XXI, the Centre for Social and Environmental Studies of the University of Bologne, the International Institute for Democracy and Electoral Assistance (IDEA) and the Civil Association for Transparency (Peru).

Authors of Articles about Topics on the Agenda

Manuel Alcántara, Raúl Alconada Sempé, Willem Assies, Natalio Botana, Fernando Calderón, Dante Caputo, Fernando Henrique Cardoso, Jean-Paul Fitoussi, Eduardo Gamarra, Marco Aurélio Garcia, Manuel Antonio Garretón, César Gaviria, Julio Godio, Felipe González, Rosario Green, Cândido Grzybowski, Osvaldo Hurtado, Enrique Iglesias, José Antonio Ocampo, Celi Pinto, Augusto Ramírez Ocampo, Rubens Ricupero, Lourdes Sola, Joseph Stiglitz, Cardenal Julio Terrazas and Francisco Thoumi.

Participants in the Round of Consultations

Argentina: Raúl Alfonsín, Jaime Campos, Elisa Carrió, Jorge Casaretto, Víctor De Genaro, Fernando de la Rúa, José Manuel de la Sota, Jorge Elías, Rosendo Fraga, Aníbal Ibarra, Ricardo López Murphy, Juan Carlos Maqueda, Joaquín Morales Solá, Hugo Moyano, Adolfo Rodríguez Saá, Rodolfo Terragno, Horacio Verbitsky and Oscar Vignart.

Bolivia: Esther Balboa, Carlos Calvo, Carlos Mesa, Gustavo Fernández Saavedra, Martha García, Fernando Mayorga, Jaime Paz Zamora, Jorge Quiroga Ramírez, Edgar Ramírez and Gonzalo Sánchez de Losada.

Brazil: Frei Betto, Luiz Carlos Bresser-Pereira, José Márcio Camargo, Fernando Henrique Cardoso, Suely Carneiro, Marcos Coimbra, Fábio K. Comparato, Paulo Cunha, Joaquim Falcão, José Eduardo Faria, Ruben César Fernandes, Argelina Figueiredo, Luiz Gonzaga Belluzo, Oded

Grajew, Cândido Grzybowski, Helio Jaguaribe, Miriam Leitão, Ives Martins, Filmar Mauro, Henrique Meirelles, Antônio Delfim Neto, Jarbas Passarinho, João C. Pena, Celso Pinto, Márcio Pochmann, João Paulo dos Reis Velloso, Clóvis Rossi, Maria Osmarina Marina Silva Vaz de Lima, Pedro Simon, Luiz E. Soares, Luiz Suplicy Hafers, Vicentinho, Arthur Virgílio and Ségio Werlang.

Chile: Andrés Allamand, Patricio Aylwin, Benito Baranda, Edgardo Boeninger, Eduardo Frei, Juan Pablo Illanes, Jorge Inzunza, Ricardo Lagos, Norbert Lechner, Arturo Martínez, Jovino Novoa, Ricardo Nuñez, Carlos Ominami and Carolina Tohá.

Colombia: Ana Teresa Bernal, Belisario Betancur, Héctor Fajardo, Guillermo Fernández de Soto, Luis Jorge Garay, Hernando Gómez Buendía, Julio Roberto Gómez, Carlos Holguín, Fernando Londoño, Antonio Navarro, Sabas Pretelt de la Vega, Jorge Rojas, Ernesto Samper, Francisco Santos, Horacio Serpa, Álvaro Valencia Tovar and Luis Carlos Villegas.

Costa Rica: Oscar Arias, Leonardo Garnier, Eduardo Lizano, Elizabeth Odio Benito, Ottón Solis, Albino Vargas and Samuel Yankelewitz.

Republic Dominican: Manuel Esquea Guerrero, Leonel Fernández Reyna, Antonio Isa Conde, Carlos Guillermo León, Hipólito Mejía and Jacinto Peynado.

Ecuador: Rodrigo Borja, Marena Briones, Joaquín Cevallos, José Eguiguren, Ramiro González, Susana González, Lucio Gutiérrez, Osvaldo Hurtado, Miguel Lluco, Alfredo Negrete, Jaime Nebot, Benjamín Ortiz, Alfredo Palacio, Rodrigo Paz, Gustavo Pinto, Mesías Tatamuez Moreno, Luis Verdesoto and Jorge Vivanco.

El Salvador: Armando Calderón Sol, Gregorio Rosa Chávez, Humberto Corado, David Escobar Galindo, Mauricio Funes, Salvador Samayoa, Héctor Silva and Eduardo Zablah Touché.

Guatemala: Marco Vinicio Cerezo, Marco Augusto García, Gustavo Porras, Alfonso Portillo, Rosalina Tuyuc and Raquel Zelaya.

Honduras: Isaías Barahona, Rafael Leonardo Callejas, Miguel Facusse, Carlos Flores Facusse, Ricardo Maduro and Leticia Salomón.

Mexico: Sergio Aguayo, Luis H. Álvarez, Manuel Arango, Raúl Benitez, Gilberto Borja Navarrete, Luis Felipe Bravo Mena, Felipe Calderón Hinojosa, Cuauhtémoc Cárdenas, Jorge G. Castañeda, Eugenio Clariond, Rolando Cordera, Santiago Creel, Carlos Elizondo, Vicente Fox, Juan Ramón de la Fuente, Amalia García, Francisco Hernández, Felipe de Jesús Cantú, Santiago Levy, Carmen Lira, Soledad Loaeza, Andrés Manuel López Obrador, Roberto Madrazo, Lorenzo Meyer, Arturo Montiel, Arturo Núñez, Mariano Palacios Alcocer, José Francisco Paoli Bolio, Beatriz Paredes, José Luis Reina, Jesús Reyes Heroles, Rosario Robles, Juan Sánchez Navarro, Sergio Sarmiento, Bernardo Sepúlveda, Luis Téllez, César Verduga, José Woldenberg and Ernesto Zedillo.

Nicaragua: Carlos Fernando Chamorro, Violeta Granera, Wilfredo Navarro Moreira, René Núñez Tellez, Sergio Ramírez Mercado and José Rizo Castellón.

Panama: Miguel Candanedo, Norma Cano, Guillermo Endara, Angélica Maytin, Martín Torrijos and Alberto Vallarino.

Paraguay: Martín Almada, Nelson Argaña, Nicanor Duarte Frutos, Pedro Fadul, Ricardo Franco, Cristina Muñoz, Enrique Riera, Milda Rivarola, Humberto Rubin, Miguel Abdón Saguier and Aldo Zucolillo.

Peru: Julio Cotler, Jorge Del Castillo, Carlos Ferrero Costa, Lourdes Flores Nano, Gastón Garatea Vori, Diego García-Sayán, Juan José Larrañeta, Roberto Nesta, Valentín Paniagua, Rafael Roncagliolo, Javier Silva Ruete, Luis Solari de la Fuente, Alejandro Toledo and Alan Wagner.

Uruguay: Diego Balestra, Jorge Batlle, Héctor Florit, Luis Alberto Lacalle, José Mujica, Romeo Pérez, Juan José Ramos, Julio María Sanguinetti, Liber Seregni and Ricardo Zerbino.

Venezuela: José Albornoz, Alejandro Armas, Carlos Fernández, Eduardo Fernández, Guillermo García Ponce, Alberto Garrido, Janet Kelly, Enrique Mendoza, Calixto Ortega, Teodoro Petkoff, Leonardo Pisani, José Vicente Rangel, Cecilia Sosa, Luis Ugalde and Ramón Velásquez.

Special Participants

Belisario Betancur, former President of Colombia; Rodrigo Borja, former President of Ecuador; Kim Campbell, former Prime Minister of Canada and President of the Club de Madrid; Aníbal Cavaco Silva, former Prime Minister of Portugal; Fernando Henrique Cardoso, former President of Brazil; Eduardo Frei, former President of Chile; César Gaviria, former President of Colombia and Secretary-General of the OAS; Felipe González, former President of Spain; Antonio Guterres, former Prime Minister of Portugal; Osvaldo Hurtado, former President of Ecuador; Valentin Paniagua, former President of Peru; Jorge Quiroga Ramírez, former President of Bolivia; Carlos Roberto Reina, former President of Honduras; Miguel Angel Rodríguez, former President of Costa Rica; Julio María Sanguinetti, former President of Uruguay and President of the Fundación Círculo de Montevideo; Ernesto Zedillo, former President of Mexico; Enrique Iglesias, President of the IADB; José Antonio Ocampo, former Executive Secretary of the Economic Commission for Latin America and the Caribbean (ECLAC) and current UN Under-Secretary General for Economic and Social Affairs; Fernando Valenzuela, Assistant Director-General for External Relations of the European Union; Guillermo de la Dehesa, former Secretary of State of Spain for the Economy; Miguel Ángel Fernández-Ordoñez, former Secretary of State of Spain for the Economy; Ernesto Garzón Valdés, President of the Club de Tampere; Antonio Álvarez-Couceiro, Secretary-General of the Club de Madrid; Fernando Carrillo-Florez, Principal Counsellor of the IADB Office in Europe; and Lucinio Muñoz, Assistant to the Secretary-General of the Club de Madrid.

Special thanks to Jacques Le Pottier, Dean of the Faculty of Economic Sciences at the University of Toulose Le Mirail, who lent his support to the project and provided access to that university's resources.

Officials of the Office
of the Administrator of UNDP

Thanks to the officials of the Office of the Administrator of the UNDP, particularly Marck Suzman, Jessica Faietta, William Orme and Victor Arango of the Communications Office of the Administrator.

Officials of the UNDP Directorate for Latin America and the Caribbean

The project staff wishes to acknowledge in particular the close collaboration of UNDP officials, especially Freddy Justiniano, Myriam Méndez-Montalvo and Enrique Ganuza, as well as Gilberto Flores, Jacqueline Carbajal, Isabel Chang, Elisabeth Díaz, Cristina Fasano, Elena García-Ramos, Lydia Legnani, Cielo Morales, Susana Pirez, Juan Manuel Salazar, Luis Francisco Thais, María-Noel Vaeza and Gemma Xarles.

Officials of the Liaison Office of UNDP
in Brussels

We thank the officials of the Liaison Office of the UNDP in Brussels, Belgium: Omar Baquet; María-Noel Vaeza; and Susana Etcheverry.

Officials of the UNDP Office in Argentina

Staff members of the UNDP Office in Argentina—the headquarters of the project—were invaluable in terms of cooperation and organizational and administrative support, notably Carmelo Angulo Barturen, Jessica Faieta, Silvia Rucks, Susana Gatto, Pablo Vinocur, José Ignacio López, Gerardo Noto, Liliana De Riz, Elba Luna, Sonia Urriza, Aldo García, Ana Inés Mulleady, María Angélica Wawrzyk, Ana Edmunds, Pablo Basz, Marcelo Bagnasco, Beatriz Martínez, Saioa Royo, Itziar Abad, Mercedes Ansotegui, Natalia Aquilino, Andrea Botbol, Cecilia Del Río, Daniela Del Río, Myriam Di Paolo, Claudio Flichman, Oscar González, Guillermo Iglesias, Beatriz López, María Inés Jezzi, Vivian Joensen, Juan Carlos Magnaghi, Marina Mansilla Hermann, Jorge Martínez, Santiago Redeci-llas, Walter Ricciardi, Ricardo Salas and Geraldine Watson.

We would like to express our gratitude to all of them.

Resident Representatives, Deputies and Assistants in UNDP Offices throughout Latin America

Jeffrey Avina, Kim Bolduc, Katica Cekalovic, Renata Claros, Juan Pablo Corlazzoli, Jorge Chediek, Juan Carlos Crespi, Ligia Elizondo, Jafet Enríquez, Niki Fabiancic, Elisabeth

Fong, Walter Franco, Roberto Galvez, Susana Gatto, Peter Grohmann, Elizabeth Hayek, José Manuel Hermida, Henry Jackelen, Lorenzo Jiménes de Luis, Thierry Lemaresquier, Carlos Lopes, Carlos Felipe Martínez, Pablo Martínez, Alfredo Marty, César Miquel, Antonio Molpeceres, Roberto Monteverde, Bruno Moro, Clemencia Muñoz, Lucien Muñoz, Adelina Paiva, Barbara Pesce-Monterio, Irene Phillip, Benigno Rodríguez, Beat Rohr, Martín Santiago, Rosa Santizo, Ilona Szemzo, Aase Smedler, Claudio Tomasi, René Mauricio Valdés, Jan-Jilles Van der Hoeven and Alfredo Witschi-Cestari.

Officials in UNDP Offices throughout Latin America

Bolivia: Patricia Cusicanqui, Christian Jetté and Cecilia Ledesma.

Brazil: Johanna Clarke de Voest Silva, Gilberto Chaves, José Carlos Libânio, Filipe Nasser and Wilson Pires Soares.

Chile: Alejandra Cáceres, Josefa Errázuriz, Eugenio Ortega, Oscar Muñoz, Carla Pietrantoni and María Teresa Vergara.

Colombia: Adriana Anzola, Alice Ayala, Carlos Mauricio García, Hernando Gómez Buendía, Daniel Igartua, Patricia Lizarazu, Amalia Paredes, Mauricio Ramírez and María del Pilar Rojas.

Costa Rica: Vera Brenes, Henry González and Arlene Méndez Solano.

Dominican Republic: Solange Bordas and Martha Elizabeth Martínez Correa.

Ecuador: José Balseca, Santiago Burbano and Norma Guerrero.

El Salvador: Esther López and Morena Valdez.

Honduras: Fátima Cruz, Doris Rivas, Karina Servellón and Lesly María Sierra.

Guatemala: Juan Alberto Fuentes, Myriam de López, Ingrid Melgar, Carmen Morales and Cecilia Zúñiga.

Mexico: Arturo Fernández, Luz Patricia Herremann and Patricia Marrón.

Nicaragua: Gloria Altamirano and Dina García.

Panama: Marta Alvarado.

Paraguay: Inés Brack and María Clavera.

Peru: Pilar Airaldi, Carolina Aragón and Mario Solari.

Uruguay: Verónica Nori and Mónica Voss.

Venezuela: Mayra Cartaya and Alberto Fuenmayor.

Participants in Seminars and Meetings

In designing the Statistical Compendium and developing the indices we were aided by the commentaries of Kenneth Bollen, Fernando Carrillo-Florez, Michael John Coppedge, Freddy Justiniano, Fernando Medina, John Mark Payne, Adam Przeworski, Ardys Robles Soto, Michael Smithson, Jay Verkuilen, Gemma Xarles and Daniel Zovatto.

In a meeting to review the Index of Electoral Democracy the following people provided expertise: Horacio Boneo, Dante Caputo, Leandro García Silva, Hernando Goméz Buendía, Freddy Justiniano, Juan Fernando Londoño, Myriam Méndez-Montalvo, Simón Pachano, Juan Rial, Thomas Scheetz, Elisabeth Spehar, Maria Hermínia Tavares de Almeida and José Woldenberg.

The following experts took part in analyzing the current state of democracy in Latin America and its future prospects: Héctor Aguilar Camín, Raúl Alconada Sempé, Soledad Alvear, Julio Angel, Sergio Bitar, Dante Caputo, Jorge Castañeda, Marcelo Contreras, Álvaro Díaz, Nicolás Eyzaguirre, Marco Aurélio Garcia, Manuel Antonio Garretón, Gabriel Gaspar, Rodolfo Gil, Alonso González, Eduardo Graeff, Katty Grez, Jorge Heine, José Miguel Insulza, Ricardo Lagos, Thierry Lemaresquier, Edgardo Lepe, Ester Levinsky, Rodolfo Mariani, Elena Martínez, Guttemberg Martínez, Gonzalo Martner, Jorge Levi Mattoso, Heraldo Muñoz, José Antonio Ocampo, Carlos Ominami, Verónica Oyarzún, Augusto Ramírez Ocampo, Juan Ramírez, Jorge Reyes, Julio María Sanguinetti, Camila Sanhueza, Joseph Stiglitz, Federico Storani, Juan Gabriel Valdéz and Isabel Vásquez.

Together with the Fundación Círculo de

Montevideo, the following people participated in the discussion on the crisis of politics: Carmelo Angulo Barturen, Danilo Arbilla, Dante Caputo, Antonio Álvarez Cruceiro, Joaquín Estefanía, Aníbal Fernández, Eduardo Frei, Felipe González, Osvaldo Hurtado, Elena Martínez, Bartolomé Mitre, Alfredo Negrete, Andrés Oppenheimer, Rodrigo Pardo, J.C. Pereyra, Rafael Poleo, Julio María Sanguinetti, Martín Santiago, Enrique Santos, Thomas Scheetz, Javier Solanas and Ernesto Tiffenberg.

The following people contributed to the analysis of democracy and the State: Diego Achard, Giorgio Alberti, Raúl Alconada Sempé, Antonio Álvarez Couceiro, José Luis Barros, Rodrigo Borja, Dante Caputo, Fernando Henrique Cardoso, Elisa Carrió, Marcelo Contreras Nieto, Alberto Couriel, Sonia Draibe, Gilberto Dupas, Gustavo Fernández Saavedra, Walter Franco, Manuel Antonio Garretón, Rodolfo Gil, George Gray Molina, Edmundo Jarquín, José Carlos Libânio, Rodolfo Mariani, Elena Martínez, Marcus Melo, Arturo O'Connell, Guillermo O'Donnell, Beatriz Paredes, Celi Pinto, Eduardo Piragibe Graeff, Márcio Pochmann, Augusto Ramírez Ocampo and Lourdes Sola.

The following participated in the discussion on civil society and drug trafficking: Carlos Basombrio, Fernando Calderón, Eduardo Gamarra, Luis Santana, Francisco Thoumi, Edelberto Torres Rivas, and Luis Verdesoto.

With regard to the discussion on democracy and multiculturalism we benefited from the views of Álvaro Artiga, Willem Assies, Santiago Bastos, Antonio Cañas, Julieta Castellanos, Isis Duarte, Galo Guardián, Francesca Jessup, Carlos Benjamín Lara, Carlos Mendoza, Arodys Robles Soto, Ignacio Rodríguez, Gonzalo Rojas, Manuel Rojas, Leticia Salomón, Edelberto Torres Rivas, Jorge Vargas and Agatha Williams.

The following experts took part in the analysis of democracy and economics: Raúl Alconada Sempé, Alberto Alesina, Carlos Amat y León, José Luis Barros, María Elisa Bernal, Tim Besley, Dante Caputo, Alberto Couriel, Ricardo Ffrench-Davis, Enrique Ganuza, Innocenzo Gasparini, Rebeca Grynspan, Eugenio Lahera, Oscar Landerretche, Thierry Lemaresquier, Manuel Marfán, Juan Martín, Elena Martínez, Gonzalo Martner, Oscar Muñoz, Arturo O'Connell, José Antonio Ocampo, Carlos Ominami, Torsten Persson, Thomas Scheetz, Jorge Schvarzer, Andrés Solimano and Guido Tabellini.

Together with the Club de Madrid, the following people participated in the analysis of democracy and globalization: Andrés Allamand, Antonio Alvarez-Couceiro, Rodrigo Borja, Dante Caputo, Fernando Henrique Cardoso, Fernando Carrillo-Florez, Aníbal Cavaco Silva, Tarcísio Costa, Miguel Darcy, Guillermo de la Dehesa, Miguel Ángel Fernández-Ordóñez, Eduardo Frei, Ernesto Garzón Valdés, Felipe González, Antonio Guterres, Carlos Lopes, Elena Martínez, Lucinio Muñoz, Carlos Ominami, Beatriz Paredes, Jorge Quiroga Ramírez and Fernando Valenzuela.

The following people participated in the discussion on conditions for the stability of the democratic institutions: Alberto Arene, Miguel Angel Barcárcel, Rafael Guido Béjar, Marcia Bermúdez, Miguel Antonio Bernal, Roberto Cajina, Antonio Cañas, Zenayda Castro, Carlos Cazzali, Elvira Cuadra, Jorge Chediek, Francisco Díaz, Mirna Flores, Dina García, Jorge Giannareas, Ricardo Gómez, Valdrack Jaentschke, Francesca Jessup, Walter Lacayo, Semiramis López, José Raúl Mulino, Isabela Orellana, Alfonso Peña, Kees Rade, Juan Carlos Rodríguez, María del Carmen Sacasa, Gabriela Serrano, Héctor Hérmilo Soto, Edelberto Torres Rivas, Arnoldo Villagrán, Knut Walter.

Meeting with the UN Secretary-General

The following people participated in the meeting in New York on 12 November 2002 with Kofi Annan, the Secretary-General of the UN: Belisario Betancur, former President of Colombia; Kim Campbell, President of the Club de Madrid (former Prime Minister of Canada); Eduardo Frei, former President of Chile; Jorge Quiroga Ramírez, former President of Bolivia: Carlos Roberto Reina, former President of Honduras; Julio María Sanguinetti, former President of Uruguay; Ernesto Zedillo, former President of Mexico; Zéphirin Diabré, Associate Administrator of UNDP; Shoji Nishimoto, Assistant Administrator and Director of Policy Development, UNDP; Elena Martínez, Assistant Administrator and Regional Director for Latin America and the Caribbean (RDLAC), UNDP; José Antonio Ocampo, former Executive Secretary, Economic Commission for Latin America and the Caribbean (ECLAC) and current UN Under-Secretary General for Economic and Social Affairs; Danilo Türk, Assistant Secretary-General, Department of Political Affairs (DPA); Marta Maurás, Director of the Office of the Deputy Secretary-General (EOSG); Angela Kane, Director of the Division for the Americas and Europe (DPA); Freddy Justiniano, Co-ordinator of the RDLAC; as well as the following project staff: Dante Caputo; Gonzalo Pérez del Castillo; Edelberto Torres Rivas; and Augusto Ramírez Ocampo.

Meeting with the Administrator of UNDP

The following people attended the meeting on 4 November 2003 with the Administrator of UNDP, Mark Malloch Brown: Elena Martínez, Assistant Administrator and Regional Director for Latin America and the Caribbean (RDLAC), UNDP; Víctor Arango, Specialist in Communications for Latin America and the Caribbean, Office of the Administrator; Magdy Martínez-Solimán, Head of the Office on Governance, BDP/UNDP; William Orme, Head of the Press and Communications Office, Office of the Administrator; Stefano Pettinato, Policy Advisor, Office of the Human Development Report, UNDP; Carmelo Angulo Bartu-

ren, Resident Representative of UNDP in Argentina; Dante Caputo, Project Director; Freddy Justiniano, Co-ordinator of the RDLAC; Myriam Méndez-Montalvo, Advisor on Governance to the RDLAC; Leandro García Silva, Consultant to the Project on Technical and Academic Follow-up; and Luis Francisco Thais, Consultant to the RDLAC.

Support in preparing Meetings and Seminars

We are grateful for the particular assistance of Isabel Vásquez, of the Fundación Círculo de Montevideo; Katty Grez and Verónica Oyarzún, of Fundación Chile XXI; Ángeles Martínez and Irene Fraguas, of the Club de Madrid; and Bernardita Baeza, Carolina Ries and Valerie Biggs, of the ECLAC.

Production and Translation

The following people assisted in transcribing the interviews in the Round of Consultations: Maximiliano Bourel, Marcelo Burello, María Eva Cangiani, Valentina Farrell, Virginia Gallo, Guadalupe Guzmán, Erika Moeykens, Josefina Pittaluga, Julia Ramos, Natalia Rosenberg, Gisela Urriza and Geraldine Watson. Federico M. Guido Calvo improved the sound quality of the recorded interviews.

Translating services were provided by Marcelo Canosa, María Esperanza Clavell, Yvonne Fisher, Liliana Hecht, Gabriela Ippólito, Claudia Martínez and Merril Stevenson. Hinde Pomeraniec was in charge of style corrections.

We would also like to extend our thanks to every person who has provided input to this Report. We apologize for any unintentional omissions.

■ Technical Note on the Electoral Democracy Index

This note describes the steps taken and the statistical tests carried out to construct the Electoral Democracy Index (EDI), a measure of political rights as related to the election of governments. Explanations are also provided of how the index is to be interpreted and used.

Construction of the EDI

The Choice of Component Items

The first step in developing the EDI, and probably the most important one, was to select its four components: the right to vote; free elections; clean elections; and elections as the means of gaining access to public office. These items were chosen because they are traditionally considered by theorists of democracy to be the main elements that define a democratic regime. They encompass numerous issues that are generally considered to be necessary for any evaluation of the democratic nature of a political system (Figure 1).

Second, these elements refer to citizens' rights, which the State is responsible for upholding and which may be interpreted clearly in the context of current theories on democracy. Hence, any problems related to issues like voter

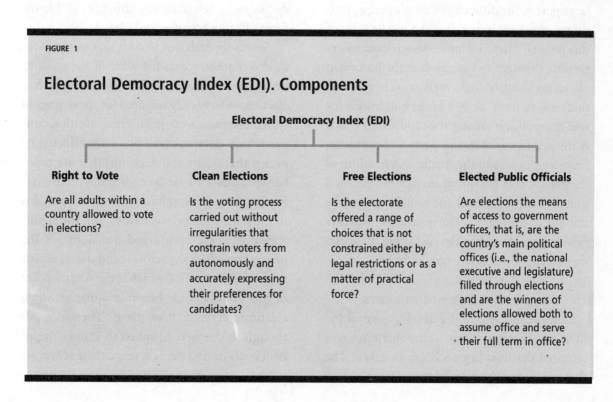

FIGURE 1

Electoral Democracy Index (EDI). Components

Electoral Democracy Index (EDI)

Right to Vote	Clean Elections	Free Elections	Elected Public Officials
Are all adults within a country allowed to vote in elections?	Is the voting process carried out without irregularities that constrain voters from autonomously and accurately expressing their preferences for candidates?	Is the electorate offered a range of choices that is not constrained either by legal restrictions or as a matter of practical force?	Are elections the means of access to government offices, that is, are the country's main political offices (i.e., the national executive and legislature) filled through elections and are the winners of elections allowed both to assume office and serve their full term in office?

turnout or disproportionate electoral representation—which are a reflection on the actions of the State as much as they are on those of its citizens—are avoided. This ensures that the index can be interpreted clearly as a measure of the extent to which the state guarantees citizenship rights regarding the political regime, as distinct from the actions of the citizens themselves. Similarly, it avoids problems related to measures whose significance is unclear with respect to the degree of democracy of the regime, such as the difference between proportional and majority electoral rules, or between parliamentary or presidential systems. Although these aspects are not unimportant, they do not provide such a clear indication of the degree of democracy in a particular regime as do the four components that were chosen.

Third, these elements allow for the use of valid and reliable data collected as recently as the previous calendar year. Accordingly, emphasis has been placed on measuring components strictly on the basis of observables and not through the use of surveys of perceptions. Therefore, some elements that could have been included were left out for 'practical' reasons.

Finally, other factors were analyzed that could have been included but were not, due in large part to the difficulty of developing appropriate measures in time for the publication of this Report. These include issues related to exercising the right to vote, such as the process of obtaining identity cards, registering to vote and then voting itself, as well as the conditions for free competition among the candidates, which is affected by variables like party and campaign financing, access to the media and freedom of the press. Other key questions concern electoral practices at the regional and local levels and the stability of the regime. The question of whether new indices should be devised using these elements is open for discussion in future.

The Measurement of Component Items

The second step in the development of the EDI—measuring its four component items—required that two key decisions be taken. The first concerned the rules of the coding process; the second concerned the actual coding process itself.

As regards the former, the scales used to measure the component items—three five-point ordinal scales and one three-point ordinal scale—were constructed firstly by establishing theoretically meaningful endpoints and then by identifying different values on the scale that were conceptually as far from each other as possible, starting from the median point. The values on the scale were chosen to reflect relevant distinctions identified in the literatures as being important, avoiding any minor variations between cases, even though these were verifiable. For cases not seen as fitting precisely any of the points on the various ordinal scales, the possibility of using pluses and minuses was introduced as a means to record intermediate values.

The scales were also put together in such a way that each point corresponded to events and situations of a relatively concrete nature and that any decisions about their coding could be taken strictly on the basis of observables. The index does not include any data based on opinion polls. Moreover, as a way to further ensure that the coding exercise was replicable, and faced with possibly arbitrary decisions, the importance of documenting the bases for coding decisions by referring to publicly available information sources was underlined.

Scores for each case in each year were not required. Rather, scores for three of the components—the right to vote, clean elections and free elections—were only required for those years in which elections were held. The conditions under which elections take place are affected by events that occur and decisions that are taken between elections, so the coding has accordingly taken into account information that pertains to the period between elections. But the significance of these events and decisions for the process via which the actors (candidates) accede to government office, which is the central point of this exercise, only becomes apparent when elections actually take place. Therefore, although scores were assigned to some components only during election years, these scores are to be taken as synthesizing a broader process.

The second decision concerns the coding process itself. In this regard, two supplementary processes were used to code the cases. An initial coding was conducted by a single coder, on the basis of extensive research and consultations with many experts over several months. In addition, the scores assigned were presented and discussed in depth in various meetings, including one with a group of experts from different spheres (politics, academia and international organizations) and different countries of North and South America (Argentina, Brazil, Canada, Colombia, Ecuador, Mexico, United States and Uruguay). These discussions led to the identification of disagreements, which led to further research, and yet further group discussions. Finally, at the end of this iterative process, the participants managed to achieve a high degree of consensus on the coding of the four dimensions of the EDI.

The Generation of a Rectangular Data Set with Normalized Scales

The third step in the construction of the EDI concerned the transformation of the scores on the component scales into a rectangular data base, that is, a data set that includes numerical scores for all cases on all variables and all years, with normalized scales.

This step involved a series of procedures. First, some fairly mechanical aspects had to be dealt with. The plus and minus signs were turned into numbers by adding and subtracting 0.33 to and from the base score (for example, 3+ became 3.33). The hyphens (-) used to indicate that the score given was not applicable, because the government was not elected, became zeros (0). Furthermore, the scores for two of the components that were assigned scores only for the year in which an election was held—right to vote and free elections—were extended to intermediate years simply by moving the score from one year on to the following years, until a new score had been assigned (either because of an election was held after a period in which there was a non-elected government, or a new election was held, or the election process was interrupted). This procedure is justified by the fact that the way in which a government originates continues to be a characteristic that affects its nature beyond the moment of its installation.

In the case of clean elections, the process was slightly more complex. This item was codified using a three-point scale to facilitate interpretation. However, the one (1) on this scale does not really represent the midpoint, as it is much closer to the two (2). Thus each one (1) was converted into three (3) and each two (2) became four (4). Furthermore, as this element makes a distinction between the values assigned to presidential and parliamentary elections, the scores have not been merely changed from election to election. The points are in fact the average of the scores awarded to the presidential and the parliamentary elections.

A second issue that was dealt with was the problem of assigning a single score per country per year. This practice is customary for reasons of parsimony and is well justified. After all, the objective of an index is to present an overall synthetic evaluation of the situation in each country. But this does imply several problems, as the situation in a country can vary substantially over 12 months and only one score is used to represent the whole period. In some cases the solution is relatively simple. Thus, when a key event such an election was held toward the end of the year, the change in status due to that event was registered in the following year. For instance, the elections held in Guatemala in 1985, which ended a period of successive military rule, took place towards the end of the year and the new government took office in January 1986. Thus, even though the scores for the component elements were logged in 1985, when the EDI was calculated, the scores were entered for 1986. When events take place in the first half of the year, they are recorded as relevant for that same year. For example, the 1994 elections in El Salvador took place in March and the government took office in June, so this change was logged for 1994. In other cases, though, the solution has proved more complex, as when an event occurring in the second half of the year was registered for that same year. This was the case, for example, with regard to the fraudulent elections that took place in May 1994 in the Dominican Republic, with the new President taking office in August. Also problematic were those cases where more than one relevant event happened in the same year. In 2000, for instance, Peru held two very suspect elections in April and May, which led to the installation of President Alberto Fujimori in July and to his resignation in November. In this case, the problematic elections were logged for 2000 and the rectification for 2001.

Third, the scales used to measure the components were normalized, that is, translated into a common metric using a simple linear norming to the unit interval:

$$\text{Normalized Value} = \text{Raw Value} / \text{Maximum Raw Value}$$

Unfortunately, nearly any choice made would have been somewhat arbitrary because there are no widely acceptable units of electoral freedom comparable to units such as kilograms or dollars. However, the choice of the normalization procedure as it was applied to the five-point ordinal scales—with the modification made to the clean elections component when transforming the scores on the component scales into a rectangular data base set, the scales used to measure four component items were five-point ordinal scales—is both transparent and justifiable.

First, all of the scales have theoretically meaningful endpoints, and can be assumed to fall within the unit interval, with zero indicating a total lack of the property and one indicating full possession of the property. That is, the lower value on the ordinal scale corresponds to the absence of the property in question, whereas the higher value corresponds to its complete presence. A case with right to vote 0 has no suffrage at all while a case with right to vote 1 after norming has complete adult suffrage, the theoretically established standard. Thus, the problem of distance relates only to the points between the endpoint.

Second, most of the scales were constructed in such a way that each point on the scale might be interpreted theoretically, and in such a way that the different values on the scale are as distant from each other as possible from a conceptual standpoint. That is, the scale values were chosen to reflect distinctions that were identified as relevant in the existent literature, avoiding verifiable but nonetheless small variations between cases. Consequently, the probability of introducing a major error is relatively small. Although there are other more sophisticated psychometric methods that could have been employed, these tend to be more complex, less accessible and heavily reliant on data; and they rarely yield significantly better results than this simple procedure.

The Choice of Aggregation Rules

The fourth step in the development of the EDI—the choice of aggregation rules that formalizes the relationship between the component elements that make up the index—was resolved through the use of a simple aggregation rule. The core insight is that the four component parts of the EDI are parts that constitute a system by virtue of the way in which they combine together and, moreover, that these four component items are so fundamental to the overall characterization of the regime that their absence would simply render the regime non-democratic. For example, as has been debated at length by theoreticians on democracy, the fact that Soviet-style systems held elections characterized by universal suffrage is totally irrelevant from the perspective of democracy, as the electorate had no choice with regard to the selection of candidates and because those elections did not grant access to offices with the capacity to wield effective power within the State. Therefore, the four component parts of the EDI are presented as individually necessary conditions, which are unsubstitutable and have equal weight. This conception is formalized by multiplying together the values of all of the components. In formal terms, then, the EDI is calculated according to the following equation:

$$\text{Electoral Democracy Index} = \text{Right to Vote} \times \text{Clean Elections} \times \text{Free Elections} \times \text{Elected Public Officials}$$

This equation draws on a key insight of democratic theory: when one component element is completely absent, the regime must be considered to be non-democratic. In effect, this formula ensures that if a value of zero is assigned to any of the four elements then the case is classified as non-democratic. This is a 'tough' standard, which may be seen as less 'forgiving' than other rules of aggregation. Thus, it bears emphasizing that precisely because this conception of the component items of the EDI as individually necessary conditions is highly demanding, it is used in conjunction with a conservative criterion in assigning zeros, indicating the total lack of a certain property, to the component items. This is so both in the sense that the scales were constructed in such a way that a zero would be called for only in the extreme cases where a property that is widely seen as vital to the existing of democracy is totally lacking, and in the sense that the evidence required for assigning a zero had to be compelling. Thus, only when democratic norms are blatantly and undisputedly disregarded would the EDI code a country as being non-democratic.

Testing the EDI

Intercoder Reliability and Error Estimates

A formal intercoder reliability test was not carried out for reasons of time. However, in order to find out if other coders might have assigned different values to the component parts of the EDI, a sensitivity analysis was conducted. This analysis relies on perturbations of the assigned codings according to an experimental design and an examination of the resulting overall "replicated" indices. Thus, it uses mathematics to create "virtual" coders that are biased in various ways, for instance downwardly biased in rating one or more components.

The results of this test showed that the EDI is quite stable—rank correlations with all the other "replications" were 0.99 or greater—and the shifts in mean and spread were quite predictable, showing a predictable negative or positive bias depending on the cell in the experimental design. This test also provided some basic error bars for the EDI based on the "replications." Generous bands for index values from around 0.25 to 0.75 are about ±0.07 and reasonably conservative bands are ±0.1. By the most conservative possible standard, the EDI values are within ±0.2. The width is reasonably constant throughout the cited interval, but the precise boundaries depend on the value of the index and are in general narrower near the endpoints. A check on the mathematics was conducted using the inversion of the well-known and highly conservative Kolmogorov-Smirnov test for the distribution function—based on entirely different mathematics—and similar results were produced.

The Robustness of Aggregation Rules

A test was conducted to compare the four possible rules of aggregation: the product of the four component parts actually used in the EDI; the minimum value of the four components on the scale; the geometric mean of the four components; and the arithmetic mean of the four components. The results showed that, whatever the rule used, the rank correlations are all very high, indicating that the general ordering of cases is preserved. But there are differences among the indices, with the arithmetic mean and the geometric mean being similar to each other, and the minimum and the EDI being similar to each other. The most important difference is between the means and the standard deviations (SDs). The arithmetic and geometric means are 0.92 and 0.91, respectively, while the SDs are 0.20 and 0.21, respectively. In contrast, the minimum and the EDI have means of 0.84 and 0.82, respectively, and SDs of 0.26 and 0.28, respectively. This suggests that the latter rules do a better job at spreading the cases out and avoiding a bunching up of cases that makes it hard to interpret their differences with much clarity.

The Dimension of the Component Items

A test of the scalability of the EDI's four component items gave a Cronbach's alpha of 0.92, suggesting that the EDI is a measure of a unidimensional phenomenon. However, when a test was performed on two periods (1960-

1985 and 1990-2002), the resulting Cronbach alphas were of 0.95 and 0.23 respectively. This indicates that while in the earlier period the components were unidimensional, this is no longer true in the post-1990 period. This finding is consistent with the theory used in selecting the aggregation rules for the EDI. In effect, it is important to note that standard additive measurement models rely on the assumption that aggregation operates on multiple parallel measurements. In contrast, because the component items of the EDI are theoretically considered unsubstitutable, the decision to aggregate up to one single score is not invalidated by any potential deviations from unidimensionality. Thus, this scalability test offers further validation for the choice of the proposed aggregation rules as opposed to the quite common additive rule.

Interpreting and using the EDI

The EDI is a 0.00-1.00 scale, with 0.00 indicating non-democracy and any number above 0.00 indicating a degree of electoral democracy, with higher scores referring to greater degrees of electoral democracy. To avoid misunderstanding, it is important to note that the index should not be interpreted as an evaluation of the actions taken by the government. It is more a measurement of the state of a system, which is affected by government action or inaction, as well as by the activities of other State agencies and social actors. Furthermore, it should be emphasized that it is the concept of *electoral* democracy that is being measured. This concept is not as limited as some might think. Therefore, although the focus is exclusively on elections that are inclusive, clean and free, it encompasses more than 'mere elections'. Not only are the conditions for holding such elections affected by developments between elections. In addition, it calls for a consideration of what happens to the governments themselves between elections.

But the EDI is by no means a broad measure of democracy. It is more a way of measuring a concept of the democratic political regime based on the most widely-shared beliefs about fundamental political rights. This is highly significant. On the one hand, it implies that any irregularity detected by the EDI should be considered an important restriction of citizen's political rights. On the other hand, the fact that a country may have scored a perfect 1.00 should not be seen to mean that it cannot improve its performance both with regard to aspects that are not covered by the index and by meeting more demanding standards for the component parts of the EDI.

The EDI may be used for comparative purposes in order to evaluate a country's own performance or to compare it with that of other countries. Either way, the evaluation of a country's own performance at different points in time is generally the easiest to interpret the data. After all, a country may have made significant improvements and still remain behind other countries if they have made even greater strides. It is important to bear in mind, though, that any comparison should be based on major differences rather than on minor ones. This is because the EDI, like any index, possesses a certain degree of measurement error, and, within the limits of that measurement error, it is unadvisable to make any conclusive assertions concerning the differences. Indeed, as was estimated through the sensitivity analysis, generous error bars for EDI values between about 0.25 and 0.75 are roughly ±0.07. Thus, any pair of cases that differ by less than this value—for example a country with an EDI of 0.85 and one of 0.92— are simply too close to validly distinguish. Hence, it is methodologically unjustifiable to offer an overly precise ranking of countries, as is commonly done in the context of other indices, which simply transforms the scores of the EDI into a ranking without taking into consideration the degree of uncertainty associated with the EDI scores.

The identification of benchmark cases that are prototypical representations of the features that are associated with a range of scores can help to give concreteness to the meaning of each number. Moreover, the EDI can be used as a flag, in the sense that the specific scores of each country invite the reader to go back to the tables on the component items to identify precisely what feature or features account for a country's score. In this way the EDI can be used as a valuable analytical tool, in that it offers a summary score that allows its users to identify the distinctiveness of each country's political regime in terms of its various component items but also in terms of the relationship among the constituent parts of the regime and their contribution to the whole.

■ Technical Note on the Indices derived from an Analysis of the Latinobarómetro 2002 Survey

Constructing the Democratic Support Index

Introduction

This note examines the source of the information, the methodological design and the statistical procedures applied in formulating the main indices and indicators used to analyze the perceptions and behavior of Latin American citizens. It accounts for the significance, usefulness and scope of these indices and indicators. The descriptions in this document supplement the tables in the Statistical Compendium. For a more detailed explanation please consult the report on the methodological and statistical procedure adopted, which consists of nine longer documents that can be found at www.democracia.undp.org (T. Benavides and J. Vargas Cullell, 2003; M. Gómez, 2003; L. Kikut, M. Gómez and J. Vargas Cullell, 2003a, 2003b; L. Kikut and J. Vargas Cullell, 2003; J. Vargas Cullell, T. Benavides and M. Gómez, 2003a and 2003b; J. Vargas Cullell and T. Benavides, 2003; and J. Vargas Cullell and M. Gómez, 2003.)

The note is divided into two sections. The first evaluates the Latinobarómetro survey as a source of information and examines the data and the analytical methods employed. The second describes in detail the methodology used to construct the Democracy Support Index (DSI)—the project's main innovation.

Opinion Poll on Democracy

The section of the Report entitled 'How do Latin Americans envisage their democracy' is based on work carried out by a team coordinated by Jorge Vargas Cullell and made up of Miguel Gómez, Lorena Kikut and Tatiana Benavides. This team devised the conceptual and methodological framework that was used to identify the pertinent indices and indicators, and analyzed the information. The main objectives were to enable a comparative study on the exercise of citizens' rights and the fulfillment of their duties in Latin America and to assess citizens' support for democracy.

This section outlines the data sources on which the Report bases its investigation. We invite specialists who wish to add to this information to consult the detailed documents on the conceptual and methodological aspects of the analysis available on the PRODDAL website (www.democracia.undp.org).

PRODDAL data are formulated on the basis of inherent conceptual developments and methodological procedures and technical applications that produces outcomes that do not necessarily correspond with those of the sources used. The indices and the indicators on citizens' perceptions and behavior utilize information from three sources:

Latinobarómetro as a Source of Information

Latinobarómetro is a comparative study carried out in all of the countries of the region. In 2002, following an agreement between UNDP and Latinobarómetro, 28 questions (62 variables) were included in the survey, and approximately one-third of the questionnaire was devoted to topics defined by PRODDAL. The survey was conducted in Spanish in 18 countries (for the first time in the Dominican Republic), using the same questionnaire and a code book. Interviews were held with 19,508 people and samples of 1,000–1,200 persons were taken in each country. All designs use some version of multiple-stage sampling and, practically in all of them, the final selection of interviewees is made on the basis of quota sampling. Therefore, the samples can be affected by statistical limitations and the known biases of quota sampling.
(See Statistical Compendium, Second Part, 'Opinion Survey on Democracy', p. 187 et seq.)

- the regular section of the opinion survey carried out by the Latinobarómetro Corporation in 2002;

- the UNDP proprietary section;[1] and

- the historical series of Latinobarómetro questions (as a secondary source).

The DSI was formulated on the basis of these sources and the conceptual and methodological developments of the Report. It was necessary to analyze the following in constructing this index:

- the overall issue of citizens' support for democracy, how to measure it and the shortcomings of the most popular method previously applied;

- orientations of citizens towards democracy, their determination and the classification of opinions;

- the size of each of the orientations, their level of political activism and the relative distance; and

- the index aggregation rule and its statistical validation.

These topics are discussed hereunder.

Data and Methodology

The main objective of the UNDP proprietary section was to allow a comparative study to be conducted on the exercise of citizens' rights and the fulfillment of their duties in Latin America. This supplemented the questions that the regular Latinobarómetro section poses on political attitudes within a wide array of categories. The indices and indicators on citizens' perceptions and behavior use information derived from three sources: the regular section of the opinion survey; the UNDP proprietary section; and, as a secondary resource, the time series. The information from the proprietary section is reflected in the tables in the Statistical Compendium. The information from the regular section is only presented in the Report once it has been duly processed and as part of an indicator or index.

Sample Design

The *Latinobarómetro 2002 Methodological Report* allows us to comment on the samples used by Latinobarómetro 2002 with a view to identifying issues that are relevant to the proper application of its findings. It is a simple valuation, since the text does not have the necessary information for a technical audit of the

1 The UNDP proprietary section consists of questions P1U to P28U.

samples, preventing us from paying attention to some potential weaknesses of the technical aspects.[2] Therefore this section's remarks are of a general nature and are unavoidably limited. Nonetheless, we are able to highlight certain factors that need to be taken into account in subsequent data management.

The following general conclusions can be drawn after analyzing the main characteristics of the designs used in each country:

- All of the designs use some version of multiple-stage sampling and, practically in all of them, the final selection of interviewees is made on the basis of quota sampling. In a couple of cases the random technique of 'the last anniversary' is used, but, in practice, the selected person is replaced if he/she is not at home or does not appear within a short time. Therefore, all samples are affected by the known limitations and biases of quota sampling, particularly by an underestimation of the persons who are less available—especially those working full-time—and an overestimation of those working on their own or at home.

- Practically all of the designs use geographical stratification and take into account the size of localities and cities. One-half of the samples use disproportionate affixation. It must be pointed out that, in itself, disproportionate affixation does not lead to problems because weighting is used to generate results that are in proportion to the reference population.

- For some countries there is a sample bias towards the urban population, resulting in over-representation of the opinions of the urban population in national averages.

In sum, it can be said that, although Latinobarómetro reflects essentially the opinions of the urban population in some countries, which can distort findings, it is undoubtedly the source of information that best reflects the views of the region's population as a whole.

Statistical Analysis

The statistical analysis carried out for the *Report on Democracy in Latin America* based on Latinobarómetro used SPSS software, version number 11. The statistical analysis methods used were simple ones. In order to establish the connection between two numerical variables, the Pearson correlation coefficient was applied, with values ranging between zero and one. In order to establish the linkage between nominal variables, the Crammer V measure was utilized. When there was an ordinal and nominal variable, the Tau-c measure was employed.

In order to bring together the various questions that, at first sight, seem to refer to the same topic, factor analysis was carried out with the aim of determining implicit dimensions, and scales were elaborated through simple addition. As an indicator of the consistency or internal reliability of the scales thus built, Cronbach's alpha coefficient was applied (coefficients of 0.70 or more are considered reliable and consistent). If such a value was not attained, the pertinent scale was disregarded. When this happened, we used each of the variables independently (as was done with the DSI).

During the information analysis process, profiling techniques were employed to examine whether the values of a dependent variable were linked to given socio-demographic factors and political attitudes. Those that had a significance equal to or below one percent were highlighted (see the Statistical Compendium).

---

2 For a critical analysis of Latinobarómetro 2002 see M. Gómez, 2003.

The countries were the units of analysis used to study support for democracy and particularly to develop the DSI and its components. Values were also obtained for Latin America as a whole (18 countries) and for three sub-regions: (a) Mexico, the Dominican Republic and Central America (Costa Rica, El Salvador, Guatemala, Honduras, Nicaragua and Panama); (b) the Andean sub-region (Bolivia, Colombia, Ecuador, Peru and Venezuela); and (c) the Mercosur (Argentina, Brazil, Paraguay and Uruguay) and Chile. In the case of the values obtained for the region and the sub-regions, the values state averages of the group of countries within the bigger unit, considering each country with the same relative weight. Consequently, the sample was not weighted with the pertinent populations in order to reach categorical conclusions on 'Latin America' or for each of the three sub-regions. Samples were not weighted for the following reasons:

- Citizens express opinions on, and make an appraisal of, the political system of which they are a part and not in relation to a Latin American political 'macro-unit'. Most of the affairs that they refer to are problems at the national level, such as the performance of democracy. Therefore national differences have the same importance/valuation. If, for this study, the population sample was weighted to identify trends in Latin America, these would basically reflect the opinions and valuations of Brazilians and Mexicans (who comprise approximately 60 percent of the total population). Both would only refer to the experience of their respective countries and not to that of Latin America.

- The sizes of the original samples for each country were not established by the Latinobarómetro Corporation with the purpose to facilitate a subsequent analysis, which, while it provides representative results for the Latin American population as a whole, gives also representative results for each of the countries included in the study. If the current consolidated database were weighted by population, the smallest countries—for instance, Costa Rica, Nicaragua and Uruguay—would receive a very small share.

- The sample designs in the countries included in the study are clearly different. As was stated in prior sections, some samples are national in scope, while others are urban—in some countries, only certain urban centers are covered. For example, the universe of Brazil's sample encompasses only certain cities and not the whole of the population; if the Brazilian sample were weighted by its population an excessive weight would be accorded to the inhabitants of these urban centers compared to the inhabitants of other countries where samples seem to be a little more 'national'.

When the profiling of persons with different orientations towards democracy was carried out, the sample was not weighted. In these cases, the results reflect the situation of the interviewees and not of Latin American citizens more generally.

Accuracy of Results[3]

All surveys based on sampling are affected by two kinds of errors: non-sampling ones;[4]

---

3 The explanation of sampling and non-sampling errors is taken from J. Vargas Cullell and L. Rosero-Bixby, 2004.
4 The non-sampling errors are those made during information collection and processing and can be controlled, for example, by constructing an appropriate measurement instrument, training survey pollsters so that they apply the instrument properly, supervising fieldwork, creating an efficient data capturing program, reviewing the questionnaire and ensuring adequate coding, and by cleaning the file. These errors cannot be quantified. However,

and sampling ones.[5] Since the results of a technical audit of Latinobarómetro 2002 are unknown, it is not possible make reference to the former. However, analysis of the latter is extremely limited, since the information included in the *2002 Methodological Report* does not the submission of sampling errors (standard errors, SE) and design effects (DE) vis-à-vis selected indices and questions. Consequently, there is a lack of information at the first observation level, and hence it is not possible to provide an opinion on the reasonableness of the accuracy of the estimates.

Overall, it can be said that, in cases like Costa Rica, the other Central American nations and Brazil, where the average size of the final cluster is not very high—around 13 interviewees—if normal roh values are assumed to be 0.02 to 0.04, the DE reaches a maximum of 1.50, which means that the cluster increases its p variance by 50 percent and the sampling error by 22 percent, figures that are fully tolerable. In other cases, though, such as Ecuador, the procedure for selecting cities or municipalities and then identify sub-samples of them, produces large clusters (50 or more interviewees) and the DE can be 3 or 4 which entails sampling errors of 1.73 percent or twice those obtained by applying the usual formula.

Total Samples, Valid Samples and Non-Replies

The size of the total sample in the 18 countries where the Latinobarómetro 2002 survey was conducted was 19,508.[6] Data for Paraguay were given a double weighting so as to simulate a sample of 1,200 persons in that country. After weighting the total sample, the size increased from 19,501 to 20,101 (Table 1). All calculations and estimates were made on the basis of this sample, which includes the double weighting for Paraguay. The following reasons justified this decision:

- to allow Paraguay to have a similar weight as the other 17 countries; otherwise, it would count as 'half a country' when the information is brought together to analyze the regional situation (Latin America) or the sub-regional situation (Mercosur and Chile); and

- if a sample of 1,200 persons were used in the same localities in which the survey was applied, the results should not be too different to those effectively obtained with the study of 600 persons if the same criteria were used and the statistical sampling techniques were appropriately applied.

By giving Paraguay a greater weight, the average results of all Latin American countries change slightly (in tenths of percentage points) and the average results of the Mercosur and Chile sub-region also vary a little (two to three percentage points). In view of the above, however, these changes would allegedly be as ex-

---

a comparison of sample results with those of the population provides an idea as to whether these errors have generated biases that deprive the sample of its representation.

5 Sampling errors happen randomly and arise as a result of interviewing a sample and not the whole of the population. When a sample is selected, it is one of many potential permutations. The variability that exists between all of these potential samples is the sampling error that could be measured if one could assess all of those samples, an obviously unrealistic scenario. In practice, what is estimated is the error on the variance obtained based on that same sample. In order to estimate the sampling error of statistical information (averages, percentages, differences and totals) the SE is calculated as the square root of the population variance of that statistics measurement. This makes it possible to measure the degree of accuracy of these statistics vis-à-vis the results obtained when having interviewed all population elements under the same conditions. In order to calculate this error it is important to consider the design used to select the sample.

6 When the study covered 17 countries, the size of the unweighted sample was 18,508. Some 1,000 more records were added with the inclusion of the Dominican Republic.

SIZE OF THE STUDY'S SAMPLE	TABLE 1
Sample	**N° of Cases**
Number of interviews or size of the unweighted sample (17 countries)	18,508
Size of the weighted sample (17 countries)	18,501
Size of the weighted sample (18 countries, including the Dominican Republic)	19,501
Size of the weighted sample (18 countries with double weighting for Paraguay)	20,101

Source: calculation by PRODDAL based on data from Latinobarómetro 2002.

pected should the study have been made on the basis of 1,200, instead of 600 interviewees.

In practice, due to 'non-replies', the valid samples are less than the total number of the interviewees and fluctuate according to the variable under consideration. The tables in the Statistical Compendium present total samples and valid samples for most variables used in the analysis. In some cases the percentage of non-replies is low, for instance, when addressing socio-demographic factors like gender or the interviewee's level of education. In other cases, though, the percentage of non-replies is high, especially when questions were grouped to shape the indices used in results analysis, leading to a smaller amount of valid samples. Table 2 presents the difference in relation to the DSI.

The Decision to omit 'Non-Replies'

From the outset, a decision was made not to consider 'non-replies'. The 'do not know' and 'do not answer' responses were brought together and described as 'missing' values. This was also done with respect to the calculation of orientations towards democracy, within the framework of the DSI. In this case, the suppression of 'non-replies' is necessary so as not to make assumptions about the attitudes of the persons placed in this category. The decision adopted is consistent with the criteria applied to the total contents of the Report. In order to carry out a multi-variable analysis and to build complex indices, the non-consideration of the 'non-replies' was a systematic option.

To avoid making a mistake due to the non-consideration of 'non-replies', the size of the sample on which the results are based or the effective sample (number of valid responses) was included. Therefore, it is always possible to rebuild original values and thus infer the volume of 'non-replies'.

Submission of Results

In the main text of the Report, the percentages shown in the tables and graphs refer to valid samples and not to total samples. In all cases, the size of the sample on which they are based, or the size of the effective sample, is included and hence it is always possible to rebuild the original values and thus deduct the volume of 'non-replies'.

In the case of tables and graphs relating to the DSI and forms of citizen participation, the valid sample includes the cases 'rescued' through the procedure described in the pertinent methodological text. The missing values or 'non-replies'—'do not know' and 'do not answer'—are excluded. As mentioned, the exclusion of 'non-replies' from the results of the data analysis is necessary so as not to make assumptions about the attitudes of people placed in that category, which can impact on the results of the multi-variable analysis and the construction of the indices.

TOTAL SAMPLES AND VALID SAMPLES FOR THE DSI USED
IN THE ANALYSIS OF LATINOBARÓMETRO

TABLE 2

Country	Total Sample	Index of Support for Democracy	
		Valid sample*	% of non-replies*
Argentina	1,200	964	19.7
Bolivia	1,242	886	28.7
Brazil	1,000	663	33.7
Colombia	1,200	768	36.0
Costa Rica	1,006	808	19.7
Chile	1,188	873	26.5
Dominican Republic	1,000	909	9.1
Ecuador	1,200	938	21.8
El Salvador	1,014	577	43.1
Guatemala	1,000	703	29.7
Honduras	1,005	747	25.7
Mexico	1,210	1,031	14.8
Nicaragua	1,016	833	18.0
Panama	1,010	794	21.4
Paraguay	1,200	1,011	15.8
Peru	1,224	856	30.1
Uruguay	1,187	926	22.0
Venezuela	1,200	928	22.7
Latin America**	**20,101**	**15,217**	**24.3**

Notes:
* After the 'rescue' of cases via the procedures outlined in L. Kikut, M. Gómez and J. Vargas Cullell, 2003 and 2003a and J. Vargas Cullell and L. Kikut, 2003.
** The values for the region differ from the total amount per country because of the automatic rounding-off of the total weighted amounts by the statistical program. The figures for total samples per country were obtained after weighting.
Source: Statistical Compendium.

*The Method used to measure Citizens'
Support for Democracy and to assess its
Shortcomings*

In the Latinobarómetro survey a question was included to gauge the loyalty of Latin American citizens towards democracy:[7]

Which of the following statements do you agree with the most?

1. Democracy is preferable to any other type of government.
2. Under some circumstances, an authoritarian government may be preferable to a democratic one.
3. For people like me, it makes no difference if the regime is a democracy or not.

Thus, persons who selected the first response are those who support democracy; those who selected the second response are those who would support its replacement by an authoritarian regime; and those who selected the third response have an ambivalent attitude, which can become a problem. If, over time, the number of persons choosing response one increases, then support for democracy allegedly augments; and, conversely, if it decreases, such support seemingly declines. The best situation for democracy in a country would be if almost all interviewees chose response one; the worst, of course, would be if most people selected response two.

The question—coded in the 2002 Latinobarómetro survey as P32ST—has been criticized

7 In the academic, political and journalistic worlds this question is addressed as a summary-measure of citizens' support for democracy and, indirectly, of the latter's 'health'; year after year the results are attentively observed.

PROPORTION OF PERSONS SUPPORTING DEMOCRACY
WITH 'UNEXPECTED' RESPONSES IN RELATION TO SUPPORT
FOR AUTHORITARIAN MEANS OF SOLVING PROBLEMS   TABLE 3

Question		Question P32ST
Question		Percentage of people supporting the democratic system which agrees with ...
P28UA	Do you agree that the President should not be limited by what the laws say?	38.6
P28UB	Do you agree that the President should secure order by force?	32.3
P28UC	Do you agree that the President should control the media?	32.4
P28UD	Do you agree that the President should bypass Congress and the political parties?	32.9
P38STB	II would not mind a non democratic government in power if it could solve the economic problems	44.9

Note: 'do not know' and 'do not answer' responses are not included. In the case of persons who say that they support a democratic system, we combine the 'disagree' and 'strongly disagree' replies to each of the assertions.

as a measure of support for democracy.[8] However, it is useful as an entry point to the topic because people adopt a *prima facie* position vis-à-vis their idea of democracy. Although the question provides a useful entry point—as an initial summary-measure of citizens' loyalty towards democracy—this does not mean that it is in itself enough to address thoroughly citizens' support for democracy or is a good indirect measure of the 'health' of a democracy.

When question P32ST is related to others that assess support for, and acceptance of, democratic rules, at first sight, the results appear to be surprising or simply inconsistent. A significant proportion of persons who say that they support democracy hold views that call into question the operation of basic institutions of democracy, such as the legislature and political parties, and support the use by the government of authoritarian means to solve a country's problems. Equally 'unexpected' results arise when examining open support for democracy in relation to, for instance, the valuation of democracy as a good system of government, or its preference vis-à-vis other socially relevant values, such as in the case of the alternative between development and democracy (Tables 3 and 4).

8 Mitchell Seligson contends that, since question P32ST does not specify the idea of democracy that people have, it has an undetermined component. He proposes to explore support for the system through an alternative series of questions (M. Seligson, 2000). Although his observation underscores the need to maintain a cautious attitude in the interpretation of outcomes, it does not necessarily invalidate the question as an entry point for examining citizens' support for democracy. The weakness pointed out by Seligson can be resolved by examining question P32ST in relation to others in the Latinobarómetro survey, particularly P30ST ("In your opinion, what does democracy mean?") and P31ST ("People often differ in their opinions regarding the viewpoints on the most important features of democracy. From the list, choose only one feature which you believe is essential to democracy").

PROPORTION OF PERSONS SUPPORTING DEMOCRACY
WITH 'UNEXPECTED' RESPONSES IN RELATION TO THEIR VALUATION
ON THE ALTERNATIVE BETWEEN DEMOCRACY AND DEVELOPMENT   TABLE 4

Question 35ST	Question P32ST
	Percentage of people supporting the democratic system that agree with the following statement
Democracy is most important	32.8
Both are equally important	20.7
Economic development is most important	46.4

Note: 'do not know' and 'do not answer' responses are not included.

With regard to these unexpected responses, there are basically two positions that can be adopted. On the one hand, they can be used as evidence to underline the fickleness of the support of people for a regime. If a preference for democracy only pertains to rhetoric, then question P32ST should be disregarded as a measure of citizens' loyalty towards the regime, due to its scarce analytical value. In this situation we would have to identify other variables to illustrate more stable behavior. In the opinion of this study, such an argument is misguided. Not only does it assume that unexpected responses always reflect inconsistent attitudes, which is not necessarily true, but also that the unexpected is not of interest to the analysis.

On the other hand, unexpected responses can constitute a starting point for a study on citizens' loyalty towards democracy. If one takes this position—which this report does—then question P32ST, which assesses 'overall' support for democracy, should be analyzed in relation to other questions that look at more specific dimensions of this support, with the purpose of determining whether unexpected responses are merely due to citizens' inconsistent attitudes or whether, taken as a whole, they point to certain patterns. In principle, the idea would be to investigate if it is possible to distinguish the sectors with consistently democratic attitudes, both in general terms as well as more specifically, from those with pro-authoritarian viewpoints.

From an inductive standpoint, exploration of the interrelationship between variables underscores the need to have a concept that will allow us to study whether attitudes towards a democratic regime really shape particular positions. Furthermore, this concept should serve as a tool with which to analyze the vulnerability of Latin American democracies. The report thus sets forth the concept of 'orientations towards democracy'.

A final point to bear in mind is that the study of orientations towards democracy in Latin America uses information from a public opinion survey. Although it is valuable material it must be noted that sometimes opinions only approximately reflect the thoughts of people. Individuals can conceal their true beliefs, questions and measurement scales can contain defects that do not allow them to fulfill the purpose for which they were designed. And even when interviewees respond candidly and the questions work out well, people's responses may not necessarily reflect the values and beliefs that may underlie their reactions vis-à-vis concrete situations for supporting democracy in the future.

The Democracy Support Index

The DSI, which was elaborated for this Report, is a summary-measure designed to gauge citizens' support for democracy.[9] It combines indicators of size, level of political activism and the distance between orientations towards democracy. It is the methodological option for analyzing this topic based on an independent reading of variables.[10] This section starts out with a description of the procedure and the tests applied to establish these orientations and goes on to describe the DSI and its components.

The orientations towards democracy are positions of support for democracy or opposition to it, identified from a set of attitudes regarding the preference for democracy and acceptance of the norms on which it is based. This concept arises from an adaptation of the theory of Juan Linz on the breakdown of democracies (Linz, 1978). Linz postulates (with respect to the survival or the replacement of a democratic regime) that citizens can be grouped into three different arrangements: political forces that are loyal to the system; those that are disloyal and are trying to overthrow it; and those that are semi-loyal, possessing contradictory and ambivalent attitudes. Linz further sets out the conditions that encourage the breakdown of democracy; he states that a regime crisis will bring down a democracy when the disloyal group manages to convince semi-loyal citizens to support its viewpoint. Orientations towards democracy follow the definitions provided by Linz (loyal, semi-loyal and disloyal). In order to make it easier for non-specialist readers to understand this analysis, though, the orientations have been re-baptized: 'loyal' citizens are called 'democrats'; semi-loyal citizens are called 'ambivalents'; and disloyal citizens are called 'non-democrats'.

The analysis of these orientations will attempt to answer the following questions: is there an anti-democratic current of opinion among Latin Americans that could constitute a social support base for a 'disloyal' political force? How prevalent is this current vis-à-vis that which supports democracy? Who are the most active people in the political life of a country: those who oppose the system or those who support it? How large is the ambivalent sector? With respect to their views, are the ambivalents closer to the opposition? How are the social bases of these currents of opinion changing in size?

The concept of orientations towards democracy is not, however, identical to that of political alignment as described by Linz. First, Linz studies historical situations in order to extract a comparative theory. The orientations represent a tool with which to approach the issue of the vulnerability of democracy when faced with the possibility of a regime crisis, assessing the degree of citizen support for democracy. Second, the orientations identify attitude patterns among citizens but do not allow direct observation of their actual behavior.

The starting point for identifying orientations towards democracy was work on the 2002 questionnaire produced by Latinobarómetro. A series of factor analyses were applied to a wide set of questions, which, in principle, measure attitudes towards democracy,

---

9 In developing the DSI we tried to stay true to the wider concept of democracy promoted by the Report: that democracy is more than just a political regime. Indeed, the questions posed to establish the orientation of persons towards democracy, on the basis of which the DSI was constructed, include attitudes towards democracy as a political regime and the representative political institutions, which, according to S. Mazzuca, refer to access to power, and towards democracy beyond the political regime, that is, the exercise of power.

10 The reading of simple frequencies of the variables was the point of entry for the analysis but not its pillar. All questions should be put into context, and should be examined in relation to others so as to have a better approach to the meaning of data. Otherwise we run the risk of formulating random constructions based on "how spectacular something is" or on the convenience of a figure. Avoiding this risk is precisely one of the purposes of the orientation analysis.

development, values and interpersonal trust. The objective was to identify those questions directly related to the issue of attitudes supporting democracy.[11] Eleven questions were selected (Table 5).

In all of the analyses, the questions consistently were separated into three groups of factors (Table 6). Factor 1 is made up of the group of delegative attitudes, and corresponds to 23.5 percent of the variance. Factor 2 comprises the degree of support for democracy as a system of government (16.5 percent of the variance). And factor 3 corresponds to support for institutions of representative democracy (13.8 percent of the variance). The accumulated explained variance was 53.8 percent.[12] Confidence tests showed that it was not useful to apply combined indices of the dimensions generated through factor analysis, for which reason each of the variables of the sample was independently studied.

The technique selected to establish, on the basis of these questions, the position of each of the interviewees on one or other orientation towards democracy was cluster analysis. This is an exploratory tool employed to resolve classification problems, since it contributes to revealing associations and structures present in the data that had not been previously observed. Its objective is to assign the cases to groups called clusters, so that the members of the same group are similar with regard to the particular characteristics selected, while the members of different groups are relatively dissimilar.

Cluster analysis can be conducted in several ways, depending on the degree of similarity and the method employed. In this case, because of the magnitude of the data base available, the calculation of Euclidian distance was used as a measure of similarity, and then the method of K-means partition was applied. This procedure requires the investigator to establish *a priori* the number of clusters (k) that he/she wishes to obtain,[13] (the Linz theory defined k=3). In general, it is preferable to base the rationale for the number of clusters selected on an existing theory, because this allows each cluster to be described and especially critical elements to be generated in order to understand their implications.

The K-means method attempts to classify quantitative variables. The 11 questions used to establish orientations towards democracy have a scale of measurement that does not reach the interval level. Nevertheless, they all show a clear directionality related to the attitude towards democracy of the persons interviewed. This is why it was considered appropriate to use this method. To this end, the variables were recoded in order to assign the same range and direction to their measuring scales. Subsequently, the recoded answers were applied to the cluster analysis.[14]

Cluster stability and reliability tests produced satisfactory results. On the one hand, different orders of the data base yielded very small variations in the 'centroids' of the 11 variables: 50 percent had standard deviations below 0.03. Furthermore, in order to assure re-

---

11 The Kaiser–Meyer–Olkin coefficient of sample adequacy for these 11 variables was 0.77, and it is considered appropriate for application in factor analysis.

12 Clustering the 11 values of interest into the three factors indicated follows the Kaiser–Guttman method (eigenvalues greater than one), although the variance explained by them is not particularly high. Percentages obtained from applying the factorial to the variables of interest are shown, without including the remaining variables originally considered.

13 The cluster analysis algorithm will generate groups once the variables in play have been defined and the rules established regarding the number of clusters to be obtained. It is important, therefore, to have a model that backs up the identification of those groups and then validates the results both theoretically and empirically, depending on the characteristics of the individuals assigned to each subset.

14 Zhexue Huang (1997) states that "the traditional approach to converting categorical data into numeric values does not necessarily produce meaningful results in those cases where categorical domains are not ordered." However, as has already been mentioned, in this case the data do have directionality and, as will be shown later, the results are relevant.

Question p32st	Which of the following statements do you agree with most? 'Democracy is preferable to all other forms of government', 'Under some circumstances, an authoritarian government can be preferable to a democratic one', 'For people like me, it doesn't matter whether we have a democratic or a nondemocratic regime'.
Question p35st	If you had to choose between democracy and economic development, which would you say is more important?
Question p37no2	In order for a country to become a developed country, do you believe that democracy is indispensable as a system of government? Or do you think it is possible to become a developed country with a system of government other than democracy?
Question p38stb	Do you strongly agree, agree, disagree or strongly disagree with the following statement? 'I would not mind a non democratic government in power if it could solve the economic problems'.
Question p39st	Some people say that without a National Congress there can be no democracy, while others say that a democracy can work without a National Congress. Which statement best expresses your viewpoint?
Question p40st	Some people say that without political parties, there can be no democracy, while others say that democracy can work without political parties. Which sentence best expresses your viewpoint?
Question p41st	Some people say that democracy permits us to find solutions to the problems that we have in the country. Others say that democracy does not help with solving problems. Which statement best expresses your viewpoint?
Question p28ua	If the country has serious difficulties, are you very much in agreement, in agreement, in disagreement or very much in disagreement that the President should not be limited by what the laws say?
Question p28ub	If the country has serious difficulties, are you very much in agreement, in agreement, in disagreement or very much in disagreement that the President should secure order by force?
Question p28uc	If the country has serious difficulties, are you very much in agreement, in agreement, in disagreement or very much in disagreement that the President should control the media'?
Question p28ud	If the country has serious difficulties, are you very much in agreement, in agreement, in disagreement or very much in disagreement that the President should bypass Congress and the political parties?

Source: Latinobarómetro, 2002.

liable results, the average of 42 results was calculated and this information was used as the initial centroids, which are applied to the cluster algorithm.[15] Also, a methodology was designed to rescue those cases missing one or two answers, increasing the number of cases eligible for study from 12,020 to 14,308 (74.9 percent of the total sample).

Cluster 1 is consistently positive in its standardized values, so it may be inferred that those individuals who fall into this subset have a democratic orientation. Cluster 2 can be classified as corresponding to ambivalent individuals, because it tends to show positive values for the dimensions of support for democracy and support for institutions of representative

15 It is important to note that once the initial centroids are introduced the result of the cluster analysis does not vary among the different subsets of the data base.

FACTORIAL LOADS FOR 11 QUESTIONS OF INTEREST
IN DETERMINING ORIENTATIONS TOWARDS DEMOCRACY

TABLE 6

Dimension	Question	Factor 1	Factor 2	Factor 3
Delegative attitudes	President is above the law	0.74		
	President imposes order by force	0.81		
	President should control the media	0.80		
	President ignores Congress and political parties	0.77		
Support for democracy as form of government	Preference for democracy		0.67	
	Democracy or development		0.58	
	Democracy indispensable for development		0.69	
	Authoritarian government acceptable if it solves problems		0.48	
	Democracy solves problems		0.57	
Support for representative institutions	Democracy without Congress			0.844
	Democracy without political parties			0.85
	Explained variance	23.50	16.50	13.80

Note: factorial loads above 0.450 only are included.

Source: calculated using data from Latinobarómetro, 2002.

democracy, but negative values for delegative attitudes. Finally, cluster 3 presents negative centroids for ten of the variables, being the only positive value very close to zero, so it may be affirmed that the citizens classified as belonging to this group have a non-democratic orientation (Table 7).

In order to verify the importance of the differences in the cluster means with respect to the variables employed to define them, a variance analysis was applied to each cluster. A post hoc study was conducted using the Scheffé test at a five percent significance level.[16] The result showed that the differences are significant for all 11 variables in the three clusters. In other words, all of the questions included in the analysis contribute to distinguishing among the three groups.

Cluster analysis grouping was validated by discriminant analysis. To this end, a random sample of approximately 30 percent of the data was taken and information on the group to which each case corresponded was assigned according to the results obtained in the clusters. Based on this, the discriminant functions were obtained and these were then applied to the remaining 70 percent of cases in order to establish which group they would fall under. With regard to the 30 percent sample, 93.4 percent of the data fell within the correct group, as assigned according to cluster analysis based on the discriminant functions generated. As for the remaining 70 percent, 92.6 percent of the cases were correctly classified, giving a rate of correct assignation for the global sample of 92.9 percent. This percentage can be consid-

16 In conducting a variance analysis, when the null hypothesis is rejected, at least one mean is accepted as being different for the groups. Post hoc methods were employed in order to establish the relationship among those means, and to detect which one, or more than one, is different and which are equal to one another. This technique is used to test the differences between data, comparing all of the possible means of matched pairs in order to identify the ones that are truly different. There are many different post hoc tests. The Scheffé test is useful to prove the significance level of all of the potential mean pairs and is recommended when the groups compared have different numbers of cases, as is the present situation (Steel and Torrie, 1996).

Dimension	Question	Standardized Centroids			Non-Standardized Centroids		
		Cluster 1 Positive	Cluster 2 Central	Cluster 3 Negative	Cluster 1 Positive	Cluster 2 Central	Cluster 3 Negative
Delegative attitudes	President above the law	0.511	-0.707	-0.004	3.09	2.01	2.63
	President imposes order by force	0.609	-0.816	-0.010	3.25	1.97	2.68
	President controls media	0.582	-0.812	0.037	3.26	2.01	2.77
	President ignores political parties and Congress	0.612	-0.755	-0.107	3.25	1.99	2.58
Support for democracy as a system of government	Preference for democracy	0.464	0.080	-0.772	3.72	3.28	2.29
	Democracy or development	0.345	-0.017	-0.438	2.47	2.00	1.47
	Democracy essential for development	0.455	0.383	-1.090	3.83	3.75	1.78
	Authoritarian government tolerated if it solves problems	0.514	-0.268	-0.416	2.88	2.17	2.02
	Democracy solves problems	0.274	0.326	-0.691	3.07	3.15	1.64
Support for representative institutions	Democracy without Congress	0.379	0.006	-0.595	3.38	2.87	1.98
	Democracy without parties	0.372	0.029	-0.572	3.32	2.85	1.94

Note: the range of values for all variables on the scale is between one (attitude most contrary to democracy) to four (attitude most favorable to democracy). Questions relating to support for representative institutions are binary, which therefore weakens their ability to discriminate.
Source: calculated using data from Latinobarómetro, 2002.

ered high, and it underlines the validity of the group assignation as a result of the cluster analysis applied.[17]

The Three Dimensions of the DSI

The Democracy Support Index is a summary-measure of citizens' support for democracy. It is constructed on the basis of assigning individuals to each cluster that identifies the three different orientations towards democracy. It combines three dimensions, which answer the following questions:

■ *What is the size of each orientation towards democracy?*
The best situation for a democracy is when the largest group of citizens falls into the subset of pro-democracy advocates.

■ *What is the degree of political activism of each orientation group?*
The best situation for a democracy is when the pro-democracy orientation group is not only the largest sector but also the most active one.

■ *What is the distance, or dissimilarity measure of the differences in opinion, among the orientations?*
The critical point to establish is whether, in general terms, the ambivalents are closer to the democrats or to the non-democrats. The best situation is when

17 The total number of cases used for the analysis is limited to the 12,020 individuals who answered all 11 questions of interest. Therefore, this analysis was conducted only for those cases in which all of the information was available. Large differences are not expected for the 'rescued' data, due to the fact that the profile of these individuals did not demonstrate much difference with respect to the profile of individuals who answered all 11 questions of interest.

the distance between the ambivalents and the democrats is significantly smaller than the one between the ambivalents and the non-democrats.

Indicators and indices of citizen support constitute interval scales. They do not have a value of absolute zero; the values express proximity to, or distance from, a given situation, but not a proportion. Because these tools are still being fine-tuned, criteria to classify them and to create intensity scales are not yet available.

First Dimension:
Size of a Given Orientation

The size of a given orientation towards democracy refers to the number of citizens belonging to a given cluster. To measure this dimension the DSI uses the proportion of democrats to non-democrats as the indicator.[18] This indicator illustrates a critical situation: whether, even though they are a minority, the democrats are in fact a larger group than the non-democrats, their 'natural' adversaries.[19]

(1) Ratio of Democrats to Non-Democrats =
$$Q_d / Q_{nd}$$

where: Q_d = the number of people with a democratic orientation; and Q_{nd} = the number of people with a non-democratic orientation.

When, in a given country or sub-region, the number of democrats is greater than the number of non-democrats, a condition that is the least desirable, the indicator has a value greater than one. The worst-case scenario is when these indicators have a value below one and close to zero. Furthermore, there are several situations of political equilibrium that generate figures close to one.

Second Dimension: Political Activism among Orientations

'Political activism' among an orientation towards democracy is understood to mean the proportion of its members who participate actively in the political life of their country. A given group is more active when a higher proportion of its members participate. For this calculation a two-step process was utilized. The first step was to establish the degree of political activism for each orientation group. The DSI derives this information from the 'Modes of Citizen Participation' (MCP), a variable that distinguishes the different types of interventions people make in the social and political life of a country, and permits several classifications depending on the researcher's preference.

MPCs are the types of interventions that citizens carry out in social and political life. One modality describes the characteristic profile of a citizen's participation activities. It is rebuilt by analyzing things that people do in the different dimensions of citizens' participation. This is a nominal classification whose categories were not envisaged as to be classified on the basis of a criterion which allows their hierarchical organization; even so, their order of presentation shows the flexible application of certain criteria.[20]

18 There are two other indicators of size, the results of which are mentioned in the Report but were not used in developing the DSI. The first is the indicator of the democratic majority. This reflects the ratio of democrats to the total (ambivalents and non-democrats), and establishes whether the democrats represent the majority or not. The indicator is equal to or greater than one, when the proportion of democrats is equal to or greater than 50 percent of citizens. The second indicator is the relative size of the democratic orientation compared with the ambivalent orientation. When it is greater than one, it indicates that the democrats are more numerous than the ambivalents.

19 This concept was adopted from the field of financial analysis, where there is an indicator called the 'acid test'. It establishes the vulnerability of a company in the short term—in other words, whether it is in a position to pay its short-term debts. It is defined as the ratio of current assets plus stock to current liabilities.

20 Overall, the order of presentation starts with certain categories where there is less personnel cost (investment of time, money), commitment and leadership and concludes with those categories which entail higher costs in staff, commitment and leadership. Finally a category is included for matching other criteria.

TABLE 8

PROCEDURE APPLIED TO DETERMINE MODES OF CITIZEN PARTICIPATION

Dimension				Description
Electoral participation	ELP	0	=	Does not vote
		1	=	Votes
Social participation	SOP	0	=	Does not collaborate
		1	=	Participates at least in one activity
Participate by contacting authorities	PCA	0	=	Does not contact
		1	=	Contacts at least one authority
Participates in collective demonstrations	PCD	0	=	Does not participate
		1	=	Participates in at least one collective demonstration
Violent participation	VP	0	=	Does not participate
		1	=	Participates in at least one violent act, regardless of the 0 or 1 in the other dimensions

Note: these dimensions can be arranged by hierarchy without making any additional assumptions. Zero and one are used to express the presence or absence of activity.

Classification of Modes of Citizen Participation

As table 9 shows, 8 modes of citizen participation were distinguished.

(2) Activism (OX) = $(Q_{mpc}X) / Q_X$

where $Q_{mpc}X$ = the number of people belonging to orientation 'X', who participate as citizens in more ways than simply by voting— modes of citizen participation include contacts established with the authorities and attending public demonstrations. In this equation Q_X = the number of people who hold orientation 'X'. 'X' can represent the democratic, ambivalent or non-democratic orientation.

The second step is to compare the activism of opposite orientations—de-mocratic and non-democratic—and to establish which group is more active. This indicator is called 'demo-cratic activism' (DA) and is the one that is used for the DSI. It is obtained by dividing the activism of the democratic group (D) by the activism of the non-democratic group (ND).

(3) DA = D Activism / ND Activism

where DA = democratic activism, D = democrats and ND = non-democrats.

If the division produces a value greater than one, democrats are more active than non-democrats, a situation that favors democracy; if the value is below one, non-democrats are more active than democrats, which is an uncomfortable situation for democracy; if the result is one, the level of activism in both groups is the same.[21]

Third Dimension: Distance between Orientations

Distance here implies greater or lesser difference in opinion as regards support or rejection of democracy among persons belonging

---

21 There are two other situations that are not analyzed: a) when activism is similar in all orientations (uniform distribution); and b) when the activism of opposed orientations (democrats and non-democrats) is similar and much greater than that of the ambivalents. Both represent potentially unstable political situations for democracy, because the democrats do not enjoy a particular advantage.

CLASSIFICATION OF MODES OF CITIZEN PARTICIPATION	TABLE 9
Name	**Description**
Does nothing	A 0 in all dimensions of citizen participation
Only votes	A 1 in ELP; a 0 in SOP, PCA and PCD
Votes and collaborates	A 1 in ELP and SOP; a 0 in PCA and PCD
Only political action	A 1 in PCA and PCD; a 0 in ELP and SOP
Voting and political action	A 1 in ELP, PCA and PCD; a 0 in SOP
Collaboration and political action	A 1 in SOP, PCA and PCD; a 0 in ELP
Voting, collaboration and political action	A 1 in all dimensions of citizen participation
Violent participation	Any combination in which violent participation is 1

to different orientations. For each variable that makes up the orientation, the indicator examines the mean affinity associated with the answers given by the members of that group. The greater the affinity, the shorter the distance, and vice versa.

The procedure used to incorporate the distance dimension into the DSI is similar to the one employed for the activism dimension. First, the distance of the ambivalent group from each of the adversaries is calculated. In order to calculate the distance between two orientations one must obtain, for each variable, the absolute value difference between their centroids (standard mean values according to cluster analysis) and then add these values together.

(4) Di(Ox/A) = Â|Cxvi-Cavil

where: Di = distance, Ox = democratic or non-democratic orientation and A = ambivalent; Cxi = democratic or non-democratic centroid in variable i; and $Cavi$ = the ambivalent centroid in variable i.

The results for democrats and non-democrats are then compared by means of the indicator of distance (ID). This indicator expresses the average distance between the non-democratic and the ambivalent orientations as a proportion of the distance between democrats and ambivalents.

(5) IDD = Di (D/A) / Di (ND/A)

where: IDD = the distance of democrats from ambivalents as a proportion of the distance of non-democrats from ambivalents; $Di(D/A)$ = the distance between democrats and ambivalents; and $Di(ND/A)$ = the distance between non-democrats and ambivalents.

If this division produces a value greater than one, the ambivalents are closer to the non-democrats; if the value is less than one, the ambivalents are closer to democrats; if the result is one, the ambivalents are equidistant from both opposing orientations. Contrary to the indicators of size and activism, in which the larger values for democrats represent optimal conditions for democracy, where distance is concerned, the ideal is for ambivalents to be as close as possible to democrats, indicating values that are more akin.

The DSI Aggregation Rule

The DSI combines the size, activism and relative distance of the three orientations. All factors are equally weighted within the index. There is no theory governing hierarchy among these elements, and there is no prior research offering specific criteria to weight the importance of each factor. So as not to introduce assumptions that are hard to justify, the option chosen was determined to be the most straightforward expression of the conceptual basis of the investigation.

(6) DSI = Size[AD] * (Activism [AC] / Distance [DI])

If, in a given country, the majority of citizens are loyal to democracy, and these citizens are more active than the rest of the people and only a small amount of distance separates them from the ambivalents, we may conclude that democracy is backed by citizens. In these circumstances, the DSI produces a value considerably greater than one. By contrast, if, in a given country, the majority of citizens are non-democrats, those non-democrats participate more than the rest of the people and are only a small amount of distance separates them from the ambivalents, we may conclude that support for democracy is fragile. In these circumstances the value of the index is well below one and close to zero. The inference is that a political system with these characteristics is more vulnerable to crisis than one that enjoys strong citizen support. Different combinations of size, degree of activism and distance arise, constituting intermediate states of strength and weakness for democracy. In situations of equilibrium, the value of the DSI is around one.

Interpreting the DSI

Given the formula used to calculate the DSI, the index can range between zero and a very high number (the number tends towards infinity in a country where all democrats are active participants and the few ambivalents are very close to their position). There is not enough knowledge on the subject to standardize this variation, in a range that fluctuates between zero and one, for example, nor to categorize values on an intensity scale. Standardization would require employing relatively sophisticated procedures based on additional assumptions.

Furthermore, creating an intensity scale would imply justifying the cut-off points between the categories defined; this will be feasible only when more observations become available (there is only 18 countries studied in one year). Nevertheless, observing how the DSI behaves in some hypothetical situations permits an initial attempt at interpretation (Table 10).

Validation and Reliability of the DSI

There are no known studies that have applied this methodology to the examination of citizen support for democracy. The analysis of orientations towards democracy cannot be replicated in the Latinobarómetro time series. Some of the variables used in this analysis come from the regular section of Latinobarómetro, but they are not included every year; other questions were elaborated specifically for the UNDP section of the survey, and therefore no prior observations exist.

Some of the questions posed to determine orientations are subject to limitations, which affect measurement. The scales for questions with two or three alternative answers do not fully adapt to cluster analysis requirements. Also the standard deviation of these variables was greater than that of other variables. These difficulties are particularly evident with respect to questions about the degree of support for institutions of representative democracy; the scale on which responses to these questions is measured is binary. Despite these limitations, as has been explained, the results obtained have proved robust.

A study on the external validity of orientation analysis was carried out. The study posed the following question (included in Latinobarómetro, 1996 and 1998): 'Would you be prepared to defend democracy should it be threatened?' The results obtained for each country were compared with the size of orientations in 2002. In general, in 1996 and 1998, those countries in which more people were prepared to defend democracy were the ones that had more democrats in 2002 (0.27 and 0.25, respectively). Additionally, they demonstrate an inverse correlation with the percentage of non-democrats (-0.29 and -0.36, respectively).

Assumptions and Limitations of the DSI

The methodology used to construct the index is based on three assumptions. The first is that orientations towards democracy are relatively stable over time. Although fluctuations within the long-term accumulated effect are not ruled out (for example, the economic deterioration of a given country). However, because these are attitudes related to a diffuse support for democracy (or rejection), one can infer that the variations are less pronounced than the variations exhibited by perceptions

EXAMPLES OF SITUATIONS AND VALUES ASSOCIATED WITH THE DSI

TABLE 10

When the DSI is above or equal to five, conditions are very favorable for democracy. In other words, democrats tend to represent the majority and to be politically more active than their adversaries, and ambivalents tend to be much closer to their position.

The opposite situation would represent conditions that are unfavorable for democracy: non-democrats represent the majority, they are more active politically and the ambivalents are much closer to their position. A value of 0.15 for the DSI corresponds to this second situation.

When the DSI is slightly above one, the situation tends to favor democracy but in a more tenuous way. The situation is unfavorable for democracy with regard to some dimension or component of the index, but this is more than compensated by the favorable result in other dimensions. Or then again, the situation may favor democracy in all three dimensions, albeit by very narrow margins. For example, a value of 1.43 for the DSI would represent a situation in which democrats are more numerous (although not in the majority) and ambivalents are slightly closer to their position, but the democrats are less politically active than non-democrats.

The DSI is a tool that still requires fine-tuning. Its current algorithm, based on the assumption that all three components are independent from one another and equally weighted, does not function adequately under some circumstances.[22] More research needs to be conducted to find valid methodological answers to the problems that the simple DSI formulation cannot resolve. Nevertheless, it should be noted that the analysis of the results obtained for the DSI in different Latin American countries during 2002 suggests that, in spite of these limitations, the index did not produce unexpected results. Furthermore, none of the DSI components demonstrated 'anomalous' behavior to the point of introducing distortions in the index's global result.

related to satisfaction with the way institutions work or the economic and social performance of the system.[23]

The second assumption is that, even when persons with a given orientation do not constitute a political force with organizational capacity, ideology and leadership, they may become one if they are faced with a polarizing political event.[24] One should recall that orientations do not help to predict people's behavior in terms of subversion or support for the system. There are a series of factors, difficult to establish a priori, that influence the transformation of attitudes into behavior.

Third, when it comes to defense of, or opposition to, the democratic system, it is assumed that ambivalents do not act on their own initiative. They are therefore a target group in the dispute between democrats and non-democrats. It is further assumed that the resistance offered by ambivalents, however great, is the same for both orientations. These two assumptions were inherited from Linz, and are a logical derivation from his position. When the political question of the day concerns the survival of democracy, there is no 'Third Way': one either defends or challenges the regime. Nevertheless, until one has to make a political choice between whether democracy survives or perishes, these assumptions cannot be said for sure to hold true. In practice, ambivalents may act on their own political initiative on a wide range of issues, even if they do not constitute a specific political force.[25]

22 For example, in a country where the number of democrats is only half that of non democrats (AD = 0.5), where non-democrats are more politically active than democrats (AC = 0.5), but where ambivalents are overwhelmingly closer to democrats than non-democrats (DI = 0.2), the DSI would be equal to 12.5. This situation is far from favorable to democracy. Maybe it is an unlikely scenario, but it is certainly possible.

23 The Latinobarómetro time series does allow evaluation of the stability of orientations towards democracy. Tests carried out with regard to the question about the economic status of the household, along with questions on the preference for democracy and satisfaction with democracy in certain years (1996, 1997, 2001 and 2002), reveal that the preference for democracy does not vary according to whether the economic position of the household is good or bad, but, rather, according to how well democracy is working.

24 A *polarizing political* event refers to an economic, political or social crisis, which creates the possibility of replacing the democratic system with a different regime.

25 One of the most important points of this study was to determine the political and social profile of ambivalents.

Finally, certain characteristics of Latinobarómetro's samples suggest that the DSI must be interpreted carefully, particularly in certain countries. The effects of including the 'rural sector' and the more impoverished urban segments are unknown.

The data from the opinion poll used for this Report were supplied by Latinobarómetro in accordance with a contractual agreement to work and collaborate with UNDP. In 2002, Latinobarómetro increased by one-third the size of its annual study, including specific questions requested by UNDP for this Report. Under the agreement between the two institutions, Latinobarómetro made available the time series from previous surveys, which were also used as one of the antecedents for the empirical base of the Report.

Bibliography

Ackerman, Bruce, 1980, *Social Justice in the Liberal State,* New Haven, Yale University Press.

————, 2004, "¿Hacia una síntesis latinoamericana?", text prepared for PRODDAL, in UNDP, *La democracia en América Latina. Hacia una democracia de ciudadanas y ciudadanos. Anexo: El debate conceptual sobre la democracia (CD ROM),* Buenos Aires, Aguilar, Altea, Taurus, Alfaguara.

Acuña, Carlos, and Catalina Smulovitz, 1996, 'Adjusting the Armed Forces to Democracy: Successes, Failures, and Ambiguities in the Southern Cone', in Jelin, Elizabeth, and Hershberg, Eric (eds.), *Constructing Democracy. Human Rights, Citizenship, and Society in Latin America,* Boulder, Colorado, Westview Press.

Adrianzen, Alberto, 1993, *Democracia, etnicidad y violencia política en los países andinos,* Lima, Peru, Instituto de Estudios Peruanos.

Aguilar Camín, Héctor, 1996, *Después del milagro,* Mexico DF, Cal y Arena.

————, 1999, "El México vulnerable", in *Nexos,* March.

Aguilar Camín, Héctor, and Lorenzo Meyer, 1990, *A la sombra de la Revolución Mexicana. Un ensayo de historia contemporánea de México, 1910–1989,* 3rd edition, Mexico DF, Cal y Arena.

Alcántara Sáez, Manuel, 2002, "Experimentos de democracia interna: Las primarias de partidos en América Latina", in Helen Kellogg Institute for International Studies Working Paper, 293, Notre Dame, Indiana, The Helen Kellogg Institute for International Studies at Notre Dame University.

————, 2004, "Partidos políticos en América Latina: precisiones conceptuales, estado actual y retos futuros", text prepared for PRODDAL, in UNDP, *La democracia en América Latina. Hacia una democracia de ciudadanas y ciudadanos: Contribuciones para el debate,* Buenos Aires, Aguilar, Altea, Taurus, Alfaguara.

Alconada Sempé, Raúl, 2004, "Seguridad jurídica y Estado democrático de derecho", text prepared for PRODDAL, in UNDP, *La democracia en América Latina. Hacia una democracia de ciudadanas y ciudadanos: Contribuciones para el debate,* Buenos Aires, Aguilar, Altea, Taurus, Alfaguara.

Almaraz Paz, Sergio, 1979, *Para abrir el diálogo,* La Paz, Los Amigos del Libro.

Almond, Gabriel, 1980, 'The Intellectual History of the Civic Culture Concept', in Almond, G., and Verba, S. (eds.), *The Civic Culture Revisited,* Boston, Massachusetts, Little, Brown & Co.

Almond, Gabriel, and Sidney Verba, 1963, *The Civic Culture,* Princeton, New Jersey, Princeton University Press.

Altman, David, 2001, 'The Politics of Coalition Formation and Survival in Multiparty Presidential

Regimes', doctoral thesis, Notre Dame, Indiana, Department of Government and International Studies, Notre Dame University.

————, 2002, 'Prospects for E-Government in Latin America: Satisfaction with Democracy, Social Accountability, and Direct Democracy', in *International Review of Public Administration,* 7(2), pp. 5–20.

Amnesty International, 2002, 'Amnesty International Website Against the Death Penalty. Abolitionist and Retentionist Countries' [http://web.amnesty.org/rmp/dplibrary.nshf/index?openview].

Anderson, Benedict, 1991, *Imagined Communities,* London and New York, Verso.

————, 1993, *Comunidades imaginadas. Reflexiones sobre el origen y la difusión del nacionalismo,* Mexico DF, Fondo de Cultura Económica.

Anderson, Perry, 1974, *Lineages of the Absolutist State,* London, New Left Books.

Andrade, Vera Regina, 1999, *Cidadania: do Direito aos Direitos Humanos,* Sao Paulo, Brazil, Acadêmica.

Annan, Kofi, 2003, *Implementation of the United Nations Millennium Declaration. Report of the Secretary-General,* A/58/323.

Aragón Reyes, Manuel, 1998, "Derecho Electoral: Sufragio activo y pasivo", in Nohlen, Dieter, Picado, Sonia, and Zovatto, Daniel (eds.), *Tratado de derecho electoral comparado de América Latina,* Mexico DF, Fondo de Cultura Económica.

Arato, Andrew, 1993, *Civil Society and Political Theory,* Cambridge, Massachusetts, MIT Press.

————, 2004, "Algunos comentarios sobre la Tesis I", text prepared for PRODDAL, in UNDP, *La democracia en América Latina. Hacia una democracia de ciudadanas y ciudadanos. Anexo: El debate conceptual sobre la democracia (CD ROM),* Buenos Aires, Aguilar, Altea, Taurus, Alfaguara.

Arbós, Xavier, 1996, *La gobernabilidad: ciudadanía y democracia en la encrucijada mundial,* 2nd edition, Mexico DF, Siglo XXI.

Arditi, Benjamín, 1992, "Elecciones municipales y democratización en Paraguay", in *Nueva Sociedad,* No. 117.

Aristoteles, 1968, *The Politics,* edition of Ernest Baker, Oxford, Oxford University Press. (Edition in Spanish: 1975, *La política,* 5th edition, Barcelona, Spain, Emecé.)

Arriagada, Genaro, 2002, "Diez proposiciones para encarar la crisis de los Partidos", in *asuntospublicos.org* (informes 201 y 206)

Assies, Willem, 2004, "Diversidad, Estado y democracia: unos apuntes", text prepared for PRODDAL, in UNDP, *La democracia en América Latina. Hacia una democracia de ciudadanas y ciudadanos: Contribuciones para el debate,* Buenos Aires, Aguilar, Altea, Taurus, Alfaguara.

Baeza, Fernández, 1998, "El voto obligatorio", in Nohlen, Dieter, Picado, Sonia, and Zovatto, Daniel (eds.), *Tratado de derecho electoral comparado de América Latina,* Mexico DF, Fondo de Cultura Económica.

Barié, Cletus Gregor, 2000, *Pueblos indígenas y derechos constitucionales en América Latina: un panorama,* Mexico DF, Instituto Indigenista Interamericano.

Barro, Robert J., and Jong-Wha Lee, 2000, 'International Data on Educational Attainment: Updates and Implications', CID Working Paper, 42, Center for International Development (CID), Harvard University [http://www.cid.harvard.edu/ciddata/ciddata.html].

Bazdresch, Carlos, and Soledad Loaeza, 1993, *México, auge, crisis y ajuste,* 3 volumes, Mexico DF, Fondo de Cultura Económica.

Beitz, Charles. R., 1989, *Political Equality. An Essay in Democratic Theory,* Princeton, New Jersey, Princeton University Press.

Bello, Álvaro, and Marta Rangel, 2002, "La equidad y la exclusión de los pueblos indígenas y afrodescendientes en América Latina y el Caribe", in *Revista de la CEPAL,* 76 (April), pp. 39–54.

Bellomo, Manlio, 1995, *The Common Legal Past of Europe, 1000–1800,* Washington DC, Catholic University of America Press.

Benavides, T. and Vargas Cullell, J. 2003. *Nota conceptual sobre participación ciudadana.* San José, prepared for PRODDAL. June 2003.

Bendix, Reinhardt, 1964, *Nation-Building and Citizenship. Studies of our Changing Social Order,* New York, John Wiley & Sons.

Berger, Peter, and Thomas Luckman, 1966, *The Social Construction of Reality. A Treatise in the Sociology of Knowledge,* New York, Doubleday.

Berlin, Isaiah, 1969, *Four Essays on Liberty,* Oxford, Oxford University Press.

Berman, Harold J., 1993, *Law and Revolution: The Formation of the Western Legal Tradition,* Cambridge, Massachusetts, Harvard University Press.

Blondet, Cecilia, 1998, *La emergencia de las mujeres en el poder. ¿Hay cambios en Perú?*

Bobbio, Norberto, 1989, *Democracy and Dictatorship. The Nature and Limits of State Power,* Minneapolis, Minnesota, University of Minnesota Press.

————, 1992, *El futuro de la democracia,* Colombia, FCE.

Bobbio, Norberto, and Matteucci, Nicola, 1988, *Diccionario de Política,* 5th edition, Mexico DF, Siglo XXI.

Boneo, Horacio, and Edelberto Torres Rivas, 2001, *¿Por qué no votan los guatemaltecos? Estudio de participación y abstención electoral,* Guatemala, IDEA/IFE/UNDP.

Borón, Atilio A., 1997, *Estado, capitalismo y democracia en América Latina,* 3rd edition, Buenos Aires, Argentina, Oficina de Publicaciones del CBC.

————, 2000, "América Latina: crisis sin fin o fin de la crisis", in López Segrera, Francisco, and Filmus, Daniel (ed.), *América Latina 2020. Escenarios, alternativas, estrategias,* Buenos Aires, Argentina, UNESCO–FLACSO–Temas Grupo Editorial.

Boschi, Renato, 2004, "Desarrollo democrático en América Latina: su condición, las percepciones de sus ciudadanos, indicadores y agenda", text prepared for PRODDAL, in UNDP, *La democracia en América Latina. Hacia una democracia de ciudadanas y ciudadanos. Anexo: El debate conceptual sobre la democracia (CD ROM),* Buenos Aires, Aguilar, Altea, Taurus, Alfaguara.

Botana, Natalio, 2004, "Dimensiones históricas de las transiciones a la democracia en América Latina", text prepared for PRODDAL, in UNDP, *La democracia en América Latina. Hacia una democracia de ciudadanas y ciudadanos: Contribuciones para el debate,* Buenos Aires, Aguilar, Altea, Taurus, Alfaguara.

Bourdieu, Pierre, 1996, "Espíritus de Estado. Génesis y estructura del campo burocrático", in *Sociedad,* 8, pp. 5–29.

Breuilly, John, 1993, *Nationalism and the State,* Manchester, UK, Manchester University Press.

Brown, Mark Malloch, 2002, *Deepening Democracy in the Developing World: An Agenda for Action in the New Millennium,* Washington, DC, Center for Global Development [http://www.undp.org/dpa/statements/administ/2002/october/21oct02.html].

Brubaker, Rogers, 1992, *Citizenship and Nationhood in France and Germany,* Cambridge, Massachusetts, Harvard University Press.

————, 1996, *Nationalism Reframed. Nationhood and the National Question in New Europe,* Cambridge, Massachusetts, Cambridge University Press.

Burdeau, Georges, 1985, 'Democratie', in *Encyclopaedia Universalis,* Paris, France.

Burns, Nancy, et al., 2001, *The Private Roots of Public Action,* Cambridge, Massachusetts, Harvard University Press.

Calderón, Fernando, 2000, *Sociedad y globalización,* La Paz, Bolivia, UNDP, Cuadernos del Futuro.

————— (ed.), 2003, *¿Es sostenible la globalización en América Latina? Debates con Manuel Castells,* 2 volumes, Buenos Aires, Argentina, Fondo de Cultura Económica.

—————, 2004a, "Las condiciones sociales de la democracia: el Estado y el régimen", text prepared for PRODDAL, in UNDP, *La democracia en América Latina. Hacia una democracia de ciudadanas y ciudadanos. Anexo: El debate conceptual sobre la democracia (CD ROM),* Buenos Aires, Aguilar, Altea, Taurus, Alfaguara.

—————, 2004b, "Notas sobre la crisis de legitimidad del Estado y la democracia", text prepared for PRODDAL, in UNDP, *La democracia en América Latina. Hacia una democracia de ciudadanas y ciudadanos: Contribuciones para el debate,* Buenos Aires, Aguilar, Altea, Taurus, Alfaguara.

Calvo, Ernesto, and Juan Manuel Abal Medina, Jr. (eds.), 2001, *El federalismo electoral argentino. Sobrerrepresentación, reforma política y gobierno dividido en la Argentina,* Buenos Aires, Argentina, INAP Eudeba.

Camargo, Pedro Pablo, 1996, *Derechos humanos y democracia en América Latina,* Bogota, Colombia, Grupo Editorial Leyer.

Canovan, Margaret, 1996, *Nationhood and Political Theory,* London, Edward Elgar.

Caputo, Dante, 2004, "Globalización, hegemonía y Democracia", text prepared for PRODDAL in UNDP, *La democracia en América Latina. Hacia una democracia de ciudadanas y ciudadanos: Contribuciones para el debate,* Buenos Aires, Aguilar, Altea, Taurus, Alfaguara.

Cardoso, Fernando Henrique, 1993, *A construçao da Democracia,* Sao Paulo, Brazil, Siciliano.

—————, 2004, "Democracia y globalización", text prepared for PRODDAL in UNDP, *La democracia en América Latina. Hacia una democracia de ciudadanas y ciudadanos: Contribuciones para el debate,* Buenos Aires, Aguilar, Altea, Taurus, Alfaguara.

Carey, John M., and Matthew Soberg Shugart (eds.), 1998, *Executive Decree Authority,* New York, Cambridge University Press.

Carey, John, Octávio Amorin Neto, and Matthew Soberg Shugart, 1997, 'Appendix: Outlines of Constitutional Powers in Latin America', in Mainwaring, Scott, and Soberg Shugart, Matthew (eds.), *Presidentialism and Democracy in Latin America,* Cambridge, Cambridge University Press.

Carranza, Elías, 2001, "Sobrepoblación penitenciaria en América Latina y el Caribe: Situación y respuestas posibles", article presented at the Technical Seminar of the Network of Programmes of UN Institutes, Vienna, Austria, 10 May.

Carvalho, José Murilo de, 2001, *A Cidadania no Brasil: O Longo Caminho,* Rio de Janeiro, Brazil, Civilização Brasileira.

Castel, Robert, 1995, *La metamorfosis de la cuestión social,* Buenos Aires, Argentina, Paidós.

Castells, Manuel, 1998, *La era de la información. Economía, sociedad y cultura,* Madrid, Spain, Alianza.

Cavarozzi, Marcelo, and Manuel Antonio Garretón (eds.), 1989, *Muerte y resurrección, los partidos políticos en el autoritarismo y la democratización en el Cono Sur,* Santiago, Chile.

Cavarozzi, Marcelo, and Juan Manuel Abal Medina, Jr. (eds.), 2002, *El asedio a la política. Los partidos latinoamericanos en la era neoliberal,* Rosario, Argentina, Homo Sapiens Ediciones, Konrad Adenauer Stiftung.

CEJA (Centro de Estudios sobre la Justicia en las Américas/The Justice Studies Center of the Americas), 2003a, "Reporte sobre el Estado de la Justicia en las Américas 2002–2003", Santiago, Chile, CEJA.

—————, 2003b, "Primer Encuentro Interamericano de Defensorías Públicas", [http://www.cejamericas.org/newsite/ingles/index_in.htm].

CELS (Centro de Estudios Legales y Sociales/Center for Legal and Social Studies), 2001, *Derechos Humanos en Argentina: Informe anual 2001,* Buenos Aires, Argentina, Eudeba.

Cerdas-Cruz, Rodolfo, Juan Rial, and Daniel Zovatto (eds.), 1992, *Elecciones y democracia en América Latina, 1988–1991. Una tarea inconclusa,* San José, Costa Rica, Instituto Interamericano de Derechos Humanos–Centro Interamericano de Asesoría y Promoción Electoral.

Coleman, James S., 1990, *Foundations of Social Theory,* Cambridge, Massachusetts, Cambridge University Press.

Collier, David, and Steven Levitsky, 1996, 'Democracy with Adjectives: Conceptual Innovation in Comparative Research', in Helen Kellogg Institute for International Studies Working Paper, 230, Notre Dame, Indiana, The Helen Kellogg Institute for International Studies at Notre Dame University.

—————, 1997, 'Democracy With Adjectives: Conceptual Innovation in Comparative Research', in *World Politics,* 49(3) (April), pp. 430–451.

Comisión Andina de Juristas (Andean Commission of Jurists), 2000, *La reforma judicial en la región andina. ¿Qué se ha hecho, dónde estamos, adónde vamos?,* Lima, Peru, Comisión Andina de Juristas.

—————, 2003, "Red de información jurídica. Sistemas judiciales" [http://www.cajpe.org.pe/rij/].

Comparato, Fabio Konder, 1989, *Para viver a democracia,* Sao Paulo, Brazil, Brasiliense.

Conaghan, Catherine, 2004, "Más allá del minimalismo: una agenda para unir democracia y desarrollo", text prepared for PRODDAL in UNDP, *La democracia en América Latina. Hacia una democracia de ciudadanas y ciudadanos. Anexo: El debate conceptual sobre la democracia (CD ROM),* Buenos Aires, Aguilar, Altea, Taurus, Alfaguara.

Conway, Margaret, 1985, *Political Participation in the United States,* Washington, DC, Congressional Quarterly Inc.

Córdova Macías, Ricardo, 2000, *Una propuesta para la reforma del Estado en El Salvador,* San Salvador, El Salvador, Fundación Dr. Guillermo Manuel Ungo.

Cornelius, Peter K., and Klaus Schwab (eds.), 2003, *The Global Competitiveness Report 2002–2003,* New York, Oxford University Press.

Cornelius, Wayne A., Todd A. Eisenstadt, and Jane Hindley, 1999, *Subnational Politics and Democratization in Mexico,* San Diego, California, Center for US-Mexican Studies, University of California.

Corrigan, Philip R.D., and Derek Sayer, 1985, *The Great Arch. English State Formation as Cultural Revolution,* London, Basil Blackwell.

Cortina, Adela, 1997, *Ciudadanos del mundo: hacia una teoría de la ciudadanía,* Madrid, Spain, Alianza Editorial.

Cotler, Julio, 1978, *Clases, Estado y nación en el Perú,* Lima, Peru, IEP.

—————, 2004, "La nacionalización y democratización del Estado, la política y la sociedad", text prepared for PRODDAL in UNDP, *La democracia en América Latina. Hacia una democracia de ciudadanas y ciudadanos. Anexo: El debate conceptual sobre la democracia (CD ROM),* Buenos Aires, Aguilar, Altea, Taurus, Alfaguara.

Cotterrell, R.B.M., 1995, *Law's Community. Legal Theory in Sociological Perspective,* Oxford, UK, Clarendon Press.

—————, 1996, 'The Rule of Law in Transition: Revisiting Franz Neumann's Sociology of Legality', in *Social & Legal Studies*, 5(4), pp. 451–470.

CPJ (Committee to Protect Journalists), 2003, 'Journalists Killed in the Line of Duty During the Last Ten Years' [http://www.cpj.org/killed/Ten_Year_Killed/Intro.html].

Crotty, W. 1991. 'Political Participation: Mapping the Terrain', in William, C., *Political Participation and American Democracy*. Westport, Greenwood Press

Dahl, Robert A., 1966, *Political Oppositions in Western Democracies*, New Haven, Connecticut, Yale University Press.

—————, 1971, *Poliarquía, participación y oposición*, Mexico DF, Rey. (Spanish edition of 1993.)

—————, 1987, *Un prefacio a la teoría democrática*, Ediciones Gernika.

—————, 1989, *Democracy and Its Critics*, New Haven, Connecticut, Yale University Press.

—————, 1999, *La democracia*, Buenos Aires, Argentina, Taurus.

Dalton, Russell J., 1996, 'Political Support in Advanced Industrial Democracies', in Norris, Pippa (ed.), *Critical Citizens. Global Support for Democratic Governance*, Oxford, UK, Oxford University Press.

Dasgupta, Partha, 1993, *An Inquiry into Well-Being and Destitution*, Oxford, UK, Clarendon Press.

De Riz, Liliana, 1992, "El debate sobre la reforma electoral en Argentina", in *Desarrollo Económico*, 126 (July–September).

De Soto, Hernando, 1984, *El Otro Sendero*, Lima, Peru, El Barranco.

Defensoria Pública da União, Brasil, 2001, "Relatório de Gestão" [http://www.mj.gov.br/defensoria/default.htm].

Deininger, Klaus, and Lyn Squire, 1998, *The Deininger and Squire Data Set. A New Data Set Measuring Income Inequality*, Washington, DC, World Bank.

Del Castillo, Pilar and Daniel G. Zovatto (eds.), 1998, *La financiación de la política en Iberoamérica*, San José, Costa Rica, IIDH-CAPEL.

Dellasoppa, Emilio E., Alicia M. Bercovich, et al., 1999, "Violencia, Direitos Civis e Demografía no Brasil na Década de 80: O Caso da Area Metropolitana do Rio de Janeiro", in *Revista Brasileira de Ciencias Sociais*, 14(39), pp. 155–176.

Di Tella, Torcuato (ed.), 1998, *Crisis de representatividad y sistemas de partidos políticos*, Buenos Aires, Argentina, ISEN.

Diamint, Rut (ed.), 1999, *Control civil y fuerzas armadas en las nuevas democracias latinoamericanas*, Buenos Aires, Argentina, Grupo Editor Latinoamericano.

Diamond, Larry, 1999, *Developing Democracy. Toward Consolidation*, Baltimore, Maryland, The Johns Hopkins University Press.

—————, 2004, "Sobre los atributos de la democracia como régimen político", text prepared for PRODDAL in UNDP, *La democracia en América Latina. Hacia una democracia de ciudadanas y ciudadanos. Anexo: El debate conceptual sobre la democracia (CD ROM)*, Buenos Aires, Aguilar, Altea, Taurus, Alfaguara.

Diamond, Larry, et al. (eds.), 1997, *Consolidating the Third Wave Democracies: Themes and Perspectives*, Baltimore, Maryland, The Johns Hopkins University Press.

Diamond, Larry, Jonathan Hartlyn, Juan Linz, and Seymour Martin Lipset (eds.), 1999, *Democracy in Developing Countries: Latin America*, 2nd edition, Boulder, Colorado, Lynne Rienner.

Domingo, Pilar, 1999, 'Judicial Independence and Judicial Reform in Latin America', in Schedler, Andreas, Diamond, Larry, and Plattner, Marc F. (eds.),

The Self-Restraining State. Power and Accountability in New Democracies, Boulder, Colorado, Lynne Rienner.

Domínguez, Jorge, 1998, *Democratic Politics in Latin America and the Caribbean,* Baltimore, Maryland, The Johns Hopkins University Press.

Domínguez, Jorge, and Abraham Lowenthal (eds.), 1996, *Constructing Democratic Governance. Latin America and the Caribbean in the 1990s,* Baltimore, Maryland, The Johns Hopkins University Press.

Dornbusch, Rudiger, and Sebastián Edwards, 1994, "La macroeconomía política del populismo latinoamericano", in Dornbusch, Rudiger, and Edwards, Sebastián (eds.), *La macroeconomía del populismo en América Latina,* Mexico DF, Fondo de Cultura Económica.

Durkheim, Emil, 1983, *Professional Ethics and Civic Morals,* London, Routledge.

Dworkin, Ronald, 1986, *Law's Empire,* Cambridge, Massachusetts, Harvard University Press.

Easton, David, 1965, *A System Analysis of Political Life,* New York, John Wiley & Sons.

————, 1975, 'The Concept of Political Support', in *The British Journal of Political Science,* 5.

ECLAC (Economic Commission for Latin America and the Caribbean), 1997, *Síntesis. Estudio económico de América Latina y el Caribe, 1996–1997,* Santiago, Chile, United Nations.

————, 1999, *Participation and Leadership in Latin America and the Caribbean: Gender Indicators,* Santiago, Chile, ECLAC.

————, 2000, *The Challenge of Gender Equity and Human Rights on the Threshold of the Twenty-First Century,* Santiago, Chile, Unidad de Mujer y Desarrollo, 27, Mayo.

————, 2001a, *Panorama social de América Latina 2000–2001,* Santiago, Chile, United Nations.

————, 2001b, *Estudio económico para América Latina y el Caribe 2000–2001,* Santiago, Chile, United Nations.

————, 2002a, *Anuario estadístico de América Latina y el Caribe 2001,* Santiago, Chile, United Nations.

————, 2002b, *Panorama social de América Latina 2001–2002,* Santiago, Chile, United Nations.

————, 2002c, *Balance preliminar de las economías de América Latina y el Caribe 2002,* Santiago, Chile, United Nations.

————, 2002d, *Estudio económico de América Latina y el Caribe, 2001–2002,* Statistical Annex in CD-ROM form [http://www.eclac.cl/DE/proyectos/eee/eee2002/index.htm].

————, 2003, *Anuario estadístico de América Latina y el Caribe 2002,* Santiago, Chile, United Nations.

————, 2004, *Panorama social de América Latina 2002–2003,* Santiago, Chile.

ECLAC, IPEA, UNDP, 2003, *Hacia el objetivo del milenio: Reducir la pobreza en América Latina y el Caribe,* Santiago, Chile.

Eisenstadt, Shmuel N., 1999, *Paradoxes of Democracy. Fragility, Continuity, and Change,* Baltimore, Maryland, The Johns Hopkins University Press.

————, 2000, 'Multiple Modernities', in *Daedalus,* 129(1), pp. 1–29.

Ely, John, 1980, *Democracy and Distrust. A Theory of Judicial Review,* Cambridge, Massachusetts, Harvard University Press.

EPIC (Election Process Information Collection), 2002 [http://www.epicproject.org].

Epp, Charles R., 1998, *The Rights Revolution. Lawyers, Activists, and Supreme Courts in Comparative Perspective,* Chicago, Illinois, University of Chicago Press.

Eurostat, PCM–BDU (Panel Communautaire de ménages–Base de données des utilisateurs).

Evans, Peter B., Dietrich Rueschemer, and Theda Skocpol (eds.), 1985, *Bringing the State Back In,* Cambridge, Massachusetts, Cambridge University Press.

Fábre, C., 1998, 'Constitutionalising Social Rights', in *The Journal of Political Philosophy,* 6(3), pp. 263–284.

Feinberg, Joel, 1973, *Social Philosophy,* Englewood Cliffs, New Jersey, Prentice-Hall.

————, 1986, *Harm to Self. The Moral Limits of the Criminal Law,* New York, Oxford University Press.

Fishkin, James S., 1991, *Democracy and Deliberation. New Directions for Democratic Reform,* New Haven, Connecticut, Yale University Press.

Fitch, J. Samuel, 1998, *The Armed Forces and Democracy in Latin America,* Baltimore, Maryland, The Johns Hopkins University Press.

Fitoussi, Jean-Paul, 2002, *La règle et le choix,* Paris, France, Editorial Le Seuil, Collection La république des idées.

————, 2004, "Globalización, mercado y democracia", text prepared for PRODDAL, in UNDP, *La democracia en América Latina. Hacia una democracia de ciudadanas y ciudadanos: Contribuciones para el debate,* Buenos Aires, Aguilar, Altea, Taurus, Alfaguara.

Flathman, Richard E., 1995, 'Citizenship and Authority: A Chastened View of Citizenship', in Beiner, Ronald, *Theorizing Citizenship,* New York, State University of New York Press.

Foweraker, Joe, and Todd Landman, 1999, *Social Movements and Citizenship Rights,* Oxford, UK, Oxford University Press.

Fox, Jonathan, 1994, 'The Difficult Transition from Clientalism to Democracy', in *World Politics,* 46(2), pp. 154–184.

Franck, Thomas M., 2001, 'Are Human Rights Universal?', in *Foreign Affairs,* 80(1), pp. 191–204.

Freedom House, 2002, 'Press Freedom Survey' [http://www.freedomhouse.org].

Freidenberg, Flavia, and Francisco Sánchez López, 2002, "¿Cómo se elige un candidato a presidente? Reglas y prácticas en los partidos políticos de América", in *Revista de Estudios Políticos,* 118 (October–December), pp. 321–361.

Frohlich, Norman, and Joe A. Oppenheimer, 1992, *Choosing Justice. An Experimental Approach to Ethical Theory,* Berkeley, California, University of California Press.

Fuentes, Carlos, 1998, 'Masters Conference', Faculty of Law and Social Sciences, University of Buenos Aires, Argentina, September.

Fuentes, Claudio, 1996, *El discurso militar en la transición chilena,* Santiago, Chile.

Fukuda-Parr, Sakiko, and A.K. Shiva Kumar (eds.), 2002, *Human Development: Concepts and Measures. Essential Readings,* New York, Oxford University Press.

Fuller, Lon L., 1964, *The Morality of Law,* New Haven, Connecticut, Yale University Press.

Furet, François, 1998, 'Democracy and Utopia', in *Journal of Democracy,* 9(1), pp. 65–81.

Gamarra, Eduardo, 2004, "La democracia y las drogas en América Latina y.el Caribe", text prepared for PRODDAL, in UNDP, *La democracia en América Latina. Hacia una democracia de ciudadanas y ciudadanos: Contribuciones para el debate,* Buenos Aires, Aguilar, Altea, Taurus, Alfaguara.

García, Marco Aurelio, 2004, "Democracia política y desarrollo en América Latina", text prepared for PRODDAL, in UNDP, *La democracia en América Latina. Hacia una democracia de ciudadanas y ciudadanos: Contribuciones para el debate,* Buenos Aires, Aguilar, Altea, Taurus, Alfaguara.

Garretón, Manuel Antonio, 1987, *Reconstruir la política. Transición y consolidación democrática en Chile,* Santiago, Chile, Editorial Andante.

————, 1997, "Revisando las Transiciones democráticas en América Latina", in *Nueva Sociedad,* 148, pp. 20–29.

————, 2000, *Política y sociedad entre dos épocas. América Latina en el cambio del siglo,* Rosario, Argentina, Homo Sapiens.

————, 2004a, "Comentario al documento 'Discusión de tres tesis para un marco teórico para el proyecto sobre el Desarrollo de la democracia en América Latina: estado, percepciones ciudadanas, indicadores y agentes'", text prepared for PRODDAL, in UNDP, *La democracia en América Latina. Hacia una democracia de ciudadanas y ciudadanos. Anexo: El debate conceptual sobre la democracia (CD ROM),* Buenos Aires, Aguilar, Altea, Taurus, Alfaguara.

————, 2004b, "La indispensable y problemática relación entre partidos y democracia en América Latina", text prepared for PRODDAL, in UNDP, *La democracia en América Latina. Hacia una democracia de ciudadanas y ciudadanos: Contribuciones para el debate,* Buenos Aires, Aguilar, Altea, Taurus, Alfaguara.

Garzón Valdés, Ernesto, 1993a, "Acerca de los conceptos de publicidad, opinión pública, opinión de la mayoría y sus relaciones recíprocas", in *Doxa,* 14, pp. 77–95.

————, 1993b, *Derecho, ética y política,* Madrid, Spain, Centro de Estudios Constitucionales.

————, 1997, 'Some Remarks on the Concept of Toleration', in *Ratio Juris,* 10(2), pp. 127–138.

————, 1999, "Derecho y democracia en América Latina", in *Anales de la Cátedra Francisco Suárez,* 33, pp. 133–157.

————, 2001, "Prólogo" a Rodolfo Vázquez, *Liberalismo, estado de derecho y minorías,* 11–26 Mexico, Paidós.

Gavíria, César, 2004, "La Carta de Navegación de las Américas", text prepared for PRODDAL, in UNDP, *La democracia en América Latina. Hacia una democracia de ciudadanas y ciudadanos: Contribuciones para el debate,* Buenos Aires, Aguilar, Altea, Taurus, Alfaguara.

Geertz, Clifford, 1980, *Negara: The Theatre State in Nineteenth-Century Bali,* Princeton, New Jersey, Princeton University Press.

————, 1985, 'Centers, Kings, and Charisma: Reflections on the Symbolics of Power', in Wilentz, Sean (ed.), *Rites of Power. Symbolism, Ritual, and Politics since the Middle Ages,* Philadelphia, Pennsylvania, University of Pennsylvania Press.

Georgetown University and the Organization of American States (OAS), 2002, "Base de Datos Políticos de las Américas" [http://www.georgetown.edu/pdba/spanish.html].

Gewirth, Alan, 1978, *Reason and Morality,* Chicago, Illinois, University of Chicago Press.

————, 1996, *The Community of Rights,* Chicago, Illinois, University of Chicago Press.

Gibson, Edward L., 1997, 'The Populist Road to Market Reform: Policy and Electoral Coalitions in Mexico and Argentina', in *World Politics,* 49(3), pp. 339–370.

Gibson, Edward L., Ernesto F. Calvo, and Tulia G. Falleti, 1999, "Federalismo redistributivo: Sobrerrepresentación territorial y transferencia de ingresos en el hemisferio occidental", in *Política y Gobierno,* 6(1), pp. 15–44.

Godio, Julio, 2004, "El componente 'parlamentarista' en los sistemas presidenciales. Ejercicio de simulación: caso Argentina", text prepared for PRODDAL, in UNDP, *La democracia en América Latina. Hacia una democracia de ciudadanas y ciudadanos: Contribuciones para el debate,* Buenos Aires, Aguilar, Altea, Taurus, Alfaguara.

Goldstein, Robert J., 1983, *Political Repression in Nineteenth-Century Europe*, London, Croom Helm.

Gómez, M., 2003, *Observaciones generales sobre las muestras de los países incluidos en Latinobarómetro 2002. San José*, document prepared for PRODDAL. June 2003.

González, Felipe, 2004, "Crisis de la política: causas y respuestas eficientes", text prepared for PRODDAL, in UNDP, *La democracia en América Latina. Hacia una democracia de ciudadanas y ciudadanos: Contribuciones para el debate*, Buenos Aires, Aguilar, Altea, Taurus, Alfaguara.

González, Luis E., 1991, *Political Structure and Democracy in Uruguay*, Notre Dame, Indiana, Notre Dame University Press.

González Casanova, Pablo, and Marcos Roitman Rosenmann (coordinators), 1996, *Democracia y Estado multiétnico en América Latina*, Madrid, Spain, Colección La democracia en México, La Jornada, Centro de Investigaciones Interdisciplinarias en Ciencias y Humanidades/UNAM.

Gratschew, María, 2001, 'Compulsory Voting' [http://www.idea.int/vt/analysis/Compulsory_Voting.cfm].

————, 2002, 'Compulsory Voting', in López-Pintor, Rafael, Gratschew, María, et al., *Voter Turnout since 1945: A Global Report*, Stockholm, Sweden, International Institute for Democracy and Electoral Assistance (IDEA)

Gray, John, 2000, *The Two Faces of Liberalism*, New York, Free Press.

Green, Rosario, 2004, "La crisis de la política en América Latina", text prepared for PRODDAL, in UNDP, *La democracia en América Latina. Hacia una democracia de ciudadanas y ciudadanos: Contribuciones para el debate*, Buenos Aires, Aguilar, Altea, Taurus, Alfaguara.

Greenfeld, Liah, 1992, *Nationalism. Five Roads to Modernity*, Cambridge, Massachusetts, Harvard University Press.

Groisman, Enrique, and Emilia Lerner, 2000, "Responsabilización por los controles clásicos", in *La responsabilización en la nueva gestión pública latinoamericana*, Buenos Aires, Argentina, Centro Latinoamericano de Administración para el Desarrollo (CLAD) and IDB.

Grzybowski, Cândido, 2004, "Democracia, sociedad civil y política en América Latina: notas para un debate", text prepared for PRODDAL, in UNDP, *La democracia en América Latina. Hacia una democracia de ciudadanas y ciudadanos: Contribuciones para el debate*, Buenos Aires, Aguilar, Altea, Taurus, Alfaguara.

Guadamuz, Andrés, 2000, 'Habeas Data: The Latin-American Response to Data Protection', in *The Journal of Information, Law and Technology*, 2 [http://elj.warwick.ac.uk/jilt/00-2/guadamuz.html].

————, 2001, 'Habeas Data vs. the European Data Protection Directive', in *The Journal of Information, Law and Technology*, 3 [http://elj.warwick.ac.uk/jilt/01-3/guadamuz.html].

Gutiérrez, C.J., 2000, "Ciudadanía", in *Diccionario Electoral*, Tomo I , San José, Costa Rica, IIDH-CAPEL.

Gutiérrez Saxe, Miguel, 1998, *Auditoría ciudadana sobre la calidad de la democracia: propuesta para su ejecución en Costa Rica*, San José, Costa Rica, Proyecto Estado de la Nación.

Gwartney, James, Robert, Lawson, Walter Block, Smita Wagh, Chris Edwards, and Veronique de Ruby, 2002, *Economic Freedom of the World: 2002 Annual Report*, Vancouver, Canada, Fraser Institute.

Habermas, Jurgen, 1996, *Between Facts and Norms*, Cambridge, Massachusetts, MIT Press.

————, 1998a, 'The European Nation-State: On the Past and Future of Sovereignty and Citizenship', in Cronin, Ciaran, and Grieff, Pablo D. (eds.), *The Inclusion of the Other. Studies in Political Theory,* Cambridge, Massachusetts, MIT Press.

———, 1998b, 'On the Relation Between the Nation, the Rule of Law, and Democracy', in Cronin, Ciaran, and Grieff, Pablo D. (eds.), *The Inclusion of the Other. Studies in Political Theory,* Cambridge, Massachusetts, MIT Press.

———, 1998c, 'Individuation through Socialization: On George Mead's Theory of Subjectivity', in Habermas, Jurgen, *Postmetaphysical Thinking: Philosophical Essays,* Cambridge, Massachusetts, MIT Press.

———, 1999, 'Introduction', in *Ratio Juris,* 12(4), pp. 329–335.

Hague, Rod, et al., 1998, *Comparative Government and Politics,* 4th edition, London, Macmillan Press.

Hair, Joseph F., et al., 1987, *Multivariate Data Analysis with Reading,* New York, Macmillan Publishing Company.

Halperin Donghi, Tulio, 1994, *La larga agonía de la Argentina peronista,* Buenos Aires, Argentina, Espasa-Ariel.

Hamburger, Philip A., 1989, 'The Development of the Nineteenth-Century Consensus Theory of Contract', in *Law and History Review,* 7(2), pp. 241–329.

Hammergren, Linn, 2002, "Quince años de reforma judicial en América Latina: Dónde estamos y por qué no hemos progresado más" [http://www.oas.org/Juridico/spanish/adjusti.htm].

Hampshire, Stuart, 2000, *Justice is Conflict,* Princeton, New Jersey, Princeton University Press.

Hansen, M.H., 1991, *The Athenian Democracy in the Age of Demosthenes,* Oxford, UK, Oxford University Press.

Hardin, R., 1989, 'Why a Constitution?', in Grofman, Bernard, and Donald Wittman (eds.), *The Federalist Papers and the New Institutionalism,* New York, Agathon Press, pp. 100–120.

Harsanyi, John C., 1975, 'Can the Maximin Principle Serve as a Principle Morality?', in *American Political Science Review,* 69(2), pp. 690–705.

Hart, Herbert L.A., 1961, *The Concept of Law,* Oxford, UK, Clarendon Press.

Hartlyn, Jonathan, and Arturo Valenzuela, 1994, 'Democracy in Latin America since 1930', in Bethell, Leslie (ed.), *The Cambridge History of Latin America,* Vol. VI: *Latin America since 1930,* Part 2: 'Politics and Society', New York, Cambridge University Press.

Hartlyn, Jonathan, Jennifer McCoy, and Thomas J. Mustillo, 2003, 'The "Quality of Elections" in Contemporary Latin America: Issues in Measurement and Explanation', an article presented at the twenty-fourth International Congress of the Association of Latin American Studies (LASA), Dallas, Texas, 27–29 March.

Held, David, 1987, *Models of Democracy,* Stanford, California, Stanford University Press.

———, 1999, 'Conclusions', in Held, David, McGrew, Anthony, et al., *Global Transformations. Politics, Economics and Culture,* Stanford, California, Stanford University Press.

———, 2004, "El estado de la democracia en América Latina", text prepared for PRODDAL, in UNDP, *La democracia en América Latina. Hacia una democracia de ciudadanas y ciudadanos. Anexo: El debate conceptual sobre la democracia (CD ROM),* Buenos Aires, Aguilar, Altea, Taurus, Alfaguara.

Held, David, and Montserrat Guibernau, 2001, 'Cosmopolitan Democracy. An Interview with David Held', in *Constellations,* 8(4), pp. 427–440.

Held, David, Guay Hermet, Soledad Loaeza, and Jean-Francois Prud'homme (eds.), 2001, *Del populismo de los antiguos al populismo de los modernos,* Mexico, Colegio de México, Centro de Estudios Internacionales.

Hill, Christopher, 1997, *Liberty against the Law. Some Seventeenth-Century Controversies,* London, Penguin Books.

Hirschman, Albert, 1970, *Exit, Voice, and Loyalty. Responses to Decline in Firms, Organizations, and States,* Cambridge, Massachusetts, Harvard University Press.

————, 1991, *The Rhetoric of Reaction,* Cambridge, Massachusetts, Belknap Press of Harvard University Press.

Hodess, Robin, Jessie Banfield, and Toby Wolfe, (eds.), 2001, *Global Corruption Report 2001,* Berlin, Germany, Transparency International.

Hoffman, Martin L., 2000, *Empathy and Moral Development. Implications for Caring and Justice,* Cambridge, Massachusetts, Cambridge University Press.

Holmes, Stephen, 1995, *Passions & Constraint. On the Theory of Liberal Democracy,* Chicago, Illinois, University of Chicago Press.

Holmes, Stephen, and C.R. Sunstein, 1999, *The Cost of Rights. Why Liberty Depends on Taxes,* New York, W.W. Norton.

Hooker, M.B., 1975, *Legal Pluralism: An Introduction to Colonial and Neo-Colonial Laws,* Oxford, UK, Oxford University Press.

Hosle, Vittorio, 1998, *Objective Idealism, Ethics, and Politics,* Notre Dame, Indiana, Notre Dame University Press.

Houtzager, Peter, and Richard Crook, 2001, 'We Make the Law and the Law Makes Us. Some Ideas on a Law in Development Research Agenda', in *IDS Bulletin,* 32(1), pp. 8–18.

Hsieh, C.C., and M.D. Pugh, 1993, 'Poverty, Income Inequality, and Violent Crime: A Meta-Analysis of Recent Aggregate Data Studies', in *Criminal Justice Review,* 18(2), pp. 182–202.

Huang, Zhexue, 1997, 'A fast clustering algorithm to cluster very large categorical data sets in data mining' [http://www.cmis.au/Graham.Williams/papers/sigmodfn.pdf].

Huber, Evelyne, and John D. Stephens, 1999, 'The Bourgeoisie and Democracy: Historical and Comparative Perspectives', in *Social Research,* 66(3).

Huber, Evelyne, Dietrich Rueschemeyer, and John D. Stephens, 1997, 'The Paradoxes of Contemporary Democracy: Formal, Participatory, and Social Democracy', in *Comparative Politics,* 29(3), pp. 323–342.

Huntington, Samuel, 1991, *The Third Wave: Democratization in the Late Twentieth Century,* Norman, Oklahoma, University of Oklahoma Press.

Hurtado, Osvaldo, 2004, 'Cultura y democracia, una relación olvidada', text prepared for PRODDAL, in UNDP, *La democracia en América Latina. Hacia una democracia de ciudadanas y ciudadanos: Contribuciones para el debate,* Buenos Aires, Aguilar, Altea, Taurus, Alfaguara.

Iazzetta, Osvaldo, 2002, *Estado y democracia: Una revision sobre un vínculo necesario,* Rosario, Argentina, Universidad Nacional de Rosario.

IDEA (International Institute for Democracy and Electoral Assistance), 2002a, 'Voter Turnout from 1945 to Date. A Global Report on Political Participation', Stockholm, Sweden, IDEA [http://www.idea.int/vt/index.cfm].

————, 2002b, 'Compulsory Voting' [http://www.idea.int/vt/analysis/Compulsory_Voting.cfm].

————, 2003, 'Global Database of Quotas for Women' [http://www.idea.int/quota/index.cfm].

Iglesias, Enrique, 2004, "Democracia y desarrollo: la política importa", text prepared for PRODDAL, in UNDP, *La democracia en América Latina. Hacia una democracia de ciudadanas y ciudadanos: Contribuciones para el debate,* Buenos Aires, Aguilar, Altea, Taurus, Alfaguara.

ILO (International Labor Organization), 2002a, 'ILOLEX Database of International Labour Standards' [http://www.ilo.org/ilolex/english/convdisp2.htm].

————, 2002b, "Pueblos Indígenas" [http://www.indigenas.oit.or.cr/].

————, 2003, 'ILOLEX Database of International Labor Standards. Ratifications of the Fundamental Human Rights Conventions by Country' [http://ilolex.ilo.ch:1567/english/docs/decl-world.htm].

ILO, Regional Office for the Americas, 2001, *2001 Labour Overview,* Lima, Peru, ILO, Regional Office for the Americas.

————, 2002, *Panorama laboral 2002,* Lima, Peru, ILO, Regional Office for the Americas.

————, 2003, *Panorama Laboral 2003,* Anexo Estadístico.

IMF (International Monetary Fund), various years, *Government Financial Statistics Yearbook,* Washington, DC, IMF.

Inglehart, Ronald, 1990, *Culture Shift in Advanced Industrial Society,* Princeton, New Jersey, Princeton University Press.

Instituto de Derecho Público Comparado, Universidad de Carlos III de Madrid, 2003, Justicia Constitucional en Iberoamérica [http://www.uc3m.es/uc3m/inst/MGP/JCI/00-portada.htm].

Inter-American Dialogue, 2003, 'Afro-Descendants in Latin America: How Many?', in *Race Report,* Washington, DC, Inter-American Dialogue, January.

International Centre for Prison Studies, King's College London, 2003, 'World Prison Brief' [http://www.kcl.ac.uk/depsta/rel/icps/].

INTERPOL, 2004, 'International Crime Statistics' [http://www.interpol.int/Public/Statistics/ICS/downloadList.asp].

IPEC (International Programme on the Elimination of Child Labor) and SIMPOC (Statistical Information and Monitoring Programme on Child Labor),

2002, *Every Child Counts: New Global Estimates on Child Labour,* Geneva, Switzerland, ITO.

IPU (Inter-Parliamentary Union), 1995, *Women in Parliaments 1945–1995: A World Statistical Survey,* Geneva, Switzerland, IPU.

————, 2003, 'Women in National Parliaments. Statistical Archive website' [http://www.ipu.org/wmne/classif-arc.htm].

Jarquín, Edmundo, and Fernando Carrillo (eds), 1998, *Justice Delayed: Judicial Reform in Latin America,* Washington, DC, Inter-American Development Bank.

Jelin, Elizabeth, and Eric Hershberg, 1996, *Construir la democracia: derechos humanos, ciudadanía y sociedad en América Latina,* Caracas, Venezuela, Nueva Sociedad.

Jessop, Bob, 1990, *State Theory. Putting Capitalist States in their Place,* University Park, Pennsylvania, Pennsylvania State University Press.

Johnson III, Ollie A., 1998, 'Racial Representation and Brazilian Politics: Black Members of the National Congress, 1983–1999', in *Journal of Inter-American Studies and World Affairs,* Vol. 40, No. 4 (Winter), pp. 97–118.

Jones, Mark P., 1995, 'A Guide to the Electoral Systems of the Americas', in *Electoral Studies,* 14(1), pp. 5–21.

————, 1997, 'A Guide to the Electoral Systems of the Americas: An Update', in *Electoral Studies,* 16(1), pp. 13–15.

Jones, P., 1994, *Rights,* New York, St. Martin's Press.

Karlekar, Karin Deutsch, 2003, *Freedom of the Press 2003. A Global Survey of Media Independence,* Lanham, Maryland, Rowman & Littlefield Publishing Group.

Kavanagh, Dennis, 1983, *Political Science and Political Behaviour,* London, Allen & Unwin.

Kelsen, Hans, 1945, *General Theory of Law and State,* Cambridge, Massachusetts, Harvard University Press.

————, 1967, *Pure Theory of Law,* Berkeley, California, University of California Press.

Keohane, Nannerl O., 1980, *Philosophy and the State in France. The Renaissance to the Enlightment,* Princeton, New Jersey, Princeton University Press.

Kertzer, David, 1988, *Ritual, Politics & Power,* New Haven, Connecticut, Yale University Press.

Kikut, L., Gómez M y J. Vargas Cullell. 2003a *Metodología empleada para determinar las orientaciones hacia la democracia de las y los ciudadanos de América Latina.* San José, document prepared for PRODDAL. June 2003.

Kikut, L., Gómez M y J. Vargas Cullell. 2003b. *Anexo: Metodología para determinar las orientaciones hacia la democracia de las y los ciudadanos de América Latina a partir de índices sumativos.* San José, document prepared for PRODDAL. June 2003.

Kikut, L., y Vargas Cullell, J. 2003. *Variables empleadas en el análisis de las orientaciones hacia la democracia y otras actitudes.* San José, document prepared for PRODDAL. June 2003.

Kinzo, María Dálva, 1996, *PMDB: Partido do Movimento Democrático Brasileiro,* Sao Paulo, Brazil, Konrad Adenuar Stiftung.

Kornblith, Miriam, 1994, "La crisis del sistema politico venezolano", in *Nueva Sociedad,* No. 134.

Krug, Etienne G., et al. (eds.), 2002, *World Report on Violence and Health,* Geneva, Switzerland, World Health Organization (WHO).

Krygier, Martin, 1997, *Between Fear and Hope. Hybrid Thoughts on Public Values,* Sydney, Australia, ABC Books.

Kucera, David, 2001, 'The Effect of Core Worker Rights on Labour Costs and Foreign Direct Investment: Evaluating the "Conventional Wisdom"', Discussion Paper 130, Geneva, Switzerland, International Institute for Labour Studies.

Kymlicka, Will, 1996, *Multicultural Citizenship,* New York, Oxford University Press.

Laakso, Markku, and Rein Taagapera, 1979, 'Effective Number of Parties: A Measure with Application to Western Europe', in *Comparative Political Studies,* 12(1), pp. 3–27.

Lacey, Nicola, 2001, 'Responsibility and Modernity in Criminal Law', in *The Journal of Political Philosophy,* 2(3), pp. 149–176.

Lagos, Ricardo, Norberto Lechner, and Rosenthal Gert, 1991, *Las Ciencias Sociales en el proceso de democratización,* Santiago, Chile, Cuadernos de Difusión.

Lagroye, Jacques, 1993, *Sociologie politique,* Paris, France, Presses de la Fondation Nationale des Sciences Politiques and Dalloz.

Lambsdorff, Johann Graf, 2001, 'Transparency International 2001 Corruption Perceptions Index', in Hodess, Robin, Banfield, Jessie, and Wolfe, Toby (eds.), *Global Corruption Report 2001,* Berlin, Germany, Transparency International.

Lamounier, Bolivar, 1989, *Partidos e Utopia. O Brasil nio Limiar dos anos 90,* Sao Paulo, Brazil, Loyola.

————, (org.), 1990, *De Geisel a Collor. O Balanco da Transica,* Sao Paulo, Brazil, IDESP/CNPq.

Lamounier, Bolivar, and Rachel Menegeghello, 1986, *Partidos y Consolidaçao democratica,* Sao Paulo, Brazil, Brasilense.

Lamounier, Bolivar, and Maria Teresa Sadek, 1991, *Depois da Transicao: Democracia e Eleicoes no Governo Collor,* Sao Paulo, Brazil, Loyola.

Landi, Oscar, 1992, *Devórame otra vez. Qué hizo la TV con la gente. Qué hizo la gente con la TV,* Buenos Aires, Argentina, Planeta.

Lane, Robert, 1988, 'Procedural Goods in a Democracy: How One is Treated Versus What One Gets', in *Social Justice Research,* 2(3), pp. 177–192.

Langton, Stuart, 1978, 'What is Citizen Participation', in Langton, S., *Citizen Participation in America,* Lexington, Massachusetts, Lexington Books.

Lechner, Norbert, 1981, "Epílogo", in Lechner, Norberto (ed*.), Estado y Política en América Latina,* Mexico DF, Siglo XXI.

————, 1991, *Capitalismo, democracia y reformas,* Santiago, Chile.

————, 1994, "Los nuevos perfiles de la política. Un bosquejo", in *Nueva Sociedad,* No. 130 (March–April).

————, 1995, "La problemática innovación de la sociedad civil", in *Espacios,* SJCR , No. 4.

————, 1996, "Estado y sociedad en una perspective democrática", in *Estudios Sociales,* 11.

————, 2000, "Desafios de un desarrollo humano: Individualización y capital social", in *Instituciones y Desarrollo,* 7, pp. 7–34.

León-Rosch, Marta, 1998, "Los registros electorales", in Nohlen, Dieter, Picado, Sonia, and Zovatto, Daniel (eds.), *Tratado de derecho electoral comparado de América Latina,* Mexico, Fondo de Cultura Económica.

Levi, Margaret, 1997, *Consent, Dissent, and Patriotism,* Cambridge, Massachusetts, Cambridge University Press.

Lijphart, Arend, 1984, *Democracies. Patterns of Majoritarian and Consensus Government in Twenty-One Countries,* New Haven, Connecticut, Yale University Press.

————, 1997, 'Unequal Participation: Democracy's Unresolved Dilemma', in *American Political Science Review,* 91(1), pp. 1–14.

Linz, Juan, 1978, *The Breakdown of Democratic Regimes. Crisis, Breakdown and Reequilibration,* Baltimore, Maryland, The Johns Hopkins University Press.

Linz, Juan, and Alfred Stepan, 1996, *Problems of Democratic Transition and Consolidation. Southern Europe, South America, and Post-Communist Europe,* Baltimore, Maryland, The Johns Hopkins University Press.

López Jiménez, Sinesio, 2002, *Ciudadanía informada y democracia: el caso peruano,* Lima, Peru, Comisión Andina de Juristas.

López-Pintor, Rafael, 2000, *Electoral Management Bodies as Institutions of Governance,* New York, Office of Development Policies, UNDP.

Lora, Eduardo, 2001, 'Structural Reforms in Latin America: What Has Been Reformed and How to Measure It', in Research Department Working Paper 466, Washington, DC, Inter-American Development Bank, December.

MacAdam, Doug, S. Tarrow, and C. Tilly, 2001, *Dynamics of Contention,* New York, Cambridge University Press.

Maier, Charles S., 1981, *Recasting Bourgeois Europe. Stabilization in France, Germany, and Italy in the Decade after World War I,* Princeton, New Jersey, Princeton University Press.

Mainwaring, Scott, and Matthew Soberg Shugart (eds.), 1997, *Presidentialism and Democracy in Latin America,* New York, Cambridge University Press.

Mainwaring, Scott, Daniel Brinks, and Aníbal Pérez-Liñán, 2001, 'Classifying Political Regimes in Latin America, 1945–1999', in *Studies in Comparative International Development,* 36(1) (Spring), pp. 37–65.

Maiorano, Jorge Luis, 2000, 'The Defensor del Pueblo in Latin America', in Gregory, Roy, and Giddings, Philip (eds.), *Righting Wrongs. The Ombudsman in Six Continents,* Washington, DC, IOS Press.

Maíz, Ramón, 2002a, *Nacionalismo y moviliza-ción política: Hacia un análisis pluridimensional de la construcción de las naciones,* Santiago de Compostela, University of Santiago de Compostela.

————, 2002b, "Nacionalismo, federalismo y acomodación en Estados multinacionales", in Safran, W., and Maíz, R. (eds.), *Identidad y auto-gobierno en sociedades multiculturale*s, Barcelona, Spain, Ariel.

Malloy, James M., 1991, "Politica económica e o problema de governabilidade democrática nos Andes Centrais", in Sola, L. (ed.), *Estado, Mercado e Democracia: Politica e economía comparada,* Sao Paulo, Brazil, Paz e Terra.

Mansbridge, Jane, 1983, *Beyond Adversary Democracy,* Chicago, Illinois, Chicago University Press.

————, 1999, 'On the Idea that Participation Makes Better Choices', in Elkin, S., and Soltan, K.E. (eds.), *Citizen Competence and Democratic Institutions,* University Park, Pennsylvania, Pennsylvania State University Press.

Margalit, Avishai, 1996, *The Decent Society,* Cambridge, Massachusetts, Harvard University Press. (Spanish edition: Margalit, Avishai, 1997, *La sociedad decente,* Barcelona, Spain, Paidós.)

Marshall, Thomas H., 1965, 'Citizenship and Social Class', in Marshall, T.H. (ed.), *Class, Citizenship and Social Development,* New York, Doubleday.

Martínez, Néstor Humberto, 1997, "Estado de derecho y eficiencia económica", in Jarquín, Edmundo, and Carrillo, Fernando (eds.), *La economía política de la reforma judicial,* Washington, DC, IDB

Marx, Karl, 1963, *Early Writings* (edited by T.B. Bottomore), New York, McGraw-Hill.

Matos Mar, José, 1993, "Población y grupos étnicos de América, 1994", in *América Indígena,* 53(4) (October–December), pp. 155–234.

Mayorga, René Antonio, 1992, *Democracia y gobernabilidad en América Latina,* Caracas, Venezuela, Nueva Sociedad.

Mazzuca, Sebastian, 1998, "¿Qué es y no es la democratización?", in *Estudios Políticos,* 19, pp. 73–122.

————, 1999, "Acceso al Poder versus Ejercicio del Poder", photocopy, Berkeley, California, University of California.

————, 2000, 'Access to Power versus Exercise of Power: Democratization and Bureaucratization in Latin America', mimeographed document, Berkeley, California, Department of Political Science, University of California.

McCoy, Jennifer, 2004, "Sobre tesis III - Sobre la democracia como organización social", text prepared for PRODDAL in UNDP, *La democracia en América Latina. Hacia una democracia de ciudadanas y ciudadanos. Anexo: El debate conceptual sobre la democracia (CD ROM),* Buenos Aires, Aguilar, Altea, Taurus, Alfaguara.

Mead, George H., 1967, *Mind, Self, and Society. From the Standpoint of a Social Behaviorist,* Chicago, Illinois, University of Chicago Press.

Meentzen, Angela, 2002, *Estrategias de desarrollo culturalmente adecuadas para mujeres indígenas,* Washington DC, Department of Sustainable Development, Indigenous Peoples and Community Development Unit, IADB.

Méndez, Juan, 2004, "Sociedad civil y calidad de la democracia", text prepared for PRODDAL, in UNDP, *La democracia en América Latina. Hacia una democracia de ciudadanas y ciudadanos. Anexo: El debate conceptual sobre la democracia (CD ROM),* Buenos Aires, Aguilar, Altea, Taurus, Alfaguara.

Méndez, Juan, G. O'Donnell, and P.S. Pinheiro (eds.), 1999, *The Rule of Law and the Underprivileged in Latin America,* Notre Dame, Indiana, Notre Dame University Press.

Méndez-Montalvo, Myriam, and Julie Ballington (eds.), 2002, *Mujeres en el Parlamento. Más allá de los números,* Stockholm, Sweden, International Institute for Democracy and Electoral Assistance.

Mesa, Carlos, 1999, *Presidentes de Bolivia: Entre urnas y fusiles,* La Paz, Bolivia, Gisbert.

Middlebrook, Kevin J. (ed.), 1998, *Electoral Observation and Democratic Transitions in Latin America,* La Jolla, California, Center for US-Mexican Studies, University of California.

Mill, John Stuart, 1962, *On Liberty,* Glasgow, Scotland, Collins/Fontana. (Spanish edition: Mill, John Stuart, 1954, *Sobre la liberta*d, Buenos Aires, Argentina, Aguilar.)

Moisés, Jose Álvaro, and J.A. Guilhon Albuquerque (organizers), 1989, *Dilemas da Consolidaçao da Democracia,* Rio de Janeiro, Brazil, Paz e Terra.

Montgomery, Tommie Sue (ed.), 1999, *Peacemaking and Democratization in Central America,* Boulder, Colorado, Lynne Rienner.

Mora y Araujo, Manuel, 1997, *Los actores sociales y políticos en los procesos de transformación en América Latina,* Buenos Aires, Argentina, CIEDLA.

Moreira Cardoso, Aldalberto, y Eisenberg, José, 2004, "Esperanza entrampada: Las perspectivas para la democracia en América Latina", text prepared for PRODDAL, in UNDP, *La democracia en América Latina. Hacia una democracia de ciudadanas y ciudadanos. Anexo: El debate conceptual sobre la democracia (CD ROM),* Buenos Aires, Aguilar, Altea, Taurus, Alfaguara.

Morley, Samuel, 2001, *The Income Distribution Problem in Latin America and the Caribbean,* Santiago, Chile, ECLAC.

Morley, Samuel A., Roberto Machado, and Stefano Pettinato, 1999, 'Indexes of Structural Reform in Latin America', in *Serie Reformas Económicas,* No. 12, Santiago, Chile, ECLAC, LC/L.1166/I, January.

Mosley, Layna, and Saika Uno, 2002, *Dataset of Labor Rights Violations, 1981–2000,* Notre Dame, Indiana, Notre Dame University Press.

Mouffe, Chantal, 1996, 'Democracy, Power, and the 'Political'', in Benhabib, S. (ed.), *Democracy and Difference. Contesting the Boundaries of the Political,* Princeton, New Jersey, Princeton University Press.

——————, 2000, *The Democratic Paradox,* London, Verso.

Moulián, Tomás, 1983, *Democracia y socialismo en Chile,* Santiago, Chile.

——————, 2002, *En la brecha. Derechos humanos. Críticas y alternativas,* Santiago, Chile, Lom.

Munck, Gerardo L., 2004, *Concepts, Indicators, and Indices. Methodological Foundations of the Statistical Compendium of the Report on Democratic Development in Latin America,* unpublished manuscript.

Munck, Gerardo L., and Jay Verkuilen, 2002, 'Conceptualizing and Measuring Democracy: Evaluating Alternative Indices', in *Comparative Political Studies,* 35(1) (February), pp. 5–34.

Murilo de Carvalho, Jose, 1991, *A Cidadanía no Brasil. O Longo Camino,* Rio de Janeiro, Brazil, Civilizacão Brasileira.

Nanda, Ved P., James Scarritt, and George Shepherd, Jr. (eds.), 1981, *Global Human Rights: Public Policies, Comparative Measures, and NGO Strategies,* Boulder, Colorado, Westview Press.

Newey, Glen, 1998, 'Value-Pluralism in Contemporary Liberalism', in *Dialogue,* 37, pp. 493–522.

Nohlen, Dieter, and Florian Grotz, 2000, 'External Voting: Legal Framework and Overview of Electoral Legislation', in *Boletín Mexicano de Derecho Comparado,* 99 (September–December), pp. 1115–1145.

Nohlen, Dieter, Sonia Picado, and Daniel Zovatto (eds.), 1998, *Tratado de derecho electoral comparado de América Latina,* Mexico, Fondo de Cultura Económica.

Nozick, Richard, 1974, *Anarchy, State, and Utopia,* New York, Basic Books. (Spanish edition: Nozick, Richard, 1988, *Anarquía, Estado y utopía,* Mexico DF, Fondo de Cultura Económica.)

Nun, José, 2001, *Democracia. ¿Gobierno del pueblo o de los políticos?,* Buenos Aires, Argentina, Fondo de Cultura Económica.

————, 2004, "Estado y ciudadanía", text prepared for PRODDAL, in UNDP, *La democracia en América Latina. Hacia una democracia de ciudadanas y ciudadanos. Anexo: El debate conceptual sobre la democracia (CD ROM),* Buenos Aires, Aguilar, Altea, Taurus, Alfaguara.

Nussbaum, Martha, 1997, 'Capabilities and Human Rights', in *Fordham Law Review,* 66(2), pp. 273–300.

————, 2000a, 'Aristotle, Politics, and Human Capabilities: A Response to Antony, Arneson, Charlesworth, and Mulgan', in *Ethics,* 111, pp. 102–140.

————, 2000b, *Women and Human Development. The Capabilities Approach,* Cambridge, Massachusetts, Cambridge University Press.

OAS (Organization of American States), 2003, 'Appendix: Inter-American Treaties: Status of Signatures and Ratifications Classified by Treaty, Country and Subject Matter' [http://www.oas.org/juridico/english/study_appendix.doc].

OAS–CIDH (Inter-American Commission on Human Rights), 2001, *Annual Report of the Special Rapporteur for Freedom of Expression 2001,* Office of the Rapporteur for Freedom of Expression [http://www.cidh.org/Relatoria/English/AnnualReports.htm].

————, 2003, 'Special Reports' [http://www.cidh.oas.org/countryrep/pais.esp.htm].

OAS–CIM (Inter-American Commission of Women), 2002, 'Quota Laws' [http://www.oas.org/cim/English/Laws-Cuota.htm].

————, 2003, 'Violence Laws' [http://www.oas.org/cim/English/LawsViolence.htm].

O'Donnell, Guillermo, 1982, *El Estado burocrático-autoritario. 1966–1973. Triunfos, derrotas y crisis,* 2nd edition, Buenos Aires, Argentina, Editorial de Belgrano.

————, 1993, 'On the State, Democratization and Some Conceptual Problems: A Latin American View with Glances at Some Post-Communist Countries', in *World Development,* 21(8), pp. 1355–1369.

————, 1994, 'Delegative Democracy', in *Journal of Democracy,* 5(1), pp. 94–108.

————, 1997a, *Horizontal Accountability and New Polyarchies,* Notre Dame, Indiana, The Helen Kellogg Institute for International Studies at Notre Dame University.

————, 1997b, *Contrapuntos. Ensayos escogidos sobre autoritarismo y democratización,* Buenos Aires, Argentina, Paidós.

————, 1998a, 'Horizontal Accountability and New Polyarchies', in Schedler, A., Diamond, L., and Plattner, M. (eds.), *The Self-Restraining State: Power and Accountability in New Democracies,* Boulder, Colorado, Lynne Rienner.

————, 1999a, *Democratic Theory and Comparative Politics,* Notre Dame, Indiana, The Helen Kellogg Institute for International Studies at Notre Dame University.

————, 1999b, 'Polyarchies and the (Un)Rule of Law in Latin America', in Méndez, Juan, O'Donnell, G., and Pinheiro, P.S. (eds.), *The Rule of Law and the Underprivileged in Latin America,* Notre Dame, Indiana, Notre Dame University Press.

————, 1999c, "Pobreza y desigualdad en América Latina. Algunas reflexiones políticas", in Tokman,

Víctor, and O'Donnell, Guillermo (eds.), *Pobreza y desigualdad en América Latina. Temas y nuevos desafíos,* Buenos Aires, Argentina, Paidós.

—————, 2000, 'Democracy, Law, and Comparative Politics', in Helen Kellogg Institute for International Studies Working Paper 274, Notre Dame, Indiana, The Helen Kellogg Institute for International Studies, Notre Dame University. Summarized version in *Studies in International Comparative Development,* 36(1) (2001), pp. 5–36.

—————, 2001a, *Human Development, Human Rights, Democracy,* document prepared for the workshop "Calidad de la Democracia", in San José, Costa Rica.

—————, 2001b, 'Reflections on Contemporary Latin American Democracies', *Journal of Latin American Studies,* (Autumn), pp. 67–82

—————, 2002a, 'Human Development/Democracy/Human Rights', presentation at the workshop entitled "Calidad de la Democracia y Desarrollo Humano en América Latina", in Heredia, Costa Rica [http://www.estadonacion.org.cr.

—————, 2002b, "Notas sobre varias 'accountabilities' y sus interrelaciones", in Peruzzotti, Enrique, and Smulovitz, Catalina (eds.), *Controlando la política. Ciudadanos y medios en las nuevas democracias,* Buenos Aires, Argentina, Temas.

—————, 2002c, *Notes on the State of Democracy in Latin America,* document prepared for the project entitled "El estado de la democracia en América Latina", under the auspices of the Regional Division for Latin America and the Caribbean, UNDP.

—————, 2003a, 'Horizontal Accountability: The Legal Institutionalization of Mistrust', in Mainwaring, S., and Welna, C. (eds.), *Accountability, Democratic Governance, and Political Institutions in Latin America,* Oxford, UK, Oxford University Press.

—————, 2004a, "Acerca del Estado en América Latina contemporánea: diez tesis para discusión",

text prepared for PRODDAL, in UNDP, *La democracia en América Latina. Hacia una democracia de ciudadanas y ciudadanos: Contribuciones para el debate,* Buenos Aires, Aguilar, Altea, Taurus, Alfaguara.

—————, 2004b, "Notas sobre la democracia en América Latina", text prepared for PRODDAL, in UNDP, *La democracia en América Latina. Hacia una democracia de ciudadanas y ciudadanos. Anexo: El debate conceptual sobre la democracia (CD ROM),* Buenos Aires, Aguilar, Altea, Taurus, Alfaguara.

O'Donnell, Guillermo., et al., 1986, *Transitions from Authoritarian Rule: Comparative Perspectives,* Baltimore, Maryland, The Johns Hopkins University Press.

O'Donnell, Guillermo, and Philippe Schmitter, 1986, *Transitions from Authoritarian Rule: Tentative Conclusions About Uncertain Democracies,* Baltimore, Maryland, The Johns Hopkins University Press.

O'Driscoll, Jr., Gerald, J. Edwin Feulner, Mary Anastasia O'Grady, Ana Eiras, and Brett Shaefer (eds.), 2003, *The 2003 Index of Economic Freedom,* Washington, DC, Heritage Foundation and Dow Jones & Co., Inc.

O'Driscoll, Jr., Gerald, Kim Holmes, and Mary Anastasia O'Grady (eds.), 2002, *The 2002 Index of Economic Freedom,* Washington, DC, Heritage Foundation and Dow Jones & Co., Inc.

Ocampo, José A., 2004, "Economía y democracia", text prepared for PRODDAL, in UNDP, *La democracia en América Latina. Hacia una democracia de ciudadanas y ciudadanos: Contribuciones para el debate,* Buenos Aires, Aguilar, Altea, Taurus, Alfaguara.

OECD (Organisation for Economic Co-operation and Development) and UNESCO (United Nations Educational, Scientific and Cultural Organization), 2003, *Literacy Skills for the World of Tomorrow,* Paris, France, OECD and UNESCO.

Office of the Comptroller and Auditor General of India, 2003, 'Mandates of SAIs [Special Audit Agencies]' [http://www.cagindia.org/mandates.htm].

Ortega R., Eugenio, and Carolina Moreno (eds.), 2002, ¿La Concertación desconcertada? Reflexiones sobre su historia y su futuro, Santiago, Chile, Lom.

Ostwald, Martin, 1986, From Popular Sovereignty to the Sovereignty of Law: Law, Society, and Politics in Fifth-Century Athens, Berkeley, California, University of California Press.

Pachano, Simón (ced.), 1998, Modernización de las instituciones democráticas: El Congreso, Quito, Ecuador, Flacso.

————, (comp.), 2003, Ciudadanía e identidad, Quito, Ecuador, Flacso.

Paniagua, Vicente, 2000, "El fraude en marcha", in Qué Hacer, No. 118.

Pastor, Robert A., 1999, 'The Role of Electoral Administration in Democratic Transitions: Implications for Policy and Research', in Democratization, 6(4) (Winter), pp. 1–27.

Patterson, O., 1991, Freedom, Volume I: Freedom in the Making of the Western World, New York, Basic Books.

Paxton, Pamela, Kenneth Bollen, Deborah Lee, and Kim Hyojoung, 2003, 'A Half-Century of Suffrage: New Data and a Comparative Analysis', in Studies in Comparative International Development, 38(1), pp. 93–122.

Payne, J., Daniel Zovatto, Fernando Carillo Floréz, and Andrés Allamand Zavala, 2002, Democracies in Development. Politics and Reform in Latin America, Washington, DC, IADB and Stockholm, Sweden, IDEA.

Pease García, Henry (ed.), 2003, La autocracia fujimorista: del Estado intervencionista al Estado mafioso, Lima, Peru, Pontificia Universidad Católica del Perú, Fondo de Cultura Económica.

Pedersen, Mogens N., 1983, 'Changing Patterns of Electoral Volatility in European Party Systems, 1948–1977: Explorations in Explanation', in Daalder, Hans, and Mair, Peter (eds.), Western European Party Systems: Continuity and Change, Beverly Hills, California, Sage.

Pennington, K., 1993, The Prince and Law, 1200–1600. Sovereignty and Rights in the Western Legal Tradition, Berkeley, California, University of California Press.

Pérez-Liñán, Aníbal, 2001, "Crisis presidenciales: Gobernabilidad y estabilidad democrática en América Latina, 1950-1996", in Instituciones y Desarrollo, Barcelona, Spain, 8 and 9, pp. 281–298.

————, 2003, 'Presidential Crises and Political Accountability in Latin America, 1990–1999', in Eckstein, Susan, and Timothy Wickham-Crowley (eds.), What Justice? Whose Justice? Fighting for Fairness in Latin America, Chapter 4, Berkeley, California, University of California Press.

Perry, Guillermo Francisco, H.G. Ferreira, Michael Walton, et al., 2004, Inequality in Latin America and the Caribbean: Breaking with History?, Washington, DC, World Bank.

Peruzzotti, Enrique, and Catalina Smulovitz, 2002a, 'Accountability social: la otra cara del control', in Peruzzotti, Enrique, and Smulovitz, Catalina, (eds.), Controlando la política. Ciudadanos y medios en las nuevas democracias, Buenos Aires, Argentina, Temas.

————, (eds.), 2002b, Controlando la política. Ciudadanos y medios en las nuevas democracias, Buenos Aires, Argentina, Temas.

Peschard, Jacqueline, 1997, La cultura política democrática, Cuadernos de divulgación de la cultura democrática, 2, Mexico DF, IFE.

Pinto, Céli Regina Jardim, 2004b, "Ciudadanía y democracia: los aportes desde una perspectiva de género", text prepared for PRODDAL, in UNDP, La democracia en América Latina. Hacia una democracia de ciudadanas y ciudadanos: Contribuciones para el debate, Buenos Aires, Aguilar, Altea, Taurus, Alfaguara.

Pinto, Céli Regina Jardim, 2004a, "El objetivo de una perspectiva de género", text prepared for PRODDAL, in UNDP, *La democracia en América Latina. Hacia una democracia de ciudadanas y ciudadanos. Anexo: El debate conceptual sobre la democracia (CD ROM)*, Buenos Aires, Aguilar, Altea, Taurus, Alfaguara.

Pinto-Duschinsky, Michael, 2002a, 'Financing Politics: A Global View', in *Journal of Democracy*, 13(4), pp. 69–86.

————, 2002b, *Money and Politics Handbook: A Guide to Increasing Transparency in Emerging Democracies*, Washington, DC, Office of Democracy and Governance, Technical Publications Series.

Pion-Berlin, David (ed.), 2001, *Civil-Military Relations in Latin America. New Analytical Perspectives*, Chapel Hill, North Carolina, University of North Carolina Press.

Poder Judicial, República Oriental del Uruguay, División de Planeamiento y Presupuesto, Departamento de Estadísticas Judiciales, 2002, *Actividad de Defensorías de Oficio en todo el país. Año 2001* [http://www.poderjudicial.gub.uy/].

Popkin, Margaret, 2001, "Informe comparativo sobre la independencia judicial en América Latina", paper presented at the International Conference: Global, Regional and National Perspective, Lima, Peru, 29–30 November.

Porter, Michael, Jeffrey Sachs, Peter Cornelius, John McArthur, and Klaus Schwab, 2002, *The Global Competitiveness Report 2001–2002*, New York, Oxford University Press.

Portes, Alejandro, 1995, *En torno a la informalidad. Ensayos sobre teoría y medición de la economía no regulada*, Quito, Ecuador.

Prebisch, Raúl, 1997, "La industrialización de América Latina", in López Segrera, Francisco (ed.), *El pensamiento social latinoamericano en el siglo XX*, Volume I, Caracas, Venezuela, UNESCO.

Preuss, U., 1986, 'The Concept of Rights and the Welfare State', in Teubner, G. (ed.), *Dilemmas of Law in the Welfare State*, New York and Berlin, Germany, Gruyter.

————, 1996a, 'The Political Meaning of Constitutionalism', in Bellamy, R. (ed.), *Constitutionalism, Democracy, and Sovereignty: American and European Perspectives*, Aldershot, UK, Avebury.

————, 1996b, 'Two Challenges to European Citizenship', in *Political Studies*, 44(3), pp. 534–552.

Prillaman, William C., 2000, *The Judiciary and Democratic Decay in Latin America. Declining Confidence in the Rule of Law*, Westport, Connecticut, Praeger.

Programa Integral de Reforma Judicial, 2003 [http://www.reformajudicial.jus.gov.ar/estadisticas/america.htm].

Proyecto Estado de la Nación, 1999, *Estado de la región. Un informe desde Centroamérica y para Centroamérica*, San José, Costa Rica, Proyecto Estado de la Nación.

————, forthcoming, *Estado de la región. II Informe de Desarrollo Humano Sustentable en Centroamérica*, San José, Costa Rica, Proyecto Estado de la Nación.

Proyecto Estado de la Nación en Desarrollo Humano Sustentable, 2001, *Informe de la auditoría ciudadana sobre la calidad de la democracia en Costa Rica*, San José, Costa Rica, Proyecto Estado de la Nación.

————, 2002, "Políticas públicas de combate al racismo y la discriminación en Centroamérica", San José, Costa Rica, Proyecto Estado de la Nación.

Przeworski, Adam, 1991, *Democracy and the Market: The Political and Economical Reforms in Eastern Europe and Latin America*, New York, Cambridge University Press.

Przeworski, Adam, Michael E. Álvarez, José Antonio Cheibub, and Fernando Limongi, 2000, *Democracy and Development: Political Institutions and Well-Being in the World, 1950–1990,* Cambridge, Cambridge University Press.

Przeworski, Adam, and J. Sprague, 1986, *Paper Stones. A History of Electoral Socialism,* Chicago, Illinois, University of Chicago Press.

Przeworski, Adam, B. Manin, and S. Stokes (eds.), 1999, *Democracy, Accountability, and Representation,* New York, Cambridge University Press.

Putnam, R., 1993, *Making Democracy Work,* Princeton, New Jersey, Princeton University Press.

————, 1995, 'Tuning In, Tuning Out: The Strange Disappearance of Social Capital in America', in *Political Science and Politics,* No. 4, pp. 664–683.

————, 2000, *Bowling Alone: The Collapse and Revival of American Community,* New York, Simon & Schuster.

Ramírez Ocampo, Augusto, 2004, "La defensa colectiva de la Democracia", text prepared for PRODDAL, in UNDP, *La democracia en América Latina. Hacia una democracia de ciudadanas y ciudadanos: Contribuciones para el debate,* Buenos Aires, Aguilar, Altea, Taurus, Alfaguara.

Rawls, John, 1971, *A Theory of Justice,* Cambridge, Massachusetts, Harvard University Press.

————, 2001, *Justice as Fairness. A Restatement,* Cambridge, Massachusetts, Belknap Press of Harvard University Press.

Raz, J., 1986, *The Morality of* Freedom, Oxford, UK, Clarendon Press.

————, 1994, *Ethics in the Public Domain. Essays in the Morality of Law and Politics,* Oxford, UK, Clarendon Press.

Reporters Without Borders, 2003, 'Worldwide Press Freedom Index' [http://www.rsf.org/article.php3?id_article=4116].

Reyna, José Luis, 1999, *América Latina a fines de siglo,* Buenos Aires-Mexico DF, Paidós.

Rial, Juan, 2000, 'Instituciones de democracia directa en América Latina' [http://www.ndipartidos.org/pdf/gobernando/democraciadirecta.pdf].

Rial, Juan, and Daniel Zovatto (eds.), 1998, *Elecciones y democracia en América Latina, 1992–1996,* San José, Costa Rica, Instituto Interamericano de Derechos Humanos–Centro Interamericano de Asesoría y Promoción Electoral.

Ribeiral, Tatiana B., and Humberto Dantas, 2003, *Participação Política e Cidadania,* Belo Horizonte, Editora Lê.

Richards, D.A., 1996, 'Autonomy in Law', in Christman, J. (ed.), *The Inner Citadel. Essays on Individual Autonomy,* Oxford, UK, Oxford University Press.

Ricupero, Rubens, 2004, "Notas sobre el impacto del comercio internacional en el desarrollo de las economías latinoamericanas", text prepared for PRODDAL in UNDP, *La democracia en América Latina. Hacia una democracia de ciudadanas y ciudadanos: Contribuciones para el debate,* Buenos Aires, Aguilar, Altea, Taurus, Alfaguara.

Rivarola, Domingo, 1993, *La sociedad conservadora,* Asunción, Paraguay, CPES.

Rivero, Oswaldo de, 2001, *El mito del desarrollo: los países inviables en el siglo XXI,* Lima, Peru, Fondo de Cultura Económica.

————, 1995, *Radicales y peronistas en el Congreso Nacional: 1983–1989,* Buenos Aires, Argentina, Centro Editor.

Rodrik, Dani, 1997, 'Democracy and Economic Performance', Harvard University, December.

————, 2000, 'Development strategies for the next century', Harvard University, February.

————, 2001, 'Four simple principles for democratic governance of globalization', Harvard University, May.

Roncagliolo, Rafael, 2000, "Elecciones del 2000: Caja de sorpresas para una teoría del fraude electoral", in *Qué hacer,* No. 118.

Rosanvallon, Pierre, 1992, *Le Sacré du Citoyen. Histoire du Suffrage Universel en France,* Paris, France, Gallimard.

————, 1995, 'The History of the Word 'Democracy' in France', in *Journal of Democracy,* 6(4), pp. 140–154.

————, 2004, "Las dimensiones social y nacional de la democracia: hacia un marco de comprensión ampliada", text prepared for PRODDAL in UNDP, *La democracia en América Latina. Hacia una democracia de ciudadanas y ciudadanos. Anexo: El debate conceptual sobre la democracia (CD ROM),* Buenos Aires, Aguilar, Altea, Taurus, Alfaguara.

Rose, Richard (ed.), 2000, *International Encyclopedia of Elections,* Washington, DC, CQ Press.

Rothstein, B., 1998, *Just Institutions Matter. The Moral and Political Logic of the Universal Welfare State,* Cambridge, Cambridge University Press.

Rouquié, Alain, Bolivar Lamounier, and Jorge Schvarzer, 1985, *Cómo renacen las democracias,* Sao Paulo, Brazil, Brasiliense.

Rueschemeyer, Dietrich, and P. Evans, 1985, 'The State and Economic Transformation: Toward an Analysis of the Conditions Underlying Effective Intervention', in Evans, P., Rueschemeyer, D., and Skocpol, T. (eds.), *Bringing the State Back In,* Cambridge, Massachusetts, Cambridge University Press.

Rueschemeyer, Dietrich, Evelyne Huber, and John Stephens, 1992, *Capitalist Development & Democracy,* Cambridge, Polity Press.

Sagasti, Francisco, Pepi Patrón, Max Hernández, and Nicolás Lynch, 1999, *Democracia y buen gobierno. Agenda Perú,* Lima, Peru, Agenda Perú.

Salomón, Leticia, 1994, *Democratización y sociedad civil en Honduras,* Tegucigalpa, Honduras.

————, (ed.), 1994, *Los retos de la democracia,* Tegucigalpa, Honduras, Cedoh.

Samuels, David, 2000, 'Fiscal Horizontal Accountability? Toward a Theory of Budgetary 'Checks and Balances' in Presidential Systems', article presented at the conference on 'Horizontal Accountability in New Democracies', The Helen Kellogg Institute for International Studies at Notre Dame University, Notre Dame, Indiana.

Santos, Wanderley Guilherme dos, 1979, *Cidadania e Justicia,* Rio de Janeiro, Brazil, Campus.

Sartori, Giovanni, 1967, *Democratic Theory,* New York, Praeger Publishers.

————, 1987a, *The Theory of Democracy Revisited. I: The Contemporary Debate,* New York, Chatham House Publishers.

————, 1987b, *The Theory of Democracy Revisited. II: The Classical Issues,* New York, Chatham House Publishers.

————, 1991, "Democracia", in *Revista de Ciencia Política,* Vol. XIII, Nos 1 and 2 , Chile, Instituto de Ciencia Política, Pontificia Universidad Católica de Chile.

Sartorius, R., 1983, *Paternalism,* Minneapolis, University of Minnesota Press.

Scheiber, H. N. (ed.), 1998, *The State and Freedom of Contract,* Stanford, California, Stanford University Press.

Schlozman, K., et al., 1999, 'Civic Participation and the Equality Problem', in Skocpol, T., and Fiorina, M., *Civic Engagement in American Democracy,* Washington, DC, Brookings Institution Press.

Schmitter, Philippe, 1992, 'The Consolidation of Democracy and Representation of Social Groups', *American Behavioral Scientist*, 35(4/5), pp. 422–449.

Schneewind, J.B., 1998, *The Invention of Autonomy. A History of Modern Moral Philosophy*, Cambridge, Cambridge University Press.

Scott, J.C., 1985, *Weapons of the Weak. Everyday Forms of Peasant Resistance*, New Haven, Connecticut, Yale University Press.

Seider, R., 2000, *Legal Pluralism and the Politics of State Formation in Mesoamerica*, London, Institute for Latin American Studies.

Seligson, Mitchell, and Córdova, P., 2000, *Auditoría de la Democracia*, Quito, Ecuador, United States Agency for International Development (USAID)–Proyecto de Opinión Pública de la Universidad de Pittsburgh.

Seligson, Mitchell, Annabelle Conroy, Ricardo Córdova Macías, Orlando Pérez, and Andrew Stein, 1995, 'Who Votes in Central America? A Comparative Analysis', in Booth, John and Seligson, Mitchell (eds.), *Elections and Democracy in Central America*, revised edition, Chapel Hill, North Carolina, University of North Carolina Press.

Sen, Amartya, 1985, 'Well-Being, Agency and Freedom. The Dewey Lectures 1984', in *The Journal of Philosophy*, 82(4), pp. 169–221.

———, 1992, *Inequality Reexamined*, Cambridge, Massachusetts, Harvard University Press.

———, 1999a, 'Democracy as a Universal Value', in *The Journal of Democracy*, 10(3), pp. 3–17.

———, 1999b, *Development as Freedom*, New York, Alfred Knopf. (Spanish edition: Sen, Amartya, 2000, *Desarrollo y libertad*, Buenos Aires, Argentina, Planeta.)

———, 2000, 'East and West. The Reach of Reason', in *New York Review*, 47(12), pp. 33–38.

———, 2003, *La libertad individual como compromiso social*, La Paz, Bolivia, Ildis. Introduction by Marc Saint-Upéry.

Serrano, Claudia, 2002, "Pobreza, Capital Social y Ciudadanía" [http://www.asesorias.tie.cl/documentos.htm].

Shapiro, I., 1996, *Democracy's Place*, Ithaca, New York, Cornell University Press.

Shklar, J.N., 1989, 'The Liberalism of Fear', in Rosenblum, N.L. (ed.), *Liberalism and the Moral Life*, Cambridge, Massachusetts, Harvard University Press, pp. 21–38.

Shue, H., 1996, *Basic Rights. Subsistence, Affluence, and U.S. Foreign Policy*, Princeton, New Jersey, Princeton University Press.

Shugart, Matthew Sobert, and John Carey, 1992, *Presidents and Assemblies: Constitutional Design and Electoral Dynamics*, New York, Cambridge University Press.

Skaar, Elin, 2001, 'Judicial Reform in Latin America. Why?', article presented at the Annual Norwegian Political Science Conference, Hønesfoss, January.

Skinner, Quentin, 1984, 'The Idea of Negative Liberty: Philosophical and Historical Perspectives', in Rorty, Richard (ed.), *Philosophy in History*, Cambridge, Cambridge University Press.

Smith, A.D., 1991, *National Identity*, Reno, Nevada, University of Nevada Press.

Smulovitz, Catalina, and Peruzzotti, Enrique, 2000, 'Social Accountability in Latin America', *Journal of Democracy*, 11(4), pp. 147–158.

Snyder, Richard, 2001, *Politics after Neoliberalism. The Politics of Reregulation in Mexico*, Cambridge, Cambridge University Press.

Snyder, Richard, and David Samuels, 2001, 'Devaluing the Vote in Latin America', in *Journal of Democracy*, 12(1) (January), pp. 146–159.

Sola, Lourdes, 2004, "Democratización, Estado e integración a la economía global. ¿Cuál es el lugar de la política democrática? La experiencia brasileña en perspectiva", text prepared for PRODDAL in UNDP, *La democracia en América Latina. Hacia una democracia de ciudadanas y ciudadanos: Contribuciones para el debate,* Buenos Aires, Aguilar, Altea, Taurus, Alfaguara.

Soros, George, 2001, "Capitalismo frente a la democracia", in *El País,* 21 December.

Stavenhagen, R., 1996, *Ethnic Conflicts and the Nation-State,* London, Macmillan Press.

Steel, R., and J. Torrie, 1996, *Principles and Procedures of Statistics: A Biomedical Approach,* New York, McGraw-Hill.

Stein, P., 1999, *Roman Law in European History,* Cambridge, Cambridge University Press.

Stepan, A., 2000, 'Religion, Democracy, and the Twin Tolerations', in *Journal of Democracy,* 11(4), pp. 37–57.

Stiglitz, Joseph, 2004, "Globalización, organismos financieros internacionales y las economías latinoamericanas", text prepared for PRODDAL in UNDP, *La democracia en América Latina. Hacia una democracia de ciudadanas y ciudadanos: Contribuciones para el debate,* Buenos Aires, Aguilar, Altea, Taurus, Alfaguara.

Stolcke, V., 1997, 'The "Nature" of Nationality', in Blader ,V. (ed.), *Citizenship and Exclusion,* London, Macmillan Press.

Stölting, E., forthcoming, 'Informal Arrangements and the Public Space: Structural Obstacles to Empirical Research', in Brie, Michael (ed.), *Formal Institutions and Informal Institutional Arrangements.*

Strasser, Carlos, 1999, *Democracia y desigualdad. Sobre la "democracia real" a fines del siglo XX,* Buenos Aires, Argentina, Clacso–ASDI.

Suny, R., 2001, 'Constructing Primordialism: Old Histories for New Nations', in *The Journal of Modern History,* 73, pp. 862–896.

Suprema Corte de Justicia, República de El Salvador, 2003, 'Organization and Responsibilities' [http://www.csj.gob.sv/organiza.htm].

Sypnowich, C., 2000, 'The Culture of Citizenship', in *Politics & Society,* 28(4), pp. 531–555.

Tamayo, Eduardo, 1996, *Movimientos sociales: la riqueza de la diversidad,* Quito, Ecuador, Agencia Latinoamericana de Información.

Tamir, Y., 1993, *Liberal Nationalism,* Princeton, New Jersey, Princeton University Press.

———, 1995, 'The Enigma of Nationalism', *World Politics,* 47, pp. 418–440.

Tanaka, Martín, 1998, *Los espejismos de la democracia: el colapso de un sistema de partidos en el Perú, 1980–1995, en perspectiva comparada,* Lima, Peru, IEP.

———, 2002, "Las relaciones entre Estado y sociedad en el Perú: desestructuración sin reestructuración, un ensayo bibliográfico", in *América Latina Hoy,* 31 (August), pp. 189–218.

Tarrow, Sidney, 2000, 'National Unification, National Disintegration, and Contention: A Paired Comparison of Unlikely Cases', Madrid, Spain, Centro de Estudios Avanzados en Ciencias Sociales.

Taylor, Charles, 1985, 'What's Wrong with Negative Liberty', in Taylor, Charles, *Philosophy and the Human Sciences. Philosophical Papers* 2, Cambridge, Cambridge University Press, pp. 211–229.

Terrazas, Julio, 2004, "Avances y límites de la democracia en América Latina, en los últimos veinte años", text prepared for PRODDAL in UNDP, *La democracia en América Latina. Hacia una democracia de ciudadanas y ciudadanos: Contribuciones para el debate,* Buenos Aires, Aguilar, Altea, Taurus, Alfaguara.

Thompson, E.P., 1975, *Whigs and Hunters. The Origins of the Black Act,* New York, Pantheon Books.

Thoumi, Francisco, 2004, "Notas sobre corrupción y drogas ilegales", text prepared for PRODDAL in UNDP, *La democracia en América Latina. Hacia una democracia de ciudadanas y ciudadanos: Contribuciones para el debate,* Buenos Aires, Aguilar, Altea, Taurus, Alfaguara.

Tierney, B., 1997, *The Idea of Natural Rights. Studies on Natural Rights, Natural Law and Church Law, 1150–1625,* Atlanta, Georgia, Scholars Press.

Tilly, Charles, 1975, *The Formation of National States in Western Europe,* Princeton, New Jersey, Princeton University Press.

————, 1985, 'War Making and State Making as Organized Crime', in Evans, P.B., Rueschemeyer, D., and Skocpol, T. (eds.), *Bringing the State Back In,* Cambridge, Massachusetts, Cambridge University Press.

————, 1990, *Coercion, Capital and European States,* Cambridge, Blackwell.

————, 1996, *Citizenship, Identity and Social History,* Cambridge, Cambridge University Press.

————, 1998a, *Durable Inequality,* Berkeley, California, University of California Press. (Spanish edition: Tilly, Charles, 2000, *La desigualdad persistente,* Buenos Aires, Argentina, Manantial.)

————, 1998b, 'Where do Rights Come From?', in Skocpol, T. (ed.), *Democracy, Revolution, and History,* Ithaca, New York, Cornell University Press.

————, 1999, 'Now Where?', in Steinmetz, George (ed.), *State/Culture. State Formation after the Cultural Turn,* Ithaca, New York, Cornell University Press.

Tironi, Eugenio, 1999, *La irrupción de las masas y el malestar de las elites,* Santiago, Chile, Grijalbo.

Tokman, Victor, and Guillermo O'Donnell (eds.), 1998, *Poverty and Inequality in Latin America. Issues and New Challenges,* Notre Dame, Indiana, Notre Dame University Press.

Torre, Juan Carlos, 1998, *El proceso político de las reformas en América Latina,* Buenos Aires, Argentina, Paidós.

Torres, Cristina, 2001, 'Ethnicity and Health: Another Perspective Toward Equity', in Pan American Health Organization, *Equity in Health: From an Ethnic Perspective,* Washington, DC, Pan American Health Organization.

Torres Rivas, Edelberto, 1981, "La nación: problemas teóricos e históricos", in Lechner, Norberto (ed.), *Estado y política en América Latina,* Mexico DF, Siglo XXI.

Touraine, Alain, 1994, *Qu'est-ce que la Démocratie?,* Paris, France, Fayard.

————, 1997, *Pourrons-nous vivre ensemble? Égaux et différents,* Paris, France, Fayard. (Spanish edition: Touraine, Alain, 1999, *¿Podremos vivir juntos?,* San Pablo, Fondo de Cultura Económica.)

————, 2000, "El Sistema y los Actores", in *Reforma y Democracia* 18, pp. 7–24.

————, 2004, "Los caminos sinuosos de la democracia", text prepared for PRODDAL in UNDP, *La democracia en América Latina. Hacia una democracia de ciudadanas y ciudadanos. Anexo: El debate conceptual sobre la democracia (CD ROM),* Buenos Aires, Aguilar, Altea, Taurus, Alfaguara.

Transparency International, 2002, '2002 Corruption Perceptions Index' [http://www.transparency.org/surveys/index.html].

Turner, B.S., 1986, *Citizenship and Capitalism. The Debate over Reformism,* London, Allen & Unwin.

Tyler, Tom, 1990, *Why People Obey the Law,* New Haven, Connecticut, Yale University Press.

————, 1994, 'Governing and Diversity: The Effect of Fair Decision Making Procedures on the Legitimacy of Government', in *Law and Society Review,* 28(4), pp. 809–831.

Uggla, Fredrik, 2003, 'The Ombudsman in Latin America (The Uses of a Toothless Watchdog)', article presented at the conference on 'Diagnosing Democracy: Methods of Analysis, Findings and Remedies', Santiago, Chile, 11–13 April.

UNDP (United Nations Development Programme), 1998a, *Integrating Human Rights with Sustainable Human Development. A UNDP Policy Document*, New York, UNDP.

—————, 1998b, *UNDP Poverty Report 1998. Overcoming Human Poverty*, New York, UNDP.

—————, 2000a, *Human Development Report 2000. Human Rights and Human Development*, New York, Oxford University Press.

—————, 2000b, *Poverty Report 2000. Overcoming Human Poverty*, New York, UNDP.

—————, 2000c, *Informe sobre desarrollo humano 2000*, Madrid, Spain, Ediciones Mundi-Prensa.

—————, 2001, *Human Development Report 2001*, New York, UNDP and Oxford University Press.

—————, 2002a, *Arab Human Development Report 2002. Creating Opportunities for Future Generations*, New York, UNDP, Regional Office of Arab States.

—————, 2002b, *Informe sobre desarrollo humano. Honduras 2002. Por una democracia incluyente*, Tegucigalpa, Honduras, UNDP.

—————, 2002c, *Informe sobre desarrollo humano 2002. Profundizar la democracia en un mundo fragmentado*, Madrid, Spain, Ediciones Mundi-Prensa.

—————, 2003, *Informe sobre desarrollo humano 2003. Millennium Development Goals: A Compact Among Nations to End Human Poverty*, New York, Oxford University Press.

—————, 2004, *La democracia en América Latina. Hacia una democracia de ciudadanas y ciudadanos:*

Contribuciones para el debate, Buenos Aires, Aguilar, Altea, Taurus, Alfaguara.

UNESCO (United Nations Educational, Scientific and Cultural Organization), Institute of Statistics, 2002a, *Literacy and Non Formal Education Sector, Estimates and Projections of Adult Illiteracy for Population Aged 15 Years Old and Above, by Country and by Gender 1970–2010, January 2002 assessment* [http://www.uis.unesco.org/en/stats/stats0.htm].

—————, 2002b, *Education Sector, Gross and Net Enrolment Ratio at Primary Level by Country and by Gender for the School Years 1998/1999 and 1999/2000, October 2002* [http://portal.unesco.org/uis/ev.php?url_id=5187url_do=do_topicurl_section=201].

—————, 2002c, *Education Sector, Gross and Net Enrolment Ratio at Secondary Level by Country and by Gender for the School Years 1998/1999 and 1999/2000, October 2002* [http://portal.unesco.org/uis/ev.php?url_id=5187url_do=do_topicurl_section=201].

—————, 2002d, *Education Sector, Gross and Net Enrolment Ratio at Tertiary Level by Country and by Gender for the School Years 1998/1999 and 1999/2000, October 2002* [http://portal.unesco.org/uis/ev.php?url_id=5187url_do=do_topicurl_section=201].

United States Department of State, 2001, *Guatemala Country Report on Human Rights Practices 2001* [http://www.state.gov/g/drl/rls/hrrpt/2001/wha/8344.htm].

UNO (United Nations Organization), 1948, *Universal Declaration of the Rights of Man*, adopted and proclaimed by the General Assembly in Resolution 217 A (III), 10 December.

—————, 2003a, 'Multilateral Treaties Deposited with the Secretary General' [http://untreaty.un.org/].

—————, 2003b, *Implementation of the United Nations Millennium Declaration. Report of the Secretary General*, A/58/323.

UNO (United Nations Organization), Commission on Human Rights, 1999, 'Resolution of the Commission on Human Rights 1999/57 on the "Promotion of the right to democracy"'.

UNO (United Nations Organization), Population Division, Department of Economic and Social Affairs, 2001, *World Population Prospects: the 2000 Revision,* New York, United Nations.

————, 2002, *World Urbanization Prospects: the 2001 Revision,* New York, United Nations.

UNODC (United Nations Office on Drugs and Crime), 2002, *United Nations Surveys of Crime Trends and Operation of Criminal Justice Systems* [http://www.unodc.org].

Valenzuela, J.S., 1992, 'Democratic Consolidation in Post-Transitional Settings: Notion, Process, and Facilitating Conditions', in Mainwaring, S., O'Donnell, G., and Valenzuela, J.S. (eds.), *Issues in Democratic Consolidation: The New South American Democracies in Comparative Perspective,* Notre Dame, Indiana, The Helen Kellogg Institute for International Studies at Notre Dame University.

Van Cott, Donna Lee, 2003, 'Latin American Constitutions and Indigenous Peoples' [http://web.utk.edu/~dvancott/constitu.html].

Varga, C., 1991, *Codification as a Socio-Historical Phenomenon,* Budapest, Hungary, Akadémiai Kiadó.

Vargas Cullell, J., Benavides T. y Gómez, M. 2003a. *Medición de la participación ciudadana en América Latina.* San José, document prepared for PRODDAL. June 2003.

Vargas Cullell, J., Benavides T. y Gómez, M. 2003b. *Nota conceptual y planteamiento analítico sobre las orientaciones hacia la democracia de las y los ciudadanos en América Latina.* San José, document prepared for PRODDAL. June 2003.

Vargas Cullell, J. y Benavides T. 2003. *Nota conceptual y metodológica sobre intensidad ciudadana.* San José, document prepared for PRODDAL. June 2003.

Vargas Cullell, J. y Gómez, M. 2003. *Medición de las percepciones sobre el apego a las normas legales con base en Latinobarómetro 2002.* San José, document prepared for PRODDAL. June 2003.

Vargas-Cullell, J y Rosero-Bixby, L. *Cultura democrática en Costa Rica: 2004.* San José: report prepared for Proyecto de Opinión Pública de la Universidad de Vanderbilt (en prensa).

Vargas Cullel, Jorge, and M. Gutiérrez Saxe, 2001, *Auditoría ciudadana de la calidad de la democracia,* San José, Costa Rica, Proyecto Estado de la Nación en Desarrollo Humano Sustentable.

Vázquez, R., 2001, *Liberalismo, estado de derecho y minorías,* Mexico DF, Paidós.

Verba, S., K.L. Schlozman, and H. Brady, 1995, *Voice and Equality. Civic Voluntarism in American Politics,* Cambridge, Massachusetts, Harvard University Press.

Verba, S., et al., 1978, *Participation and Political Equality,* Cambridge, Cambridge University Press.

Verdesoto C., Luis F., 1989, "El sistema de partidos politicos y la sociedad civil en Ecuador", in Meyer, Lorenzo, and Reyna, José Luis (co-ordinators), *Los sistemas políticos en América Latina,* Mexico DF, Siglo XXI Editores and Tokyo, Japan, United Nations University.

Villey, M., 1968, *La Formation de la Pensée Juridique Moderne,* Paris, France, Montchrestien.

Waldron, J., 1999, *Law and Disagreement,* Oxford, UK, Clarendon Press.

Walker, Thomas, and Ariel Armony (ed.), 2000, *Repression, Resistance, and Democratic Transition in Central America,* Wilmington, Delaware, Scholarly Resources.

Wallack, Jessica, Alejandro Gaviria, Ugo Panizza, and Ernesto Stein, 2003, 'Electoral systems data set' [http://www.stanford.edu/~jseddon/].

Ward, Gene, 2002, "Requisitos de divulgación en el financiamiento de partidos políticos y campañas electorales", article presented at the Inter-American Forum on Political Parties, Vancouver, Canada, 4–6 December.

Weale, A., 1983, *Political Theory and Social Policy,* New York, St. Martin's Press.

Weber, Max, 1978, *Economy and Society. An Outline of Interpretative Sociology,* 1, Berkeley, California, University of California Press. (Spanish edition: Weber, Max, 1944, *Economía y sociedad,* Mexico DF, Fondo de Cultura Económica.)

————, 1997, *El político y el científico,* Madrid, Spain, Alianza.

Weffort, Francisco, 1981, *¿Por qué democracia?,* San Pablo, Brazil, Brasiliense.

Whitehead, Laurence, 2001, 'Some Significant Recent Developments in the Field of Democratization', paper presented at the World Political Science Congress, Quebec, Canada.

————, 2002a, *Democratization. Theory and Experience,* Oxford, UK, Oxford University Press.

————, 2002b, 'Notes on Human Development, Human Rights, and Auditing the Quality of Democracy', written comments presented at the workshop on 'Quality of Democracy and Human Development in Latin America', Heredia, Costa Rica.

————, 2004, "Comentario sobre las tres tesis", text prepared for PRODDAL in UNDP, *La democracia en América Latina. Hacia una democracia de ciudadanas y ciudadanos. Anexo: El debate conceptual sobre la democracia (CD ROM),* Buenos Aires, Aguilar, Altea, Taurus, Alfaguara.

WHO (World Health Organization)–UNICEF (United Nations Children's Fund), 2000, *Global Water Supply and Sanitation Assessment 2000 Report,* Geneva, Switzerland, WHO and New York, UNICEF.

WHO (World Health Organization), Department of Nutrition for Health and Development, 2002, 'WHO Global Database on Child Growth and Malnutrition' [http://www.who.int/nutgrowthdb/].

Wightman, J., 1995, *Contract: A Critical Commentary,* London, Pluto Press.

Wilkie, James W. (ed.), 2001, *Statistical Abstract of Latin America,* Vol. 37, Los Angeles, California, UCLA Latin American Center.

Willis, Eliza, Christopher Garmen, and Stephan Haggard, 1998, 'The Politics of Decentralization in Latin America', in *Latin American Research Review,* 34(1), pp. 7–56.

World Bank, Legal and Judicial Reform Practice Group, 2003, 'Legal and Judicial Sector at a Glance: Worldwide Judicial and Legal Indicators' [http://www4.worldbank.org/legal/database/Justice/].

Young, I.M., 1995, 'Polity and Group Difference: A Critique of the Ideal of Universal Citizenship', in Beiner, R., *Theorizing Citizenship,* Albany, New York, State University of New York Press.

Yrigoyen Fajardo, R., 1999, *Pautas de coordinación entre el Derecho Indígena y el Derecho Estatal,* Guatemala, Fundación Myrna Mack.

Zermeño, Sergio, 1978, *México, una democracia utópica,* Mexico DF, Siglo XXI.

————, 1998, *La sociedad derrotada,* Centro de Investigaciones interdisciplinarias en Ciencias y Humanidades/UNAM.

Zovatto G., Daniel, 2003, "Dinero y política en América Latina: Una visión comparada", in Instituto Federal Electoral de Mexico DF (eds.), *Dinero y contienda política electoral,* Mexico DF, Fondo de Cultura Económica.

■ Abbreviations

CLAD	Centro Latinoamericano de Administración para el Desarrollo (Latin American Centre for Development Administration)
CELADE	Latin American and Caribbean Demographic Centre Population Division
ECLAC	Economic Commission for Latin America and the Caribbean
EPIC	Election Process Information Collection
IADB	Inter-American Development Bank
IDEA	International Institute for Democracy and Electoral Assistance
ILO	International Labor Organization
IMF	International Monetary Fund
IPEC	International Programme on the Elimination of Child Labor
IPU	Inter-Parliamentary Union
JSCA	Justice Studies Center of the Americas
LASA	Latin American Studies Association
OAS	Organization of American States
OECD	Organisation for Economic Co-operation and Development
SIMPOC	Statistical Information and Monitoring Programme on Child Labour
TI	Transparency International
UNDP	United Nations Development Programme
UNESCO	United Nations Educational, Scientific and Cultural Organization
UNICEF	United Nations Children's Fund
UNO	United Nations Organization
UNODC	United Nations Office on Drugs and Crime
WB	World Bank
WHO	World Health Organization

■ Contents of Boxes

Contents of Tables

■ Contents of Graphics

■ Contents of the CD-ROM included with this Report

REPORT: DEMOCRACY IN LATIN AMERICA

STATISTICAL COMPENDIUM

■ Introduction

▪ Democracy and Civil Citizenship: Civil Rights

Table 62. Children: Economically Active Children, and Unconditional Worst Forms of Child Labor, 2000

Table 63. Indigenous Peoples: International Treaties, Multicultural and Language Rights, 2002

Right to Life, Physical Integrity and Security (Tables 64-65)
Table 64. Homicide, c. 2000

Table 65. The Death Penalty, 1990-2002

Administration of Justice (Tables 66-67B)
Table 66. Access to the Courts I: Public Expenditures, Number of Judges and Public Defenders, c. 2000

Table 67A. Rights of the Accused and Imprisoned: Prison Population, Detainees Awaiting Sentencing, Occupancy Level, and Categories of Prisoners, c. 2002

Table 67B. Rights of the Accused and Imprisoned: Prison Population, Detainees Awaiting Sentencing, Occupancy Level, and Categories of Prisoners, c. 2002

Right to a Free Press and to Information (Tables 68-70)
Table 68. Press Freedom, 1993-2002

Table 69. Violence Against Journalists, 1990-2002

Table 70. Right of Access to Public Information and Habeas Data, 2002

■ Democracy and Social Citizenship: Social Rights

Poverty and Indigence (Tables 71-74)
Table 71. Poverty and Indigence I: Households and Individuals, 1980-1999

Table 72A. Poverty and Indigence II. Individuals 1989/ 1990-2001

Table 72B. Poverty and Indigence II. Individuals 1989/ 1990-2001

Table 73A. Poverty and Indigence III. Households, 1977-2000

Table 73B. Poverty and Indigence III. Households, 1977-2000

Table 74. Poverty and Indigence IV. Poor Households in Urban and Rural Areas, 1989-2000

Inequality (Tables 75-76)
Table 75. Inequality I: Gini Coefficients, Total, Urban and Rural, 1989-2000

Table 76. Inequality II: Income Distribution by Quintiles in Urban Households, 1979-2000

Jobs (Tables 77-81)
Table 77. Employment I: Open Unemployment Rate in Urban Areas I. Total, 1990-2002

Table 78. Employment II: Open Unemployment Rate in Urban Areas II. Male and Female, 1990-2000

Table 79. Employment III: Real Urban Minimum Wages, 1990-2001

Table 80. Employment IV: Real Industrial Wages, 1990-2001

Table 81. Employment V: Size of the Informal Sector by Category of Workers, c. 2000

Health (Tables 82A-86)
Table 82A. Health I: Infant Mortality (Total, Male and Female), 1970-2000

Table 82B. Health I: Infant Mortality (Total, Male and Female), 1970-2000

Related Socio-Economic Factors

■ **References to Sources for the Indicators**

SECOND PART

Public Opinion Study about Democracy

■ **Technical Note on the Indices derived from an Analysis of the Latinobarómetro 2002 Survey: Constructing the Democratic Support Index (DSI)**

■ **Democratic Support Index**

■ Political Citizenship

■ Civil Citizenship

▣ Social Citizenship

▣ Latinobarometro Questionnaire 2002